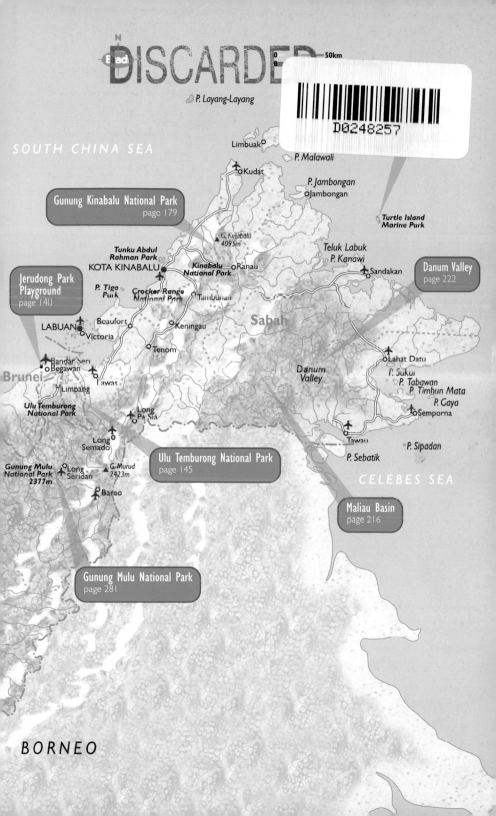

DISCARDED

N

Brad

0   50km

SOUTH CHINA SEA

P. Layang-Layang

Limbuak

oKudat

P. Malawali

P. Jambongan
oJambongan

Gunung Kinabalu National Park
page 179

Turtle Island
Marine Park

G. Kinabalu
4095m

Teluk Labuk
P. Kanawi

Tunku Abdul
Rahman Park

KOTA KINABALU

Kinabalu
National Park

oRanau

Sandakan

Danum Valley
page 222

**Jerudong Park
Playground**
page 140

P. Tiga
Park

Crocker Range
National Park

Tambunan

Sabah

LABUAN

Beaufort

Victoria

Keningau

Danum
Valley

Lahat Datu

P. Sukui
P. Tabawan
P. Timbun Mata
P. Gaya

Tenom

Brunei

Bandar Seri
Begawan

Tawas

Limbang

Semporna

Ulu Temburong
National Park

Long
Pa Sia

Long
Semado

Tawau

P. Sipadan

Ulu Temburong National Park
page 145

P. Sebatik

Gunung Mulu
National Park
2377m

Long
Seridan

G. Murud
2423m

Bareo

CELEBES SEA

Maliau Basin
page 216

Gunung Mulu National Park
page 281

BORNEO

Borneo
Don't
miss...

Sepilok orang-utan sanctuary
Sabah
(ST) page 206

Brunei's capital: Bandar Seri Begawan
Omar Ali Saifuddin Mosque
(TT) page 129

Gunung Mulu National Park
Limestone pinnacles, Sarawak
(RD/TIPS) page 281

Pristine coral reefs
Semporna Islands, Sabah (GAR/TIPS)
page 717

Forest canopy walks
Danum Valley, Sabah
(NG) page 222

Modern versus traditional

above left Malay fast food at the Gadong *pasar malam* (night market), Bandar Seri Begawan (TT) page 127
above right Town fashion (TT) page 80
below Masjid Jamek mosque, Brunei (BT) page 142

above   Hunting with a blow pipe for monkeys (ADI/TIPS)
below left Iban chief with traditional tattoos and his fighting cock (LIT/TIPS) page 18
below right A traditional communal longhouse — or *baruk* — built by the Bidayuh people, Sarawak
            (LIT/TIPS) page 17

AUTHOR

Tamara Thiessen is a freelance writer, photographer and broadcaster from Australia. Over the past two decades she has worked across news, current affairs and programme production for the Australian Broadcasting Corporation, SBS Multicultural Services, Deutsche Welle and Agence France Presse; and as a freelance correspondent in Europe. She has written for numerous newspapers including the *Toronto Globe & Mail*, the *Montreal Gazette*, the *Sydney Morning Herald*, the *Melbourne Age*, *Sunday Business Post* (Ireland), the *South China Morning Post* and *Singapore Straits Times*. Amid constant globetrotting, her travel-inspired reports

and photographs have been published in magazines worldwide including *Condé Nast Traveller*, *Islands*, *Ulysse Magazine* (France), *GEO Australasia* and the in-flight publications of US Airways, Delta Airlines, Air Emirates, SN Brussels, Jet Star, LAN Airlines and Air Jordan. She has contributed to the Eyewitness Travel Guides to Australia and Style City Europe, and is working on her first travel book *Planet Ends: Beyond Temptation in Tasmania*.

CONTRIBUTING EDITOR

Kara Moses is a primatologist and freelance writer. She has contributed to a number of books, including *Primates of the World* by Ian Redmond, and writes articles about primates and environmental issues for publications such as *BBC Wildlife Magazine*.

AUTHOR'S STORY

I was born on remote and wild Tasmania and ever since islands have been part of my make-up. I'm drawn to points of isolation and the 'otherness' they so often bring. And so it was that in the mid-1990s I started dreaming of Borneo.

Back then I had asked a native Malaysian where the most beautiful places in his country were. He drew a map of Sabah and Sarawak for me and told me how extraordinary, but threatened, their forests and animals were. Clutching that scrap of paper, the desire to visit Borneo simmered away for another couple of years, but my love for Borneo was a *fait accompli*. When I finally got there, the country was everything and more my friend had described. The wildlife and people were spectacular, but both face challenges to their environment.

Many agree that one of the most unbearable, heart-rending tragedies of the world today is the destruction of the beauty and uniqueness of places like Borneo. Whilst some of the changes to the natural environment and traditional ways of life are inevitable and necessary, some are not. Like much of the developing word, the Malaysian peninsular is becoming increasingly taken over by Western food and cultures and, as a result, Borneo's singularity – its natural beauty, cultural richness and traditional village lifestyles – stands out even more. Those lucky enough to visit the island, whether travelling from London, New York or Sydney, will hopefully be inspired to help protect this extraordinary island of forested fantasies.

PUBLISHER'S FOREWORD   *Hilary Bradt*

The first Bradt travel guide was written in 1974 by George and Hilary Bradt on a river barge floating down a tributary of the Amazon. It was followed by *Backpacker's Africa*, published in 1979. In the 1980s and '90s the focus shifted away from hiking to broader-based guides to new destinations – usually the first to be published on those places. In the 21st century Bradt continues to publish these ground-breaking guides, along with guides to established holiday destinations, incorporating in-depth information on culture and natural history alongside the nuts and bolts of where to stay and what to see.

Bradt authors support responsible travel, with advice not only on minimum impact but also on how to give something back through local charities. Thus a true synergy is achieved between the traveller and local communities.

First published December 2008

Bradt Travel Guides Ltd, 23 High Street, Chalfont St Peter, Bucks SL9 9QE, England
www.bradtguides.com
Published in the USA by The Globe Pequot Press Inc, 246 Goose Lane,
PO Box 480, Guilford, Connecticut 06475-0480

Text copyright © 2008 Tamara Thiessen
Maps copyright © 2008 Bradt Travel Guides Ltd
Illustrations © 2008 Individual photographers and artists
Contributing editor: Kara Moses

ISBN-13: 978 1 84162 252 1
British Library Cataloguing in Publication Data
A catalogue record for this book is available from the British Library

Photographs Anne Noris/Natural Visions (AN/NV), Arco Digital Images/TIPS (ADI/TIPS), Brian Rogers/Natural Visions (BR/NV), Brunei Tourism (BT), Chris Thompson (CT), David Pendleton (DP), Eloyhouse (E), Franco Banfi/WaterFrame (FB/WF), Guido Alberto Rossi/TIPS (GAR/TIPS), Jean-Philippe Trenque (JPT), Jeff Collett/Natural Visions (JC/NV), Ken Soh (KS), Luca Invernizzi Tettoni/TIPS (LIT/TIPS), Mark Strickland/Waterframe (MS/WF), Matthias Bergbauer/WaterFrame (MB/WF), Meor Amir Zariman Bin Jabir (MJ), Nick Garbutt (NG), Nina Kleven Pedersen (NKP), Paul Thomsen/ Wikicommons (PT/W), Paulo Kawai (PK), Quentin Walls (QW), UnderwaterTimes (UWT), Reinhard Dirscherl/TIPS (RD/TIPS), Reinhard Dirscherl/WaterFrame (RD/WF), Reto Kuster (RK), Ronald Pudin (RP), Sabah Tourism (ST), Slim Sreedharan/Natural Visions (SS/NV), Tamara Thiessen (TT), Yann Guichaoua/TIPS (YG/TIPS)
Front cover Male proboscis monkey (NG)
Back cover Iban chief (LIT/TIPS); Wildlife watching, Menanggol River, Sabah (NG)
Title page Outer-lying island (ST); Bajau Laut boys eating papayas, Kampung Mengkabong (TT); Hibiscus flower, Crocker National Park (TT)
Maps Dave Priestley, Maria Randell

Typeset from the author's disk by Wakewing
Printed and bound in Malta by Gutenberg Press Ltd

Acknowledgements

My immeasurable appreciation goes to the Sabah and Sarawak tourism boards, Brunei Tourism and Royal Brunei Airlines without whose extensive help I could never have realised the travels necessary to write the book. In a similar vein my gratitude goes to the local tour operators, particularly TYK Adventure Tours, SI Tours and Borneo Divers in Sabah, and Sunshine Borneo Tours & Travel in Brunei, for their incredible guides, local knowledge and on-the-ground support; likewise to the innumerable hotels, resorts and guesthouses who generously offered me Bornean hospitality par excellence during my travels. I would also like to thank the many local language and cultural organisations who assisted me with information, as well as several notable experts on Borneo who freely gave of their time and knowledge to make invaluable contributions to the guidebook: archaeologist Peter Bellwood for clarifying the complex and sometimes very confusing Bornean prehistory; Dr Glen Reynolds and Sir Peter Crane for their insights into Borneo's natural history and conservation; anthropologist Victor King; and archaeologist Huw Barton.

I would like to thank Kara Moses for editing the manuscript, Adrian Phillips at Bradt Travel Guides for the opportunity to write and publish this book and my project manager Emma Thomson for her patience, support and dedication to get this book into shipshape form.

Finally thanks to everyone else I have encountered in Malaysian Borneo and Brunei, especially to the people of the island whose culture and spirit and warmth – along with the heavenly natural world – make it the most memorable place in my ostensibly short, but highly privileged, history of world travels.

FEEDBACK REQUEST

Every effort has been made to ensure that the details contained within this book are as accurate and up to date as possible. Inevitably, however, things move on. Any information regarding such changes, or relating to your experiences in Borneo – good or bad – would be very gratefully received. Such feedback is invaluable when compiling further editions. You can email the author directly at e traveltt@hotmail.com or send your comments to Bradt Travel Guides Ltd, 23 High Street, Chalfont St Peter, Bucks SL9 9QE, England

Contents

LIST OF MAPS

Introduction

Borneo – the very name conjures up an image of sultry island mystery, maritime escapade and swampy, steamy jungle adventure. Situated at the junction of four seas in the heart of southeast Asia, its history is one of fierce headhunters and pirates, vast migrations and seafaring invasions. The name 'Borneo' is believed to be a European transformation of *Bruni*, a once-powerful Muslim trading post on the west coast of the island … known today as Brunei.

The third-biggest island in the world after Greenland and New Guinea, Borneo houses three nations: Brunei, Malaysia and Indonesia. Throughout its rich and colourful history, the island has been regarded as remote and mysterious – an isolation fuelled over time by talk of pirate-ridden seas, inhospitable landscapes, turbulent politics and rumours of savage natives. Even today it takes an extra two hours to reach Borneo from mainland Asian airports. Yet the very things which once made the island inaccessible are now part of its great attraction. The rich tribal vestiges, exotic jungle and remoteness of Borneo are making it a prime destination for those seeking both cultural and natural authenticity.

With over 200 indigenous tribes and large Chinese and Malay populations, Borneo represents a fascinating chapter in the world's ethnographic history. The two Malaysian states of Sabah and Sarawak, and the self-ruled Sultanate of Brunei – the areas this guide covers – each have their own stories to tell, but are inextricably linked to each other by history. All three came under British influence at some stage, which has left lasting impressions, and were the site for significant human migrations.

Borneo's natural wonders are undoubtedly its greatest and most famous asset. As a 'biodiversity hotspot', its variety and richness of life is unparalleled. Just 10ha of Bornean rainforest can support 700 species of tree – as many as are found across the whole of North America! The island is home to as many bird species as Europe and as many mammals as Australia, including Asia's only great ape, the orang-utan. Over 5,000 of Borneo's plant species are not found anywhere else in the world, and 500 animal species are unique to the island.

Like many paradises, however, the very thing that makes Borneo so unique is that which threatens its existence. The island's bountiful natural endowment and traditional cultures have been seriously eroded over the last half-century; up to half of its tropical forests have been lost, and much of its extraordinary flora and fauna and traditional ways of life have been pushed towards extinction.

The urgency for conservation has not waned over the past three decades. Local organisations, international scientists, media and tourists have all helped to turn up the heat on those that threaten Borneo's forests, assisting natives who have long been fighting to save their island. As the world slowly wakes up to the consequences of environmental destruction, and the conservation of tropical forests and biodiversity become increasingly prominent on the world's agenda, hopefully what remains of Borneo will be preserved for future generations to continue to enjoy.

Part One

GENERAL INFORMATION

Country Official name: Borneo. The states of Sabah and Sarawak are known as Eastern Malaysia, while Brunei Darussalam is the official name of the Sultanate of Brunei. Kalimantan is the Indonesian section of Borneo (not covered in this guide).
Location Straddling the equator between 4–7°N and 4°S in southeast Asia. Bordered by the South China Sea to the northwest, the Sulu Sea to the north, the Celebes Sea to the east, the Makassar Strait to the west and the Java Sea to the south. It is part of the Malay Archipelago.
Size 743,294km²; the world's third-largest island.
Capital In Malaysian Borneo, Kota Kinabalu is the state capital of Sabah and Kuching the capital of Sarawak; Bandar Seri Begawan is the capital of Brunei.
Climate Equatorial-tropical; average daily temperatures 28°C (coast), 21°C (highlands).
Population Borneo's total population including Indonesian Borneo is 16 million. Three million live in Sabah, 2 million in Sarawak, and around 372,000 in Brunei.
Population growth per year Brunei and Saba 3.1% average, Sarawak 2.3%
Official language Malay
Religion Islam is the official religion of Malaysia, but Christianity and Buddhism are also widely practised, along with Hinduism, Taoism and tribal religions. Brunei is predominately Muslim.
Life expectancy Malaysia 76 years (women)/71 years (men); Brunei 78 years (women)/73 years (men)
Government Malaysian Borneo is a democracy; Brunei a constitutional monarchy.
Currency Malaysian ringgit (MYR), Brunei dollar (BND)
Exchange rate US$=3.50MYR, €1=4.80MYR, £1=6.04MYR; US$=1.47BND, €1=2.00BND, £1=2.53BND (October 2008)
National flags Malaysia: 14 red and white horizontal stripes with blue rectangle in upper left corner containing a yellow star and moon crescent. Brunei: parallel bands of black & white on yellow background with the red state crest in centre.
National emblems Malaysia's state ensign (Lambang Negara) depicts a shield guarded by two tigers, crowned by a yellow crescent depicting Islam and the motto Bersekutu Bertambah Mutu ('Unity is Strength'). The National Crest of Brunei illustrates the red royal umbrella and flag, crescent of Islam, hands of welfare, wings of peace, with the slogan 'Always in service with God's guidance'; 'Brunei Darussalam' means 'abode of peace'.
Tourist information Sabah Tourism Board (www.sabahtourism.com), Sarawak Tourism Board (www.sarawaktourism.com), Brunei Tourism Board (www.tourismbrunei.com)
Public holidays 1 January (New Year's Day); 20 January * (Awal Muharram , first day of Muslim calendar); 29–30 January* (Chinese New Year); 23 February (National Day Brunei); 31 March (Prophet Muhammad's birthday); 6 April, Sabah & Sarawak only (Good Friday); 1 May (Labour Day); 30–31 May (Tadau Ka'amatan – Harvest Festival); 1–2 June (Pesta Gawai, Sarawak Gawai Festival); 2 June (Birthday of Malaysian King); 15 July (Sultan of Brunei's birthday); 31 August (National Day); 9 September, Sarawak only (Birthday of Head of State); 16 September, Sabah only (Birthday of Head of State); 8 November* (Deepavali Hindu light festival); 20 December (Hari Raya Qurban); 25 December (Christmas Day).
* Indicates variable dates

1

Background Information

GEOGRAPHY

Straddling the Equator between 4–7°N and 4°S, Borneo is three times the size of Great Britain – a total of 743,294km². Sabah, Sarawak and Brunei between them account for less than a quarter of the island, with the Indonesian region of Kalimantan occupying the rest of the island (NB: Indonesian Borneo is not covered in this guide).

Surrounded by several straits and four oceans, Borneo is a generous blob among dozens of island spots and specks in the humid, tropical zone of Southeast Asia. The South China Sea lies to the northwest, the Sulu Sea to the north, the Celebes Sea to the east and the Java Sea to the south. The island is located east of the *Semananjung Malaysia* – Peninsular Malaysia – where the Malaysian capital Kuala Lumpur is situated; the two Malaysian states on Borneo – Sarawak and Sabah – are often referred to as 'East Malaysia'.

The shape of Borneo represents that of a dog: its ears point upwards towards the Philippines; a paw extends across the Makassar Strait to Sulawesi; a tail juts westward towards Singapore and feet dip down towards Jakarta. Often considered to be extremely mountainous, over half of Borneo is actually covered by swampy, waterlogged coastal areas of less than 150m elevation. Only 5% of the island lies above 3,000m (approximately 9,000ft) and most mountain peaks are around 2,000m (approximately 6,000ft). Many of these lie near Borneo's rooftop, *Gunung* (Mount) *Kinabalu*, the 4,095m mountain in the northwestern tip of Sabah. The tallest peak in southeast Asia between the Himalayas and Papua New Guinea, Mount Kinabalu towers high over Sabah. The presence of this colossal granite eruption qualifies Borneo as the 'sixth-highest island in the world'.

MALAYSIAN BORNEO Malaysian Borneo is composed of two states: Sabah and Sarawak.

Sabah Sabah occupies the northern chunk of Borneo, forming the head of the 'dog'. Many rivers spring from Sabah's mountainous interior, and the surrounding hills are criss-crossed by an extensive network of river valleys. Nearer the coastal plains are lower-lying swampy hills. Sabah's chant *'negeri di bawah bayu'* ('land below the wind') comes from its location – just south of the typhoon belt which occasionally blights the Philippines, in the equatorial doldrums.

Sarawak Sarawak is a land of rivers; rivers narrow and wide run through the countryside and cities in an incredible navigable network of 3,300km. The state's 55 rivers provide a vital link between the coast and remote interior, and are still the only means of transport to some places today.

BRUNEI A small enclave of a nation squashed between Sabah and Sarawak's frontiers, the 5,765km² of Brunei account for less than 1% of the total land area of Borneo. A mini-Borneo even within such physical constraints, it combines wide coastal plains of mangrove, *nipa* and peat swamp, rainforest and hilly terrains. In comparison with the 720km and 1,600km coastlines of Sarawak and Sabah respectively, Brunei's *Laut China Selatan* runs for just 161km along the South China Sea.

POPULATION DENSITY AND DISTRIBUTION Northern Borneo is very sparsely populated by Asian standards, with on average 17 people per km², compared with 74 on Peninsular Malaysia. A third of the island's 16 million people live in Sabah, Sarawak and Brunei. Historically, the population was divided between coastal and inland dwellers – most early human settlements were concentrated along the coast and on riverbanks. Until the late 19th century, the hinterland was relatively uninhabited, whilst the coast and floodplains of major rivers were densely populated. Though these patterns still exist today, the distinction has faded with soaring urbanisation. In the mid-1970s about 15% of Sarawak's population lived in towns and cities – today that figure is 50% and rising. Much the same can be said for Sabah, where today about half of the population live in urban areas, compared with 20% in 1970. This rapid evolution is having major repercussions on the environment, through urban waste problems and coastal and river pollution.

CLIMATE

The climate of Borneo is equatorial-tropical, and distinguished by marked wet and dry seasons: the wet season (or 'northeast monsoon') generally runs from November to March, the dry season (or 'southwest monsoon') from May to October. Official start and end points vary though, and there is a variable period of transition between seasons. In the wet season, there is usually some rainfall every day and there can also be violent storms, monsoon winds, flooding, landslides and torrential rains.

Half of the annual rainfall on Sarawak's greater west coast falls between December and March, and the hilly slopes of the Kelabit Highlands (inland Sarawak) receive the highest annual rainfall – more than 5,000mm. The wettest months tend to be January and February, which are then directly followed by the driest – March and April.

In Sarawak, which is closest to the Equator, there is little variation in day length throughout the year. There is only a seven-minute difference between the shortest and longest days.

The sun rises and sets at around the same time every day between 06.00 and 18.00. Sunshine is bountiful, but a typical day will usually have some cloudy periods as well. The climatic exception is Mount Kinabalu which has varying alpine microclimates, and can be quite chilly at the top.

HISTORY

The following sections are a brief summary of the island's history. For more information see the titles listed in *Further information, Appendix 2*, page 292.

RAINFOREST TREASURES – EARLY TRADE WITH INDIA AND CHINA There is evidence to suggest that India was trading with southeast Asia from as early as 290BC, with Chinese traders joining the continental market around AD1000. During this period of internationalisation, Borneo's tribes were gradually drawn into networks of trade in spices, camphor, precious woods and other exotic forest products.

The 11th–13th centuries saw an explosion of trade between China and the Indo-Malaysian archipelago in forest products, metals, gemstones and spices. A whole gamut of exotic export products came from the Bornean rainforests: beeswax for ointments, aromatic woods for incense, rubber, resin and rattan.

Some of the Chinese merchants settled in Borneo's ports. Excavations in the Sarawak River delta (south of Kuching) show evidence of a sizeable Chinese settlement, dated to the 10th–13th centuries. Other excavations in Brunei and Sabah suggest the Chinese were trading ceramics for spices even earlier than this.

Borneo polities remained independent of each other until recent times, but important Islamic sultanates were established from the 14th and 15th centuries onwards in Brunei and the Sulu Archipelago (southern Philippines). The Hindu and Buddhist kingdoms of western Indonesia during the first millennium had little influence in Malaysian Borneo.

MALAY CULTURE AND EARLY EMPIRES Malay culture was embedded into Borneo from the 7th to 13th century, propagated by trading empires. During this period, the maritime empire of *Srivijaya* ruled supreme, controlling international sea trade across the Malay archipelago. Originating in Sumatra, the influence extended through Borneo, with many Sumatran Malays said to have settled on the island during this time.

In the 14th century, Srivijaya ceded to the Java-based Hindu empire *Majapahit*. Borneo absorbed some Hindu influences, traces of which remain today. The Majapahit Empire started to topple at the end of the 15th century.

ENTER ISLAM It was around this time that Islam got a foothold in Borneo, though its presence had been felt since the 13th century. Muslim trading states had become established in Sumatra, Java, Malacca and the Moluccas (the spice islands of Ternate and Tidore).

Malay language and culture, and Islam, proceeded to flourish along the coasts of what are today Sabah and Sarawak, as vessels from Malaya and Sumatra anchored in port. Traders, teachers and missionaries all played a hand in the implantation of Islamic culture and civilisation in the region. Islam spread to Brunei under the influence of trade, and the sultanate came to act as a centre of Islamisation for other parts of Borneo. Smaller Muslim-Malay states gradually emerged all over the island during the 17th century, some converting purely for strategic and mercenary reasons, as they had done earlier to Hinduism and Buddhism. The Sultanate of Brunei ruled over much of northern Borneo until the 19th century, through some significant territorial tugs of war.

Throughout this period, Borneo's economic influence was still marginal on a regional scale. The southern Philippines area of the Sulu Islands emerged as a powerful late 18th-century sultanate, and attempted to wrench parts of northern Borneo under its control. The Sultan of Brunei is said to have failed to honour an agreement to cede Sabah to Sulu, and the effects of these chronic territorial tensions are still felt today.

WHITE RAJAHS AND RANEES – EUROPEANS IN BORNEO The Portuguese were the first Europeans to set foot in Borneo, and the Spanish attacked Brunei in 1578, briefly occupying the port. However, no external power gained total control over the country, despite continual tugs of war. Instead it was the Sultanate of Brunei that ruled over much of what is today Sabah and Sarawak for over two centuries, through a court of noble envoys, *Raja* (princes) and locally appointed Malay chiefs.

However, the sultans' methods were met with resistance. Under the weight of rebellion and piracy, Brunei's control over the region waned and colonial forces expanded to fill the vacuum created by the receding empire. The British saw power in Borneo as a way of protecting British shipping routes to China, and got a footing in northern Borneo through a series of naval coups to protect the weakened sultanate. From the mid 19th century, Borneo was to be carved up territorially between European powers: the British in the north, and the Dutch in the south. In spite of a reputation as a haunt for pirates, home to headhunters and rife with tropical diseases, competition was fierce for the last piece of available land in the area – what is today Sabah.

The foundations of Sabah Sabah at that stage did not exist – it fell within the Sulton of Brunei's territories. However, the sinking sultanate was forced to hand over several parts of its empire which it could no longer control and in the mid 1860s, a ten-year lease of Sabah was agreed with the American consul to Brunei, Claude Lee Moses. Sadly he did nothing more than run off to Hong Kong with the cession fees! British trading arrangements had far more lasting repercussions.

The birth of the BNBC In 1875, Gustavus Baron Von Overbeck, the Austrian consul in Hong Kong, won the deeds to the American Trading Company. Austria wasn't interested in a colonial acquisition and Overbeck turned to a London-based merchants firm run by Alfred Dent. Backed by Dent's money, they gained leases from the Sultan of Brunei for some 50,000km² of northern Borneo territory. A deal with the Sultan of Sulu won them another chunk of land, and the foundations of the British North Borneo Company (BNBC) were laid. Overbeck sold out to Dent and the company was officially baptised with a Royal Charter in 1881.

The BNBC was allowed freedom to administer as it saw fit, but heavy taxes on everything from rice to boats and birds' nests evoked resentment and resistance from Sabahans. However, none were successful (despite some credible efforts), and the BNBC administered the region of British North Borneo – known today as Sabah – until it became a British protectorate in 1888.

Meanwhile, in Sarawak... Brunei's need to seek outside support for protection was also the key to the beginning of a decisive era in Sarawak's history. In 1839, James Brooke – a Bengal-born, former British army officer and gentleman adventurer – sailed up the Sarawak River on his schooner *The Royalist*.

Here he encountered Raja Muda Hassim, a consort of the sultan who had been sent to suppress an uprising of exploited Malay and Dayak against the sultanate. The coastal and river dwellers had been hit with taxes, their men forced into working in the antimony mines, their women and children into slavery. With the situation spiralling out of Brunei's control, the junior prince begged Brooke to help him regain order. He was rewarded with land and the title of Rajah – ruler – of Sarawak in 1841. Thus began a somewhat unlikely chapter in Sarawak's history, which was to leave a lasting impression. For nearly a century, three generations of the Brooke family – hailed as the 'White Rajahs' – reigned over the state.

The Brooke empire spreads The Sultan of Brunei grew to be reliant on the British, and on Brooke, to help protect his sultanate. Brooke successfully suppressed the pirates which frequently wreaked havoc in coastal and river areas, enabling him to secure more land under his control as he worked his way up the coast. Some pirate-quashing missions were excessively brutal, sparking disapproval from Britain and even resulting in a commission of enquiry, though he was later acquitted. The Anglo–Brunei Treaty was signed in 1848, guaranteeing British control of trade along the northwest coast, free trade and access to Brunei ports. It also prevented the sultan ceding territory to any other nation without British consent – giving the British a tight grip on authority in the region.

And spreads... From its origins as a small riverside settlement, by the 1890s the White Raj had expanded through much of Sarawak, devouring territories from Kuching south to the Indonesian border and all the way north to Limbang. Even the BNBC ceded land to the Brookes. A lot of this expansion was driven by James Brooke's nephew, Charles, who succeeded him in 1868. As well as significantly extending the territory, no-nonsense Charles formed the *Council Negari* (State Council), boosted the economy and straightened out unruly tribes.

Charles Brooke was in turn succeeded by his son, Charles Vyner Brooke in 1917. Unlike family members before him, Vyner Brooke felt the Brooke dominion in Sarawak was something of an anachronism and chose to work in co-operation with a Supreme Council, diminishing the family's autocratic power. This decision was bitterly resented by the next in line, Anthony Brooke, who saw inheritance of his uncle's legacy as his birthright. Anthony stormed off to Singapore. The Brooke dynasty continued in Sarawak for over a century, until Japanese invasion on Christmas Day 1941.

For better and for worse, the European presence had a major impact on tribal and Malay societies in Borneo. Most historians agree that the biggest effect of colonial rule was the eradication of headhunting, bloody inter-tribal feuding, piracy and slavery. Over the first half of the 20th century, British rulers in Sabah and Sarawak promoted economic development, improved public welfare, and introduced infrastructure, bringing transport, healthcare, education and industry. Government and society were transformed, with Western taxation and law systems and territorial borders established.

WORLD WAR II IN BORNEO The Japanese invaded Borneo on Christmas Day 1941, and occupied several areas of Sabah and Sarawak until liberation by Australian

Ten thousand leeches as big as pencils walking all over you ... And big baboons [Orang-utans] screaming in the jungle of the night, wild pigs and crocodiles. And I'd think this is it, I'm going. You could feel yourself dying.

Comment by Australian POW Rex Blow at Memorial Park, Sandakan

Rex Blow was one of six Australian survivors of the atrocious Sandakan to Ranau 'death marches' of 1945, in which some 500 British and Australian POWs were forced to march 260km through hell and towards death, on the cusp of liberation.

forces in 1945. Hundreds of British, Australian, Chinese and other Allied troops died a brutal death at the hands of the invaders. According to the Sandakan Memorial Park, 'The POWs under the Japanese suffered brutally appalling living conditions, hard labour and death.'

Rebellion against the Japanese, led by the Chinese, showed some initial success, but the Japanese won with brute strength – guerillas on the ground were no match for Japanese bombs. Headhunting was quickly resumed during the occupation. Some 1,500 Japanese heads were collected, *paranged* (a *parang* is a steel sword) with glee – prized by the Dayaks (natives) for being 'nice round heads with good hair and gold teeth'. Though the Brooke regime had actively extinguished this brutal tradition, it was actually encouraged by Tom Harrisson (future curator of the Sarawak Museum) who famously parachuted into the jungle and recruited 1,000 Kelabit tribesmen to fiercely attack the Japanese.

There are many recorded instances of bravery and humanity towards the Allied troops by Sabah's and Sarawak's indigenous populations. They built shelter for escapees, provided them with medical supplies and helped them across enemy lines.

The aftermath of war The towns and economies of northern Borneo were badly hit by the war, as was the tenability of both Chartered Company rule in North Borneo and Brooke administration in Sarawak. The BNBC did not have the resources to rebuild after the devastation of the war which had levelled Sandakan and Jesselton (now Kota Kinabalu). It sold its assets to the British government, and in 1946 the British Protectorate of North Borneo became a Crown Colony. Political parties sprang up, squabbled, then joined forces, resulting in the Sabah Alliance. Sabah actually became an independent country for 16 days before joining the Malaysian federation.

When the Japanese surrendered, Sarawak was placed under Australian military administration and Charles Vyner and Sylvia Brooke took exile in Australia. In return for a large pension, claimed one account, he retired to England. In 1946, upon his urging, the State Council voted to cede Sarawak to Britain and the old Raj became a British Crown Colony, remaining so until the formation of Malaysia in September 1963.

MERDEKA! Malaysia had gained independence from Britain in 1957. Tunku Abdul Rahman, the prime minister of the freshly independent federation of Malayan states, was pushing for a wider alliance – to include Sarawak, North Borneo, Singapore and Brunei. Though Brunei snubbed the federation, the others signed up for the expanded federation in 1963, allowing Sabah and Sarawak their rightful *merdeka* (independence) from foreign rule. Singapore subsequently quit the federation in 1965, but the others remained.

THE FALL OF AN EMPIRE

In his book *Sylvia, Queen of the Headhunters: An Outrageous Englishwoman and her Lost Kingdom* Philip Eade attributes the downfall of the Brooke dynasty in part to Ranee Sylvia, Vyner Brooke's wife. 'She did nothing to dispel the impression that Sarawak was populated by headhunters and lotus eaters, and saw to it that her position as Ranee remained enshrouded in myth. Her peculiar status and activities were endlessly celebrated by the press, but the Colonial Office had long regarded her as "a dangerous woman".'

Drawing in part on Sylvia Brooke's autobiography written in the 1940s, his book is full of fascinating insights into some of the real machinations of the Brooke Borneo people's relationship, including their last night spent in a longhouse among rows of smoked Japanese heads, and their departure when the Ranee wrote: 'hundreds of little boats lined the river banks, and behind the boats the crowds were so dense they looked like a forest of dazzling flowers with their golden sarongs and little coloured coats... I would have felt further from tears if some of them had denounced us and called down curses on our heads instead of invoking this gracious and merciful benediction, this unanimous affection'.

After the Brookes returned to London, and the Privy Council, according to Eade, 'ordered the annexation of Sarawak to the British Crown' in July 1946, Sylvia wrote that: 'shorn of our glory ... [they were] faced with adjusting to a world in which we were no longer emperors but merely two ordinary, ageing people, two misfits...'

Brunei's decision to opt out of the federation meant that not only was it the only Muslim dynasty to re-establish itself after independence, it was also the only one to remain a British protectorate in the post-war years and not become a British Crown Colony. Brunei turned to partial self rule from 1959 until 1984, when it regained its independence and returned to sovereign rule.

GOVERNMENT AND POLITICS

SABAH AND SARAWAK Sabah and Sarawak are among the 13 states which, together with three federal territories (the capital Kuala Lumpur, Labuan Island and Putrajaya), make up the Federation of Malaysia. Malaysia is a constitutional monarchy, with two chambers of democratic parliament – the *Dewan Negara* (State Council) and the *Dewan Rakyat* (People's Council). The East Malaysian states of Sabah and Sarawak elect their own state legislative assembly to decide on state affairs, but fall under national jurisdiction for all federal matters, and share the same King.

Monarchy The king, or *Yang di-Pertuan Agong* ('paramount ruler'), of Malaysia acts as leader of the Islamic faith and official head of state. The latter role is largely

BORNEO'S GOVERNMENT AND POLITICS AT A GLANCE

Malaysia's prime minister (Datuk Seri Utama) Abdullah Ahmad Badawi
Malaysia's king Sultan Mizan Zainal Abidin
Sabah's chief minister (Datuk Seri) Musa Haji Aman
Sabah's head of state Tun Ahmadshah Abdullah
Sarawak's chief minister Abdul Taib Mahmud
Sarawak's head of state Tun Abang Muhammad Salahuddin Abang Barieng
Brunei's sultan and prime minister Hassanal Bolkiah

symbolic, and in reality the king has little legislative control – similar to the British monarch. His powers include a say in appointing the prime minister and granting parliamentary dissolution, acting on the advice of the legislature. The *Yang di-Pertuan Agong* is selected every five years by the nine hereditary sultans of Malaysia. The states without a hereditary sultan appoint their own state figureheads – Sabah and Sarawak both have a *Yang di-Pertua Negeri* ('head of state'), appointed by the king, on the advice of the federal government. Those governors join the other states in the 'Conference of Rulers' to elect the *Yang di-Pertuan Agong*.

Government Loosely based on the British system, Malaysia has three levels of government – federal, state and local. In the federal sphere, executive power is vested in a prime minister who, along with (the two houses of) parliament, is elected every five years. The Senate-like *Dewan Negara* (State Council), is partly elected by the king, partly by the state parliaments, whilst the House of Representatives-style *Dewan Rakyat* (People's Council) is chosen by a national vote.

Legislative power is divided between federal and state governments. While the majority of political matters are decided at a federal level, Sabah and Sarawak like the other 11 Malaysian states have exclusive jurisdiction over matters of local government, land, forestry and agriculture. Sabah and Sarawak also enjoy special autonomy from the federal government, akin to the special position of Northern Ireland in the United Kingdom's set-up. As well as its own head of state, each state also has its own constitution and elected assembly. The state assembly is led by a chief minister (*menteri besar*) and cabinet, and legislates on matters outside the federal parliament sphere.

Local government At a local government level, the many levels of administration are befitting of an English-inspired system of government. In Sarawak, the 13 state divisions are administered by district officers which are further divided and administered by Sarawak administrative officers. Beyond that, at the level of *kampungs* (villages), local affairs are taken in charge by the *ketua kampung* (village chief), also known as the *penghulu*.

Immigration When Sabah and Sarawak surrendered self-government to become part of Malaysia, one thing they both kept hold of was absolute power over their immigration laws. This means that even Malaysians from the peninsula have to produce passports and fill out immigration forms when entering Sabah and

MERDEKA! MERDEKA! MERDEKA!

It features in the name of shopping plazas, football fields, hotels, hairdressers and banks throughout Sabah and Sarawak. *Merdeka*, meaning independence, was the cry echoing through what is now the Merdeka Stadium in Kuala Lumpur on 31 August 1957, when independence was proclaimed and the Malaysian flag raised. The bid for independence was led by Tunku Abdul Rahman Putra Al-Haj, who headed the delegation of Malaysian ministers who negotiated the deal through to completion.

While the relationship of Sabah and Sarawak with the federal government may be generally ambivalent, public enthusiasm for Malaysian independence and for the concept of nation seems very strong if the *Merdeka*-count can be taken as an indication. A similar thing could be said for the frequency of crests, coats of arms, flags and other patriotic displays.

FLAGS AHOY!

THE MALAYSIAN FLAG The 14 red and white horizontal stripes on the flag represent the 13 Malaysian states, plus the federal entity. The flag is known as *Jalur Gemilang* or 'Stripes of Glory'. The blue rectangle to the upper left is meant to unify these different states and people. Within it there is a yellow star and moon crescent. The 14 points of the star again represent the federation; the crescent symbolises Islam; and the yellow is the dab of royalty and rulers.

THE FLAGS OF SABAH AND SARAWAK Since 1988 Sabah has had its own flag with the state symbolised by a black silhouette of Mount Kinabalu and its five divisions by the five colours: red, white, royal blue, zircon blue and icicle blue. Sarawak's flag, the *Bendera negeri Sarawak*, was also adopted by the state parliament in 1988. It uses the same colours as that of the Brooke Rajah flag – red, yellow and black – minus the Christian and monarchist symbols of a cross and a crown. The yellow star in the middle of the flag has nine points standing for the number of administrative divisions at the time, though today there are 11. The Sarawak flag was first raised at the National Day parade in Kuching in 1988. The unveiling of the flags probably marked a refreshed sense of state nationalism after 25 years of being parts of Malaysia.

Sarawak. This small bureaucratic hiccup is a shred of nominal autonomy in Malaysian Borneo. The trail-blazing prime minister of the 1990s, Dr Mahathir Mohamad, described it as being totally out of step with the idea of a single nation, and his contention over the immigration issue was just one of many thorns in the often prickly state–federal relationship between east and west Malaysia.

Political parties Malaysia is governed by a coalition of 14 political parties, the *Barisan Nasional* (National Front), led by the predominant United Malays National Organisation (UMNO). The UMNO has held power since Malaysia's independence in 1957 – currently holding two-thirds of the parliamentary seats – and the Prime Minister of Malaysia has always been from this major Malayan group. All other parties in the coalition represent a different ethnic group. Two other prominent parties are the MCA – the Malaysian Chinese Association – and MIC – the Malaysian Indian Congress. The MCA is the largest of several Chinese parties, each of them representing factions of the large and diverse Chinese community. It has been riddled for years by bitter squabbles.

BRUNEI With the sultan as self-elected, supreme executive authority, Brunei is an independent 'constitutional' sovereignty. Sultan Haji Hassanal Bolkiah is not only sovereign ruler, but also prime minister, defence minister, finance minister and head of the Islamic faith. Under the country's 1959 constitution he was invested with full executive authority, later amended to include full emergency powers. His brother, Prince Jefri Bolkiah, was finance minister until he caused a financial and personal scandal, squandering millions on a line-up of playboy acquisitions – his super yacht was called *Tits*, complete with two tenders, *Nipple I* and *Nipple II*!

The sultan's son – the crown prince and would-be 30th sultan – Haji Al-Muhtadee Billah – is the senior minister at the prime minister's office, while one of the sultan's brothers holds the foreign affairs portfolio. The other ministerial posts are shared among a close group of allies, personally hand-picked by his majesty. There are no elections. The sultan is advised on national policy by several councils, which he appoints – a Council of Cabinet Ministers, Religious Council, Privy Council, a Council of Succession and a Legislative Council.

Political parties Ever since a 1962 coup aimed at gaining political democracy, Brunei has been ruled by strict decree of the sultan, with zero tolerance of political parties – countenanced for a few years in the mid-1980s, but outlawed again in 1988.

The Brunei Solidarity National Party (PPKB) first registered in 1985 but has been largely inactive since; the Brunei People's Party (PRB) has been banned since 1962, and the Brunei National Democratic Party lost its government registration in 1988. The sultan is said to be making efforts to allow for democracy and public participation in political processes, in recognition that the country has to opt for less isolationism and more global in-touchness for economic and political survival. So far there has been no major public call for dissident political parties to come forth and make themselves heard.

JUDICIARY AND LAW

SABAH AND SARAWAK In judicial affairs, both Sabah and Sarawak have a High Court which comes under the supreme jurisdiction of the Malaysian Federal Court and Court of Appeal. All these courts took a page out of the British judicial system. In Sarawak James Brooke established a Court of Justice in 1841, and Charles Brooke established a more developed court system in 1870, adding a Supreme Court, Magistrates' Court and Native Court.

Today, both states have special laws dealing with Indigenous affairs, dealt with by the Native Courts. Various ordinances deal with Native Customary Rights (NCR) (see box below) and claims of native communities to ancestral land. State governments have introduced many new laws to seriously curb (or 'tighten their claws' as one critic put it) on Native Customary Rights. Well before the British set up courts, or the Malaysian Constitution was born, the indigenous communities had their own complex body of customary law called *adat* which governed their daily lives and socio-economic dealings. This was only recognised in a very limited manner by the NCR.

BRUNEI Brunei has a dual legal system, combining elements of English common law and court structure with Islamic sharia law – known in Malay as *syariah*. The majority of cases are handled by the Supreme Courts system which includes a Magistrates Court, High Court, Intermediate Court and Court of Appeals. The final court of appeal for civil cases only can be made through the Judicial Committee of the Privy Council which sits in London. The Syariah courts co-exist with the Supreme Courts and deal particularly with family law matters such as Muslim divorces, and questions of Malay-Muslim custom.

ECONOMY

SABAH AND SARAWAK Historians have said that Borneo was somewhat neglected during European presence. In Sarawak, the White Rajah did nothing to encourage large-scale private enterprise or capitalist investment, and the British government were not keen on investment. Sarawak and Sabah entered the Malaysian Federation as disadvantaged, politically undeveloped and marginal territories. Since then they have become something of an 'offsite production centre' for Malaysian primary industry, producing timber, petroleum, palm oil, rubber and other raw materials for export.

Since the 1980s, Malaysia has transformed itself into a major industrial force and southeast Asia's third-richest country. Sabah and Sarawak are developing at a much slower rate. Unlike Peninsular Malaysia, there is very little secondary industry, though there are signs of a small Silicon Valley developing in the greater Kuching area.

A sharp and divisive issue in Sabah and Sarawak has been that of indigenous land rights, known officially as 'Native Customary Rights' (NCR). On many occasions, it has pitted native people up against unbridled commercial forces and heavy-handed government projects such as logging and hydro schemes, often with grave consequences for natives – from misappropriation to total deprivation.

In theory, Native Customary Rights in Sarawak have been well established since as far back as James Brooke's times. The first White Rajah referred to indigenous land rights as 'the indefeasible rights of the Aborigines'. In reality, native people have been uprooted and relocated at will by the government, with little judicial recourse, and natives' rights have been whittled away rather than bolstered. 'Although the state has often conceded that the natives do have some customary rights on land surrounding their longhouse and on nearby cultivated areas, it has consistently disputed the natives' claims to the "high forest", where hunting, fishing and gathering of forest products by community members take place. Naturally, it is in these high forest areas that logging concessions and dam building activities often take place,' says Sahabat Alam of Friends of the Earth Malaysia.

'Indigenous peoples have not been granted titles under Sarawak land legislation for much of their lands,' Douglas Sanders wrote in *Indigenous Law Bulletin* in 2002. Sanders is an indigenous rights specialist and professor of law at the University of British Columbia. 'The Indigenous majority of Sarawak has not been able to control the State government and its development agenda. The government is based on an alliance of Malays, Chinese and coastal tribal peoples, while the issues of land rights, logging and plantations affect the interior tribes. Sarawak is prosperous. Its wealth is primarily based on massive logging operations, and the logging companies are usually controlled by Chinese businesspeople. Many Indigenous people work in the harvesting operations. In this process, native customary land rights are largely ignored. Where titles have been granted to native tribes, they can be appropriated without consent under amendments passed a few years ago designed to facilitate the establishment of pulpwood and palm oil plantations.'

The Sarawak government has put the onus on indigenous people to prove that they cultivated land prior to 1958, in order to be able to lay claim to it as ancestral land. With the help of NGOs, native communities have done so using community mapping and hand-held GPS units. After having some success in their claims, in 2001 the government introduced new laws requiring all permissible land surveys to be conducted only by those licensed with the Land Surveyor's Board. 'Without any map to indicate the extent of their land, communities will be increasingly powerless to oppose the claims of logging, oil palm and other companies on their land,' says Sahabat Alam, describing the laws as unprecedented worldwide.

The differences of standards of living and earnings between Malaysian Borneo and the peninsula has lessened since the 1990s, when one-third of Sabah's residents lived in poverty, though 2005 still saw Sabah ranked as Malaysia's third-poorest state. Despite a wealth of natural resources, growth rates and GDPs in both Sabah and Sarawak (GDP US$3,000) are still lower than the Malaysian average (US$5,000), and five times less that of neighbouring Brunei (US$15,000) (based on 2005 figures). The wealth generated from agriculture and forestry is said to largely bypass the chronically poor, particularly indigenous communities in rural areas.

Agriculture, forestry and fishing have underpinned Sabah and Sarawak's economies for decades. However, since the early 2000s, tourism has been the fastest-growing sector of Sabah's economy, and the fourth foreign revenue earner after palm oil, crude petroleum and plywood. Tourism in Sarawak is also catching up.

In Sabah, agriculture provides about one-third of the state's GDP, a third of the jobs and a third of the state's export earnings. Palm oil, cocoa and rubber are the three biggest agricultural industries. The state is Malaysia's biggest crude cocoa producer, providing 70% of the national crop, and rubber is the third most important commercial crop. Both rubber and cocoa beans are sent to Peninsular Malaysia for downstream processing into high value-added products.

For now, the timber industry is still the backbone of Sarawak's economy. The value of Sarawak's wood exports increased by 26% to 9.1 billion MYR in 2006 from 7.2 billion MYR the previous year. The timber industry is also a major employer in the state. In 2007 it provided jobs to 40% of people employed in the state. Sarawak also grows 95% of Malaysia's black pepper, which sees the country ranked as the world's fifth-largest pepper producer with an annual yield of around 20,000 tonnes.

Palm oil In the last ten years, palm oil has overtaken forestry as the biggest export (and environmental issue) in Sabah (see *Monoculture* box, *Chapter* 7, page 201). Sabah produces over a quarter of Malaysia's palm oil and the controversial crop is the state's biggest earner, reaping 37% of total revenue, and exceeding 7RM billion in 2004.

More and more farmers are converting to oil palm cash crops with its high yields and quick returns. Though there is currently little secondary industry, that picture may be changing as biofuel companies set up camp in southeastern Sabah, investing in research and development of palm oil as a potential renewable energy source.

As indigenous tribes are encouraged to convert their forested land, palm oil plantations are springing up all over Sarawak too, and it is quickly catching up with Sabah in terms of production – contributing 50% of the world's billion dollar palm oil market. Sarawak plans to double its plantations to one million hectares by 2010, as the palm oil industry gradually replaces the timber industry.

BRUNEI Despite having one of Asia's highest per capita incomes, Brunei's GDP per capita has been on a downward trend since the mid-1990s. It dropped by about 15% in the following decade and economic growth was a 'modest' 2% per year. Per capita GDP was US$18,300 in 2002, down from the 1980 heydays of over US$20,000. Still, alongside its Bornean neighbours Brunei's wealth glows. Brunei is the wealthiest country of the 57-member Organisation of Islamic Countries, and the fourth-richest country in Asia.

A small nation with an intensively resource-based economy, Brunei's main economic and social fuel are the extensive oil and gas fields which account for over half of its economic activity and three-quarters of its exports. The oil and gas business has been the main catalyst of economic growth since 1975. Nearly 95% of crude oil produced is exported – about 90% as liquefied natural gas (LNG), the rest used to generate electricity supply in Brunei.

Brunei's oil-rich economy, says its government, affords its population high living standards 'resulting in positive social indicators such as high literacy rates, longer life expectancy, and low unemployment and crime rates. The government provides for all medical services and subsidizes rice and housing.' This is clearly visible– the ubiquitous villas, cars and gold jewellery; however, such relative wealth does not seem to be actually transferred to other social indicators such as life expectancy (despite the claims of the government). Sabah, Sarawak and Brunei shared similar figures in the mid-70s.

Meanwhile, life expectancies of the petroleum and natural gas resources are as low as 20 years. In 2005, UNESCO recognised the need for Brunei to innovate and diversify with science and technology to counter the foreseen fall in oil riches. It concluded that Brunei's non-oil and gas sectors were not very developed. Currently, oil and gas account for 90% of exports and 40% of the country's GDP. The government's 'economic diversification program' has targeted international finance, tourism, transport, logistics and ICT as potential growth areas.

PEOPLE

ORIGINS AND PREHISTORY As the midpoint between China, the Indonesian Archipelago and the Pacific region, Borneo is an age-old sea crossroads of southeast Asia; southerly migrations through the island are known to have taken place tens of thousands of years ago. The thoroughfare left its footprints on the population of Borneo to become what it is today: a human rainbow of racial intensity and multi-hued traditions.

The racial mosaics of Sabah and Sarawak are quite different in their intricacies. However, the people of Borneo are believed to originate from a common ancestral stock, along with the people of Sumatra, Java, Bali, Sulawesi Island, the Philippines and the Malay Peninsula. Scant information is available about the precise period of arrival of the ancestors of today's indigenous people to Malaysian Borneo, though it is believed to have started around the 15th century. Some earlier tribes were wiped out through clan warfare or simply moved on to other places.

Early hunter-gatherers There is evidence of human presence in Borneo as far back as 45,000 years ago; one of the most important archaeological finds of the 20th century was near the west coast of Sarawak. A 40,000-year-old human skull, along with stone tools, animal bones and human burials, was unearthed at the mouth of the Niah Caves. The immense cave has been described as the most important archaeological site in Asia. The discovery, made by Tom Harrisson in 1958, confirmed the presence of prehistoric hunter-gatherers in Borneo. Similar remains have also been found in caves in southeastern Sabah. Since 1958, the area surrounding the caves has been granted national park status (see *Chapter 12, Northern Sarawak*).

Austronesian migrations Despite the evidence of such early *Homo sapiens* in Borneo, the linguistic ancestors of today's native populations are believed to have settled more recently. Austronesians migrating through Taiwan and the Philippines from around 2500BC are believed to have settled in Borneo, the Philippines and Indonesia. People with closely related Austronesian languages also settled the Malay Peninsula, other parts of the Malay Archipelago and the Pacific Islands, to as far as Hawaii, New Zealand and Easter Island.

The early Austronesian-speaking migrants who moved to the Philippines and Borneo from Taiwan around 2000BC took with them knowledge of 'weaving, bark-cloth making, pottery, pigs, dogs, rice, and finely polished stone tools', says Professor Peter Bellwood from the Australian National University School of Archaeology and Anthropology. People originally settled in lowland coastal areas, with shifting agriculture and rice production becoming ingrained in their culture. Only with the advent of metal-use, iron in particular, were tribes able to penetrate the forests further inland.

The story of the Austronesian-speakers tells of one of the most remarkable migrations in human history, from which people in the area of southern China 4,000–5,000 years ago set out and settled vast parts of southeast Asia. Today, over

In Sarawak, the collective name *Dayak* is given to all the indigenous tribes (and is also sometimes used to refer to all indigenous people of Borneo). Its origin is debatable but it has been widely used to denote inland-dwelling people as opposed to the Malay coastal populations. The word Dayak is not considered derogatory – it is used in the press and in public, in reference to Dayak issues and events. Many indigenous people including settled agriculturalists and forest nomads use it themselves to affirm their indigenousness both politically and culturally, and to differentiate themselves from the rest of the population

The closest equivalent in Sabah is the *Kadazandusun*, an umbrella term for the largest native population which includes many ethnic subgroups and represents about a fifth of the population.

300 million people are estimated to speak Austronesian languages, populating a large chunk of the planet from Madagascar though to New Zealand and Hawaii. These people 'share over 1,000 related languages that derive from a common linguistic homeland in Taiwan', Professor Bellwood says in his 1997 book *Prehistory of the Indo-Malaysian Archipelago*. 'Before Christopher Columbus and the explosive expansions of Hispanic languages and English, the Austronesian language family was by far the most widespread in the world.'

Today There are now over two dozen major ethnic groups living in Malaysian Borneo, and a handful of such groups in Brunei. Between them, they speak over 80 different dialects. Like Malaysia as a whole, Sabah and Sarawak have large contingents of Malay, Chinese and Indian populations, but are distinguished by a much wider variety of other ethnic groups. Brunei on the other hand has a big Malay majority.

ETHNIC GROUPS AND INDIGENOUS PEOPLES Borneo's ethnic make-up is colourful and multi-layered, having been touched by various influences over the centuries. For every different type of landscape – highland, lowland, coast and interior – there are different indigenous tribes and dozens of sub-tribes. There are around 70 different ethnic communities between Sabah and Sarawak alone. Brunei is predominantly Malay but also has Chinese, Indian and indigenous populations such as the Iban and Murut.

Sarawak Sarawak's population is made up of 27 different ethnic communities, speaking 45 different languages and dialects. Around 50% of the population are indigenous races, 28% are Chinese and 21% Malay (*Melayu*).

Iban The major ethnic group of Sarawak are the Iban, who migrated *en masse* from deep within the Kalimantan hinterland from the 16th century through to the 19th. A nomadic yet territorial group, they successively annexed large parts of Sarawak, from the southern border region right up through the centre of the state, eventually reaching the coast. Around 30% of the Sarawak population today is Iban – a much smaller number also migrated to Brunei. The Iban were referred to by 19th century Europeans as 'sea Dayak' – sea natives – erroneously, because they were in fact an inland, river-dwelling people. It is believed the confusion could have arisen from their superior boating skills, which they picked up from other tribes during their years of commandeering the coast – or their dabblings in piracy alongside the Malays at this time. The Ibans' name was also synonymous with both

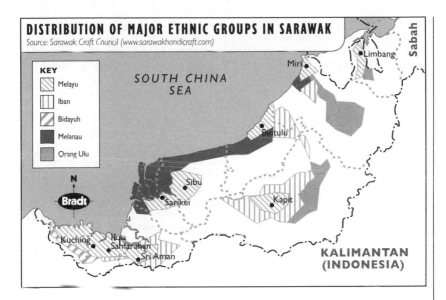

DISTRIBUTION OF MAJOR ETHNIC GROUPS IN SARAWAK
Source: Sarawak Craft Council (www.sarawakhandicraft.com)

KEY
- Melayu
- Iban
- Bidayuh
- Melanau
- Orang Ulu

SOUTH CHINA SEA

Sabah

Limbang

Miri

Bintulu

Sibu

Sarikei

Kapit

N

Bradt

Kuching

Nou Samarahan

Sri Aman

KALIMANTAN (INDONESIA)

headhunting and hunter-gathering; the success of an Iban man at these traditional activities would be proudly spelt all over his body in the form of tattoos. The first Iban settlements in Sarawak were at Lubok Antu, south towards the Indonesian border. Many still live in and around this area, sometimes in longhouses on the banks of rivers, several hours' boat journey from the nearest town. Some Iban homes are now furnished with modern, Western, luxuries such as televisions and fridges, afforded by employment in local timber and oil industries. As shifting cultivators, they originally built their homes near navigable rivers designed to last as long as their exploitation of rice farming in the area before moving on to pastures new. Whilst they have modernised, many still live in a longhouse community with up to 20 families per home, subsisting primarily on rice, fish and jungle food (plus *tuak* – rice wine), and are as river-savvy as ever.

Bidayuh The Bidayuh, meaning 'people of the interior', live in the hinterland regions of southwest Sarawak, pushed back from the coast by Iban invasions and pirate attacks; the Europeans dubbed them the 'land Dayaks'. However, their gentle-mannered and timid nature belies their warrior past – in their circular community houses or *baruk*, which rose over a metre off the ground, skulls of their enemies were displayed as headhunted trophies. Their (living) guests traditionally slept out in the *baruk*, with the severed heads in place of paintings on the walls! These houses are thus sometimes distastefully and simplistically translated as 'head houses'. The trophy heads were only ever gained from retaliation attacks however. As peace-loving people, the Bidayuh would only attack when provoked rather than out of sheer bloodthirstiness.

The Bidayuh people are masters of building with bamboo, expertly fashioning the dried stalks of the plant into a huge range of implements, from farming tools and cooking utensils to musical instruments, not to mention utilising its properties for their ingenious water system. This gravity-based plumbing system not only provides water for the longhouses but also waters the fields of growing rice and vegetables in times of little rain. Existing in just a small slither in the Samarahan District, the Bidayuh number 135,000 – about 8% of the population.

The Kayans, Ibans, Kenyah and Kelabits all have strong tattoo traditions. The Kayans have been described as the creative force behind most tattoo designs. Kayan men carved highly stylised designs of animals – hornbills, dogs, scorpions – onto wooden blocks that could be easily transferred onto skin and shared between villages. Tattoos were collected like passport stamps, as proof and souvenirs of journeys. It was the Kayan women however that traditionally applied the tattoos. These were usually made from soot or charcoal, and occasionally impregnated with special materials believed to make the tattoo more powerful, such as a piece of meteorite or animal bone. Kayan women would be adorned with their first tattoo as they passed into adulthood, although the most intricate designs were reserved for those of higher class and greater wealth. A design unique to the Kayan is the talisman (*lukut*) on the wrists that is believed to prevent the soul from escaping the body. In Iban society, men apply the tattoos, often after a successful headhunting expedition. Indeed, tattoos in all Dayak societies often have more than a mere decorative purpose – they can be symbols of status, success and wealth.

Orang Ulu The remainder of the population is made up of various tribes, including the coastal **Melanau**, the **Kelabit** people who live in the highlands of northeast Sarawak near the Indonesian border and several ethnic minorities who live in the interior. Collectively these upriver races are called the **Orang Ulu,** literally 'people of the headwaters'. They number about 100,000 and account for 6% of Sarawak's population. The name 'Orang Ulu' was originally attributed to the larger **Kayan** and **Kenyah** tribes who live in the Upper Rejang and Upper Baram river areas, but included smaller contiguous groups including the Kajang, Kejaman, Punan, Penan and Ukit. The term now embraces other mid- and lower-river people such as the Berawan and Murut, the Lun Bawang, Lun Dayeh and the Kelabits.

Kayan Another headhunting group who migrated from Kalimantan into Sarawak, the Kayan gradually moved, or were forced by other tribes, way up north. Some among the population of 15,000 still live in longhouses along the 400km-Sungai Baram and its tributaries, and the lower Sungai Tubau in the Kapit Division. Kayan women have tattoos on their hands and legs – the men wear leopard's teeth in their ears. Though it is becoming increasingly rare to see, they once all had earlobes hanging down towards their shoulders extended with the help of brass and other metal weights. Like other tribes, their greatest skills grew from their lifestyle and many of those in Sarawak were buoyed along by rivers. The Kayan traditionally carved their boats from a single block of *belian* (ironwood) – the strongest tropical hardwood.

Kenyah The Kenyah people are closely related to their Kayan neighbours, and brutally rivalled the Ibans together as age-old allies. For centuries both have also practised shifting cultivation of dry rice in the upper parts of the Baram River. It's believed they could be the first of the aboriginal groups in Sarawak, preceding the Iban, after migrating from the Sungai Kayan (Kayan River) area of East Kalimantan where many of their cousins still live.

Sabah In Sabah about 39 different indigenous groups account for 50% of the population.

Kadazandusun This is the largest group, encompassing several distinct sub-tribes including the **Rungus** and the **Dusuns** of Tuaran, Ranau and Tambunan, all of

DISTRIBUTION OF MAJOR ETHNIC GROUPS IN SABAH

KEY

- Rungur
- Bajau
- Orang Sungei (KD sub-tribe)
- Murut
- Kadazan (Rungus sub-tribe)

SOUTH CHINA SEA

SULU SEA

CELEBES SEA

Kudat · Kota Delud · Kota Kinabalu · Ranau · Penampang · Yambunan · Kota Klias · Labuan F.T. · Beaufort · Tenom · Long Pa Sia · Sandakan · Sukau · Lahad Oayu · Tawau · Semporna

N

Bradt

whom speak very closely related dialects. With varying degrees of Chinese physical similarities, they are believed to have migrated from southern China thousands of years ago. Formerly known as *Duson*, meaning village or orchard people, this was construed as an uncomplimentary name given by Malay coastal dwellers, and was changed to Kadazan in the 1970s. Once farming people – and fierce headhunters – the Kadazandusun communities are concentrated mainly along the west coast and in the hinterland areas of Penampang, Ranau, Tambunan and Keningau through to the Sarawak border. As Sabah's population rises, so the Kadazandusun's shrinks – in the 1970s they were a large majority at over 30% of the population. That has since fallen to around 19% of Sabah's three million-plus people.

Politically, the group refers to itself as Kadazandusun – sometimes written as Kadazan-Dusun – though some official population counts still separate them as the Kadazan and Dusun. Many of the individual races would never identify with anything but their proper tribal name: **Dusun**, **Rungus**, **Lotud**, **Minokok**, **Tambanuo**, **Tindal** and **Orang Sungai** ('river people'), and it's far more courteous to do the same.

Bajau This is the second-biggest ethnic group in Sabah, representing 13% of the state population. Like Kadazandusun, Bajau is a collective term for several ethnic groups, all of them originating from the Philippines and the Sulawesi coast of Indonesia: the **Bajau**, the **Illanun**, **Suluk**, **Obian** and **Binadan**. With a history of seafaring migrations, and partly of piracy, they are still largely a coastal-dwelling people, with large communities on both the east and west coasts of Sabah.

Murut The Murut people represent the third-largest indigenous group – about 50,000 live in the hinterland of Sabah's west coast and in the Kinabatangan river

The Penan tribe have been making international headlines since the 1980s, when the consciousness of the devastation of Borneo's forests and indigenous traditions first started to break through island barriers. Many Penan were among those arrested for protesting against logging; despite being inherently shy people, having had little contact with the world beyond the forest until recent years, their determination to do something about the all-out war on their forest homes made them go public.

The Penan are among the only hunter-gatherers remaining in southeast Asia, and the last tribe in Borneo still living this traditional lifestyle. They live in groups of 20–30 in the upper Rejang river area and along the Sungai Baram in central Sarawak, and around Sungai Limbang in northern Sarawak. The Penan use blowpipes to kill deer and wild boar, moving to new areas when their supply of wild sago flour starch (which they make from sago palms) runs out; they supplement their diet with wild fruits, jungle roots and plants. Their shyness of the world outside the forest, and of sunlight, is reflected in the paler shades of their skin in comparison with other tribes. There is common confusion between them and the less numerous, dialectally distinct Punan.

Prince Charles of Great Britain caused outrage in Malaysia when he accused the country of collective genocide with regards to the Penan. The Malaysian government maintained that it simply wanted the Penan to integrate with society for their own sake, attempting (unsuccessfully) to lure the hunter-gatherers to settle with luxurious longhouses; meanwhile, the logging continued.

The dispute continues, with Penan leaders maintaining that without the forests they 'become poor and lose our homes, with no hope of good jobs. Our children are robbed of their future and their heritage. We have the right to live in the lands of our ancestors, just as you do.'

According to Malaysian and international law, the Penan do have rights to their land and should be consulted before any logging can proceed; but these rights are often openly violated.

Worryingly, they also face another threat: in October 2008 a document outlining the construction of 12 hydroelectric dams was accidentally published on the internet. If the plans are approved, the dams would puts the homes of 1,000 Penan, Kelabit and Kenyah peoples under water, as well as parts of the Mulu National Park World Heritage site.

area. There are also tribes of Murut in Sarawak and Brunei. Dressed in black and sporting multi-coloured beads, they are longhouse dwellers and many still live traditionally, their houses close to rivers and with high levels of community co-operation. A good illustration of Borneo's kaleidoscopic culture is that even as such a relatively small slice of the population, the Murut are broken down into 14 sub-ethnic groups speaking 12 dialects, some of whom do not understand each other. Living in and alongside forests, the Murut are great botanical healers – each community has its own herbalist, a *mongugusap,* wiser old men or women who use plants – roots, barks and leaves – and animals to cure a variety of ailments. From diarrhoea to diabetes and high blood pressure, it seems that when you have an intimate knowledge of the forest, there's a natural cure for everything.

Brunei Only 12% of Brunei's population is made up of indigenous tribes, though the 'Malay' majority (73%) are actually Melanaus and Kedayan – people indigenous to northern Borneo. **Muruts**, **Ibans**, **Dayaks** and **Dusuns** form the tiny slice of Brunei's indigenous population.

Melayu (Malay) Originating from Yunnan, China, the Malay people first reached the Malaysian Peninsula around 2000BC. Due to many influences from the neighbouring areas like Java, Sumatra, the Indian subcontinent, China, the Middle East and the West, the cultures of the Malaysian Peninsula have been shaped and reshaped. This is probably due to the strategic position for trade, consequently influencing its custom and social identity.

The Malays are the largest ethnic group in Bornean Malaysia, accounting for more than 50% of the population. In Sabah and Sarawak however, that figure is closer to 25%. The Malay population in Brunei is highest, at 73%. Malays started arriving in Borneo from the 1400s, from trading kingdoms in Sumatra (Indonesia). Nearly all of them settled on Borneo's shores and subsisted as fishermen. Today the Malay *kampung* (villages) still cling largely to the coast. Some of those *kampung* in the Kuching area are named after Javanese towns from where the locals sprang. The Malays are known for their gentle mannerisms and rich arts heritage.

'The main defining characteristic of "Malayness" is the Islamic religion,' writes Victor T King in *The Peoples of Borneo*, adding 'one of the most important distinctions in Borneo is between those who are Muslims and those who are not'.

Not all Muslims however are Malay. Some major ethnic groups such as the Bajau in Sabah and the Melanau in Sarawak have converted to Islam but many still maintain their own cultural identity. Their Malay conversion from Hinduism and Theravada Buddhism to Islam began in the 1400s, largely influenced by the decision of the royal court of Malacca.

The Federal Constitution of Malaysia defines a Malay as someone who practises Islam and Malay customs, speaks the Malay language and is the child of at least one parent who was born within the Federation of Malaysia before independence on 31 August 1957.

The question of 'Malayness' is quite a paradox, especially when it appears that the origins of many 'Malay' people in Borneo lay with the island's indigenous tribes. Large numbers of the island's Malay population are believed to descend from Dayak tribes who converted to Islam from the 16th century onwards. Such a switch is called *masuk Melayu* – to convert to Malay.

Chinese In Sabah, Sarawak and Brunei, the diverse Chinese communities represent the second-largest race of people and the largest non-indigenous group – 30% in Sabah and Sarawak and 15% in Brunei. Although evidence of Chinese settlements dating to the 10th and 11th centuries have been found, most of the ancestors of today's Chinese population came as settlers in the 18th century, during the early years of the British North Borneo Chartered Company in Sabah and the White Rajah's reign in Sarawak (see *History*, *Chapter 1*, page 5). Most of them were Hakka Christian farmers, and this is still the biggest Chinese race in Sabah. There are also populations of Cantonese, Mandarin, Teochew, Hokkien, Hainanese and Henghua, each with their own dialects.

From Sabah's east coast to Sarawak's west coast, the Chinese colour Malaysian Borneo's and Brunei's towns red with their festivities, urban mentality and businesses. In Sabah, many Chinese have intermarried with other races, in particular with the large Kadazandusun population; there are prevalent Sino-Kadazan and Sino-Dusun subcultures in Sabah, with people who practise both Kadazandusun and Chinese customs. Today, with typical industriousness, the Chinese are strongly represented in the services and retail sectors and have turned small shops into multi-million-dollar businesses. Thousands of others operate coffee shops and restaurants.

LANGUAGE

The language map of Borneo is as much of a mosaic as the ethnic one. Throughout Malaysian Borneo and Brunei, there are around 100 different regional and tribal dialects spoken. *Bahasa* is Malay for language, so English is *Bahasa Inggeris*, French *Bahasa Perancis*, etc.

The official national language of Malaysia is Malay – *Bahasa Melayu*. Another slightly different version is *Bahasa Malaysia*. Although mutually understandable, they are not entirely the same. There are also some state variations of Malay – *Bahasa Sarawak* is Sarawakian Malay, spoken like a dialect with only a sprinkling of different words, but enough to surprise visitors from the peninsula. *Bahasa Malaysia* and *Bahasa Melayu* are similar to *Bahasa Indonesia* and can pretty much be understood from Sumatra to the Philippines.

While Malay may be the national language of Malaysia, it is far from being the true *lingua franca* in Malaysian Borneo. In Sabah, for example, only a quarter of the population are Malay and the state harbours more than half of Malaysia's indigenous languages – the estimated 39 ethnic communities speak some 55 different languages in 80 dialects. There are four major linguistic families: *Dusunic, Murutic, Paitanic* and *Sama-Bajau*.

TRIBAL LANGUAGES Many tribal languages, as throughout Borneo, are thought to descend from the Austronesian and Malayo-Polynesian language family

Dusun usually describes himself generically as a *tulun tindal* (landsman), or on the West Coast, as a Kadazan.' We can therefore safely say that the word Kadazan was already in existence before any towns or shops were built in the Penampang District, and that Kadazan politicians did not invent the word in the late 1950s and early '60s. Thus the most likely explanation for the term Kadazan is that it means 'the people'.

Rutter also offers us the explanation as to how the word 'Dusun' came to be applied to the largest ethnic group in Sabah.

> The pagans are usually divided into two main tribes, which are given the distinguishing names of Murut and Dusun. These names are however never used by the tribes themselves, but appear to have been applied to them by the Muhammadan invaders.
>
> The name 'Murut' is derived from the Bajau word *belud* meaning 'hill' and 'Dusun' is the Malay word for 'orchard'. So that *Orang Murut* and *Dusun* respectively meant 'men of the hills' and 'men of the orchards.

Rutter seems to suggest that the word *dusun* was used by the Bajaus of Sabah's west coast in referring to the native people of Penampang and Papar. When the first white men came to the shores of Sabah, the first people to meet them were the Bajaus or Malays, and when the white men asked, 'Who are the natives living in the Penampang and Papar areas?' they would have replied with 'Orang dusun', meaning villagers or orchard people. The white men, not knowing the real meaning of the word *dusun*, believed that these people were in fact called Dusun. This was how Dusun came to be applied to the largest indigenous ethnic group of Sabah.

This is an edited version of Richard F Tunggolou's account of the origins of the names Kadazan and Dusun, reprinted with thanks to the Kadazandusun Language Foundation, a vigorous promoter of indigenous culture and language in Sabah. The writer hoped that his article, first published in 2004, would 'make the blurred picture of the ongoing question on the origins and meanings of the names Kadazan and Dusun clearer'.

trees, due to the Austronesian settlement of the island around the third millennium BC. Even in one minority group such as the Bidayuh in Sarawak, there are a dozen dialects, and some do not even understand each other. Sabah's largest linguistic group, the Dusunic, is splintered into 14 dialects including Dusun, Rungus and Bisaya. Due to imperial influence, English is spoken fluently by more Kadazans in Sabah than any other ethnic group. A similar situation occurs with the Iban in Sarawak. With the decline of the Kadazan language and other tribal vernaculars, the Sabah state government introduced policies to try and counter their extinction, including encouraging public schools to start teaching indigenous dialects. The Kadazandusun Cultural Association (e *www.kdca.org*), and the Kadazandusun Language Foundation (e *www.klf.com.my*) are both very involved in language issues, and their offices and websites are useful reference points for many other cultural links.

CONSERVING LANGUAGE AND CULTURE A study conducted in the mid 1980s showed that mass-media, urbanisation, the education system, intermarriages and language prestige were all having their effect on the decline of indigenous languages in Sabah. Since then things have got worse, but the cultural vigilance has gained ground as echoed in the following verse. It is written in Dusun dialect and kindly translated to English by Dr Benedict Topin from the Kadazandusun Cultural Association (KDCA).

Born from the British military's time in Borneo when there was a need to find mutual comprehension with the Malay people and the indigenous tribes, a common linguistic ground was struck in what became known as 'Bazaar English'. This hybrid expression was so called because of its use in trading in small street bazaars and at markets (it was also useful on buses and riverboats). The hybrid tongue borrows words from many languages. With globalisation and the rise of English language, it has grown into an increasing muddle of Malay, English, Chinese and Dusun words. People just mix it up as they like – it really should be called *Bizarre* English!

Atagak o boros, atagak o koubasanan	Lose our language and we will lose our culture
Atagak o koubasanan, atagak o kointutunan	Lose our culture and we will lose our identity
Atagak o boros, atagak o pirotian	Lose our language and we will lose our understanding
Atagak o pirotian, atagak o puinungan, pisohudungan om pibabasan	Lose our understanding and we will lose our harmony, co-operation and peace
Atagak o pibabasan, atagak o piobpinaian	Lose peace and we will lose our brotherhood and sisterhood
Atagak o piobpinaian kopitongkiad o rikoton do rusodon.	Lose our brotherhood and sisterhood and we will be dispersed in our journey towards common destiny.

RELIGION AND SPIRITUALITY

Over the centuries Borneo has been visited by many different traditional faiths and spiritual beliefs, just as it has by ethnic tribes, traders, explorers, migrations and missionaries. All these influences have brewed a rich religious life which plays an integral part in culture and society. Under the official seal of Islam there are other mainstream religions and many fascinating, though fading, rituals of tribal devotion to extensive spirit worlds.

LINGUISTIC DIVERSITY IN NORTHERN BORNEO

with Peter Martin
Like the biodiversity in northern Borneo, the linguistic diversity is wonderfully rich. Malay, in one form or another, is used along the coastal strip and in the towns. There are distinct varieties of Malay in Brunei, Sabah and Sarawak and English is spoken in major urban areas. But beneath the surface of Malay and English, there is an abundance of linguistic diversity, which encompasses major languages such as Iban (Sarawak and Brunei), Bidayuh (Sarawak), Kadazandusun (Sabah), Tutong (Brunei) and several varieties of Chinese. Many of the languages of the three northern Borneo states have not been described in detail, and remain unwritten. There is also considerable evidence that there is a shift away from some of these languages to a form of Malay.

Peter Martin is Professor of Linguistics and Education, University of East London, and has written widely on language issues in Brunei and Sarawak. He is editor of Shifting Patterns of Language Use in Borneo, *and co-editor of* Language Use and Language Change in Brunei Darussalam

RELIGIOUS HISTORY

Islam The religion came to the trading states controlled by Brunei's rulers from the late 13th century. Within a couple of centuries, the people were converting en masse to the religion of powerful Muslim merchants. Prior to that Buddhism and Hinduism were widely practised, as well as indigenous spiritual rituals.

In the 18th and 19th centuries, Islamic faith spread like wildfire into the hinterland areas of present-day Sabah and Sarawak, and many indigenous people converted. Religion reinforced the divisions between state-based and tribal society.

Christianity With the arrival of Europeans came the pressure of conversion to Christianity for Islam to compete with. This had profound effects on indigenous cultures. Thousands of Iban and Orang Ulu people including the Kelabits and Kayan turned to various denominations of Christianity and many of these former headhunters now celebrate Christmas Day.

Even the most remote ethnic communities were taken under the wings of Christianity. The same thing happened with Sabah's Kadazandusun peoples. In the process some indigenous religions were sent the way of extinction. Religious conversion was not just God-driven; it was used to improve law and order, to erode the power base of Muslim sultanates, reduce slavery and headhunting, and socialise people who were used to living in warring factions. As odd as it may seem today, headhunting was very central to the spiritual beliefs of all those tribes who engaged in it.

RELIGION TODAY Islam is the official religion of Malaysia, enshrined in the Constitution. Buddhism and Christianity are also prevalent along with Hinduism, Taoism and tribal religions. Important dates on the Muslim, Buddhist and Christian religious calendars are nationally observed with public holidays, as are major spiritual celebrations of indigenous peoples. In Malaysian Borneo, Islam is less widespread due to the greater imprint of Christianity. Sabah and Sarawak are the only two Malaysian states to celebrate Easter – about a quarter of their populations are Christian, compared with just 2% of the population in western Malaysia; one-third are of Islamic faith and over 17% are Buddhists and Taoists. Mosques, Buddhist temples, Catholic and Anglican churches are seen in cities and countryside. Large numbers of indigenous peoples including the Kadazandusun in Sabah and Iban in Sarawak have converted to Christianity, and the Bajau in Sabah and Melanau in Sarawak to Islam. Many maintain their animistic and other traditional belief systems as well, not only in private but as a key part of public celebrations. Death rituals, harvest festivals, effigies for healing and tattoos all play a part.

Islam in Borneo In Muslim-dominated cities and towns, the chants of Islamic prayer resonate through streets at dawn, and seep eloquently into skies at dusk. In Brunei, Islam is far more predominant – two-thirds of the population are practising Muslims. If you see the sign *KUDAT* in hotels, on the ceiling or table or in a bedside drawer, the arrow alongside it is not pointing out an emergency exit, but the direction of Mecca. One of the five pillars of Islam is that Muslims must make a pilgrimage – a *hajj* – to Mecca, the birthplace of Islam, once in their lifetime. By doing so, men are bestowed with the title *Hajji* and women *Hajja*. Such trips to Saudi Arabia are only possible for a relatively privileged few in poorer southeast Asian Muslim countries. In Brunei there are many *hajji* and *hajja*. Among them is the sultan, with *Hajji* just one of the words in his seemingly endless title.

Religious harmony As freedom of religion heats up as a pointed social and political issue in Muslim-dominated western Malaysia, the situation in eastern Malaysia (ie: Malaysian Borneo) seems to have progressed through its inherent greater religious diversity. In general, the religious atmosphere is one of tolerance and inter-religious respect. The different cultures and religions are relatively harmonious and it is common for people, in public and in private, to celebrate with those of different faiths. Often different religious beliefs coexist among different generations of one family, spiritual occasions are celebrated together by different indigenous groups and some of them such as the Kadazandusun *Tadau Ka'amatan* (harvest festival) in Sabah and the *Gawai Dayak* (the Iban harvest festival in Sarawak are highly communal. It's hard not to be touched by this peaceful coexistence; Sabah is one of the few places left on earth where many faiths live together in harmony.

TRIBAL BELIEFS

Iban The Iban's spirituality is believed to be something of a fusion of animism, Hinduism and Buddhism, brewed centuries back. Though hundreds of Iban converted to Christianity, the public signs of their traditional beliefs are still very potent through their festivals – the *Gawai Dayak* harvest festival, *Gawai Kenyalang* hornbill festival and *Gawai Antu* festival of the dead. The Iban dances – highly intuitive narratives – are punctuated by an array of mythical figures depicting relationships between the natural, spirit and human worlds. The *kenyalang*, or hornbill, is sacred to the Iban because the hornbill's nest, *tansang kenyalang*, is the abode of their supreme god of war *Aki Lang Sengalang Burong* – also known as 'the earth tremor which trembles and causes the full moon to fall'. In his earthly form, the Iban god takes the form of the eagle-like bird of prey, the Brahminy kite (*Haliastur Indus*).

Orang Ulu The Kayan, the Penan and the Kenyah wear cloaks of Christianity of varying denominations, but their animist beliefs live on in the supreme Bungan cult – an adaptation of their spirit-dominated worlds – and Bungan celebrations.

Melanau Old rituals remain very vividly in the minds and practices of many indigenous folk. The Melanau in Sarawak are a good example – two-thirds of them at least have converted to Islam, yet they still take part in some very feisty displays of animistic worship, and use carved wooden figurines to heal people. Journalist Diana Rose, who was born in the Melanau heartland of Mukah on Sarawak's west coast, says this: 'The original religion of the Melanau people was *Liko* meaning "people of the river". In the *Liko* religion, life and the environment are one. Followers worship the spiritual world including the superior *tou* spirits and the

ANIMISM

Many indigenous spiritual beliefs fall within the world of animism, where souls and spirits are attributed to animals, plants and various objects. Some academics have rejected the term animism, as with paganism, accusing it of depreciating traditional belief systems as simplistic and illiterate, especially when applied to Africa. There does not seem to be the same adversity to the term in Borneo and people use both animism and paganism to describe some very complex belief systems and ceremonies hinging on spirits and souls, magic and myth, spells and charms, and powerfully symbolic rites linked with birth, harvest and death. Indeed, animism is said to be more developed, elaborated and intellectualised among the Ibans and related tribes of Borneo than anywhere else in the world. The beliefs are so varied they actually defy a one-word definition. (See *Tribal beliefs* above for some brief descriptions.)

A common practice among the indigenous tribes of Borneo, until the first decades of the 20th century, was 'headhunting'; bands of young men would venture out to surrounding villages to collect the heads of enemies or other tribes. The freshly collected heads would be skinned and dried, smoked over a fire or boiled, and then hung up for all to see in the longhouse. The dried skulls were believed to possess powerful spiritual properties, providing vital transfusions of energy for villages. Heads were thought to be able to ward off evil spirits, disease and misfortune, whilst offering protection, fruitful crops and favourable weather. An unhappy head was capable of bringing terrible woes such as plagues, fires and droughts, so they were well looked after with offerings of food and blessings. Heads were the focus of much ritual, symbolising the procreative power of nature: the Kayan and Kenyah tribes in central north Borneo regularly held large festivals to honour the heads.

Heads were believed to lose their potency over time, so fresh heads were always required to replenish a village's spiritual energies. Although the practice has been all but eradicated, there are still the occasional reports of headhunting. Nowadays however, young male Dayaks are more expected to do a *bajalai*, or journey, to prove their worth rather than accomplish a successful headhunting mission. Many tribes still embrace and celebrate their headhunting histories however, using replica heads made out of coconut shells.

lesser *belum* spirits that cause sickness. The pagan Melanau use effigies of sickness spirits when practising healing. Many Melanau today are Christian and Muslim, though they still celebrate traditional festivals, most notably *Kaul*.' (See *Chapter 11, Central Sarawak*, page 266, for more.)

Kadazandusun Among the major ethnic groups of Sabah, the spirit world has reigned supreme. The best illustrations of this are the rituals of **Tadau Ka'amatan**, the rice harvest festival. The Kadazandusun believe that rice has a spirit, called *Bambarayon* or *Bambaazon*, which rejuvenates and ensures the bounty of next year's harvest. The thanksgiving festival is held to welcome the rice spirit back, to restore spirits that were lost in careless harvesting, to nourish the rice spirit with offerings of food, and for merrymaking and friendship. The whole thing is underscored by a legend and the need to fight off famine through worship.

Rituals carried out during and around the festival include the *Bobohizan* (priestess) selecting seven stalks of the best rice from the paddy before the festival begins. These are then presented to the owner of the rice field after the harvest, and symbolise the homecoming of the rice spirit. The most important part of the festival however is the *Magavau* ceremony, which takes place in the paddy under the first full moon after the harvest. *Magavau* involves a hunt for lost or strayed rice spirits who have been disturbed by mishandling of the crop or by pests. A sword-wielding male *Bobohizan* leads the ceremony followed by a chain of female *Bobohizans* who chant ritual verses to summon home the missing spirits. Triumphant, piercing cries peel out over the paddy when a spirit is recovered. See *Public holidays and festivals* on page 74 for more on Tadau Ka'amatan.

CULTURE

Forget the opera, theatre and grand literary occasions. The performing arts of Malaysian Borneo and Brunei are found (often free of charge) in the streets and in the people. The costumes, crafts, dance and music are steeped in tradition. Far from being consigned as museum pieces, the traditional customs of music, dance and rhythm are alive and kicking. Of course, there are organised indoor (and outdoor) performances, shows, festivals and orchestras, but they lack some of the verve of the raw performances.

MUSIC, SONG AND DANCE Everywhere you go in Borneo, each different culture is sung out with its own unique rhythm. Between all the various ethnic cultures – indigenous, Chinese and Malay – there is a rich tradition of instrumental music, song and dance performances. Music and dance most often go together; many dances are deeply symbolic and in some cases tied strongly to spiritual worlds and ceremonies.

Gongs and other instruments
Gongs are a big feature of cultural performance and music ensembles in Malaysia, in both indigenous and Malay music. There are many different types of gong.

Bruneians introduced the *kulintangan* into Sabah, which is played among ethnic groups of the Kadazandusun peoples on the west coast and the Muslim Bajau on the east coast. It looks like a series of brass casseroles lined up – eight small, knobbed gongs in xylophone-form which several players gong-chime away in turn.

In Brunei a stringed lute, the *gambus,* is played to the beat of Malay dances such as *joget* and *zapin*. Its hollow body is made from *nangka*, which is covered with lizard or goat skin and the neck coated with a thin wooden veneer. Three pairs of brass or gut strings are traditionally plucked with the claw of an anteater. There's a *Pesta Gambus* festival held every year on Sabah's west coast among the Brunei-Malay community and there are *Pesta* gongs all over the place.

Song and dance in sickness and health
Music and dance are central to Malay festivities. The *joget* is most common, a dance of lively tempo with lots of hand and leg movement, performed by couples in brilliantly coloured traditional silk dress. Its origins lie in Portuguese folk dance, having infiltrated Malay culture during the Malacca spice era. The dance is just as heated, but graceful as well, and there are several regional variations and adaptations.

The Bajau of Sabah perform dance rituals such as the *magamboh* to offer thanksgiving, though this is now an extremely rare dance performance. Dance may also be used to heal a sick member of the community, sometimes accompanied by an elaborate bath, visits to the graves of ancestors and prayers for the sick person and their family. The community as a whole takes note of the issue at hand, joining together at times of hardship and worry. After offering thanks and seeking blessing from the gods, the gong is struck and its resonant chime heralds the beginning of the dance.

Keeping the music alive
While Western influences are said to be having an altering effect (not all negative) on Dayak music and dance in Sarawak, efforts are under way to conserve traditional art forms. A big effort has been made recently to revive the Bajau dance traditions among young people after it was realised that most of

THE LEGEND OF HUMINODUN

The legend of Tadau Ka'amatan is that of Huminodun. Huminodun was the only daughter of the god Kinoingan, who sacrificed her (by cutting her up into many pieces) to end a great famine. It's her flesh and blood which are attributed to bountiful crops today – not only rice crops but coconuts, maize and yams.

INSTRUMENTAL BORNEO

Seri Insan Secondary School
The students from Seri Insan Secondary School in Kota Kinabalu provided these insights into Sabah's musical landscape – they live up to being 'bright human beings' as the school's name proclaims. According to them, four main groups of instruments feature in Sabah's traditional musical culture: *membranophones* (drums), *idiophones* (bronze or brass gongs), *aerophones* (flutes) and *chordophones* (string instruments).

Like many other cultures, there are many types of vocal music including love songs, battle songs, epic tales and ritual chanting. Instrumental music is as rich and complex as vocal music, with a variety of solos and ensembles. Instruments may be played by either men or women.

Most gong ensembles have a drum to emphasise the main rhythmic patterns. Drums from the interior region around Tambunan are called *karatung*. Also known as *gandang* or *gondang*, these are usually cylindrical in shape with a single head of cowhide or goatskin bound to the body. The most common types of *idiophones* are bronze or brass gongs. Every gong has a name denoting its sound or the rhythm it plays. A gong ensemble consists of seven to eight gongs, depending on the community. One such ensemble is the *sopogandangan*, which is played as an accompaniment to *magarang* dancing in Tambunan, or *sumazau* in Penampang.

Sabah has a wide variety of traditional *aerophones*, including short bamboo end-blown mouth flutes called *suling*; longer nose flutes known as *turali*; jaw's harps named *turiding* and *sompoton*, or mouth organs.

One of the *chordophones* used in Sabah is the *tonkungon*, a tube made either from a node or large *poring* bamboo. A large hole is cut in the back or in the top to enhance resonance and thin strips are cut in the surface to form strings or chords.

them could perform rap and hip hop, but not the traditional *tambawan* – performed by women only – and the *lellang* – by men only, and the graceful *limbaian*.

Shamans and storytelling in dance and music Music is an important medium in many spiritualist ceremonies. The *kulintangan* is still used in some rituals presided over by the Kadazandusun *Bobohizan* (or *Bobolian,* depending on the tribe). Music and crafts are threaded together too, as are music and storytelling. The traditional Iban women's dance – *ngajat indu* – is performed with costumes of woven *pua kumbu* cloths. Iban music and dance tells many stories of their past as virile combatants. In the *ngajat lesong* dance, the protagonist warrior displays his might by picking up a 20kg block of wood with his mouth, then dances round with it posed on his chin. The *ngajat pahlawan* is a dance to welcome the victorious warrior home after a successful week of headhunting.

Dances celebrate death, life and birth. The *datun julud*, an Orang Ulu dance, tells of the happiness of a prince when he was blessed with a grandson. From this grew a tradition; the Kenyah tribe, whose village consists of just one longhouse, perform it to welcome guests. The dancing is accompanied by the sounds of the *sape*, and much clapping and singing. 'A common aspect of the Kayan and Kenyah tribes is the singing of the *parap*, a folklore song relating expressions of love, happiness, loneliness and anger, while singing praises for the beauty of nature and all living things,' says the Sarawak Tourism Board.

Other tribes dance to appease spirits, to ask them for harvest blessings and for spiritual healing. Others pass legend and folklore through generations. In Malaysia's leading online newspaper *Malaysiakini.com*, Sim Kwang Yang wrote of *with Heidi Munan, cultural researcher and Honourable Curator of Beads at the Sarawak Museum. She has lived in Kuching for over 30 years.*

'The Dayaks of Borneo have long had a vibrant beadwork culture. Beads were believed to impart their two salient properties – physical strength and brilliance – to the wearer. Small glass beads were brought by traders from distant lands, which added to their mystical value. The manufacture and use of bead-worked garments and ornaments was traditionally linked to a person's status within society. This applies particularly to the people of Central Borneo, where the most potent designs were restricted to the aristocracy. Beadwork itself was gender-defined in that only women threaded the beads, but men designed the patterns. Today, many old taboos and restraints have become obsolete. Not so the craft of beadwork – beadwork is produced for sale in the coastal towns; some young designers incorporate traditional design in their fashion creations. Much beadwork is still done for home use and at regional festivals the young women are covered in more beads than their grandmothers ever dreamt of owning! The skills are passed from mother to daughter and materials are readily available. In sum, beadwork is flourishing in Borneo.'

Bead culture is strong in Sarawak's Kayan, Kenyah, Bidayuh and highland Kelabit communities, and among Sabah's Rungus population. In her book, *Beads of Borneo*, Heidi Munan explains that, excluding beads made from bone, teeth, seed and stone, many beads used in tribal crafts have long been imported. From as early as the 6th to the 12th century, trade with China and India brought beautiful, exotic beads. An ancient Kelabit headhunting song says that 'strangers came to buy pork and sell beads'. Later, Dutch and English explorers brought glass Venetian and Bohemian beads.

Iban storytelling: 'They have a whole legion of folk lore and myths ... a myth of creation, and legends of heroes and titans which bear some resemblance to the ancient Greek myths. Since the Ibans have no written language, their myths and legends are handed down from generation to generation by word of mouth. The telling and retelling of stories, sometimes through the lyrical form of the *Sampi* recitals that go on for hours at a time, make the Ibans great orators.... To call them merely animists is a little unfair. They certainly have a sort of pantheistic idea, in which the jungle and the land are alive with spirits.'

CRAFTS The cultural landscapes of Sabah, Sarawak and Brunei are woven in beads, fibres, fabrics and plants of many colours, shapes and forms. Every tribe has its distinctive craft and skills. The Kadazandusun are known for their hand-woven rattan baskets and bamboo musical instruments; the Rungus and Kelabits for their beadwork; the Murut for their blowpipes; and the Bajau for their colourful woven mats and food covers, *tudung dulang*. Indigenous crafts often wear a very strong mark of local flora – like part of a geo-cultural identity. Whether they have been made from forest woods or wickers, or the leaves or hard shells of tropical fruits, many of these things could not be truly replicated anywhere else.

With the vegetative world as intensely varied as it is in Borneo, there has always been quite a range of construction and crafting materials – different woods are used for boats, houses, musical instruments, hunting objects, and tools; rattan was woven into rope, baskets, bird cages, mats and crates; *nipa* palm fronds used for thatched roofs; bamboo for musical instruments. Many of these 'functional' objects can appear to be quite simple – yet their often ingenious and attractive

Beads of varying value were used to mark out social status between the indigenous aristocrats, and the middle and lower classes within tribes. Among the Kelabits for example, lower classes were rarely allowed to wear beads or bear traditional motifs, says Heidi. 'Aristocrats would buy or exchange slaves with different families, using beads as a form of payment. If you were captured during tribal war, your family may have used beads as ransom payment.' With so much power accorded to these little gems, beads were also used in a spiritual sense – for example during agricultural rites to bless planting and harvesting of crops.

The Kelabits, both men and women, still live out the bead tradition and are busy handing it on to younger generations. Women regularly wear bead necklaces and belts made from peppercorn beads; on special occasions such as weddings, they don the bead caps called *pata* made from the noble *ba'o rawir* – drinking straw beads. Men sport *kabo* – red seed bead bobble – with their Sunday suits or *batik* shirts.

Beaded creations have become popular among tourists with a couple of major downsides – rising prices, fake productions and the loss of antique beads to far off lands. 'Short of breaking the beads,' says Heidi, 'it's hard to tell the difference.' The proliferation of fakes is getting to a point that the Kelabits were even reported to be looking at a certification system, with the authenticity of bead creations authorised by the Pemanca or high chief of the Kelabit community.

Personally I don't care if the beads I buy are not old – I would rather those artefacts be kept among those who made them. However, I do not want cheap, machine-made replicas. A traditionally made creation hanging close to you is something to treasure.

New *pata* caps sell for around 1,000MYR while an antique one can fetch well over 20,000MYR. Individual antique beads can cost from 300–1,000MYR. Heirloom beads are priceless.

design qualifies them as traditional art, as much as the more intricate and embellished items made from precious materials.

Weaving Much of traditional life endures in Borneo; arriving in Melanau heartland in the region of Mukah, coastal Sarawak, you may see women sitting near the river weaving all kinds of basketry and traditional *terendak* sun hats from the fronds of sago palm – not only an economic staple but a cultural filament too.

Baskets are made by every tribe, using rattan, bamboo, *nipa* leaves and pandanus. Pandanus (screw pines) fruits are crafted not only into foodstuffs but their sheaths and fibre into many household items: *tikar pandan* (pandan mats) are made by the Kadazans of Papar on Sabah's west coast. The patterns on these, having once probably been more sober, are being turned out in many colourful patterns, woven into dining and drink mats to sell to tourists, but that doesn't mean they lose their inborn crafted quality and authenticity. The Kadazandusun people also weave many rattan baskets, and purses covered in beads. The woven wonders of Borneo are not only sold to visiting foreigners however – Malaysia provides 30% of the world's rattan.

Fabrics Different cloths (*kain*) form the basis of diverse woven handcraft traditions. The Iranun, an ethnic minority originally from the southern Philippines who live in small pockets on the east and west coasts of Sabah, traditionally used *kain dastar* as headgear during festive celebrations. Now they use the heavily motifed fabrics to make *dastar* purses, sashes and more. The Iranun community in Kota Belud, two hours north of Kota Kinabalu, are said to have gone further – combining the *dastar* tradition with that of *songket* – which uses gold coloured threads – to create *sampin songket dastar*, an amazing fusion of the gold-coloured threads and motifs. *Songket* originated among the Malayans of Brunei. There are lots of woven fabrics and cloth in Brunei; only here you may encounter real gold thread so make sure you have your purse with you. *Kain songket* ('cloth of gold') is discussed more later in the guide, as are Sabah's and Sarawak's *Pua Kumba* weaving with its plant and animal motifs.

COSTUMES The striking black velvet elegance of the Kadazandusun people attending a festival with their elaborate trimmings and embroidery stand out among the many beautiful costumes which go with ceremony, dance and music all over Sabah, Sarawak and Brunei.

According to the Kadazandusun Cultural Association, the men's jacket and trousers bear some Chinese influence. 'There are three different styles of blouses for the women. One is a blouse with short sleeves – *sinuangga* – worn by young ladies. Another is a blouse with three-quarter length sleeves – *sinompukung* – worn by middle-aged ladies for daily or casual use. The third one – *kihongon* – is worn by elderly women and female ritual specialists or priestesses during ceremonies.' The blouses are worn over a long cylindrical black skirt – *tapi*. Traditionally it was plain black cotton but rather striking renditions are trimmed with gold *siring*. The outfit is usually in silk and velvet for ceremonial occasions and cotton for day wear. Mass-made versions are appearing to sell to tourists. Likewise the men's long-sleeved shirt, *gaung*, and black trousers, *souva*, have been dollied up with gold buttons, and trimming.

The men wear some very fancy headgear: the *siga* is a conical hat made out of hand-woven cloth, *kain dastar*, which is then folded or twisted in a number of distinctive ways including *hinopung* – python form – and *kinahu* – pot-holder style.

Like many cultures, the Kadazandusun top off their couture with lots of accessories: brass and silver spiral bracelets (*tiningkokos*); hairpins (*titimbak*) to decorate and fasten the hair bun of women's often very long dark hair; necklaces (*hamai*), earrings (*simbong*) and brooches made with gold coins (*paun*). The more *himpogot* or silver 'dollar belts' a person is wearing, anything from one to three around the waist and hips, the more wealthy they are. Men wear a black, or sometimes coloured, waist sash (*kaking*). As for the *Bobohizan* priestess, her outfit is one of total feathered splendour. If you love costumes get hold of *An Introduction to the Traditional Costumes of Sabah*, see page 293.

The costumes of Borneo's tribes reflect their ethnic diversity: the noble formality of Malay outfits; the simple black sarongs and bodices of the Rungus, emblazoned in multi-hued black beads; and the strikingly beautiful, pom-pom-strung poncho and silver-feathered headdress of the Iban.

2

Practical Information

WHEN TO VISIT

WEATHER There are frequent mentions of wet and dry monsoons (and which to avoid) but in my opinion there isn't a clear-cut best period to visit Borneo. Each season has its advantages and drawbacks, and none of these are so critical that they necessitate planning an entire trip to either coincide with or avoid them. The dry season ('southwest monsoon') generally occurs from May to October, though huge downpours and floods can occur in June and July. The wet season ('northeast monsoon') is generally from November to April, and whilst monsoon rains can make life difficult and uncomfortable, they can quickly clear to blue skies in December. Unfortunately, as almost everywhere across the globe, notable climate change and seasonal unpredictability is becoming a reality.

Particularly for active and adventure holidays, the time the weather is most likely to hinder your travel plans is the wet season. Heavy rains and general bad weather may cause flights into remote regions to be cancelled and travel by boats may be affected. Those who plan to do a lot of trekking should be prepared for short bursts of wet weather at any time of the year. During the northeast monsoon, seas can be extremely rough; in January 2007, a tour company boat capsized off the north coast of Sabah because of a sudden change in weather conditions. Conversely, if there is not enough rain, travel upriver by boat is impeded. In the hotter periods with lower rainfall, river trips may be partly self-propelled as travellers are called on to get out of the longboats and push – upstream.

CROWDS As far as crowds go, it is best to avoid school holiday periods and major festive celebrations. The busy-ness of these periods can not only make it hard to find accommodation, but may also make the hotels very noisy, so if you are seeking peace and quiet then consider visiting at another time. The main school holidays are usually the last week of May to the last week of June, and six weeks from mid-November through to the end of December. There are also one-week holidays around mid-March and late August.

WHAT KIND OF HOLIDAY?

Whether you are travelling solo, with a group, or as a family, on a package holiday or independently, the variety that Borneo offers means almost everyone can find what they are looking for in a holiday. The high standard of hotels, health and safety and relative ease of transport by air, road and river enable a trouble-free holiday to be had by all. The highlands, remote river areas and challenging peaks also offer scope for the more adventurous traveller. For those who prefer beach and sun, Borneo is a perfect beach-filled package-holiday destination, with the added attractions of diverse culture and wildlife. A handful of tour operators offer high-end tailormade tours combining the best of Sabah, Sarawak and Brunei. The cost of travelling between these places is relatively cheap. Nevertheless, a consideration if you are on a budget and/or time-restricted is to only visit one Malaysian state. Both Sabah and Sarawak offer enough variety of wildlife, scenery, social life and activities to form a holiday on their own. If I had to generalise, I would probably recommend Sabah for those looking for a cultural beach holiday with islands, diving and mountains, and Sarawak for remote river and highland experiences and greater cultural colour in cities and towns.

If you are lucky enough to have more time and money then you can afford to branch out (but avoid making the common mistake of trying to see too much), whether you organise the transfers yourself or pay a tour company to do the work for you. If you have a special interest, be it diving, trekking or birdwatching, it is a good idea to opt for a tailormade tour or design your own trip using specialist local operators. For details, see *Activities* on page 36.

HIGHLIGHTS AND ITINERARIES

Once you have decided what you want out of your Borneo trip, you can start to think about where you want to go. The special interests outlined below should help you create an itinerary, be it focused on Borneo's culture and ethnic groups, the jungle and its wildlife, beaches and coast, highlands and islands, or a varied mix of all. Given the ease and frequency of air travel it is common for tour operators to propose week-long itineraries which cherry-pick from the best of Borneo across Brunei, Sabah and Sarawak, but I would always emphasise quality over quantity. If you only have a week at hand, stick to just one Malaysian state, perhaps with a stopover in Brunei. If you have ten days to two weeks, you can spend some time travelling between Sabah and Sarawak, via Brunei, and see some highlights in each. If you plan to do this, your main choice is whether you want to experience the mega-mountain (Mount Kinabalu), jungle and river trip with some smaller cultural bites, or would prefer a big taste of Borneo's people, cities, countryside and villages with a smaller glimpse of nature – or you may have one particular activity in mind. Many of the focal points outlined below usually offer natural and cultural experiences in one. Whether you are climbing mountains, lying on beaches, or going upriver, you will encounter some of Borneo's vivid ethnic history somewhere along the way.

FAUNA AND FLORA The flora and fauna hotspots of Borneo are so numerous and varied that is impossible to categorise them, but below is a brief key to some major attractions and lesser-known wonders.

Ulu Temburong National Park, Brunei Whether done as a day trip or with an overnight stay, the journey to the Temburong National Park, which begins on the riverbanks of Brunei's capital, forms half the wonder of the trip. Meandering through a network of waterways, mangrove and tropical rainforest, you will enjoy a cultural immersion as you pass through the town of Bangar and witness the incredible boating skills of the Iban people. The walk to the suspension bridge in the park will put you at dizzying heights with views over Brunei and Malaysian Borneo.

Gunung Kinabalu Park, Sabah The steamy alpine world in which Borneo's Gunung (Mount) Kinabalu sits can be enjoyed whether you climb to the peak or not. The complexity of vegetation in the 75,370ha World Heritage park is apparent even on a shorter trek – through its rainforest and lower montane areas, around park headquarters, and other parts such as Poring Hot Springs. The butterfly- and bloom-filled park has been designated as a Centre of Plant Diversity for Southeast Asia by UNESCO, and is exceptionally rich in species.

Bako National Park, Sarawak A wonderland mix of mangroves, peat swamp, heath and lowland rainforest, with epic coastal rock formations. On the fauna front, highlights include bright green snakes, bearded pigs and the proboscis monkey. About 150 of the pendulous-nosed, pot-bellied creatures live here (see *Chapter 3, Natural History*, page 103). The trails are excellent (as long as a tree doesn't fall on you, which is what happened to me when I visited!). It's on the back doorstep of Kuching, about 40km away.

Danum Valley The closest you will get to the 'Heart of Borneo' (see *Natural History*, page 117) without heading deep into the Maliau Basin. Here you may see gibbon, orang-utan, long-tailed macaque, bearded pig, sambar deer, rhinoceros hornbill, maroon langur, western tarsier, clouded leopard, red leaf monkey and a diversity of birds – though you may need to stay for a few days to catch a glimpse of such a wide variety of wildlife, rather than just doing a one-hour safari on the back of a (rather noisy) truck.

Orang-utan encounters The huge appeal of this charismatic primate attracts many people to Borneo; seeing one is often at the top of their agenda. Orang-utan rehabilitation centres and sanctuaries (Sepilok in Sabah, and Semenggoh in Sarawak) are an easy option for quick sightings. Other wild places to see them (and vast amounts of other wildlife) include the Tabin Wildlife Reserve on Sabah's east coast, the floodplain of the Lower Kinabatangan River and the Danum Valley Conservation Area.

Proboscis monkeys The proboscis monkey comes in a close second as the most popular primate to see in Borneo. They can be seen in mangrove and peat swamp forests such as the Lower Kinabatangan and Klias Wetlands in Sabah, along Brunei's waterways and in the Bako National Park in Sarawak.

River safaris The boat journey along the Sungai Kinabatangan, Sabah's longest river, is awe-inspiring with its remoteness, natural richness and other-worldly beauty. For wildlife and birdwatching it is one of Borneo's most intense experiences, and the various lodges along the river (in their varying degrees of rustic) leave you with a bolstering feeling of being in deep jungle for a night or two. Late-afternoon boat trips lead up tributaries of the river to see shy proboscis monkeys and macaques. The world-scale preciousness of the area has unfortunately not protected it from forestry and palm oil invasion, but conservation and community development work is taking place. You can stay with river-living (*orang sungai*) communities, which boosts local economy.

Journeys along Sarawak's rivers are journeys into ethnography rather than nature. You can travel through the Taman Negara Batang Ai in the southeast, and the Sungai Rendang in central Sarawak, and up through central Sarawak to Kapit and Belaga.

ISLANDS AND BEACHES If you are looking for coasts, beaches and diving then without doubt Sabah is the place to head, especially the islands off its north and east coast.

CITIES AND CULTURE With its intensely Islamic faith, river tranquillity, royal riches, mosque silhouettes and Malay culture and cuisine, **Bandar Seri Begawan**, Brunei's capital, offers a snapshot of Borneo's history and ethnic colour – with rainforests, ocean and wildlife on its doorstep too. **Kuching**, Sarawak's main city, is mesmerising in its oriental and antiquated airs, yet neighbourly and friendly. The Sungai Sarawak runs through the centre and the indigenous Iban and Bidayuh cultures are woven through its watery fabric. **Kota Kinabalu**, Sabah's capital, is more the modern resort, a Côte d'Azur of Borneo where people party late into the night. **Sandakan**, Sabah's original capital, is dilapidated on stilts and cloaked in lush hills. An ocean crossroads of migrants, it exudes maritime charm.

Cultural shows The dance performance at the **Sarawak Cultural Village** remains an absolute highlight: a joyous insight into a cross-section of Malay, Chinese and indigenous dance. It is a mainstream tourist attraction, but there are many small, singular shows. For an all-in-one cultural taste, this is well delivered and high quality.

SCENIC DRIVES
East coast, Sabah Often referred to as 'cowboy towns', the settlements on the coastal stretch from Tawau to Lahad Datu and Semporna are not only the springboard to some incredible islands and to the Danum Valley inland, they are in themselves an offbeat and vivid cultural experience, taking you from thriving Chinese-dominated port cities, businesses and restaurants to Muslim-operated outdoor markets and exotic flavours. The seafood on the east coast is the best in Borneo.

Kudat Peninsula, Sabah Without doubt, the whole region north of Kota Kinabalu offers one of the most leisurely opportunities for driving over several days in Borneo. Culminating in the Kudat Peninsula and the so-called 'tip of Borneo', the ride takes in markets and towns, coast and countryside. More difficult, but not impossible, is to do the journey by bus: regional buses connect the towns.

Pan-Borneo A stretch that is more off the beaten track of tourist operators is that between Kuching and Brunei. If you are in a car, take the Pan-Borneo Highway, heading north to Miri. You can also take a mix of coaches, buses and boats to do the trip. Highlights along the way are the Chinese city of Sibu, the Melanau people's stronghold of Mukah, the Niah Caves, and the best sago and fish salads in the world. See *Chapter 11, Central Sarawak*.

ACTIVITIES

Borneo is better known for its wildlife than extreme outdoor adventure, but there is still plenty of adventure to be had, often alongside the nature experience. Boasting Malaysia's three highest mountains, Sabah attracts mountaineers from near and far, though the Malaysian massifs are less of a challenge for climbers. Adventures encompassing natural wonders can be experienced through diving, white-water rafting, rugged jungle treks and off-the-beaten-path mountain climbing. Good locations include Sabah's Kinabalu Park and Maliau Basin, and the Kelabit Highlands of Sarawak. A few local Sabah and Sarawak companies specialise in a mix of light to medium intensity outdoor adventure, such as mountain-biking, rafting, trekking and rock-climbing excursions.

TREKKING Due to Borneo's highly bureaucratic national parks and reserves, arduously humid climate, dangers of walking alone and advantages of local knowledge, it may well be better to use a tour organiser for well-established treks. Permits, insurance and guides are obligatory in Gunung Mulu National Park in

Sarawak and Kinabalu Park in Sabah. Unfortunately for those who prefer to be independent and unrestricted, you can't just turn up and trek because of the need to book trekker's accommodation and a guide in advance. Gunung Mulu and Kinabalu Park do not have extensive trail networks; instead there are one or two major routes and a few shorter walks around park headquarters, though these are usually fairly limited. This is common throughout the national parks and reserves of Borneo, unlike those in Europe, North America and Australia that often have a system of well-marked trails that can be followed independently. Outside of national parks however, in areas like the Danum Valley conservation area, walks tend to be of the 'well-marked nature trail' kind. A serious 'wilderness' adventure is the Maliau Basin: rugged terrain, sleeping in tents and lots of leeches, though it is quite expensive as this is only available as an organised trip (See *Chapter 8, Southeast Sabah*, page 216). Another relatively little known area just north of here is the Imbak Canyon.

There are plenty of other, more relaxed places for trekking around Borneo. The Kelabit Highlands provide an opportunity to trek through a highland landscape and rich culture, permit- and guide-free. This is an established tourist route. Other areas include the Penrissen Highlands south of Kuching and the Crocker Range. It is possible to organise your own trek around these areas. For details of where to obtain topographic maps, see *What to take*, below.

Day hiking There are many other parks and reserves with easy to medium grade trails where you can experience a good mix of lowland and hill rainforest. These make nice half/full-day walks. Good areas include the Tawau Hills Park, Tabin Wildlife Reserve and Sepilok Forest Reserve on the east coast of Sabah; and the Bako, Lambir Hills, and Similajau parks in Sarawak. Nearly all of Sarawak's 18 parks (most of which are around Kuching) have at least a couple of decent tracks, and Bako and Lambir Hills have 10–12, though few exceed three or four hours. Sarawak provides more for day hikers than Sabah; its many national parks are well set up, with good park information, maps trails and rangers. The national parks website (*www.forestry.sarawak.gov.my/forweb/homepage.htm*) is also very user-friendly with details of every park and reserve, conservation and wildlife information and information on upcoming events.

There are also areas that are just enjoyable to walk around. The Santubong Peninsula just north of Kuching is one – there are a few trails over the mountain including the Mount Santubong Summit Trek (see *Chapter 10, Southern Sarawak*, page 248). Be aware that this walk is quite challenging and requires good fitness levels. Some of my most pleasant walks through mountain scenery have been along country roads, through *kampungs* alongside national parks. In Sabah especially, there are plenty of interesting paths to follow that are off the usual tourist routes. Always take safety into consideration whilst walking; it is not advisable to walk alone and some wildlife can be dangerous.

Jungle adventure treks Organised jungle adventures range from youth-oriented survivor-camp trips (which combine hiking with edgy survival activities such as eating snakes), to straightforward treks. Highlights include the Headhunter's Trail in northern Sarawak, the Salt Trek in the Crocker Range, parts of the Sandakan-Ranau death-march trail and (more costly) trips into the heart of Borneo and remote places such as the Maliau Basin. All local tour groups involved in outdoor adventure organise such trips.

MOUNTAIN ADVENTURE For more serious mountain adventures, see some of the tour operators outlined below. A good website to search for adventure-based tours is www.adventuresportsholidays.com. For keen climbers and mountaineers another interesting site to visit is www.borneoclimbing.com, maintained by Wilfred Tok Beng Cheong – a key member of the **Mountaineering Society of Singapore** and a regular guide on Mount Kinabalu. His **Adventure Factors Mountaineering Centre** (AFMC) (*Sabah;* e *info@adventurefactors.com*) provides technical climbing courses, mountain treks and adventures including rock climbing and abseiling. The centre also runs programmes for light, intermediate and serious trekkers on the summits and slopes of Mount Kinabalu.

For really off-the-beaten-track Kinabalu climbs, the hardcore climber heads to the Eastern Plateau, via Bowen's Route or Kotal's Route. Both were apparently pioneered during the Royal Society expeditions on the mountain in the mid 1960s. Some of the adventure tour operators organise these routes.

Rock climbing and abseiling The granite peaks of Mount Kinabalu are the main attraction for rock-climbing enthusiasts in Sabah; in Sarawak, the limestone crags and sandstone environs of the Mulu Caves in the north, and the Fairy Caves near the town of Bau (40 mins from Kuching) are popular for caving and climbing. The official Malaysian tourism portal, www.virtualmalaysia.com, states: 'Routes here [Mount Kinabalu] are generally conventional, although there are a handful of lines with fixed gear. Most of the routes in Malaysia are bolted sport climbs on limestone crags, with some exceptions on granite walls.' Climbing is possible throughout the year.

A website of interest to climbing enthusiasts is www.borneoclimb.com, the personal page of veteran outdoor adventurer, Basil Lung. Kota Kinabalu-based Basil is an associate guide of the TYK Adventure Tours (see page 44). For youth adventure activities and camps, contact **Outward Bound Sabah** (*Locked Bag 181, 88745 KK, Sabah, Malaysia;* \ *088 750311;* e *obsabah@outward.po.my*). According to their award-winning adventure tour guide, Tham Yau Kong, rock climbing is still a relatively new pastime in Sabah, and most of the facilities which exist are for beginners and training. 'Until recently, Mount Kinabalu seemed to be the only place for rock climbing. Now Singaporean rock climber Wilfred Tok has set up a programme to assist foreign climbers and encourage local people to try it too. Located in Inanam, the challenge begins with a trek from Kampung Kirrongu. The path leads to a natural rock face where participants are trained in the basics of rock climbing, from dressing correctly to scaling the heights. The night is spent camping by a stream. The next day is spent climbing and abseiling. The thrill is incomparable!'

In early 2008, **Wilfred Tok's Adventure Factors Group** (*Lot 126, 1st Floor, Wisma Sabah, Jalan Tun Fuad Stephens, 88400 Kota Kinabalu, Sabah, Malaysia;* \ *88 268 126;* e *info@adventurefactors.com; www.mountaintorq.com*) announced the launch of Mountain Torq Via Ferrata (borrowed from the Italian expression for a high Alp pathway), labelled 'the world's highest mountain path' and the first to be built on Mount Kinabalu, southeast Asia's highest summit.

CYCLING AND MOUNTAIN BIKES Neither Sabah nor Sarawak are easy for road cycling – there are no dedicated cycle routes on main roads, neither in the main cities nor the countryside. There are however, some great off-road mountain-bike adventures to be had. 'The Crocker Range is quite a challenge, and Kota Kinabalu to the east coast of Sabah makes a good one-week trip,' says Tham Yau Kong. 'People think Sabah is easy for cycling, but don't underestimate how hard the humidity and heat can make it.'

As the adventurer-founder of TYK Adventure Tours, Tham is well known, and a good point of call for cycling enthusiasts (e *thamyaukong@thamyaukong.com; www.thamyaukong.com*). In the late 1990s he created the eco-friendly cycling

DIVING IN BORNEO

This information has been compiled with the help of various specialist operators, particularly China-based writer and diver, William Moss, who has written for *Asian Diver* magazine among others. You will find a lot of colourful writing, thorough information and fabulous Borneo dive photos on his website (www.imagethief.com). This brief overview is intended to help you to choose the dive location best suited to your level and interests. More details on the particular marine environments, dive operators and lodgings are found in relevant destination chapters.

DIVE DESTINATIONS In Sarawak, you can dive off the coast around Miri, and further north in Brunei. It is Sabah however, that tops the list of Borneo's best dive destinations. Good dive spots are found between the west coast islands of Labuan and Layang Layang, Lankayan off the north coast and Sipadan, Mabul and Kapalai off the east coast. According to Moss, the diving attractions in Sabah include reefs, atolls and lagoons; shore diving and drift diving; and lots of pelagic life. 'The area off of Tawau and Semporna is particularly rich, featuring the islands of Mabul, Kapalai, and Sipadan. Any diver planning a trip to the area should divide their time between these locations – a week of dives will yield an amazing diversity of marine life of all sizes and shapes.'

The east coast islands in the Sulawesi and Celebes seas have brought both fame and infamy to Bornean diving. Lying in territorial waters between Indonesia and Malaysia, the area is considered by some to be dangerous and foreigners are often advised against visiting and diving in the area (see *Safety* below). In April 2000, Sipadan made world headlines when an extremist Filipino Muslim group kidnapped a group of European tourists from the Borneo Diver's Resort. All accommodation on Sipadan has since closed, on both security and environmental grounds, and Sipadan is under constant military surveillance. Most diving accommodation is now found on other islands, but Sipadan remains a marine-lovers magnet.

DIVING SEASON Rough weather during the northeast monsoon season may affect diving conditions and ease of travel by boat. William Moss maintains that diving can be enjoyed all year round, though some inhabitants may be seasonal visitors, such as Layang Layang's hammerheads. Some say that April to July is the best time to dive.

DIVING CONDITIONS Surface water temperatures range from 24–31°C. A 3mm suit is sufficient for most diving conditions, though many people dive in skin-suits. Visibility averages around 20m but varies considerably, from 6–10m inshore to 15–30m+ at offshore locations.

ACCOMMODATION Lodgings on the islands are usually closely linked with particular dive operators. Staying overnight on one of the islands is a memorable experience. The difference in price between staying on an island or choosing to stay on the mainland and make dive trips each day depends on many things. A lot depends on the package you negotiate with an operator. If you pre-book your whole trip through an international dive operator, try and negotiate a price that includes all diving, equipment, accommodation, transfers and meals. Most of the local dive operators with island-based accommodation will offer this in any case. One of the best general information websites to help make a selection is www.divetheworldmalaysia.com. It details dive sites, accommodation listings and more.

Practical Information ACTIVITIES

2

business 'Eco Tourism on Pedals', and was one of the founders of the Mount Kinabalu International Mountain Bike Race and other cycling challenges. Along with his cycling associates, he claims to have entered the 'Malaysia Book of Records' for being the first group to mountain-bike-circumvent Mount Kinabalu, and believes mountain biking as a sports tourism activity will get big in Borneo.

In Sarawak the area around Kuching in particular is excellent for mountain-bike adventure (see *Chapter 9, Kuching*, page 230), as are the parks and rainforest reserves west towards Sematan and north towards the Santubong Peninsula and Damai Beach. This is where the Rainforest Cup mountain-bike event is held each year, and there is a Battle of Borneo event at Mulu. Brunei has several reserves with mountain-biking trails, starting right in the city. See *Chapter 4, Brunei*, page 144.

RAFTING The two main rivers for rafting in Sabah are the Sungai Padas and Sungai Kiulu rivers in the hinterland of the west coast. According to operators, both are certified as Grade 3 and Grade 2 respectively in the international white-water rafting grading system. Indigenous people, with their amazing water navigation skills, quickly caught on to white-water rafting in the 1980s. The dry season is the best time for novices. Rivers can swell to Grade 4 during the wet season, more suited to more experienced rafters. Outside of the wet season, the Sungai Kiulu is too low for rafting so the Padas gets most of the crowds during other times of the year. Kiulu rapids include 'Headhunter', 'Adrenaline Flow' and 'Merry Go Round'. Make sure you go with a licensed operator, some of which are listed below. The standard Padas excursion is a day trip but longer trips can be arranged with accommodation at the Padas River Lodge in Rayoh. The basic trip provides a safety and technical briefing and life jackets. Experienced rafters can arrange for a custom-made trip. In Sabah, operators will arrange transport from Kota Kinabalu through the Padas Gorge. Bring a change of clothes, warm layers, a waterproof jacket and well-fitting shoes or diving boots. Spectacle wearers should bring something with which to anchor glasses, whilst contact-lens wearers are advised to wear spectacles to avoid lens contamination.

BIRDWATCHING Susan Myers runs **Birding Worldwide** (see *International tour operators* on page 42), and is the author of soon-to-be-published *Field Guide to the Birds of Borneo*. Susan generously shares her trip reports online (*http://users.wired.net.au/susan*) to help independent birders organise their trip. She says that in Sabah, 'The birding is out of this world.' During a 17-day trip to five key sites, she once recorded 230 species. 'This included some highly sought-after species, such as the giant pita, storm's stork, Bornean bristlehead and Whitehead's trogon.' Local Bornean bird specialists offer 1–12-day trips. There are several bird sanctuaries (run by the Wildlife Department) in Sabah, three or four on the west coast and in Kota Kinabalu itself.

GOLF Sabah's long, indented coastline is marked by an increasing number of world-class resorts, and the golf courses which accompany them. Many are found along the west coast around Kota Kinabalu (eg: Sutera Harbour) and north towards Tuaran (eg: the Dalit Bay Golf and Country Club, and Karambunai Resorts Golf Club); and further north on the Kudat Peninsula. There are also cooler-climate mountain-foothill golf clubs in the Mount Kinabalu Park area. Details of some are found in relevant chapters. A directory can be found online at the Sawadee travel site (*www.malaysia.sawadee.com/sabah/golf.html for Sabah, www.malaysia.sawadee.com/sarawak/golf.html for Sarawak*). The UK's *Golf Today* magazine also has a comprehensive online course directory (*www.golftoday.co.uk*).

CULTURAL HISTORY If archaeology, ethnography and anthropology are your main interests, then you should visit the Niah Caves in northern Sarawak, the Sarawak and Sabah state museums, the Islamic museums of civilisation and art and the mosques and museums of Brunei. The whole of northern Borneo is one incredible outdoor ethnographic museum, with living cultural displays everywhere. There are also several brilliant local indigenous cultural associations mentioned in the guide worth making contact with.

i TOURIST INFORMATION

SABAH AND SARAWAK The worldwide offices of Tourism Malaysia are a good starting point for information, but the websites of the individual tourism boards for the two states should also be consulted, and their offices contacted, for more dedicated, up-to-date information.

Sabah Tourism Board 51 Jln Gaya, KK; 🕿 6088 212121; e info@sabahtourism.com; www.sabahtourism.com. The website is simple but easy to navigate, with a search bar uncovering detailed information on all the attractions, tour operators & practicalities.

Sarawak Tourism Board 6th & 7th Floors, Bangunan Yayasan, Jln Masjid Kuching; 🕿 +6 082 423600; e stb@sarawaktourism.com; www.sarawaktourism.com. A fresh white & green website, if a little cluttered & with very small text.

Tourism Malaysia (*www.tourism.gov.my*) The website has a link to all overseas offices of the Malaysia Tourism Promotion Board. Some of the major ones are listed below.

Australia 355 Exhibition St, Melbourne, 🕿 03 96543177; Ground Flr, MAS Building, 56 William St, Perth, 🕿 08 94810400, e mtpb.perth@tourism.gov.my; Level 2, 171 Clarence St, Sydney, 🕿 02 92994441/2, e mtpb.sydney@tourism.gov.my
Canada 1590–1111, West Georgia St, Vancouver; 🕿 604 6898899; e mtpb.vancouver@tourism.gov.my; www.malaysiatourism.ca
France 29 Rue des Pyramides, Paris; 🕿 01 42974171; e mtpb.paris@tourism.gov.my

Germany Weissfrauenstrasse 12–16, Frankfurt am Main; 🕿 69 460973420; e info@tourismmalaysia.de; www.tourismmalaysia.de
UK 57 Trafalgar Sq, London WC2N 5DU; 🕿 207 9307932; e mtpb.london@tourism.gov.my or info@tourism-malaysia.co.uk
USA 818 West Seventh St, Suite 970, Los Angeles, 🕿 213 6899702, e mtpb.la@tourism.gov.my, www.tourismmalaysiausa.com; 120 East, 56th St, Suite 810, New York, 🕿 212 7451114/5, e mtpb.ny@tourism.gov.my or mtpb@aol.com

BRUNEI Information about travel in Brunei is best obtained through the central **Brunei Tourism** office in Brunei itself. Overseas, **Royal Brunei Airlines** offices and Brunei **High Commissions** and **Embassies** (listed under *Red Tape*, below) are useful sources of information.

Brunei Tourism Jln Menteri Besar, BSB, Brunei Darussalam; 🕿 673 2382822/2382832; e info@tourismbrunei.com; www.tourismbrunei.com. A stunning website with gorgeous visuals & excellent content design.

Royal Brunei Airlines 49 Cromwell Rd, London SW7 2ED; 🕿 207 5846660; e lonrba@rba.com.bn
Royal Brunei Airlines Level 14, BT Tower, 1 Market St, Sydney; 🕿 02 82675300; e rbasyd@rba.com.bn

TOUR OPERATORS

There are many advantages of using local tour operators: first and foremost, because they provide in-depth local knowledge and add a strong personal touch to travels. Secondly, employing local people and companies helps the local economy, creates jobs and is far more energy efficient than operations run offshore. Familiarise yourself with local operators in the areas you plan to visit. Local operators can help whether you are organising the whole thing independently and just calling on an agent for ticketing and hotels, or want someone to take the entire weight off your shoulders by providing a start-to-finish itinerary. What an international company might gain on sleekness, they can lose on authenticity and depth. Some international tour operators work alongside locals ones, employing local guides rather than running the whole show themselves; these are indicated below. It especially pays to contact Bornean operators regarding special interest tours. Some are found below, others in individual chapters, but a good list and links to many of Sabah and Sarawak's tour operators can be found on the Sabah and Sarawak Tourism board's websites (*www.sabahtourism.com; www.sarawaktourism.com*), as well as that of Malaysia Association of Tours and Travel Agents (MATTA) (*www.matta.org.my*).

INTERNATIONAL

Birding Worldwide ☎ +61 3 93878734; e enquiries@birdingworldwide.com.au; www.birdingworldwide.com.au. An Australia-based international bird tour group that has been leading tours to Asia for 20 years, including dozens to Borneo & Peninsular Malaysia. They will do tailormade bird tours. Work with Victor Emanuel Nature Tours (see below).
Intrepid Travel ☎ UK +44 1 373 826 611/+44 2 073 546 162; US & Canada +18 668 478 192; Australia +13 00 364 512; New Zealand +09 5 200 972; e info@intrepidtravel.com; www.intrepidtravel.com. For environmentally conscious, independent travellers who want to travel in a group or on a budget. Intrepid offers several tours of Borneo; all are outlined on their website with itineraries, prices, trip notes & more.

Based in Australia, but with sales offices in New Zealand, UK, Ireland, US & Canada. Green image boosted with several responsible travel awards, & on target to become carbon neutral by 2009. Women make up about two-thirds of its clientele.
Victor Emanuel Nature Tours ☎ +1 512 328 5221; f +1 512 328 2919; e info@ventbird.com; www.ventbird.com. America's largest specialist bird (and natural history) tour company.
World Expeditions www.worldexpeditions.com. Adventure & outdoor travel with offices in the UK, US, Canada, Australia & New Zealand. Offer a 9-day 'Borneo Flora & Fauna' trip, plus Mount Kinabalu climbs. For individual telephones & emails see the website.

AUSTRALIA

Gecko's Adventures (Peregrine Adventures) 380 Lonsdale St, Melbourne; ☎ +61 3 8601 4444; e websales@peregrine.net.au; www.geckosadventures.com. Borneo treks & safaris operated by the 'groovy young thing' part of Peregrine Adventures, with small groups, good prices & local guides.
Borneo Tour Specialists Lower Ground Floor, 100 Clarence St, Sydney; ☎ +61 2 3221 5777;

e travel@borneo.com.au; www.borneo.com.au. Pre-set & tailormade trips with several detailed itineraries & extensive country information on its website. Reservations office based in Brisbane.
Go See Touring 13/71 Racecourse Rd, Ascot, Queensland; ☎ +61 7 3868 4760; e reservations@goseetouring.com; www.goseetouring.com. The 13-day itinerary focuses on 'nature, wildlife & Australian war history'.

CANADA

50plus Expeditions 760 Lawrence Av, Toronto; ☎ +1 866 318 5050; e office@50plusexpeditions.com; www.50plusexpeditions.com. Specialise in adventure travel for people over 50. Comprehensive 15-day trip of Borneo inc Sabah, Sarawak & Brunei.

Deep Discoveries PO Box 73, Mulhurst Bay, Alberta, Canada; ☎ +1 780 389 3658; e info@deepdiscoveries.com; www.deepdiscoveries.com. Alberta-based dedicated dive & adventure travel specialist.

UK

Adventure Alternative ↘ +44 (0) 28708 31258, (Ireland) ↘ 04870 831258; www.adventurealternative.com. For mountain adventure, this Northern Ireland-based company has a 14-day 'Roof of Borneo Adventure' that goes way off the over-beaten Mount Kinabalu climb to take in the Eastern Plateau & the North Ridge. This is only for the seriously mountain-at-heart — 12 days are spent climbing & camping, with highly experienced expedition leaders. They also do a 3-week 'Borneo Trilogy' adventure which takes in trekking in the Kelabit Highlands in Sarawak. Aptly described as 'non-technical trekking' — to distinguish it from the more demanding Mount Kinabalu Climb & white-water rafting in Sabah.
Audley Travel New Mill, New Mill Lane, Witney, Oxon; ↘ +44 (0)1993 838100; www.audleytravel.com. Audley won Best Tour Operator in the 2006 Guardian, Observer & Guardian Unlimited Travel Awards. 'Tailor-made journeys for the discerning traveller.' Upmarket trips run by country specialists.
Borneo Travel www.borneo-travel.com; UK website for Borneo-based **TYK Adventure Tours** (see *Borneo tour operators* below). If you are looking for an adventure & outdoor holiday, this award-winning venture has survival, mountain-biking & trekking tours as well as offering tailormade tours for activities such as birdwatching, rock climbing & rafting.
Chaka Travel 98 University St, Belfast; ↘ 02890 232112; e mark@chakatravel.com; www.chakatravel.com. For golfing holidays in Sabah.

USA

Dive Borneo ↘ +1 618 529 8033; e info@diveborneo.com; www.diveborneo.com. Associate of the above, with many dive packages in Borneo. Both are linked to www.emalaysiatravel.com, a service destination travel specialist with lots of information on Malaysia.
Go Borneo ↘ +1 888 359 8655; e info@goborneo.com; www.goborneo.com. With extensive Borneo knowledge, & using local guides, the group offers adventure & family packages, & day tours.
Jodi's Jungle Adventures 38th St New York; ↘ +1 212 537 6298; e jodi@junglejaunts.com;

BORNEO
Sabah and Sarawak

Borneo Adventure 55 Main Bazaar, Kuching; ↘ +60 082 245175; e info@borneoadventure.com; www.borneoadventure.com. Upmarket ethical, this Sarawak-based company has wildlife-, adventure- & culture-focused tours in Sarawak & in Sabah as well as custom-made trips. It says it is 'dedicated to

Exodus Holidays Grange Mills, Weir Rd, London SW12 ONE; ↘ +44 (0)845 863 9600; e sales@exodus.co.uk; www.exodus.co.uk. Family-friendly adventure holidays with small-to-medium groups under tour leaders & local guides. 14-day 'Trails of Borneo' tour requires good fitness, includes 3 days of walking, & a mix of hotels, lodges, camping & mountain huts.
Nature Trek Cheriton Mill, Cheriton, Alresford, Hants; ↘ +44 (0)1962 733051; e info@naturetrek.co.uk; www.naturetrek.co.uk. Wildlife tour specialist with 2 Borneo itineraries, focusing on orang-utans, birds & the rainforest. Their 21-day tour which they describe as a 'birdwatching extravaganza' takes in top birdwatching sites in Sabah: Kinabatangan, Mount Kinabalu & Danum Valley. There are very good reviews of the trip. All their tours are guided by specialised tour leaders, who are trained naturalists, environmental scientists, ecologists, etc.
Saga Holidays ↘ +44 (0)800 096 0078; e reservations@saga.co.uk; www.saga.co.uk. Cushy package group holidays for the over 50s. Offer a 14 day Borneo rainforest adventure with a tour 'manager'. Save with online bookings.
The Travel Collection Kuoni Hse, Dorking, Surrey; ↘ +44 (0)1306 744311 (sales), +44 (0)1306 744319 (helpdesk); e tours@travelcollection.co.uk; www.travelcollection.co.uk. Part of the Kuoni Travel group, 10-night Borneo holiday of orang-utan focus, based in 1 luxury hotel north of KK with options & extensions.

www.jodisjungleadventures.com. Quirky, personalised trips run by an American woman with extensive life experience in the Sarawak region, in conjunction with Sarawak operator Borneo Adventure.
World Of Diving & Adventure Vacations 301 Main St, El Segundo, California; ↘ +11800 GO DIVING/1800 46 34846; e mail@worldofdiving.com; www.worldofadventure.com. Specialises in diving trips to Sabah's east coast islands with 7-day round trips from Los Angeles to Tawau all inclusive.

providing our clients with ethical tourism products that are sustainable', & steps this way with an ethnically diverse group of very professional guides, its own eco-lodges & very practical & in-touch information on its website.

Borneo Birds e ckleong@borneobirds.com. Associated with TYK, but running his own bird show, is resident Bornean bird specialist, Chun Kiong Leong. Tailor-makes trips from 1 day to 2 weeks & has a 12-day tour taking in Manukan Island, Tabin Wildlife Reserve, the Kinabatangan River & Kinabalu Park.

Borneo Divers & Sea Sports 9th Floor, Menara Jubili, 53 Jln Gaya, KK; ☏ +60 088 222226; e info@borneodivers.com; www.borneodivers.com. A very established & extremely reputable tour operator with a training institute in KK offering courses of all levels. I have heard of people getting good discounts for a Mabul Island dive package (inc accommodation etc) having first done the PADI course.

Borneo Eco Tours Lot 1, Pusat Perindustrian, Kolombong Jaya; Mile 5.5, Jln Kolombong, KK; ☏ +60 088 438300; e info@borneoecotours.com; www.borneoecotours.com. Launched in 1991 by well-known eco-author Albert Teo, the group has 40 excellent guides/specialists, 15 AC vehicles, speedboats, river boats & rafting equipment. Many awards to its name for its conservation & responsible tourism efforts. Vast choice of nature & cultural tours, treks & activities, all well outlined & easily booked on its site. Value packages & a budget corner. Operates the Sukau Rainforest Lodge & Borneo Backpackers in KK.

Borneo Nature Tours Blk D, Lot 10, Ground Flr, Sadong Jaya Complex, KK; ☏ +60 088 267637. Adventure & nature tours with the operator of the Borneo Rainforest Lodge in the Danum Valley Conservation Area. Heading out from there, they organise adventure treks into the Maliau Basin Conservation Area, deemed the 'lost world' of Sabah.

Borneo Ultimate Sports Adventure Tours (BUSAT) Lot G29, Ground Flr, Wisma Shopping Centre, KK; ☏ +60 088 225188/225199; e borneoultimate@hotmail.com; www.borneoultimate.com.my. Another Sabah-based operator big on bike adventures & bike/ rafting day trips & packages. 'Kinabalu Mountain & Rafflesia & Waterfall' day-biking trips, at easy & intermediate levels, as well as 2–4-day tours of all kinds – some involving biking, rafting & camping. Dedicated & locally tuned.

Intra Travel Service ☏ +60 088 261558; e enquiry@intra-travel.com.my; www.intra-travel.com.my. Upmarket Sabah-based company aimed at incentive travel sector. Member of the International Eco Tourism Society & American Express Travel Service Network, & PATA (Pacific Asia Travel Association). Its activities focus on jungle activities within the Tabin Wildlife Reserve in northwest Sabah, nature & adventure programmes,

theme parties, team-building exercises, aerial sightseeing, special interest eco-adventures, golf tours, diving tours, hotel & transportation bookings.

Outdoor Treks ☏ +60 82 36 3344; m +6012 8886460; e best@bikcloud.com; www.bikcloud.com. The kind of youthful, enthusiastic & down-to-earth company that draws in the film production crews & adventure travel programmes. They are familiar with a whole lot of mountain-bike trails within 1–100km from Kuching's central business district, as well as kayaking, guided nature treks, rock climbing & caving. Sarawak based.

Pulau Sipadan Resort & Tours 484 Bandar Sabindo, PO Box 61120, Tawau 91021; ☏ +60 897 65200; e kapalai@tm.net.my; www.dive-malaysia.com; www.sipadan-resort.com, www.lankayan-island.com. Packages based around their dive resorts on Lankayan & Kapalai islands, as well as their Sepilok Nature Resort. Very professional set-up, popular with families for their child-friendliness & fun. Confusing number of websites!

SI Tours 10th Flr Wisma Khoo Siak Chiew, Sandakan Town; ☏ +60 089 673502/03; e info@sitoursborneo.com; www.sitoursborneo.com. Local company specialising in adventure, wildlife & cultural tours. Package itineraries & custom tours to Kinabatangan, Gomantong Caves & Turtle Islands National Park. Guides are passionately local & mostly well-informed. The company is deeply committed to the environment & indigenous communities – & creating jobs for them.

TYK Adventure Tours Lot 48–2F, 2nd Flr, Beverly Hill Plaza, Jln Bundusan, Penampang; ☏ +60 088 720826/088 727825; e tykadto@tm.net.my; www.tykadventuretours.com. Small operators with responsible travel written all over them. Based in west coast Sabah – KK, Mount Kinabalu, Crocker Range – but do nature & adventure trips all over Sabah. The multi-ethnic team from the director down is hands-on involved in tours, each with their own particular forte. Cycling & rafting trips, survival camps, village & longhouse stays & extended trekking. Also have a group of associated experts (eg: historians) increasing their local knowledge. Organise the **Miki Survival Camp** in the foothills of Mount Kinabalu (see page 189).

Wildlife Expeditions ☏ +60 089 219616 (Sandakan), +60 088 246000 (KK); e enquiry@wildlife-expeditions.com; www.wildlife-expeditions.com. Sabah-based operator with a large range of reasonably priced half/full-day & overnight excursions from KK, Sandakan, Brunei, Kuching & Miri to all the best places of interest. Pretty big-scale, established operator, they work with Brunei Tourism & mid-market package-holiday operator Kuoni (*www.kuoni.co.uk*), upmarket Saga (see above under

Brunei

Sunshine Borneo Tours & Travel No 2 Simpang 146, Jln Kiarong, Kampung. Kiulap, Bandar Seri Begawan, Brunei; ☎ +673 2446812/3; e sales@ exploreborneo.com; www.exploreborneo.com. The local partner for Royal Brunei Airlines, sold overseas as Golden Touch Holidays through RBA offices

UK operators) & Go See Touring (see Australian operators). 7-day wildlife tour of Borneo plus shorter itineraries. They have a Kinabatangan River lodge.

(e goldentouch@rba.com.bn; www.bruneiair.com). A very Bruneian, highly conscientious, concerned & punctual operator, do day trips & excursions within Brunei. Also have a branch in the lobby arcade of the Empire Hotel & Country Club in Jerudong (☎ +673 2610578).

RED TAPE

VISAS AND ENTRY REQUIREMENTS

Malaysian Borneo Every person entering Malaysia must possess a valid national passport or internationally recognised travel document recognised by the Malaysian government. If not, they must obtain a document in lieu of a passport by applying at any Malaysian diplomatic mission abroad. Citizens of the UK, Ireland, USA, Canada and Australia are issued a three-month visa on arrival, at no charge, with a possible extension of two months. Most western Europeans receive a three-month visa on arrival. Citizens of Israel and the former states of Yugoslavia are required to apply for special approval from the Ministry of Home Affairs before entering Malaysia.

Brunei No visa is required for residents of the USA (90-day entry), the UK, Ireland, Germany, Austria, New Zealand, Singapore, Malaysia, the United Arab Emirates, Oman and Korea (30-day entry) and residents of Belgium, France, Italy, Spain, the Netherlands, Luxembourg, Denmark, Norway, Sweden, Poland, Canada, Peru, Japan, the Philippines, Indonesia and Thailand (14-day entry).

Australians are granted visas on arrival for visits of up to 30 days. A single-entry visa costs US$20 and lasts for ten days; a multi-entry visa lasts for 30 days and costs US$30; a 72-hour transit visa costs US$5.

If you require a visa and arrive into Brunei by road from Sabah or Sarawak, be aware that you must have Brunei dollars on you (which can be withdrawn from a bank in Malaysia) to pay the visa fee. There are no ATM machines at the immigration checks, and they do not take credit card payments.

CUSTOMS Brunei customs laws include particular rules relating to alcohol, which you cannot buy anywhere in the country. Non-Muslims over 17 years of age can bring in two bottles of liquor (about two litres) and 12 cans of beer, which has to be declared to customs upon arrival. Passengers over 17 can carry in 200 cigarettes, 60g of tobacco, 60ml of perfume and 250ml eau de toilette.

The trafficking of drugs in Brunei carries the death sentence.

ⓔ EMBASSIES AND CONSULATES

ABROAD Embassy opening hours vary greatly and are generally from 08.00–16.30 Monday–Friday but it is always best to ring ahead and check.

Malaysian diplomatic missions

Australia Malaysian High Commission Canberra, 7 Perth Av, Yarralumla; ☎ +61 2 6273 1543; e malcanberra@netspeed.com.au

Canada Consulate General of Malaysia, Suite 1805, Terasen Centre, No 1111, West Georgia St, Vancouver; ☎ +1 604 685 9550; e mwvcouvr@axion.net

Ireland Embassy of Malaysia, Level 3A-5A, Shelbourne Hse, Shelbourne Rd, Ballsbridge, Dublin; ☎ +353 1 6677280; e mwdublin@mwdublin.ie
New Zealand High Commission of Malaysia; 10 Washington Av, Brooklyn, Wellington; ☎ +64 4 3852439/+64 4 8015659; e mwwelton@xtra.co.nz

UK Malaysian High Commission, 45–46 Belgrave Sq, London SW1X 8QT; ☎ +44 2 072 358 033; e mwlon@btconnect.com
USA Embassy of Malaysia, 3516 International Court, NW Washington, DC; ☎ +1 202 572 9700; e malwashdc@kln.gov.my. Also consulate generals in New York & Los Angeles.

Brunei's diplomatic missions

Australia High Commission of Brunei Darussalam, 10 Beale Cr, Deakin, ACT; ☎ +61 2 6285 4500/02 6285 4501; e Bruneihc@spirit.com.au
Canada High Commission of Brunei Darussalam, 395 Laurier Av East, Ottawa, Ontario; ☎ +1 613 2345 656
France Embassy of Brunei Darussalam, 7 Rue de Presbourg, Paris; ☎ +33 1 53 64 67 60/+33 1 53 64 67 61; e ambassade.brunei@wanadoo.fr

UAE Villa No 1, Plot 8, Abu Dhabi E-33, St 27; ☎ +971 2 4486999; e kbdauh98@amirates.net.ae
UK High Commission of Brunei Darussalam, 19-20 Belgrave Sq, London SW1X 8PG; ☎ +44 20 75810521; e bruhighcomlondon@hotmail.com
USA Embassy of Brunei Darussalam, 3520 International Court, NW Washington, DC; ☎ +1 202 2371 838; e info@bruneiembassy.org; www.bruneiembassy.org

IN MALAYSIA Foreign embassies in Malaysia are in Kuala Lumpur (see *www.kln.gov.my*). The British Council is on the ground floor of the Api-Api Centre in Kota Kinabalu.

Australia Australian High Commission, 6 Jln Yap Kwan Seng; ☎ +60 3 2465555
Austria Austrian Embassy, 7th Floor, MUI Plaza Building, Jln P Ramlee; ☎ +60 3 2484277
Belgium Belgian Embassy, 8A Jln Ampang Hilir; ☎ +60 3 2625733
Canada Canadian High Commission, 7th Floor, OFK Plaza, 172 Jln Ampang; ☎ 03 2612000
China Chinese Embassy, 229 Jln Ampang; ☎ +60 3 2428495
Denmark Danish Embassy, 22nd Floor, Wisma Angkasa Raya, 123 Jln Ampang; ☎ +60 3 2416088
France French Embassy, 192–196 Jln Ampang; ☎ +60 3 2484122
Germany German Embassy, 3 Jln U Thant; ☎ +60 3 2429666
Italy Italian Embassy, 99 Jln U Thant; ☎ +60 3 4565122

Japan Japanese Embassy, 11 Persiaran Stonor, Off Jln Tun Razak; ☎ +60 3 2427044
The Netherlands Dutch Embassy, 4 Jln Mesra, off Jln Damai; ☎ +60 3 2485151
New Zealand New Zealand High Commission, 193 Jln Tun Razak; ☎ +60 3 2382533
Singapore Singapore High Commission, 209 Jln Tun Perak; ☎ +60 3 2616277
Sweden Swedish Embassy, 6th Floor, Wisma Angkasa Raya; ☎ +60 3 2485433
Switzerland Swiss Embassy, 6 Persiaran Madge; ☎ +60 3 2480622
UK British High Commission, 185 Jln Ampang; ☎ +60 3 2482122
USA US Embassy, 376 Jln Tun Razak; ☎ +60 3 2489011

The UK also has **Honorary British Consuls** in Sabah (Kota Kinabalu) and in Sarawak (Kuching).

Sabah Mr Peter Mole; ☎ +60 88 253 333; m +60 (0)19 882 3978; e peter.mole@pekah.com

Sarawak Mrs Valerie Mashman; Kuching; ☎ +60 82 250 950

IN BRUNEI All the following embassies are along the riverfront area of Bandar Seri Begawan city centre (🕐 *09.00–17.00 Mon–Fri*).

Australia Australian High Commission, Level 6, Dar Takaful IBB Utama Bldg, Jln Pemancha; ☎ +673

2229435; e austhicom.brunei@dfat.gov.au; www.bruneidarussalam.embassy.gov.au

Canada Canadian High Commission, 5th Flr, Mc Arthur Building, No 1 Jln McArthur; ☏ +673 2220043; e hicomcda@ppl.brunet.bn; www.brunei.gc.ca
New Zealand The New Zealand High Commission in Kuala Lumpur is accredited to Brunei, Level 21, Menara IMC, 8 Jln Sultan Ismail; ☏ +673 32078; e nzhckl@streamyx.com; www.nzembassy.com
UK British High Commission, 2nd Flr, Block D, Kompleks Yayasan Sultan Haji Hassanal Bolkiah, Jln

Pretty, Bandar Seri Begawan; ☏ +673 2222231; e brithc@brunet.bn; www.britishhighcommission.gov.uk/brunei
USA Embassy of the United States of America, 3rd Flr, Teck Guan Plaza, Jln Sultan (corner of Jln McArthur); ☏ +673 2220384; e amembassy_bsb@state.gov, http://bandar.usembassy.gov

GETTING THERE AND AWAY

✈ **BY AIR** The main international airports in Borneo are in Bandar Seri Begawan (the capital of Brunei), Kota Kinabalu (Sabah's capital city) and Kuching (Sarawak's capital), so your choice of airline will partly be determined by your proposed itinerary.

Flights from the UK, US, Europe, Australia, New Zealand

Royal Brunei Airlines The only non-stop long-haul flights to Borneo are provided by Royal Brunei Airlines (*www.bruneiair.com*). RBA operate direct flights to Brunei's capital Bandar Seri Begawan from the UK and Australia. There are four flights weekly between Auckland, New Zealand via Brisbane; from London there are four direct weekly flights to Bandar Seri Begawan, as well as three flights via Dubai.

In June 2008 the airline moved to improve flights to Brunei from regional and international destinations and the new flight schedule includes daily services from Bandar Seri Begawan and Miri to Singapore, Bangkok, Kuala Lumpur, Jakarta, Hong Kong, Kota Kinabalu and Kuching.

On the latter two routes there are 17 weekly flights between Bandar Seri Begawan and Kota Kinabalu, and five flights to Kuching. As a result, RBA offers the smoothest connections to the rest of Borneo.

Malaysia Airlines (*www.malaysiaairlines.com*) Malaysia Airlines (MAS) has introduced twice-weekly direct flights from Sydney to Kuching in Sarawak, adding to the twice weekly Perth–Kuching flights. Other than that, relatively smooth connections to Borneo are assured by MAS, from destinations all around the world via the Malaysian capital Kuala Lumpur.

MAS operate non-stop flights between Kuala Lumpur and London, Amsterdam, Paris, Rome, Zurich, Frankfurt, Stockholm, New York, Los Angeles, Buenos Aires, Sydney, Perth, Adelaide, Brisbane, Melbourne, Auckland, Dubai, Cape Town and Johannesburg. There are connecting flights from Kuala Lumpur to Kota Kinabalu, to Labuan Island, to Sarawak's capital Kuching and its second-biggest city Sibu, and to Brunei's capital, Bandar Seri Begawan. From Kota Kinabalu, MAS has connections to towns including Tawau, Lahad Datu and Sandakan in Sabah, and to Kuching, Miri, Mulu, Limbang, and Sibu in Sarawak. Some international flights with MAS arrive in Kuala Lumpur too late to catch the onward flight to Borneo on the same day and require an overnight stay.

Singapore Airlines (*www.singaporeair.com*) This is a very good choice for travelling to Borneo. Some choose it not only for quality of service but because a stopover of the kind mentioned above is not necessary. The airline flies non-stop to Singapore from London, Manchester, New York, Los Angeles, San Francisco, Moscow, Rome, Milan, Copenhagen, Paris, Frankfurt, Zurich, Athens, Brisbane, Sydney, Melbourne, Perth, Adelaide, Auckland, Christchurch, Dubai, Abu Dhabi,

Johannesburg and Cape Town, Tokyo and Beijing. Singapore Airlines also has flights in the UK from Aberdeen, Newcastle, Belfast, Glasgow, Edinburgh, Leeds/Bradford and Teesside passing-by London. With as little as one-hour transit, there are then connecting flights to Kota Kinabalu, Kuching and Brunei. Sometimes the connecting flight to Borneo is on code share with Malaysia Airlines or Silk Air (*www.silkair.com*), a Singapore Airlines subsidiary.

Jet-Star Australia's low cost airline Jetstar (*www.jetstar.com*) launched direct flights in both economy and business class between Kuala Lumpur and Sydney with the promise of more Malaysian destinations to come.

Other carriers Flying from the US to Hong Kong, Cathay Pacific passengers could then link with the one-a-day direct flights to Kota Kinabalu, operated by the Hong Kong-based Dragon Air (*www.dragonair.com*) which is part of the Cathay Pacific group. This is also an option for those flying on Continental Airways to Hong Kong. If you fly Delta Airlines (*www.delta.com*) they have non-stop flight to Taipei, in Taiwan, then on to Kota Kinabalu with MAS.

Flights from Asia

Malaysia Airlines If you are starting your trip from within Asia, or flew into Asia with another international carrier, MAS and AirAsia fly from Kuala Lumpur to Kota Kinabalu, Kuching and Bandar Seri Begawan in Brunei. RBA have flights from Kuala Lumpur to Brunei. MAS also have flights to Sabah and Sarawak from several Asian ports including Hong Kong, Singapore, Tokyo, Seoul, Taipei, Manila and Bandar Seri Begawan.

AirAsia Air Asia (*www.airasia.com*) is one of the best-serviced (though not most punctual) low-cost airlines in Asia. They have many direct connections from Kuala Lumpur to Kota Kinabalu, Sandakan and Kuching. They also have direct flights to Kota Kinabalu from Bangkok (allowing connections with Thai Airways, Qantas or British Airways flights among others).

If you fly into Hong Kong from London with BA or from the US, as mentioned above, or with Qantas you can then fly with Dragonair (*www.dragonair.com*) on their once-daily flights to Kota Kinabalu.

Which airline? If sheer quality and comfort of service are your priorities, for long-haul trips it is hard to beat the track record of Singapore Airlines and Malaysia Airlines (with a special star for the price-quality rapport of Economy long-haul). For price, MAS are very competitive. Forecasted upgrades of RBA's fleet should add another notch of comfort to their overall ratings. The cheapest flights on Just the Flight (*www.justtheflight.co.uk*) often turn up Malaysian Airlines, Air Emirates (via Dubai) and Qatar Airways (via Doha), so if you are not fussed about taking a direct flight – or are even searching to enjoy an exotic stopover – the latter two could be entertained. Transit flights can also be taken via Bangkok (Thai Airways), Hong Kong (Cathay Pacific) Taipei, Kaoshiung, Manila, Cebu, Seoul, Singapore and Tokyo. These trips can be very tiring, involving two transfers, unless you use the trip to stop over in a couple of interesting places.

For checking general flight prices and availability, good sites include www.expedia.com, www.justtheflight.co.uk, www.webjet.com.au, www.travelocity.com and www.travelocity.co.uk. For online travel agents, try www.trailfinders.com, www.statravel.com, www.flightcentre.au and www.flightcentre.com. For airline quality checks and star rankings in all brackets, from first class to budget airlines, see Skytrax (*www.airlinequality.com*).

The airline you choose should also tie in with your itinerary and where you want to start your trip. Royal Brunei Airlines makes it easy for an in-and-out of Brunei if coming from the UK or Australia. From there, internal flights are readily available to Sabah and Sarawak's capital cities.

✚ HEALTH *with Felicity Nicholson*

PREPARATIONS Preparations to ensure a healthy trip to Borneo require checks on your immunisation status: it is wise to be up to date on tetanus, polio and diphtheria (now given as an all-in-one vaccine, Revaxis, that lasts for ten years) and hepatitis A. Immunisations against typhoid, hepatitis B and rabies may also be recommended. Hepatitis A vaccine (Havrix Monodose or Avaxim) comprises two injections given about a year apart. The course costs about £100, but may be available on the NHS; it protects for 25 years and can be administered even close to the time of departure. Hepatitis B vaccination should be considered for longer trips (two months or more) or for those working with children or in situations where contact with blood is likely. Three injections are needed for the best protection and can be given over a three-week period if time is short for those aged 18 or over. Longer schedules give more sustained protection and are therefore preferred if time allows. Hepatitis A vaccine can also be given as a combination with hepatitis B as 'Twinrix', though two doses are needed at least seven days apart to be effective for the hepatitis A component, and three doses are needed for the hepatitis B. This is only available for those aged 18 or over.

The newer injectable typhoid vaccines (eg: Typhim Vi) last for three years and are about 85% effective. Oral capsules (Vivotif) are currently available in the US (and soon in the UK); if four capsules are taken over seven days it will last for five years. They should be encouraged unless the traveller is leaving within a few days for a trip of a week or less, when the vaccine would not be effective in time.

Vaccinations for rabies are especially important for travellers visiting more remote areas, especially if you are more than 24 hours from medical help and definitely if you will be working with animals (see *Rabies*, page 53).

Ideally you should visit your own doctor or a specialist travel clinic to discuss your requirements if possible at least eight weeks before you plan to travel.

Good starting points for general health and safety advice are foreign embassies. See the travel advice on the British Foreign and Commonwealth Office website (*www.fco.gov.uk*). The International Society of Travel Medicine (*www.istm.org*), emedicine.com (*www.emedecine.com*) and The Travel Doctor (*www.traveldoctor.co.uk*) are also useful for medical and health information.

FIRST-AID KIT
- A good drying antiseptic, eg: iodine or potassium permanganate (don't take antiseptic cream)
- A few small dressings (Band-Aids)
- Suncream
- Insect repellent and bite treatment
- Aspirin or paracetamol
- Antifungal cream (eg: Canesten)
- Anti-diarrhoea tablets such as Imodium
- Rehydration sachets
- Ciprofloxacin or norfloxacin, for severe diarrhoea
- Tinidazole for giardia or amoebic dysentery (see below for regime)
- Antibiotic eye drops, for sore, 'gritty', stuck-together eyes (conjunctivitis)

Dr Jane Wilson-Howarth

Long-haul air travel increases the risk of deep vein thrombosis (DVT). Although recent research has suggested that many of us develop clots when immobilised, most resolve without us ever having been aware of them. In certain susceptible individuals, though, large clots form and these can break away and lodge in the lungs. This is dangerous but happens in a tiny minority of passengers.

Studies have shown that flights of over five and a half hours are significant, and that people who take lots of shorter flights over a short space of time form clots. People at highest risk are:

- Those who have had a clot before – unless they are now taking Warfarin
- People over 80 years of age
- Anyone who has recently undergone a major operation or surgery for varicose veins
- Someone who has had a hip or knee replacement in the last three months
- Cancer sufferers
- Those who have ever had a stroke
- People with heart disease
- Those with a close blood relative who has had a clot

Those with a slightly increased risk:

- People over 40
- Women who are pregnant or have had a baby in the last couple of weeks
- People taking female hormones or other oestrogen therapy
- Heavy smokers
- Those who have very severe varicose veins

- Alcohol-based hand rub or bar of soap in plastic box
- Condoms or femidoms

TROPICAL DISEASES

Malaria This is a serious and potentially fatal disease transmitted by mosquitoes, for which there is no vaccine. There are hugely differing estimates of the prevalence of malaria in Borneo, ranging from 'successfully eliminated' to 'widespread'. Most sources agree that the risk is greater in more remote areas and fairly low in urban and coastal regions.

Current recommendations for prophylaxis are Malarone, doxycycline or Lariam for those travelling to rural areas of Borneo and unless none of the medication is suitable for you then you would be advised to take them. Seek medical advice as to which is the most appropriate for you and follow the regime recommended carefully. That said, no malaria tablets are 100% effective and so you should always take precautions against mosquito bites. This includes wearing trousers and long-sleeved shirts particularly between dusk and dawn. Apply insect repellents containing around 50–55% DEET to exposed skin at the recommended intervals, and when necessary sleep under a permethrin-impregnated bed net. These may not be provided so it is wise to take your own, especially if you are visiting remote areas.

Early diagnosis of malaria is essential for effective treatment, so if you suspect you or a companion has contracted the disease then seek medical help as soon as

- The very obese
- People who are very tall (over 6ft/1.8m) or short (under 5ft/1.5m)

A deep vein thrombosis (DVT) is a blood clot that forms in the deep leg veins. This is very different from irritating but harmless superficial phlebitis. DVT causes swelling and redness of one leg, usually with heat and pain in one calf and sometimes the thigh. A DVT is only dangerous if a clot breaks away and travels to the lungs (pulmonary embolus). Symptoms of a pulmonary embolus (PE) include chest pain that is worse on breathing in deeply, shortness of breath, and sometimes coughing up small amounts of blood. The symptoms commonly start three to ten days after a long flight. Anyone who thinks that they might have a DVT needs to see a doctor immediately who will arrange a scan. Warfarin tablets (to thin the blood) are then taken for at least six months.

PREVENTION OF DVT Several conditions make the problem more likely. Immobility is the key, and factors like reduced oxygen in cabin air and dehydration may also contribute. To reduce the risk of thrombosis on a long journey:

- Exercise before and after the flight
- Keep mobile before and during the flight; move around every couple of hours
- Drink plenty of water or juices during the flight
- Avoid taking sleeping pills and excessive tea, coffee and alcohol
- Perform exercises that mimic walking and tense the calf muscles
- Consider wearing flight socks or support stockings (see *www.legshealth.com*)
- Take a meal of oily fish (mackerel, trout, salmon, sardines, etc) in the 24 hours before departure to reduce blood clotability and thus DVT risk

If you think you are at increased risk of a clot, ask your doctor if it is safe to travel.

possible. Symptoms are flu-like and may include fevers, chills, muscle and joint aches, headache, tiredness, nausea, vomiting, and occasionally diarrhoea. The only consistent feature is a high temperature of 38°C or more and that alone should also make you suspect malaria. It can develop as much as one year after exposure so continue to be vigilant upon your return and seek medical advice if you develop flu-like symptoms.

For further advice and malaria information see www.fitfortravel.nhs.uk/destinations/malaysia.htm; www.preventingmalaria.info and www.traveldoctor.co.uk/malaria.htm.

Other diseases There are occasional outbreaks of hand, foot and mouth disease (HFMD) across Malaysia. The most recent large-scale outbreaks were in Sarawak in July 2006. However, this viral infection occurs worldwide particularly during the late summer and early autumn. It most commonly affects young children and in the main is not a serious infection. The risk of HFMD can be reduced by taking good personal hygiene precautions.

- Wash hands frequently, especially before eating, after using the toilet, and after nappy changes.
- Ensure contaminated surfaces are cleaned with disinfectant.
- Ensure contaminated tissues and other materials are disposed of appropriately.

There are periodic outbreaks of dengue fever (for which there is no vaccination). This viral infection is spread by day-biting mosquitoes. It causes a feverish illness with headache and muscle pains like a bad, prolonged, attack of influenza. There may be a rash.

Japanese encephalitis is another viral disease transmitted by infected mosquitoes. Vaccination is recommended for those likely to be frequently exposed to bites during long stays, repeated visits or if staying in rural infected areas for four weeks or more. The disease is endemic, with small numbers of cases occurring all the year round, in Eastern Malaysia (Sabah and Sarawak), but in addition epidemics occur following the start of the rainy season in Peninsular Malaysia (April to October) when mosquitoes are most active. Vaccination comprises a course of three doses the last of which should be taken at least ten days before a long-haul flight. Another reason to ensure that you visit your doctor well in advance of your trip.

WATER In Malaysia water is treated, but it is still best to avoid drinking tap water. You would also be advised to clean your teeth with bottled water and to avoid ice in drinks.

AIR QUALITY Malaysia, and in particular Sarawak, periodically suffers from smoke haze pollution. Hazardous air quality levels are reached due to extensive burning of forests in neighbouring Indonesia. The Malaysian Department of Environment (*www.doe.gov.my*) offers more information on this.

FOOD There are strict laws and health standards for food preparation, though this doesn't necessarily equate to high standards of cleanliness in coffee shops. Establishments with a grade A or B are usually of a good standard; anything of grade C or lower may be less than satisfactory.

Travellers' diarrhoea There is always a risk of getting a dose of travellers' diarrhoea; perhaps half of all visitors will suffer and the newer you are to exotic travel, the more likely that will be. By taking precautions against travellers' diarrhoea you will also avoid typhoid, paratyphoid, hepatitis, dysentery, worms, etc. Travellers' diarrhoea and the other faecal-oral diseases come from getting other peoples' faeces in your mouth. This most often happens from cooks not washing their hands after a trip to the toilet, but even if the restaurant cook does not understand basic hygiene you will be safe if your food has been properly cooked and arrives piping hot. The most important prevention strategy is to wash your hands before eating anything. You can pick up salmonella and shigella from toilet door handles and possibly bank notes. The maxim to remind you what you can safely eat is:

PEEL IT, BOIL IT, COOK IT OR FORGET IT

This means that fruit you have washed and peeled yourself, and hot foods, should be safe but raw foods, cold cooked foods, salads, fruit salads which have been prepared by others, ice cream and ice are all risky, and foods kept lukewarm in hotel buffets are often dangerous. That said, plenty of travellers enjoy fruit and vegetables, so do keep a sense of perspective. If you are struck, see box opposite for treatment.

Shellfish, crabs and some larger fish can be affected by 'red tide' – an algal bloom that produces harmful toxins. These can become incorporated into other sea creatures and may be harmful if consumed by humans. The Health Ministry issues warnings when this occurs, and restaurants follow their advice.   Larger seafood restaurants in Borneo with their own tanks still trade during these periods.

TREATING TRAVELLERS' DIARRHOEA

Dr Jane Wilson-Howarth

It is dehydration that makes you feel awful during a bout of diarrhoea and the most important part of treatment is drinking lots of clear fluids. Sachets of oral rehydration salts give the perfect biochemical mix to replace all that is pouring out of your bottom but other recipes taste nicer. Any dilute mixture of sugar and salt in water will do you good: try Coke or orange squash with a three-finger pinch of salt added to each glass (if you are salt-depleted you won't taste the salt). Otherwise make a solution of a four-finger scoop of sugar with a three-finger pinch of salt in a 500 ml glass. Or add eight level teaspoons of sugar (18g) and one level teaspoon of salt (3g) to one litre (five cups) of safe water. A squeeze of lemon or orange juice improves the taste and adds potassium, which is also lost in diarrhoea. Drink two large glasses after every bowel action, and more if you are thirsty. These solutions are still absorbed well if you are vomiting, but you will need to take sips at a time. If you are not eating you need to drink three litres a day plus whatever is pouring into the toilet. If you feel like eating, take a bland, high carbohydrate diet. Heavy greasy foods will probably give you cramps.

If the diarrhoea is bad, or you are passing blood or slime, or you have a fever, you will probably need antibiotics in addition to fluid replacement. A dose of norfloxacin or ciprofloxacin repeated twice a day until better may be appropriate (if you are planning to take an antibiotic with you, note that both norfloxacin and ciprofloxacin are available only on prescription in the UK). If the diarrhoea is greasy and bulky and is accompanied by sulphurous (eggy) burps, one likely cause is giardia. This is best treated with tinidazole (four x 500mg in one dose, repeated seven days later if symptoms persist).

RABIES Rabies is carried by all mammals (beware the village dogs and small monkeys that are used to being fed in the parks) and is passed on to man through a bite, scratch or a lick of an open wound. You must always assume any animal is rabid, and seek medical help as soon as possible. Meanwhile scrub the wound with soap under a running tap or while pouring water from a jug. Find a reasonably clear-looking source of water (but at this stage the quality of the water is not important), then pour on a strong iodine or alcohol solution of gin, whisky or rum. This helps stop the rabies virus entering the body and will guard against wound infections, including tetanus.

Pre-exposure vaccination for rabies is ideally advised for everyone, but is particularly important if you intend to have contact with animals and/or are likely to be more than 24 hours away from medical help. Ideally three doses should be taken over a minimum of 21 days, though even taking one or two doses of vaccine is better than none at all. Contrary to popular belief these vaccinations are relatively painless.

If you are bitten, scratched or licked over an open wound by a sick animal, then post-exposure prophylaxis should be given as soon as possible, though it is never too late to seek help, as the incubation period for rabies can be very long. Those who have not been immunised will need a full course of injections. The vast majority of travel health advisers including WHO recommend rabies immunoglobulin (RIG), but this product is expensive (around US$800) and may be hard to come by – another reason why pre-exposure vaccination should be encouraged.

Tell the doctor if you have had pre-exposure vaccine, as this should change the treatment you receive. And remember that, if you do contract rabies, mortality is 100% and death from rabies is probably one of the worst ways to go.

DOCTORS There are two medical systems in Malaysia. Both public and private health care are widely available and of a high standard. Private health care is very inexpensive. You can arrange to see a doctor easily at a medical centre or surgery, or ask your hotel to organise a doctor to visit you there. It is more expensive than public health care, but you are guaranteed a high level of service, and English-speaking staff. Medical staff administer most medication on the spot so you shouldn't need to go to a pharmacy as well. Health centres and hospitals are listed in the relevant guide chapters. For a full list of hospitals and district health officers in Sabah and Sarawak, see the Malaysian government portal (*www.moh.gov.my/MohPortal/govhospPublic.jsp*).

BRUNEI Brunei is relatively free from malaria and other tropical diseases. It is outside the typhoon belt, has no active volcanoes and is not prone to earthquakes or other major natural disasters.

TRAVEL CLINICS AND HEALTH INFORMATION A full list of current travel clinic websites worldwide is available on www.istm.org/. For other journey preparation information, consult ftp://ftp.shoreland.com/pub/shorecg.rtf or www.tripprep.com. Information about various medications may be found on www.emedicine.com/wild/topiclist.htm.

UK

Berkeley Travel Clinic 32 Berkeley St, London W1J 8EL (near Green Park tube station); ℡ 020 7629 6233; ⊕ 10.00–18.00 Mon–Fri; 10.00–15.00 Sat.
Cambridge Travel Clinic 41 Hills Rd, Cambridge, CB2 1NT; ℡ 01223 367362; f 01223 368021; e enquiries@travelcliniccambridge.co.uk; www.travelcliniccambridge.co.uk; ⊕ 10.00–16.00 Mon, closed Tue, 12.00–19.00 Wed–Thu, 11.00–18.00 Fri, 10.00–16.00 Sat.
Edinburgh Travel Health Clinic 14 East Preston St, Newington, Edinburgh EH8 9QA; ℡ 0131 667 1030; www.edinburghtravelhealthclinic.co.uk; ⊕ 09.00–19.00 Mon–Wed, 9.00–18.00 Thu & Fri. Travel vaccinations & advice on all aspects of malaria prevention. All current UK prescribed anti-malaria tablets in stock.
Fleet Street Travel Clinic 29 Fleet St, London EC4Y 1AA; ℡ 020 7353 5678; www.fleetstreetclinic.com; ⊕ 08.45–17.30 Mon–Fri. Injections, travel products & latest advice.
Hospital for Tropical Diseases Travel Clinic Mortimer Market Centre, 2nd Flr, Capper St (off Tottenham Ct Rd), London WC1E 6AU; ℡ 020 7388 9600; www.thehtd.org. Offers consultations & advice, & is able to provide all necessary drugs & vaccines for travellers. Runs a healthline (℡ 020 7950 7799) for country-specific information and health hazards. Also stocks nets, water purification equipment & personal protection measures.
MASTA (Medical Advisory Service for Travellers Abroad), at the London School of Hygiene &

Tropical Medicine, Keppel St, London WC1 7HT; ℡ 09068 224100 www.masta-travel-health.com. This is a premium-line number, charged at 60p per minute. For a fee, they will provide an individually tailored health brief, with up-to-date information on how to stay healthy, inoculations & what to take.
MASTA pre-travel clinics ℡ 01276 685040. Call for the nearest; there are currently 30 in Britain. They also sell malaria prophylaxis memory cards, treatment kits, bednets, net treatment kits, etc.
NHS travel website www.fitfortravel.scot.nhs.uk. Provides country-by-country advice on immunisation & malaria prevention, plus details of recent developments, & a list of relevant health organisations.
Nomad Travel Store 3–4 Wellington Terrace, Turnpike Lane, London N8 0PX; ℡ 020 8889 7014; f 020 8889 9528; e turnpike@nomadtravel.co.uk; www.nomadtravel.co.uk; walk in or appointments ⊕ 09.15–17.00 everyday with late night Thu. Six stores in total country wide. As well as dispensing health advice, Nomad stocks mosquito nets & other anti-bug devices, & an excellent range of adventure travel gear.
InterHealth Travel Clinic 157 Waterloo Rd, London SE1 8US; ℡ 020 7902 9000; e askus@interhealth.org.uk www.interhealth.org.uk; ⊕ 09.00–17.00 Mon–Fri. Competitively priced, one-stop travel health service by appointment only.
Trailfinders Immunisation Centre 194 Kensington High St, London W8 7RG; ℡ 020 7938 3999

www.trailfinders.com/travelessentials/travelclinic.htm;
🕘 09.00–17.00 Mon, Tue, Wed & Fri,
09.00–18.00 Thu, 10.00–17.15 Sat. No
appointment necessary

Irish Republic
Tropical Medical Bureau Grafton St Medical Centre,
Grafton Buildings, 34 Grafton St, Dublin 2; 📞 1

USA
Centers for Disease Control 1600 Clifton Rd, Atlanta,
GA 30333; 📞 (404) 498 1515 or (800) 311 3435;
e cdcinfo@cdc.gov; www.cdc.gov/travel. The central
source of travel information in the USA. Each
summer they publish the invaluable Health
Information for International Travel

Australia, New Zealand, Singapore
TMVC (Travel Doctors Group) 📞 1300 65 88 44;
www.tmvc.com.au. 22 clinics in Australia, New
Zealand and Thailand, including: *Auckland*
Canterbury Arcade, 170 Queen St, Auckland; 📞 9
373 3531; *Brisbane* Dr Deborah Mills, Qantas
Domestic Building, 6th Flr, 247 Adelaide St,
Brisbane, QLD 4000; 📞 7 3221 9066; f 7 3321

Canada
IAMAT (International Association for Medical
Assistance to Travellers) Suite 1, 1287 St Clair Av
W, Toronto, Ontario M6E 1B8; 📞 416 652 0137;
www.iamat.org

South Africa
SAA-Netcare Travel Clinics e travelinfo@
netcare.co.za www.travelclinic.co.za or
www.malaria.co.za. Twelve clinics throughout South
Africa.

Switzerland
IAMAT 57 Chemin des Voirets, 1212 Grand-Lancy,
Geneva; e info@iamat.org; www.iamat.org

Travelpharm The Travelpharm website
(*www.travelpharm.com*) offers up-to-date guidance on
travel-related health and has a range of medications
available through their online mini-pharmacy.

671 9200. Has a useful website specific to tropical
destinations: www.tmb.ie.

IAMAT (International Association for Medical
Assistance to Travelers): 1623 Military Rd, #279
Niagara Falls, NY 14304-1745; 📞 716 754 4883;
e info@iamat.org; www.iamat.org. A non-profit
organisation with free membership that provides
lists of English-speaking doctors abroad.

7076; *Melbourne* Dr Sonny Lau, 393 Little Bourke
St, 2nd floor, Melbourne, VIC 3000; 📞 3 9602 5788;
f 3 9670 8394; *Sydney* Dr Mandy Hu, Dymocks
Building, 7th Flr, 428 George St, Sydney, NSW 2000,
📞 2 221 7133; f 2 221 8401
IAMAT PO Box 5049, Christchurch 5, New Zealand;
www.iamat.org

TMVC Suite 314, 1030 W Georgia Street, Vancouver,
BC V6E 2Y3; 📞 905 648 1112; www.tmvc.com. One-
stop medical clinic for all your international travel
medicine & vaccination needs

TMVC NHC Health Centre, Cnr Beyers Naude &
Waugh Northcliff 📞 0 11 214 9030;
www.traveldoctor.co.za. Consult the website for
details of clinics.

SAFETY

British, US and Australian authorities issue warnings against travelling around the
coast of East Malaysia, particularly the islands off the east coast of Sabah. These
islands have been the site of political tensions and volatility as territorial disputes
between Indonesia and Malaysia bubble (see *Diving in Borneo* box, page 39).
Tourists have been the target of kidnappers in the past. Accommodation on some
islands has been closed and the area is under constant military surveillance.

URBAN SAFETY AND CRIME There is a relatively low risk of being mugged or robbed,
but be sensible in keeping personal belongings close to you, and be on the lookout for

pickpockets in markets. Be warned that some streets and roads, even in the state capitals, are very unkempt – keep an eye out for large cracks and holes. The low crime rate of Brunei comes in large part from government stability and economic prosperity.

ANIMALS There are several poisonous snakes on Borneo, both terrestrial and marine (see *Chapter 3, Natural history*, page 110). Caution must be taken at certain beaches. There are no deadly mammals, but jungle walks should be done with guides rather than alone.

DISABLED TRAVELLERS After contacting a couple of major UK and US associations which deal with disabled travel and being told they did not have Borneo covered, it appears that up until now there has not been a lot of call for them to do so. This is likely to change as Borneo receives more tourists. For the time being, travelling on public transport, especially small town buses, would not be easy. Most four–five-star hotels claim to have facilities for the disabled including wheelchair access and 'adapted' rooms. The lack of dedicated disabled-friendly tours to Borneo doesn't mean your chosen tour company will not do the job for you and create an itinerary. If you are travelling independently the best thing is to contact the Sabah and Sarawak tourism offices for assistance and recommendations once you have a basic itinerary planned. They can also answer specific questions and contact hotels and other businesses directly. Use the various associations (see below) as your advocates so that they know there is a demand for such information. For further information see Mobility International USA (*www.miusa.org/ncde/intlopportunities/malaysia*) as well as www.canbedone.co.uk; www.disabledtravelers.com and www.able-travel.com.

FAMILIES A family of five I know recently returned from a trip to Sabah. With children aged between eight and 16, the prospect of climbing Mount Kinabalu was approached with mixed feelings. Their itinerary also included a survivor camp in a village and a mix of budget beach resorts and luxury coastal hotels. They came back having loved all of it – wowed by the mountain, surprised by some of the beach litter, but healthy, happy and perhaps a little wiser. On the whole, Malaysian Borneo is safe, sunny and friendly and makes an inexpensive, educational, adventurous and exotic family holiday.

It's not a destination to just soak up some sun – there is so much more on offer. A volunteer family holiday, living and helping out in one of the villages, would be a fantastic experience.

Many city hostels – especially the 'lodge' kind – have family rooms from 115MYR with breakfast included. With their lounges, sun decks and other travellers for company, these may provide a more fun atmosphere than the small room, square-wall environment of a shoestring hotel which have family rooms from 100–150MYR. If you have more to spend, and want more privacy, then there are family rooms in most of the hotels. Another good option are serviced apartments. Beyond the cities, there are beach resorts which have self-contained family rooms (or just pay for two or three rooms for your brood, they can be so cheap), mountain resorts with chalet accommodation (sometimes self-contained), longhouse rentals or family-friendly homestays.

SINGLE TRAVELLERS Many of the advantages and disadvantages of travelling alone in Borneo are not very different from doing so in other places. I found, particularly in luxury hotels, the staff grilled me as to whether it was 'just *one* for breakfast?' – 'I'm not hiding anyone' is my usual reply. If you are seeking peace and quiet take a book or a newspaper.

Practically speaking, single travellers get heavily penalised in Malaysian and Bruneian hotels. There are virtually no single rates – either there is no difference in price between a single and double, or the difference is negligible. A better choice is to stay in the places where single does pay – homestays, bed and breakfasts, hostels, budget to mid-range beach resorts, and the occasional hotel suite or apartment which offer a single rate suitably priced for the 'flash packer'. Even if you have more to spend these are generally more friendly places, and many offer the chance to upgrade to a bigger or more comfortable room. All that said, if you do want a hotel environment, shoestring to budget hotel rooms start at between 60MYR and 120MYR and you will have a lot of space. Just make sure that if you are paying for a double room you are getting one. The same price bracket in some country hotels may get you anything from a superior room to a suite.

GAY AND LESBIAN TRAVELLERS One of the most highly regarded gay and lesbian associations active in Borneo is Utopia Asia (*www.utopia-asia.com*). Its general advice for travellers in Malaysia is: 'Gay life in Malaysia as in other Asian countries is blossoming, despite conservative religion-based discrimination and outdated colonial era laws. Former Deputy Prime Minister, Anwar Ibrahim, was famously removed from office by a trumped-up sodomy conviction that was reversed by Malaysia's High Court in 2004. Muslims, both local and visitors, are also subject to religious law which may (though rarely does) punish gay or lesbian sexual activity with flogging and imprisonment with imprisonment. Even though religious law does not apply to non-Muslims, Islam is the state religion under Malaysia's constitution and thus homosexual citizens face official discrimination. Police may arrest any person (Muslim or not) for having sex in a public place (such as cruise spots). Visitors are well advised to respect Malaysian law and customs while they are guests in the country. Having said that, police generally have not detained foreigners during raids on local gay businesses, focusing instead on ethnic Malay customers, almost 100% of whom are considered Muslim at birth by law.

See Utopia Asia's *Utopia Guide to Malaysia*, which has listings for the gay and lesbian scene in 17 cities including Kota Kinabalu and Kuching. The guide can be ordered online (*www.utopia-asia.com/utopiaguide/utopiaguides.htm*) and includes gay scene city maps and listings of organisations, bars, discos, spas, accommodation and restaurants, with a special section highlighting venues that are particularly welcoming to women.

Kota Kinabalu is definitely Borneo's capital of camp. Whilst there are no overtly gay hotels, there are some which are discreetly so and others which are gay-friendly. There are some well-known gay and lesbian bars and nightclubs in Kota Kinabalu. Kuching is far more conservative. Brunei is unfortunately much less tolerant of homosexuality, and the gay community is mostly 'undercover'. The nearest place where public displays of affection can be shown without the fear of being arrested is Miri in Sarawak.

WHAT TO TAKE

What you take is dependent on what kind of holiday you are planning as much as personal tastes. Rather than provide an exhaustive list of what to take, I have listed a few things you may not want to do without!

MAPS Whilst basic tourist maps of towns are available in Borneo, it is best to bring your own maps for the rest of your trip. Maps should be as detailed as is relevant for what you want to do – see *Getting your bearings*, page 64. This is especially important if you are travelling independently on trekking trips and going to places such as Kinabalu Park – maps available at the park are not very good on scale and legend. **Periplus Publishing** (*www.peripluspublishinggroup.com*) produce travel maps of Sarawak and Sabah at a scale of 1:1,000,000, including Kota Kinabalu, Kuching and Bintulu city plans. Periplus also do good language books – various Behasa, Melayu-Behasa and Inggeris dictionaries including a good pocket one.

CLOTHES It's amazing just how little clothing you need in the tropics. I packed relatively lightly for an eight-week stay on my last trip to Borneo with about 12 different outfits in total: daytime and evening wear, casual and smart. My wardrobe included two pairs of shorts, two pairs of cotton trousers, three skirts, two dresses, ten short-sleeved tops and two long-sleeved ones. All of them were very light and loose apart from one thermal top for the mountain. You can easily get by wearing the same thing day after day, as long as it is clean, cool and non-clingy. The best materials are thin pure cotton, linen and silk, as well as cotton-silk and cotton-nylon mixes. Avoid scratchy materials such as viscose and rayon or heavy viscose-elastane combinations. A couple of light long-sleeved tops or cardigans would not be necessary if it weren't for the air conditioning which can be polar in planes, buses, hotels and restaurants! If you are planning on visiting Kinabalu Park, this will then double up as one necessary clothing layer. Mount Kinabalu is the only place mentioned in this guide which never gets colder than 15°C, and you will need to take some thermal and waterproof clothing for an ascent (see *Chapter 6, West Coast Sabah,* page 178).

You will never need jeans. Denim weighs a tonne, does not dry easily and is uncomfortable in hot and humid climates. Trousers for the evening should be chosen carefully to avoid getting hot and sticky. For most evenings, skirts and sundresses are the best bet for women, smart shorts for men. Light trousers are smarter for restaurant settings; these will also be necessary in the air-conditioned environments. For daytime, 100% fine cotton or linen skirts or shorts, or beach wear such as sarongs in quick-drying fabrics are the best things. Outdoor-gear skirts and shorts from Colorado and Patagonia are perfect. Avoid black – you will feel hot in it no matter what.

You will not need any more than four pairs of shoes – including walking shoes, sandals and a pair of open, evening shoes if you wish. Avoid anything closed or tight, as your feet may swell up. A better alternative to trainers (running shoes) would be quality walking sandals, which could be worn with long socks if you wish. Good walking sandals in breathable leather are great for walking around bigger cities in heat; some also swear by crocs for this. Quality flip-flops such as Nike's are made for walking around cities and are very comfortable, and also great for the beach.

$ MONEY

EASTERN MALAYSIA
Currency The currency of Sabah and Sarawak is the Malaysian ringgit (MYR). Notes come in denominations of 1, 5, 10, 50 and 100RM. One ringgitt comprises 100 sen. Coins come in 5, 10, 20 and 50 sen denominations. The exchange rate in October 2008 was such that (approximately) US$1 = 3.50MYR, €1 = 4.80MYR, £1 = 6.04MYR.

Exchanging and spending Foreign currencies and travellers' cheques can be readily exchanged at banks and at licensed money exchanges in larger cities, as well as at hotels and some department stores. Credit cards (Visa, MasterCard, American Express and Diners Club) are widely accepted in hotels and bigger restaurants and businesses, but not in small local shops. Payment by credit card becomes more difficult the further from major cities you go, as does the possibility of exchanging money and cashing travellers' cheques. ATM machines are scarce outside of cities and medium-sized towns.

Major national Malaysian banks with branches in Sabah and Sarawak include Bumiputera Commerce and RHB Bank. Bank hours are generally 09.30–16.00.

Until 2005, the Malaysian ringgit was equal in value to the US dollar (in response to the Asian financial crash). People still commonly quote in dollars in marketplaces and shops, so if you are quoted an unreasonably high price this could be the explanation. The difference between 1MYR and US$1 is more than three-fold. Ask if you are unsure.

BRUNEI The Brunei dollar (BND) is equal in value to the Singapore dollar which is also legal tender in Brunei. The dollar comes in 1, 5, 10, 50, 100, 500 and 1,000 denominations; coins come in 1, 5, 10, 20 and 50 cents. All major credit cards are accepted throughout the country. Most Bruneian banks are government sanctioned to handle traveller's cheques and currency exchange.

CARRYING CASH In both Malaysia and Brunei, it is advisable to always carry some cash, especially when travelling in the countryside. ATMs can be hard to come by and unreliable, even at airports.

BUDGETING

Borneo caters pretty well for all budgets, and is particularly good value for those with less money to spend. Other parts of Asia may be cheaper, but they have a greater choice of 'high-end' products and services. Borneo has a great choice of budget accommodation and food. It is possible to live inexpensively whatever your budget. The hotels, car hire, tours and trips are likely to be your biggest expenditures. There are so many good hotel deals, and much inter-bleeding of categories between budget/mid-range and mid-range/upmarket you can easily upgrade a notch or two for some hotel nights.

UPMARKET Four–five-star hotels generally charge 450–600MYR or more for a double room. For this price you can enjoy 20–30m^2 (or more) rooms/suites, business lounges and other privileges that come with top-end accommodation. The food in coffee shops and markets is the best available; however, if you prefer to dine in air-conditioned restaurants there are plenty to choose from. A daily spend of US$120–150 will allow for upmarket hotels with extras, top-range food and tours and car hire.

MID-RANGE In the lower mid-range there are some very good deals to be had on two–three-star hotels, especially with online promotions. Many hotels offer deals like a superior double room with breakfast, for two people on two nights for 300MYR; this works out to just 75MYR (around US$20/£10) per person per night for bed and breakfast. With some day tours using local operators and dining in hotel restaurants, an average daily budget might be US$60–80 (around £30–40/€40–50).

To upgrade slightly: some upper mid-range (and even some more upmarket) hotels offer rates of 300–400MYR for a double room. Add occasional car hire to this, and a daily budget may be in the region of US$80–100 a day.

SHOESTRING/BUDGET If you are on a tight budget, the best option is to stay in hostels, homestays and no-star hotels; eat street food from stalls and markets and dine at coffee shops; take buses and ferries, and flights with AirAsia, and wing it on your own to visit local places rather than take guided tours. The food available at markets for 1–3MYR is delicious, and in coffee shops you won't need to pay any more than 10MYR for a good meal including soft drinks. In Brunei, prices are around double. In either country, you can eat very well for US$5 at the markets.

If you are on a restricted budget but can go that extra bit further, budget hotels may be an option. A single/double room will cost 50–60MYR. You will be able to eat at a few more coffee shops than markets, and choose a (budget) tour company for the occasional half- or full-day excursion. Budget options are outlined in each guide chapter.

I think it's feasible to live comfortably enough off 110–150MYR a day (approximately US$32–45/£20–25/€25–30).

GETTING AROUND

✈ **BY AIR** Though travelling distances within each Bornean state are not especially long, many people rely on air travel for longer journeys (such as west- to east-coast cities). This is partly because it is there – flights to the major cities and towns are abundant and cheap – and partly because of the state of most of the roads. Why spend six hours travelling in a car if you can fly in 40 minutes? With many remote inland areas and a 1,000km western coastline marked by four major cities (Kuching, Sibu, Bintulu and Miri), flights are even more common in Sarawak. If speed and convenience are what you are looking for, then flying is a good option. If you are concerned about the environmental effects of air travel, or want to take in the scenery between towns (and brave the roads!), then see below for other options.

Established or no frills? With the slogan 'Now Everyone Can Fly' plastered all over their bright red aircraft, AirAsia (*www.airasia.com*) are loved for liberating the skies and contributing to aviation democracy with their affordable prices. However they are also loathed for the frustrations they create through chronic delays, and a rather blasé attitude towards customers – though not without typical Asian politeness. The increasingly competitive prices offered by MAS are making it hardly worthwhile enduring the relative discomfort and disarray of AirAsia to save a few pennies. However as with all low cost airlines, the prices do make it very attractive and AirAsia are more friendly, professional and comfortable than Ryanair – more on a par with easyJet or German Wings. MAS are far more reliable, if a little more expensive. Their safety record and policy is unwavering; they allow 20kg for domestic flights (compared with AirAsia's 15kg); they have on-board refreshments and assigned seats; and they allow ticket changes. If a flight is cancelled by AirAsia on the other hand, you have the option of either taking another flight later that day or losing your ticket. If you arrive at the AirAsia check-in desk any later than 30 minutes ahead of departure they are uncompromising, but if they keep *you* waiting for an hour, no apologies are offered. All that said, I do know a lot of people who swear by them, rather than at them – and who fly frequently and cheaply. Just be prepared for the delays! Overall, the choice provided by the two is fantastic.

Fares With MAS fares can be as low as 99MYR from Kuala Lumpur to Kuching, Sibu, Bintulu and Miri (all in Sarawak); 129MYR from Kuala Lumpur to Kota Kinabalu and Labuan; 39MYR from Kota Kinabalu to Miri, Labuan, Tawau and Sandakan, and from Kuching to Sibu. MAS also offer specials to foreigners such as the 'Discover Malaysia Pass', offering travel to three destinations within Malaysia, for US$199. The deal allows a return trip from Kuala Lumpur to Borneo (flying into Sabah and out of Sarawak) and one internal Borneo flight.

AirAsia fares for the same period were as low as 29.99MYR Kuching to Sibu, 69.99MYR Kuching–Miri, and 49.99MYR Kuching–Kota Kinabalu, but there is a huge amount of price variation and it pays to check regularly, and to book online.

Rural air services (RAS)

All rural air services (RAS) in Sabah, Sarawak and Labuan are operated by MASWings, a new subsidiary of Malaysia Airlines. Under their former operator – FlyAsianXpress (FAX), a subsidiary of AirAsia – scheduled flights were renowned for being cancelled or delayed, because of repairs, breakdowns or bad weather. As one guide commented 'some people say that FAX Airlines stands for Flight Always Cancelled!' The rural services use propeller-driven 19-seat Twin Otters and Fokker F-50s, but the latter are due to be replaced by ATR 72 aircraft in 2009. While their management of the rural services has not yet stood the test of time, their parent company have a pretty impressive track record, so hopefully the change in management will bring improvements. The MASWings network will cover 21 destinations in Sabah and Sarawak, with 451 flights scheduled per week. 72 weekly Fokker F-50 flights and nine Twin Otter flights within Sabah; 168 Fokker F-50 flights and 146 Twin Otter flights within Sarawak; and 51 Fokker F-50 flights and five Twin Otter flights between Sabah and Sarawak.

BY CAR

The cost of car rental is similar to Western prices: around 100–150MYR a day. Perhaps with the exception of the longest trips from west to east in Sabah, or north to south in Sarawak, trips by car offer a good mix of independence, ease and maximum viewing along the way. Car journeys are particularly economical in Brunei where petrol costs 50 cents a litre, about 20BND to fill a tank. Prices are double that in Sabah and Sarawak, where petrol costs around 1.9MYR a litre, or 90MYR a tank. (Just about everything else works in the opposite sense – double the price in Brunei!) Most national driving licences (UK, US, Australian) can be used in Malaysia for three months, beyond which you require either a Malaysian driving licence or an annually renewable International Driving Permit.

Roads All major roads are dual carriageways; there are no multi-lane expressways. The speed limit is 100km/h on open roads. Distances are now metric, but there are still vestiges of the former imperial system as far as the location of some places goes (see *Getting your bearings*, page 64). The major routes are all of decent (and improving) quality. Minor roads can vary enormously, and if you are driving around a lot you will encounter some pretty bumpy roads, as well as totally unsealed sections, as you travel between towns or through plantations and rural areas. Most routes leading into developing towns or rising tourist attractions are either undergoing roadwork or earmarked for improvement.

Rules In Malaysia you drive on the left-hand side of the road and the cars are right-hand drive. Road signs are not brilliant – in their regularity or clarity, in cities or on highways. Things are better in Sarawak where the British influence is more noticeable, and international signage is far more common on major routes, especially on the west coast Pan-Borneo Highway. Two road signs you will see a lot are *AWAS* (slow) and *Dilarang Masuk* (private – no entry).

With the low population density it is easy to manoeuvre on the open road, though it is more difficult in cities – streets are small and quite congested. Due to strict licence conditions and enforcement, road safety seems very high and I have been impressed by the quality of driving. All licences have to be renewed annually and public service vehicles require a special licence. Expect police checks and road blocks, especially in southeast Sabah towards the Indonesian border, where they are checking for illegal trafficking of people and general contraband.

Inter-state travel Travelling between states by car is possible; it depends on your itinerary, how much time you have, and whether you want to make the road trip part of your journey and get a feel for the landscape. The Pan-Borneo Highway, *Lebuh raya Pan Borneo* (also referred to as the Trans Borneo Highway), links Sabah to Brunei and to Sarawak.

Although long road trips can be enjoyable, it is worth bearing in mind the practicalities of travelling between states, described here by a friend who tried it: 'It takes eight to ten hours to drive from Kota Kinabalu to Brunei town, which involves between three and five river crossings using a ferry – adding to the time and cost of the journey. And there is always the risk of having your passport taken at one of the numerous checkpoints.' If you are heading for Sarawak, you have to take this same route and travel through Brunei, as there is no direct road once you reach Lawas through to Miri, which makes it a convoluted journey. From Kota Kinabalu to Miri is a 12-hour drive; continuing south to Kuching would make at least a 20-hour journey.

Immigration checkpoints Between Sabah, Sarawak and Brunei, these are found at: Sindumin, Sabah to Merapok in Sarawak; Tedungan in Sarawak to Kuala Lurah in Brunei; and Sungai Tujoh in Brunei to Sungai Tujuh Miri in Sarawak. The Tedungan to Kuala Lurah is one of the busiest, with waits of up to an hour. Sungai Tujoh (being the only place where holders of Frequent Traveller Cards can pass between Brunei and Sarawak) can also involve nightmarish waits as Bruneians head to the border for a weekend in Miri. Avoid it on long weekends when up to 1,500 cars will pass in a day. The Bruneian checkpoints in particular are not well staffed. There also checks involved in the ferry crossing from Lawas in Sarawak to Labu in Brunei and from Puni in Brunei to Limbang in Sarawak.

Further road information, key distances and estimated driving times are included in the relevant chapters of this guide. Sabah Tourism also has an interactive distance chart online (*www.sabahtourism.com/distancechart/distancechart.html*).

BY BUS While buses provide a cheap, comfortable form of transport which can be both fun and effective, the urban bus system in both Sabah and Sarawak is a bit of a shambles. Problems include too many bus companies, no central bus terminal and confusion (at least for the outsider) of where to take each type of bus from. The situation is improving in the capital cities as the infrastructure evolves, but in smaller towns buses are not the best option.

Town buses *Bas mini* (minibuses) ply city and suburban areas but also do some longer inter-city journeys. The vehicles are generally numbered rather than named, with a route diagram at key bus stops. Different bus companies usually operate particular patches, serving specific towns and surrounding areas.

Long-distance buses Air-conditioned 'express buses' for long-distance trips leave from a different terminal from town buses. In bigger cities these are usually located in the suburbs and referred to as the long-distance bus station. Several coach and express bus operators vie for longer journeys, both intra- and inter-state. All these choices don't necessarily mean travelling by bus is easy though. Long-distance bus stations (even in smaller towns) can be very inconveniently located, meaning you also have to take a minibus to the city or town centre. Tour operators use comfortable, 8–12-seat, air-conditioned recreational buses, for which they must have a licence.

Long-distance buses can be a very cost-effective (though not necessarily time-effective) way of travelling. For example, to cross Sabah from Kota Kinabalu to the east coast city of Tawau (roughly 12 hours) costs 50MYR, including a meal. Inter-state travel by bus is more complicated – for example, travelling between Miri (Sarawak) and Bandar Seri Begawan (Brunei) involves changing buses four times and crossing two rivers by ferry. More details of all these journeys are given in the relevant chapters.

My advice would be to limit bus journeys to four or five hours. Air fares of less than 50MYR between Kota Kinabalu and Kuching make anything more than this feasibly avoidable on a budget. Another option would be to stop off at places along the way and break the bus journey up. This is a great way to see smaller places you would otherwise miss, but depends on whether you have the time.

BY BOAT

Ferries Ferries are an efficient and interesting way of travelling in Borneo. Some of the main links are: Brunei to Sabah (via Labuan Island); Brunei to Limbang in Sarawak; Kota Kinabalu to Brunei (via Labuan); and Labuan to Menumbok in Sabah. There are various operators, and both passenger and car ferries. One of the best websites to check ferry timetables and prices is **Labuan Tourism**'s homepage (*www.labuantourism.com.my*) as Labuan is a centre of ferry passage between Sabah and Brunei.

The overall trip by ferry between Brunei's capital and Sabah's capital can be done in about four hours, travelling via Labuan Island. There are no direct ferries. Have your passport on hand as you will go through immigration. If arriving in Brunei, have the necessary money on you for the visa. There are several daily departures and the fare from Kota Kinabalu through to Brunei will cost between 60 and 80MYR, depending on which ferry and ticket class you take. Child transport generally costs between 30–40% less.

There are also regular ferries between Labuan and Limbang and Lawas in Sarawak, and to Sipitang in southern Sabah. Ferries leave Brunei for Limbang – a half-hour journey – with the option of continuing by road (bus or car) north to Sabah or south through Sarawak.

River transport Boats are an integral part of the public transport system, especially in Sarawak (which boasts 55 rivers). Boats are used to travel across and along rivers, over bays, into jungles and to remote villages, though the boat journey itself can be as much a part of a trip as the destination.

Small fibreglass vessels are often used for river excursions, twin-engine motorboats for transfers. Speedboats and water taxis are also common. Larger, high-tech express boats are used for longer trips, and are a common and vital way of travelling into central Sarawak's interior. They are also the most important form of public river transport between towns on (or near) Sarawak's west coast. The trips by tribal boats are by far the most memorable though, and may be in small wooden sampan or dugout longboats (*temuai*) used by the Iban and other river-dwelling tribes.

As air travel replaces the absolute need for extensive longboat trips, especially to reach hinterland areas of Sarawak, such journeys are really only within reach of the independent traveller with enough cash to pay for the wonder of doing a six- to ten-hour river trip or an overnight custom-made adventure. Two-hour trips are a common feature of packaged river safaris and tours for both budget and upmarket travellers. If you are travelling independently, do everything you can to suss out the local public boat services to reach nearby towns, villages and islands. These are not always well publicised; information can be found at the public jetties.

MAPS For some reason, maps in Sabah and Sarawak are of poor quality and very difficult to get hold of. The owner of one award-winning tour company in Sabah told me of his joy when he visited London in the 1990s and found the best maps of Sabah he had ever seen! Things have no doubt improved since then, but if the quality and availability of tourism maps – especially in Sabah – are any indication, then you are well advised to bring your own maps. If you are just visiting the cities then the tourist maps will probably be sufficient, but if you want more detail or have a special interest – mountaineering, general touring, self-drive, nature-spotting – bring maps with sufficient details to suit your needs.

Apparently 'due to many requests', Sabah Tourism will soon be issuing a tourist map of the state for visitors. The Kota Kinabalu city map they provide is reasonably useful, but Sabah Tourism have, until recently, been unable to provide town and city maps for other destinations. Sarawak Tourism (again) does a much better job. Their large fold-out map of the state does not give topographic detail fit for hiking, but does show rivers, mountains and small towns. On the reverse side there is an excellent Kuching city map, city/town maps of Sibu, Miri, Bintulu, Kapit and Sarikei, and maps of the Damai Beach area and Gunung Mulu National Park. Brunei is only afforded basic detail on the map. Pick one up from tourist offices in any of the towns mentioned above.

DIRECTIONS Road signs are as elusive in Borneo, as are street names. In Kota Kinabalu and its coastal surrounds, there are hardly any signs along major roads, and if you ask people (including local tour guides) which road or street you are on, they usually shrug their shoulders. The same is found in small towns; you might find that one street in the town has a name, but no-one ever uses it. Locals generally orient themselves in relation to a landmark – the name of a bank, a shopping centre, or a business of some kind. So if you need directions, ask where a certain place is, rather than which street it is in.

TOWN, VILLAGE AND ROAD NAMES A village (such as Kundasang, just south of Kinabalu Park) is a *kampung,* sometimes spelt *kampong.* A small town (such as Ranau, a few kilometres from Kundasang) is known as a *pecan.* A medium-sized town is a *bandar,* and a big city is a *bandarayar.* A village on water is a *kampung ayer* (pronounced 'eye-er'). Roads are mostly called *jalan* (abbreviated to *jln*). Lanes and pathways are *lorong* and avenues are *lebuh.* Long *jalan* can change name three times along one city strip. Confusingly, tourism offices (and sometimes locals) switch between referring to streets in Malaysian and English. *Jalan Bazaar* in Kuching varies rather erratically between its real name and the Anglicised version 'Main Bazaar' on maps.

TOWN LAYOUT AND ADDRESSES Sabah, Sarawak and Brunei's town centres have been traditionally built into 'shop-lots'. Shops, bazaars, coffee shops and all kinds of other traders occupy these wall-to-wall blocks of shops. Shopping centres too are comprised of shop-lots. Addresses for hotels, restaurants and offices will often take the confusing format of 'Ground Floor, Block 3, Lot BG, 38 Kompleks Kuwasa, Jalan Karamunsing'.

Kompleks are commercial centres, usually with a mix of businesses and shops. Shopping centres and some department stores are called *Wisma* (eg: Wisma Merdeka).

Despite kilometres now being the accepted measure of distance, addresses for places outside of town are often given in terms of miles from the nearest city or town centre. So 'Mile 8' means eight miles from, for example, Sandakan. However, you will also see 'Km 8' (etc) as a point of reference; it depends on the locality.

HOTELS The Malaysian Tourism Minister, Datuk Seri Tengku Adnan Tengku Mansor, has started toughening up criteria for national hotel ratings, because the department had received many complaints from locals and tourists saying that Malaysian hotels were not up to standard. It's difficult to make blanket statements about hotel standards. However, if the tourism minister says there is a problem with Malaysian hotel standards on a national level, these problems are even more acute in Malaysian Borneo.

The 'Hotel Monitoring Team' of the Ministry of Culture, Arts and Tourism (MOCAT) keep an eye on the 992 registered hotels and more than 2,200 tourist accommodation premises nationwide. To receive any kind of rating, hotels must be MOCAT registered. MOCAT also has another grading system, the **Orchid** classification, for all lodgings which don't qualify for star ratings. This applies to budget hotels, family-owned 'resorts', homestays, bed and breakfasts, hostels and inns. You can expect a three-Orchid resort to be very comfortable and clean, perhaps with a pool, Wi-Fi and other facilities. For a full list of star- and Orchid rated hotels in Sabah and Sarawak, see www.etourz.com.

The **Malaysian Association of Hotels** (*www.hotels.org.my*) issues hotel star ratings. Some budget hotels have a no-star rating; you can check to see if they are registered or have any other classification – the **Malaysian Budget Hotels Association** (MBHA) website (*www.budgethotel.org.my*) has a member directory. There may also be a booking system up and running by the time of publication of this edition. There is a Sabah branch of the MBHA in Papar, southeast of Kota Kinabalu (\ 088 915273; e versus@pc.jaring.my).

In Brunei, the **Brunei Association of Hotels** (*www.hotelsofbrunei.com*) issues star ratings to registered hotels, and its website has descriptions of (and links to) its members, including everything from budget to luxury establishments.

In reality Overall, accommodation choices in Borneo are few and standards pretty low. The tourism industry in Sabah, Sarawak and Brunei openly admits to the lack of a truly high-end product – even the capital cities only have a handful of top-class hotels each. In each accommodation category there is generally less comparative quality to their foreign counterparts with regard to facilities and service; a 'five-star' hotel might more closely resemble a four- or even three-star by international standards.

Outside of big cities and business towns – Bandar Seri Begawan, Kota Kinabalu, Kuching, Sibu and Miri – the tourism industry is still in its early stages of development. Accommodation choices in smaller or lesser-known places may be very limited. You might choose to stay in the nearest city and make day trips out to these places. If the authentic experience of rainforest, countryside or small towns is what you are looking for though then the no-star hotels, rustic resorts or homestays will provide just that.

Despite lower standards of quality, the renowned Asian hospitality is amplified by the island friendliness, even if some would prefer less warmth and more service. As the tourism industry continues to grow in Borneo, things are improving all the time.

Rates Standards may be lower, but the good news is that prices are also lower. There are many bargains to be had, particularly in the two–three-star bracket. There are many hotels of this standard, so you can shop around for the best deal. Rates quoted are usually inclusive of a standard 10% service charge and 5–10% government service tax. Good hotels will make this clear on their website, but if you are unsure then ask.

2

Some hotels quote a 'weekend rate' of up to 30% less – particularly business hotels in smaller towns where they need the weekend business.

Booking The best deals are found on the internet, especially for independently run hotels in cities. Many offer 'promotional rates', which may be 30–40% less than the published rates, or have extra nights or services added. If you are travelling independently it is advisable to book ahead, especially during the peak foreign visitor months (June–September) and Malaysian school holiday periods (see *When to visit,* page 33). A couple of good domestic booking sites include the **Hotels Association** (*www.hotels.org.my*), though it tends to favour three–five-star hotels and some of the ratings seem exaggerated. A good general Malaysian travel site with a reservations system is **CUTI** (*www.cuti.com.my*), endorsed by Tourism Malaysia.

Check-out In hotels, check-out time is generally 12.00. Be aware that if you are on a tour and have transfers by plane, boat and bus or excursions, local tour operators often start days very early, with check-out sometimes as early as 06.00 or 07.00. Check-in at hotels is generally from 14.00.

Payment Four- and five-star hotels, and some two- and three-stars, accept a wide variety of credit cards (AmEx, Visa, MasterCard, Diners Club, etc). Expect to pay by cash or cheque for most jungle lodges, homestays and family-owned resorts.

Entertainment and internet For all hotels, a major new criterion being imposed by the MOCAT is Wi-Fi access on all floors of a hotel building. Most four–five-star hotels will have a high-speed internet connection in rooms, and Wi-Fi in the lobby and public areas, though many impose a charge for the service. Modern budget hotels, two–three-star business hotels and backpackers' hostels/lodges are more are more likely to be connected than conservative, small-town hotels. Only high-end hotels, a handful of mid-range and exceptional one–two-stars will have 'Astro' (satellite) television. Even when there is a large choice of channels, access to the BBC may be excluded – the best have CNN, BBC, Discovery Channel, Disney and Cinemax Movies.

Room service Room service in Malaysia is very affordable. Prices vary, but you may get several good-quality main-course dishes for 7–9MYR in a three-star hotel, or 15–18MYR in a four–five-star. Menus usually include Malay, Chinese, Western and sometimes Indian dishes. Family hotels will usually have a kids' menu. Western food is much more expensive – pork chops or fish and chips may cost around 30–40MYR in a mid-range hotel whereas you can feast on rice, noodles and satay delicacies for half the price. Breakfast menus are very variable and can often be disappointing. A decent bread-and-cereal-based breakfast is hard to come by (three–five-star hotels usually do a better Western-style breakfast) and the Asian cuisine can be equally disappointing. Even some luxury hotels may have no more than bread, cakes, muesli and a few other cereals; the best will have multi-ethnic smorgasbords.

Smoking in hotels Though smoking rates in much of the rest of the world are decreasing, in Malaysia they are rising – particularly amongst young people. However, the hotel industry is an international one and Malaysian hotels are increasingly following the international trend of forbidding smoking inside them, Smoking is still tolerated in some public spaces such as hotel lobbies. Four-five star hotels will have several dedicated non-smoking floors, whilst others vary in their smoking policies.

Accommodation listings are laid out in decreasing price order, under the following categories: Luxury, Upmarket, Mid-range, Budget and Shoestring. Serviced apartments, hostels and homestays are grouped together and also listed in decreasing price order. The following key (also on the inside front cover) gives a further indication of prices. See Budget below for advice on choosing accommodation categories to suit your pocket.

$$$$$	600MYR +	£100 +	US$180+
$$$$	450–600MYR	£75–100	US$115–180
$$$	300–450MYR	£50–75	US$80–115
$$	150–300MYR	£25–50	US$40–80
$	<150MYR	<£25	<US$40

Sports facilities Gyms in hotels with less than a luxury rating are few and far between, so make the most of them when you get the chance if you are trying to keep fit whilst travelling. The heat makes it tough to run outdoors. Three–five-star hotels, better homestays and beach lodges may have swimming pools. Other noteworthy fitness centres are included where relevant later in the guide.

NATURE LODGES AND ISLAND RESORTS Most major tour operators specialising in nature and/or diving tourism also manage their own lodgings in key locations, or are affiliated with particular lodges or resorts. This creates something of a monopoly – the accommodation on offer will be controlled by the same people running the tours. This is not necessarily a bad thing, except when the only accommodation on offer is not of an acceptable standard. The standard of lodgings on river and jungle trips is fairly rustic, ranging from basic forest camp to clean and comfortable dwellings. Most lodgings have generator-powered electricity. There is no luxury option, but the basic living conditions are part of the experience.

Coastal and island resorts are less basic than river and forest lodges, with better food, services and accommodation. There are some luxury island resorts.

National parks Accommodation in national parks tends to be very basic. In Sabah and Sarawak there are often no cooking facilities, which is very limiting as it means you have to drive to a nearby town for food.

LONGHOUSE STAYS It is possible to stay as a guest in the longhouses of several tribes, most commonly Sabah's Rungus and Sarawak's Ibans. In Sarawak, you can stay in quiet remote areas to experience local life. Some longhouse accommodation is purpose-built for those wanting the traditional feel without living among a family. Most longhouse accommodation in Sarawak is in the Skrang, Lemanak, Batang Ai and Rejang river areas. Longhouses can be booked directly or through a tourist office. Many organised tours, such as hiking, river safaris and cultural trips include a longhouse stay.

Longhouse facilities are usually basic. A two-person room will usually include pillows, mattresses, mosquito nets, bed sheets, towels, blankets and slippers. A modern communal bathroom or traditional bathing facilities are provided for guests. Food will often be fresh fish and vegetables, which may have been gathered from the jungle. Activities may include hunting, fishing, making jewellery and cooking. The threat of malaria is greatest in the most remote upriver areas. The

Health Department carries out regular checks; if malaria is detected then tourism authorities are alerted and visits to affected areas are suspended.

HOMESTAYS It is also possible to stay with a family in their home as part of the 'homestay' programme. This is a very up close and personal way of experiencing the lifestyle of local people and you may not have much privacy. Similar in principle to a bed and breakfast, homestay programmes may be run by an individual family or by a whole *kampong* (village) and can be booked through tourist offices. A homestay directory can be found at http://travelmalaysiaguide.com/homestay.

BED AND BREAKFASTS 'True' bed and breakfasts are rare in Borneo, as homestays offer a similar equivalent. A few are listed on www.insite.com. They can be as cheap as a hostel but offer more services than a budget hotel, such as a pool and out-of-city calm.

✕ EATING AND DRINKING

FOOD Food is an essential part of culture, and Borneo's mixture of cultures creates a fragrant broth of cuisines. I hope this chapter will help you to avoid the tongue-tied moments I have experienced trying to order food, not knowing with any certainty what I have just ordered and am about to eat!

Malaysians and Bruneians are nations of eaters. Whilst there are distinct food cultures, it is impossible to separate them. For example, rice (*nasi*) and noodles (*mee*), are staples of both Malay and Chinese cuisines and are almost impossible to avoid. Both Chinese and Malay dishes use noodles heavily, in *laksa* and other soups, or in main-meal noodle dishes. Freshly made *mee* comes in various forms: large white or yellow ribbon wheat noodles, spaghetti thin noodles and clear vermicelli noodles. In some shops you can choose the ones you want from the masses hanging at a noodle stall at the entrance which is part of the shop. Then you have to decide on the style you want them cooked – the big differences being 'wet' (with sauce) or 'dry' (without); fried (*goreng*) or not fried; spicy or mild. Increasingly, dried noodles are being used, so when you get the chance to taste the real thing then do so. *Sedap dimakan!* (Bon appetit!)

Malay food Malay cooking is spicy, salty and thick with flavour, in keeping with all the cultural influences that have infused it over the centuries. Sambal and satay are two staples of Malaysian cuisine. Satay is marinated and barbecued chicken, beef or lamb skewered on bamboo sticks – typical 'fast' Malay food, eaten from street stalls and markets. Usually it's served with salad and a peanut sauce. Sambal puts the spice in Malay food; all kinds of ground chilli pastes are used to flavour dishes or are served as a condiment. Sambals can be sweet – *sambal manis* – or hot – *sambal olek* – or fishy – *sambal belacan* (shrimp) and are flavoured with the gamut of typical Malay spices.

Rice (*nasi*) Typical breakfast fare is *nasi lemak* – literally fat, or tasty rice, but it isn't as fatty as it sounds – the rice is actually soft, steamed, aromatised with coconut milk and pandan leaves, and garnished with spicy fried anchovies, sliced cucumber, peanuts and hard-boiled egg. From the market it will be wrapped traditionally in a banana leaf; at a café or restaurant you might serve up the rice and various side dishes yourself. There are many other *nasi* dishes: *nasi kuning* – yellow rice with egg, coconut and cucumber; *nasi goring* – fried rice; *nasi ayam* – rice with slithers of steamed or roasted chicken; *nasi campur* – mixed rice; and if you are vegetarian ask for *nasi dengan sayur* – rice with vegetables.

Noodles Popular Malay noodle dishes are *mee goreng*, spicy fried thick noodles; *mee mamak*, spicy-hot fried yellow noodles; and *mee rebus*, thick blanched noodles in a gooey, sweet and spicy sauce, served with hard-boiled eggs and green chillies.

Curry Typical fish, chicken and vegetable curries are *kari ikan, kari ayam, kari sayur*, respectively. These are gently spiced and cooked with a light dose of coconut.

Meat Beef and chicken appear often. The first is the basis of the famous tangy coconut *beef rendang*, served with turmeric rice (*nasi kunyit*), while red cooked chicken, *ayam masak merah*, is a casserole of chicken pieces in tomato.

Seafood Prawns (*udang*) and fish come in many forms. Whole, grilled, fresh fish is known as *ikan panggang*. The best places to eat seafood are small coastal restaurants where you order and eat barbecued fish, prawns, and squid – *sontong panggang* – by the weight, often for as little as 2MYR per 100g in very small seafood towns on the coast. Prawns from the sea, or giant river prawns, are served whole and spicy in *sambal udang*, with lashings of shrimp and tamarind paste, chilli, garlic and shallots.

Vegetables There are many vegetable dishes in a Malay spread; *sayur campur* (mixed vegetables) includes carrot, cabbage, broccoli, cauliflower and beans cooked in a light oyster sauce. The same vegetables but stewed in coconut is *sayur lodeh*. Individual dishes of 'local vegetable', which may mean roots collected from the jungle that morning, feature on many rural and urban tables. These may include *midin*, dark green fern tops called *pucuk paku*. Shoots of all kinds are served up – cucumber, yam and *pucuk rajah*, emperor shoots.

Fusion One of the most widespread fusions is Indian-Muslim *mamak* (uncle's) cuisine. The dishes are mostly served up at food stalls and small Indian-Muslim eateries or 'Islamic restaurants'. They serve up *mamak* specials such as tandoori chicken and fish-head curry, often round the clock. The fast-food varieties are *roti canai* (after its area of origin, Chennai in India) – famous, flaky, oily unleavened bread, cooked on an open grill. *Roti canai* (*pronounced chan-eye*) is often served with a side dish of curry for dipping the bread in – vegetarians can have it with *dhal* (split pulses). The *roti canai* translates into various other forms including *roti telur* – egg roti filled with egg and onion – again served with curry or *dhal*. *Murtabak* is wrapped *roti canai*, filled with minced meat, egg and onion.

A fusion of Malay and Chinese food is *nyonya* (grandma's) cuisine. It combines the spices of Malay food with marinated, sour Chinese style and results in dishes like the tangy and fishy *assam laksa*.

Chinese food With such a large Chinese population, many cities in Borneo have restaurants specialising in all kinds of Chinese food – Cantonese, spicy Szechuan, Teochew and Hakka. At traditional coffee shops and street stalls meat dumplings, steamed sweet or savoury buns (*pau*) and rice porridge (*moi*) are often served for breakfast, with *dim sum* popular for lunch. One of the most delicious staple Chinese noodle dishes is *char kway teow*, flat rice noodles with beansprouts, egg, chilli and shrimp (or chicken). Monosodium glutamate (MSG) is used in very liberal doses in some places. Just ask for your food without if this is how you prefer it.

Soup Noodle soups are popular at lunch. *Wantan mee* is a noodle soup, with floating stuffed envelopes of prawn or pork; *mee suah* has fish balls or pork in it; and *tom* *yam* is a spicy shrimp noodle soup. A famous Hokkien herbal soup is *bak kut teh* – literally 'pork bone tea'. *Laksas* of many kinds are common at Chinese coffee shops, and are served with prawn, chicken or egg. Fish and chicken clay pots with noodles are also a popular choice.

Vegetarian There are many soybean-, soybean curd- and tofu- (*tau foo*) based dishes in soups, noodle dishes, clay pots and curries.

Fish/seafood Chinese do great fresh seafood from small stalls, coffee shops and restaurants, serving up dishes such as sweet and sour fish, deep-fried fish with mango sauce, butter prawns, black pepper crab and oyster fried with egg.

Sweet stuff Look out for cake shops (*kedai kek*) making their own Chinese baked goods such as *siew pao* (baked bun with chicken), yam pastry buns, egg custard tarts, steamed red bean cakes, lotus and red bean yeast buns and *hakka* soybean cakes.

Indigenous foods Every ethnic group has its traditional cuisine tied closely to their way of living, whether this is inland or by the sea. Coastal cuisine features many sago and coconut dishes and marinated seafood salads, whilst people living inland eat much rice and freshwater fish. Wild fruits and vegetables are used as much as home-grown crops. You may get to taste traditional dishes of indigenous people when visiting smaller towns and *tamu* markets and if staying in homes and longhouses. Wonderful and weird specialities abound, such as the bamboo-shoot pickle – *bosou hobang* – of the Murut in Sabah. Kadazandusun love their tangy pickles from mango and other fruits. This is not to forget fermented rice wine – called *tuak* by the Iban in Sarawak but also *lihing* among the Kadazandusun in Sabah. You will need to eat well to offset the effects of this!

Fruit The fruit bowl is always full: with bananas (*pisang*) of many kinds (also try the *pisang goreng*, fried bananas at the market); rambutan; jackfruit; jungle fruits such as the sweet, pulpy and aromatic *tarap* (*artocarpus odoratissimus*); and *cempedak* – a cousin to the jackfruit – both are big, with thick husks full of pod-shaped fruits.

DRINK The typical coffee shop *harga minuman* (drinks list) may look something like this, with prices ranging from 1 to 2MYR in most places.

Kopi o – black coffee with sugar
Kopi o kosong – black coffee no sugar
Kopi c susu – coffee with condensed milk
Kopi-si - coffee with unsweetened (Carnation) milk
The o - black tea with sugar
Ping so kopi o ping – black sweetened iced coffee
Kopi o kosong ping – black iced coffee unsweetened
Kopi-si ping – iced coffee with unsweetened milk
Air limau – lemon water drink
Teh tarik – 'pulled' tea: very strong and sweet, brewed black tea with condensed milk

EATING OUT Food is readily available, often of exceptional quality (in both freshness and flavour), and very cheap. Market food can easily outstrip restaurants and is available at night markets, food courts, or *taman seleras* – parks full of open-air restaurants. Any formal or fine dining takes places in Western and international restaurants. The best advice is to eat local and eat fresh.

Coffee shops 'Coffee shops' are entrenched in Malaysian culture. Most of them started out as coffee shops, serving local coffee and food, with morning dumplings and noodles. Many still do so, but *kedai kopi* (sometimes called *kopi tiam* in Chinese, or simply *kedai*) shops also serve all the food and drinks on the Malaysian cultural menu. These 'coffee shops' lack an accurate name that truly describes them, but they loosely come under the umbrella of *kedai makanan dan minuman* – food and drink shops. They are on every street corner and are mostly open-fronted, except those in hotels which are more likely to be enclosed and air conditioned. Menus usually include all kinds of noodle and rice dishes; curry; bains-marie (stainless steel, water-filled food warmers) dishes if it's a Malay shop and soups, dumplings and *laksa* made on the spot if it's Chinese. Overall, it is very cheap, top-quality food. I found that the best coffee shops were full of locals and open-fronted, with plastic chairs and linoleum tables. In the middle of the tables there is often a jar of homemade *lada* – a soy, salt and chilli mix ready for heaping on top of your food.

Many hotels have air-conditioned coffee shops serving Malay and Chinese food to locals. In these down-to-earth places you can eat very well and very cheaply. More international hotel coffee shops have a Western touch.

Food courts Nutritious, tasty food to go is available from shopping-centre food courts, usually on the top floor – where there may be one or two dozen shops preparing all kinds of food. It's either cooked on the spot, in the case of noodles and in most Chinese places, or pre-prepared and kept warm in bains-marie (especially with Malay and Indo-Malay kitchens) full of chicken, fish, pork and vegetable curries and stews; roasted meats; steamed greens with chilli and prawn paste. The store keeper will ladle dishes of your choice onto a plate of rice, or you can choose your own in a food court. All of this can be eaten there or as take-away (*bungkus*).

Restaurants Restaurants can be small, simple diners serving Malay, Indonesian, *Mamak* or Chinese food, not much different from a *kedai*, through to air-conditioned fancier places. Hotels have several dining choices, from coffee shops to restaurants, offering both Western and local food. In bigger hotels, there will be several diners catering to local and Western tastes, or both. Chinese restaurants are often large clamouring places, but they can also be some of the best seafood restaurants. Any trendy, obviously international establishment will be a restaurant rather than a coffee shop, unless it is a café or bistro, though this is very avant-garde in Borneo. Fine dining places tend to be very dated; think 1970s-80s.

Smoking in restaurants Generally, there are no non-smoking rules or set-aside spaces, other than in shopping centres. Some individual restaurants may have a non-smoking policy, especially more Western or international places. Coffee shops

SURVIVAL GLOSSARY	
Tanpa perasa	no monosodium glutamate
Tanpa garam	without salt
Tambah	add
Sedikit	less or a little
Kurang	less (eg: *kurang manis* – less sweet)
Minyak	oil/fat
Tidak	no

If you don't want sugar in anything, just add *kosong* – empty.

tend to have more smoke-free air as they are open-fronted. Although smoking rates among Malaysia's youth are increasing, most restaurants don't actually have many smokers.

Western fast food Look out for the familiar logos – they won't be far away in main cities!

Street food *Gerai makan* (food stalls) are all over the place, in the streets and markets, along roadsides and highways, by day and night. They sell many noodle and rice dishes cooked on the spot, as well as pre-prepared packages of *nasi lemak* and other rice dishes: *murtabak*, *roti canai*, satays, etc – most have their speciality. There are large open-air or covered public spaces full of *gerai makan* stalls, and semi-permanent food kitchens set up every day in some towns. Sometimes known as *taman selera* ('appetite parks'), these are somewhere between a stall and makeshift coffee shop.

Similar to the night markets, you will often find a whole lot of small food shops – *kedai* – cooking up food around an open area with tables and chairs, usually with some kind of nice outlook. Roadside *gerai* sell smoked meats, grilled corn on the cob, *puding kelapa* (a gelatinised coconut dessert), prawn crackers, nuts, bananas and drinks.

Markets (Pasar) The main food markets by night are the *pasar malam*, evening markets which have many *gerai makan*. There are also wet markets, dry markets, central markets, night markets, *tamu* and Ramadan markets. Wherever there is a market there is food in multitude forms: fresh, dried, raw, cooked, aromatic, wild, exotic; a huge array of produce for preparing food at home; fruits and nuts; Chinese pastries and buns. Usually a market will have some *gerai makan* food stalls pretty close by, if not under the same roof.

Eating out practicalities

Cleanliness Local councils grade places as 'A', 'B' or 'C' class. The lowest-grade coffee shops and small restaurants are usually fine, though more 'fancy' restaurants with a C grade are best avoided. 'C'-rated coffee shops can have filthy toilets but great food. Others pride themselves on having the cleanest loos in town. The *gerai makan* stalls are all subject to food hygiene laws and regulation, as far as the preparation, utensils and ingredients go.

Halal There are hundreds of halal eateries in Malaysia, from street stalls to coffee shops and restaurants. No non-halal products will be served in these restaurants – this includes pork, any pork by-products (such as lard), and (if they are fully halal) alcohol. All the food should, in theory, have been produced in accordance with Islamic law, including all vegetables, spices and meats.

Service As long as you can convey what you want simply, most Malay and Chinese will understand. Things are generally cooked as you watch – this is helpful if you are vegetarian or have allergies or special diet needs.

Tipping Service charges are included in bills and tipping is not customary.

Prices Meal prices range from 2–3MYR at a market stall, double that in a coffee shop, to 20–40MYR for a main course in a restaurant. The more you dine in five-star international-style hotels, the more the prices increase.

PUBLIC HOLIDAYS AND FESTIVALS

Public holidays in Eastern Malaysia generally fall into two categories, national and state, both of which embrace religious celebrations, cultural festivals and dates of major national importance. Brunei also has public holidays to mark significant state dates such as political independence, the sultan's birthday and religious occasions. Probably more important than the state occasions, and celebrated in a far more personal way, are the religious and ethnic celebrations – though these differ between Eastern Malaysia and Brunei. The sultan is 'our Sultan' in Brunei – he is part of the people's daily lives, so his birthday is a big event. The same can't be said of the Malaysian king, who has less of an impact in Sabah and Sarawak than on the peninsula. Major state-wide celebrations mark important dates on the spiritual calendars of indigenous people, and of the Chinese, Malay and Indian populations who observe Buddhist, Muslim, Hindu and Christian traditions. Festive rituals often combine a high level of spirituality and prayer, with colour, joy and feasting – but that doesn't exclude commercialism. The general racial harmony which exists throughout Borneo leaks through to the festivals. People of different faiths celebrate with their friends on major holy days and in Sabah and Sarawak there are some specific inter-cultural celebrations heartily enjoyed by all.

There are some seven major religious and cultural celebrations across Eastern Malaysia and Brunei which are marked by a public holiday. They are listed below, along with other public holidays to mark state occasions. Public holidays rarely cause business to come to a standstill, at least not shops. Banks and government offices close, but shopping centres will remain open for at least half the day, varying from place to place. The advantage of Borneo being so multi-faith is that only those who are truly celebrating the day for their culture or religion will stop completely. The shopping god is increasingly present – open all hours.

PUBLIC HOLIDAYS IN SABAH, SARAWAK AND BRUNEI

1 January	New Year's Day
20 January (variable date)	*Awal Muharram* (*Maal Hijrah*), first day of Muslim calendar
29–30 January (variable date)	Chinese New Year (Brunei: 29 January only)
23 February	National Day Brunei
31 March	Prophet Muhammad's birthday
6 April	Good Friday (Sabah & Sarawak only)
1 May	Labour Day
12 May (variable date)	Wesak Day (height of Buddhist calendar)
30–31 May	*Tadau Ka'amatan* (Harvest Festival) Thanksgiving to the rice spirits of the Kadazandusun (Sabah & Labuan only)
1–2 June	*Pesta Gawai*, Sarawak Gawai Festival (Sarawak only)

2 June	Birthday of Yang di-Pertuan Agong, Malaysian king
15 July	His Majesty the Sultan of Brunei's birthday
31 August	*Hari Kebangsaan* (National Day). Celebration of Malaysian independence, Merdeka, 1957
9 September	Birthday of Yang di-Pertua Negeri Sarawak's head of state (Sarawak only)
16 September	Birthday of Yang di-Pertua Negeri Sabah's head of state (Sabah only)
13–14 October (variable date)	*Hari Raya Aidilfitri.*
5 November	Ramadan end of Muslim fasting (Brunei)
8 November (variable date)	*Deepavali* Hindu light festival
20 December	*Hari Raya Qurban*
25 December	Christmas Day

CHINESE LUNAR NEW YEAR The Chinese New Year is full of festivity and friendship, thanksgiving and hopes of prosperity – and cries of *Kong Hee Fatt Choy!* ('Happy New Year!'). After a month of preparation, in which homes are loudly decorated with lanterns, firecrackers, and calligraphy, guests laden with gifts of mandarins and oranges visit, ready for much feasting and games of *mah-jong*. Much celebration also takes place in the Chinese temples, making this an ideal time to visit one. The dates vary from year to year according to the lunar calendar; beginning on the first day of the full moon and lasting for a fortnight. Like other Chinese festivals celebrated in Sabah, Sarawak and Brunei, the New Year festival is strong on symbolism and folklore, dance and colour – especially red. The highlight of the public festivities is the 'lion dance' – troupes of dragon-like figures prance through the streets to the beats of drums, warding off evil spirits, ushering in fortune and frightening the mythical lion away.

WESAK DAY This is the most important date on the Buddhist calendar marking the birth, death and enlightenment of Buddha. It is marked by prayers, offerings and chanting; and the release of doves and tortoises at Buddhist temples. Another magical time to head to a temple.

TADAU KA'AMATAN (Harvest Festival) Each district of Sabah holds its own various festivities for this big event, the height of the indigenous calendar in Sabah. The celebrations can go on for the entire month of May culminating during the Grand Finale on 30 and 31 May at the Kadazandusun Cultural Association Hall (KDCA) in Penampang, just south of Kota Kinabalu. Tadau Ka'amatan, in indigenous tongue, sometimes translates to *Pesta Kaamatan* in Malay. It is celebrated by the Kadazandusun and Murut communities in Sabah.

DEEPAVALI The Hindu Festival of Light, a triumph of good over evil, is held on the seventh month of the Hindu calendar. Houses are decorated with lights, old debts settled, sweets sent to friends, new clothes purchased, and all the Sikh temples (Gurdwaras) conduct prayer services and serve vegetarian food.

HARI RAYA AIDILFITRI Also called *Hari Raya Puasa*, this is a day of celebration held at the end of the month-long Muslim fast of Ramadan. The fasting ends on the first sighting of the new moon, in the tenth month of the Muslim calendar, *Syawal*.

HARI KEBANGSAAN The Malaysian National Day marks Malaysian independence in 1957 when the Union Jack was lowered and Malaysian flag hoisted to mark the end of colonial rule. It is marked by street parades in the capital cities, though celebrated less flagrantly than on Peninsular Malaysia.

ANZAC DAY Because of how strongly World War II was felt in Borneo, the tradition of remembering the servicemen and women of the war is upheld in Sabah from the west to the east coast. It is held on 25 April, and many families from overseas make a pilgrimage to Sabah during this time. Contact Catherin Chua of the Sandakan Municipal Council (**e** *Catherin.Chua@sabah.gov.my*) for more information.

🛒 SHOPPING

By far the most wonderful places to shop, for anything, are the markets, *pasar*. A visit to the marketplace is possibly one of the most authentic cultural experiences you can have – experiencing the sights, sounds and smells of true local culture and an amazing range of produce, from fresh fruit and fish, jungle vegetables and speciality foods, to clothes and handicrafts.

Every region, city and town will have several markets: the *pasar besar* is the main market, often held daily in cities and in towns, and once a week in some country districts. The *pasar besar* in cities and large towns is often held undercover, and increasingly in new two- to three-storey buildings, incorporating several different traditional markets, such as the 'wet market' (*pasar basah*) which sells fish and meats, and other food, regional produce and handicraft markets. The *pasar malam* is a night market – some are food-only, others offer a mix of produce. Some towns also have specific craft markets – *pasar pertukangan*. Larger ones in the cities are flooded with Filipino and Indonesian produce, though as always the best things are those found close to the source. You can always bargain in the marketplace.

You are more likely to find a priceless memento of your travels in more rural markets. Some of the most beautiful and authentic items you can buy are woven textiles, bamboo and rattan baskets, beaded jewellery from shell, glass and plant seeds, pottery, carved wooden bowls and batik. In Brunei you will find more brass, gold and silver than beads and bamboo. See *Chapter 1, Culture*, page 27, for more on traditional handicrafts and markets. Local shopping tips can be found in the guide chapters.

TAMU A rural market, the weekly *tamu*, was apparently introduced by the British North Borneo Company to create a communal meeting place and ease ethnic tensions through trade. Both the name and the custom have spread to Brunei and to Sarawak but *tamu* are still most common in Sabah where they are held on a varying day of the week from place to place. A growers market, crafts market and commercial bazaar all in one, each one is unique, shaped by the cultural and agricultural environment. Farmers and fishermen bring their produce (including water buffalo). Traders pile their stalls high with an exotic array of strangely shaped and wonderfully coloured produce: kitchen and clothing wares; bric-a-brac; home-grown, homemade and jungle-reaped produce. The *tamu* remain a vital part of social and trading life rather than a tourist attraction – though some have become more tourist oriented – and the best ones are often those with the fewest tourists. My best memories include those of Ranau, Kudat, Tuaran in Sabah; Sibu, Serian and Miri in Sarawak; and Brunei's *tamu*. There is also a *tamu besar* – a major *tamu* – held once a year in the *tamu*'s town of origin, Kota Belud.

GENERAL SHOPPING There are shopping plazas, supermarkets, electronic stores and pharmacies all over the cities and towns. City and town shops (*kedai*) – food and retail stores, electronics and clothes shops – are often clustered into large blocks of 'shop-lots', sometimes around a public square in smaller towns, but also in multi-storey shopping centres. New plazas, malls and commercial centres (*kompleks*) are popping up in the capital cities and coastal towns. Between the dozens of city shop-lots and older shopping centres packed with shop-lots, you will find just about everything you need. However, neither Malaysian Borneo nor Brunei has the exciting department-store shopping or the modern emporiums which exist in Singapore, Hong Kong, Bangkok and increasingly in Kuala Lumpur. There is little in the way of local or imported quality couture or food items, and department stores lack any major pizzazz though things are clearly changing. Some of the malls (especially the older ones) are more like massive shop-lots – cluttered and not very attractive. Nonetheless, items are relatively cheap. There are once-yearly major sales, but every day is a sale with the 'Buy One Free One' slogan applied to clothing, jewellery and food things.

Tax-free shopping Labuan is a duty-free shopping and tax haven, and duty-free shops at airports are very good. Brunei is tax-free too, but you won't find duty-free spirits and wine on the shelves there.

ENTERTAINMENT

The karaoke craze has not escaped Borneo, though it is now declining in favour of trendy, international bars and clubs in Sabah and Sarawak. These hip hangouts are also eroding the tradition of a hotel-based nightlife in Kota Kinabalu and Kuching. The live music scene is thriving, though music is a bit behind the international times. Traditional dance and music performances are one of the most heartening forms of entertainment. Brunei, being alcohol-free, has a quieter night scene, but there is evening fun to be had at markets.

For anyone interested in the real cultures of Borneo, the best form of art-based entertainment are the festivals, and the dance and music performances. These are very regional – Sabah, Sarawak and Brunei organised – but also very local in their nature. Each town and ethnicity will have cultural performances and pesta (festivals) celebrating dates and events dear to them. The local tourism offices are the best place to check for a list of upcoming events. Sabah and Sarawak tourism also have online events listings.

ℓ MEDIA AND COMMUNICATIONS

NEWSPAPERS Sabah, Sarawak and Brunei have their own newspapers. There seems to be little demand for international newspapers. Even in four–five-star hotels in the capital cities it is standard practice to hang a regional paper such as the *Sabah Times,* the *Daily Express,* the *Borneo Post* or the *Sarawak Tribune* on your door – it is very rare to be offered international papers. If you love your daily newspapers you may find the *International Herald Tribune* in mixed bazaars of some towns, and a couple more choices in good English-language bookstores in the capitals, though these are likely to be back copies. Local newspapers are quite British tabloid in look and thin on content, especially foreign coverage. The *Daily Express* is considered to be the best newspaper in Sabah. The most prevalent English language newspaper in Sarawak is the *Borneo Post*, which also has a section in Behasa Melayu, and by far the best foreign coverage. The weekend version is the *Sunday Post.* The Malaysian national English-language newspaper *New Straits Times* also circulates. In Brunei there are three daily newspapers: the Malay-language *Media Permata* and English-language *Brunei Times* and *Borneo*

Bulletin; this being the best. A punchy, political online Malaysia-wide newspaper is Malaysia Now (*www.Malaysiakini.com*). The state-run Malaysian news agency is Bernama (*www.bernama.com*). An interesting Brunei blog is the Weekly Brunei Resources (*http://bruneiresources.blogspot.com*).

RADIO Radio stations in Sarawak seem to reflect the cultural diversity far better than television, with day-long or half-day services in Bahasa Malaysia, Mandarin, Hakka, Hokkien, English, Iban and Bidayuh and half-day broadcasts in Kayan and Kenyah. Some of these are broadcast by WaiFM, others by the local radio station of Radio Television Malaysia (RTM). Sarawak FM has 24-hour Malay broadcasts. Sabah also has RTM radio and some English content on its FM stations – Hitz, Era and Mix FM. Radio Television Brunei (RTB) operates three radio stations – two in Malay, one switching between English, Mandarin and Hindustani programming. Commercial radio station Kristal FM is bilingual English–Malay and also operates cable television, Kristal Astro.

TELEVISION Malaysian Borneo receives two government-run (RTM) Malay television channels TV1 and TV2 and privately owned stations such as TV3, NTV7, (these are very common in hotels), 8TV and TV9. Satellite Astro TV is very popular and provides channels such as CNN, BBC, Star World Movies, Cinemax Movies, Vision 4 (movies), Star Sport, and Japanese and Chinese channels, but even in hotels which provide this service the choice of available channels varies and can be extremely minimalist in two three-star hotels. Radio Television Brunei has one television station with largely Malay-language broadcasts.

TELECOMMUNICATIONS

Telephone dialling codes All local dialling codes in Sabah and Sarawak start with three digits, such as 088 for Kota Kinabalu. The Malaysian dialling code (covering Sabah and Sarawak) is +60. If calling from overseas, drop the first zero of local numbers (eg: +6 088 334567). When in Malaysia, dial the whole number if calling from outside that town or region. Drop the local prefix only when in the town or city itself. The dialling code for Brunei is +673.

Public phones Malaysia's national telephone company is Telekom Malaysia Berhad (TM). Together with private-owned Citiphone it provides payphone booths in the city and countryside. You can use either coins or pre-paid phone cards with these. Calling cards, which function by code, are widely available from phone shops but also street stores, in 5MYR, 10MYR and 20MYR denominations.

Mobile phones Called 'hand phones' in Malaysia, these are revered like a national sport. On business cards the number is preceded by 'HP'. Most people have two or three hand phones, often ringing at the same time. There are telephone shops everywhere – you will see them plastered with flags and stickers of the companies they deal with. Major service providers are **Celcom**, **Maxis** and **DiGi** which have expansive chains of stores and dominate roadside billboards. If you want to put a Malaysian SIM card in your phone (much cheaper for internal calls) it will cost 10–30MYR depending on the provider. Celcom charged 30MYR in 2007. Code-induced top-ups for whatever provider you are with can be purchased in shops or by phone. The government introduced new laws in 2007 making it compulsory to register the SIM number with a name, so take your passport along. **Hot Link Maxis** pre-paid mobile phone cards are very popular and their rates are better than Celcom for overseas calls providing '20 sen/min to 20 countries' (around US6 cents per minute to many countries including the UK, US, France and Australia).

However, it is not the best option for making domestic calls. If you are travelling in Malaysia, top up with 100MYR before leaving, your account stays active for up to eight months.

INTERNET AND WI-FI Borneo has started to embrace the rest of Malaysia's enthusiasm for high-tech and internet communications, though the service is slower than on the peninsula. The two major Malaysian internet service providers are TMNet and Jaring, the latter being more prevalent in Eastern Malaysia. In large and small cities and towns it is usually very easy to find internet cafés, charging from 2 to 4MYR per hour; some offer decreased rates for the second or third hour, and offer a free drink. There are also quite a few cafés that offer free Wi-Fi internet for customers. See *Accommodation*, page 65, for information on internet in hotels.

BUSINESS

In Brunei Darussalam, contact the **Ministry of Industry and Primary Resources** (*One-Stop Agency, Ministry of Industry & Primary Resources, BSB;* ❯ *+673 2380026; www.brunei.gov.bn/about_brunei/business.htm*) about all business opportunities.

In Sabah, contact the **Department of Industrial Development and Research** (*7th & 8th Floors, Block C, Wisma Tun Fuad Stephens, Karamunsing Centre, Kota Kinabalu;* ❯ *+60 088 215035; www.sabah.gov.my/didr/english/WhySabah.htm*). Their website has a good section on doing business in Sabah.

LIVING IN BORNEO

Not all tropical destinations offer the combination of natural and cultural riches that Borneo does. The sunshine, islands, jungle, food and outdoor adventure are enough to tempt anyone to live there on a more permanent basis. But is it actually viable to realise such an exotic dream? There are many factors to consider and all are fairly personal decisions. A practical issue might be the climate – how well do you fare when humidity is high? Though I can survive happily in such conditions I do find that my sportier habits become somewhat subdued – sport should generally be done indoors to escape the heat. The isolation of living in more remote areas, and of living in such a different culture, may be a blessing or a curse for you.

There are sizeable expat communities in Brunei and Miri in Sarawak, working in the oil industry (oil fields and research). There may be scientific jobs available at forest research institutes and centres, and universities in both Brunei and Malaysian Borneo, as well as primary and secondary schoolteaching in foreign and Malaysian schools.

In terms of culture and lifestyle, plus points of living in Borneo include the simplicity of life, the warmth of the people, the rich culture and religious and cultural tolerance. With the friendly nature of the people, colonial traces and omnipresence of English language (not to mention the economic benefits), foreigners are warmly welcomed.

You may experience quite a cultural shock, but this in itself is an adventure just as travelling is. Many of the obstacles of settling into daily Malaysian Borneo life are as relevant today as when Heidi Munan, a Swiss-born, New Zealand-educated author wrote *Culture Shock! A Guide to Customs and Etiquette, Borneo* in 1988 (revised 1992). It's a great book – personal and straight-talking. There will be some administrative frustrations: transport, roads and communication may not be up to the standard to which you are accustomed, but not to such an extent that life is impossible. You will soon enjoy the easier-going pace! I feel it is enriching being surrounded by other languages and cultures, and English is widely spoken in the circles where you need it most: health, education and commerce.

MALAYSIA MY SECOND HOME (*23rd Floor, Menara Datuk Onn, Putra World Trade Centre, Kuala Lumpur; www.mm2h.gov.my*) Increasing numbers of people are being wooed to Borneo for the lifestyle. The 'Malaysia My Second Home' programme is a government initiative aimed at attracting foreigners to invest in Malaysia by buying a second house there. As well as the cheaper house prices, the programme promotes the low crime rates, political stability, favourable climate, low risk of natural disasters and access to quality education as tempting reasons to sign up.

The programme is open to foreigners of all race and religion. Those aged below 50 are required to make a minimum deposit of 300,000MYR; over-50s must put up 150,000MYR or provide proof of a monthly offshore income of 10,000MYR. After a year, money can be withdrawn from the account for house purchase, education, medical expenses, etc, as long as a minimum balance of 60,000MYR is maintained. You must also take out Malaysian medical insurance and provide a full medical report. If your application is accepted, the Immigration Department grants you a 'Social Visit Pass' and multiple-entry visa, which allow you to come and go as you please. These are initially valid for ten years but can be renewed thereafter.

Recently it was announced that applications would only be accepted through licensed MM2H 'agents' — they have been overwhelmed with requests. Over-50s wanting to live in Sabah or Sarawak can still apply directly to their immigration departments.

Immigration departments

Department of Immigration Sabah Tingkat 6, Bangunan Wisma Dang Bandang, Jln Tuanku Abdul Rahman, 88550, Kota Kinabalu; ☎ +60 088 80700

Department of Immigration Sarawak Tingkat 1&2, Bangunan Sultan Iskandar, Jln Simpang Tiga, 93550, Kuching; ☎ +60 082 245661

Housing is available in both rural and urban areas and ranges from terraced and semi-detached houses and bungalows to chic flats and apartments. There are an increasing number of luxury apartment and condominium developments, especially in Kuching and Kota Kinabalu and nearby coastal areas, specifically aimed at foreign investors. Prices are therefore skyrocketing, but they are still relatively low. Look at the real-estate section of one of the online daily newspapers (see *Media and communications* above) to get an idea.

STUDYING IN BORNEO

There are many opportunities in Sabah, Sarawak and Brunei for pre-tertiary and tertiary studies, through student-exchange programmes, years abroad and short-term student tourism programmes. There is both a state education system and private schools including international schools, universities, private colleges and expatriate schools (British, American, French and German).

MALAYSIAN BORNEO In Sabah, the **Yayasan Sabah Group** (*Tun Mustapha Tower, Yayasan Sabah HQ, PO Box 11623;* ☎ *+60 088 326300;* e *ysinfo@ysnet.org.my; www.ysnet.org.my*) is a progressive education foundation which has information on secondary- and tertiary-level scholarships under its education development programme.

A website which posts student exchanges, study options and participating schools and institutions in Malaysia is www.studymalaysia.com.

Useful national education contacts with links to Eastern Malaysia are the **Ministry of Higher Education** (☏ +60 03 88835000 www.mohe.gov.my) which has a focused Department of Private Education; the **National Accreditation Board** (☏ +60 03 7968 7002; www.lan.gov.my); and the **Malaysian Association of Private Colleges and Universities** (MAPCU) (☏ +60 03 86569981; www.mapcu.com.my).

Major universities include the **Universiti Malaysia in Sabah** (*Locked Bag 2073, 88999 Kota Kinabalu;* e crd@ums.edu.my; www.ums.edu.my), the **Universiti Malaysia in Sarawak** (UNIMAS) (*Jln Datuk Mohd Musa, 94300 Kota Samarahan, Sarawak;* ☏ (+60) 082 581388; f +60 082 665088; www.unimas.my).

The **British Council** in Malaysia (*Wisma Selangor Dredging, 142C Jln Ampang, 50450 Kuala Lumpur;* www.britishcouncil.org.my) is a good point of contact for inquiries about secondary school cultural exchanges. Australia's **Curtin University of Technology** (www.curtin.edu.my) also has a campus in Miri, Sarawak.

BRUNEI English-medium degrees offered at the **Universiti Brunei Darussalam** (UBD) (www.ubd.edu.bn) include education, mathematics and computer science; electronics and electrical engineering; geography/economics major; management studies; and public policy and administration.

CULTURAL ETIQUETTE

NAMES AND TITLES Malay people will address you by your first name, so I immediately got baptised Miss Tamara. It's at once very respectful and warm. Most people would not be offended if you called them by just their first name instead of adding *Encik* (Mr/Sir) or *Puan* (Mrs, Lady). While there are many formalities in Malaysian society, the people are also personable by nature and fairly laid-back about such things. It is appropriate to address people formally in written correspondence and on formal occasions.

Chinese people are addressed by their surnames – which appear before their given names. So a lady named Chia Wei Li would be addressed as 'Ms Chia'. Many Chinese people have English names though, such as a friend of mine Ivy Yap. Officially she would be 'Ms Yap', but everyone simply calls her Ivy. In my experience most people are not fussy about these things except in official circles where formalities must be observed.

DRESS Women who visit Muslim Brunei are requested to dress modestly in keeping with local customs. The same applies to Muslim-dominated parts of Sabah and Sarawak. Elsewhere, many women wear a *tudung* (a hair scarf), whilst some bare arms and legs. It is best to avoid baring too much flesh.

GREETINGS The customary Malay greeting is the *salam*: the person greeting you reaches out and grasps your hand gently whilst bringing their right hand to their chest. This graceful gesture means sweetly 'I greet you from my heart'. Hotel and restaurant staff and people in the streets and at marketplaces may greet you with an eclipsed version of this – just the hand to the heart bit. It is good manners, and greatly appreciated, to return the gesture. The reciprocated greeting is called *bersalaman*. Muslim members of the opposite sex do not generally touch in greetings. Chinese people tend to shake hands in the more traditional way. It is quite rare to see couples showing public displays of affection.

GESTURES It is deemed impolite to refuse food and drink (including rice wine!) by saying 'no' or shaking the head. If you can, accept a little; to refuse, touch the plate or glass lightly with the right hand. Use the right hand when giving and receiving objects or passing something, particularly food. The right hand is also used when eating with one's fingers. You should never point Western-style – instead curl the four fingers of your right hand inwards and point with the thumb.

BEHAVIOUR Malaysians are gracious, polite people that may be offended by boisterous behaviour; Chinese people are usually more outgoing. It is courteous to respect these cultures and behave appropriately.

ALCOHOL AND FOOD Muslims do not drink alcohol. It may be offensive to offer alcohol to a Muslim or drink it in their presence, though some restaurants and hotels openly encourage you to bring your own – but don't expect them to pull the cork for you! Discretion is the key.

During the Islamic fasting month of Ramadan, Muslims fast between sunrise and sunset (for about 12 hours); it is inconsiderate to blatantly eat and drink in their company during this time. If someone insists you do so, that's fine – this is Malaysian politeness. Muslims only eat halal food, and no pork.

MOSQUE DECORUM Mosques have strict non-Muslim visiting hours that avoid prayer times; these vary between places. Most mosques, temples and other places of worship ask all visitors to remove their shoes before entering. This also applies to Malaysian homes, homestays, guesthouses and public areas of some resorts. Some mosques provide robes and/or headscarves for female visitors. Remember to be respectful to rules and traditions. Avoid passing in front of a person who is praying, making lots of noise, or touching the Koran (the Muslim holy book).

LONGHOUSE DECORUM Longhouse dos and don'ts vary between ethnic groups and even between individual communities. Remember that longhouses are people's homes rather than museums, and you are a guest. Enter a longhouse only when invited to do so; be friendly and introduce yourself – first to the chief (the *rumai*); don't enter or peep into sleeping quarters (*sirang*) or other private rooms unless invited to do so; do not enter a longhouse during times of mourning or as it is being built (this is considered to bring bad luck); never walk under a longhouse; upon your departure, say goodbye to everyone and thank them for their hospitality.

GIVING SOMETHING BACK

The best way to 'give something back' can be done before you even arrive in Borneo, with your choices of holiday operators. As well as volunteer projects (outlined below), the tour operators you choose will dictate how 'responsible' your holiday can be, whether they are organising your entire trip or you are travelling independently. Using local tour operators does not guarantee local development, but several are committed to helping local communities. By choosing such responsible operators, you can directly help community development initiatives such as homestay programmes, or conservation efforts such as tree planting.

A good example of such responsible tourism is the work of **SI Tours** on Sabah's northeast coast. When you stay at their forest lodges or choose them as a day-trip host, they send 1MYR to a local village. Money is used to help families buy school uniforms and bags for their children and improve their homes. SI Tours also source food and other products locally, boosting the local economy.

TYK Adventure Tours aim to demonstrate to local people that long-term benefits of tourism outweigh the short-term gains of cash crops, helping to change the 'slash and burn mentality' of communities and protect the environment. By involving indigenous communities in local tourist ventures such as native rafting and survival camps, the safeguarded environment becomes the livelihood.

If you book your trip with an international operator, ensure that they are working with local communities, operators and NGOs. Those that bear the stamp of responsible travel are usually legitimate. **Intrepid Travel** (*www.intrepidtravel.com*) are a shining example.

For more information and links, try **Responsible Travel** (✆ +44 01273 600030; *www.responsibletravel.com*), a Brighton-based ecotourism travel directory that includes adventure travel, orang-utan conservation tours and volunteer programmes.

CARBON OFFSETTING Carbon emissions generated from your trip can be offset at www.atmosfair.de, a legitimate company recommended by *BBC Wildlife* magazine. The travel industry is the fastest-growing contributor of CO_2 emissions – mostly due to air travel. Conservation International (*www.conservation.org*) offer lots of helpful advice about carbon emissions, calculating your eco-footprint, and reducing your negative impacts on the environment. Al Gore's (2006) film *An Inconvenient Truth* offers more information on the negative repercussions of travel, and ways of limiting them, as does the book *The Weather Makers* by Tim Flannery.

VOLUNTEER VACATIONS There are many volunteer programmes to choose from in Malaysian Borneo, from conservation to teaching and village development. A good place to look for volunteer programmes in Sabah and Sarawak is **Travel Tree** (*www.traveltree.co.uk*). More student-oriented sites include www.realgap.co.uk and www.gapyearforgrownups.co.uk. In the US, **I-to-I** (*www.i-to-i.com*) runs Borneo summer camps and volunteer programmes for 16–19 year olds. **Raleigh International** (*Raleigh Hse, 3rd Floor, 2007 Waterloo Rd, London;* ✆ +44 020 7371 8585; ✉ *info@raleigh.org.uk; www.raleighinternational.org*) calls itself an 'international development charity'. Its expeditions in Sabah call on volunteers from the UK, Malaysia and other countries, who get incredible life experience while working on community and environmental projects, as well as some real adventure.

NATURE CONSERVATION Enormous efforts are being made for conservation by a great number of organisations. Leading the way is **WWF** (*www.panda.org*), with teams of international and Malaysian scientists active in dozens of projects for fauna and flora conservation. See *Chapter 3*, page 117, for more information on WWF's trailblazing 'Heart of Borneo' project. They publish many invaluable reports on Borneo's biodiversity and work alongside international universities and research institutes. They are in constant need of funds – see their website for details of how you can help.

There are also many small Malaysian local groups making a big difference. Some are in need of volunteer experts – **Wild Asia** (*www.wildasia.net*) has a 'Naturalist in the Lodge' programme which places volunteers in Borneo's wildlife lodges to boost their natural history knowledge base.

Other organisations, as well as general nature sites, post jobs on their websites. **Wildlife Extra** (*www.wildlifeextra.com*) is a British-based web wildlife magazine with links to wildlife volunteer and paid jobs, projects, wildlife holidays and lots of good causes and campaigns. The website www.greenvolunteers.com is a good guide and source of information on worldwide nature conservation volunteer programmes.

Sometimes the best way to help is with a donation to appeals such as the **Sepilok Orang-utan Appeal** (*Charbury, Orestan Lane, Effingham, Surrey;* ✆ +44 0771 863 6022; e *info@orangutan-appeal.org*) – you can adopt an orphaned orang-utan at Sabah's foremost orang-utan rehabilitation centre.

The **Malaysian Nature Society** *Persatuan Pencinta Alam Malaysia* (*www.mns.my mns@mns.my*) has many conservation and community projects in Sabah and Sarawak. Its website links to grassroots organisations and their upcoming events and activities. To support them you can volunteer, join or donate.

Friends of the Earth Malaysia (✆ +60 42 276930) or *Sahabat Alam Malaysia* (SAM) carry out many grassroots, community activities in Borneo and are involved in environment and community issues. They have an office in Marudi, in the Baram river area in Sarawak, but their main office is in Penang.

Borneo is one of **Conservation International**'s biodiversity 'hotspots' (*1919 M Street, NW Suite 600 Washington, DC 20036;* ✆ (202) 9121 000/1(800) 4062306; e *hotspots@conservation.org; www.biodiversityhotspots.org; www.conservation.org*). There are plenty of suggestions about how you can help on their website.

Forests Monitor (*69a Lensfield Rd, Cambridge CB2 1EN; www.forestsmonitor.org*) is an NGO working with traditional communities of the world to lobby against activities destroying their habitats. You can donate to their appeals and volunteer with projects.

INDIGENOUS RIGHTS AND CULTURAL CONSERVATION The Borneo Project (*1771 Alcatraz Av, Berkeley, California CA 94703;* ✆ 510 547 4258; *www.borneoproject.org*) is a major advocate for indigenous rights, rainforest protection and sustainable community development in Borneo. Established in 1991, they have helped indigenous people with native land claims, legal aid, reforestation and rural development primarily in Sarawak. A non-profit organisation sponsored by Earth Island Institute, it works closely with local groups who initiate and oversee various projects while a volunteer advisory board in the US gathers resources and educates audiences about the rainforests and people of Borneo. One recent reforestation scheme brought nine Penan, Kayan and Iban communities together: 'The villages share skills and strategies in reforestation of timber trees, coffee, pepper, rattans, medicinal plants, fruit trees, and vegetable gardening. Nine new nurseries have been constructed and are well on their way to rejuvenating degraded rainforests.' Other programmes focus on legal aid, community mapping (for claims to ancestral lands) and indigenous pre-schools.

The **Borneo Research Council** (*www.borneoresearchcouncil.org*) draws together a worldwide network of humanitarian field academics with an expertise in the history, language, culture, performing arts, etc, and are keen to recruit volunteers. The Sabah Museum and Sarawak Museum have many different research projects and departments in cultural heritage. **Survival International** (*6 Charterhouse Bldgs, London EC1M 7ET;* ✆ +44 020 7687 8700; e *info@survival-international.org; www.survival-international.org*) do a lot of work protecting indigenous peoples of the world, including those in Borneo.

Tropical Forest Research The following are research institutes and organisations dedicated to unravelling the mysteries of Borneo's nature as well as conserving it. Many areas of Borneo's natural wonders remain unstudied and not fully understood. There is a great need for this research, and there may be opportunities for you to contribute your own knowledge.

The **Royal Botanic Gardens, Kew** (England) (e *info@kew.org; www.kew.org*) is a world leader in botany and plant conservation. At least one of its research teams works in Borneo; it also relies on 500 affiliated researchers, students and volunteers, collaborating in the UK and overseas to build the knowledge base. Information is beautifully presented, for both children and adults on its website.

LOCAL ORGANISATIONS Organisations working on a local level are always in need of extra help, through volunteers and donations. Check out the **Institute of Biodiversity and Environmental Conservation** at Universiti Malaysia Sarawak (*www.ibec.unimas.my*), the **Institute for Tropical Biology** and the **Borneo Marine Research Institute** at the Universiti Malaysia Sabah (*www.ums.edu.my*); Sabah's **Wildlife Department** (*www.sabah.gov.my/jhl*) carries out conservation projects all over the state with the university and NGOs; **Sabah Forestry** (*www.forest.sabah.gov.my*) and **Sarawak Forestry** (*www.sarawawforestry.com*) have various national park activities and sustainable forest research programmes.

GIVING GIFTS Small gifts are a nice way of showing gratitude to hosts. These may be 'exotic' things from your own home country that are not available in Borneo. When visiting longhouses or other traditional communities, the custom is to present gifts to the village chief (*penghulu*) or longhouse chief (*tuai rumah*) so that it can be shared around.

THE KAMPUNG TOGUDON PROJECT

One of Raleigh International's highly commendable projects of 2007 'Kampung Togudon', was aimed at constructing a small brick hostel for a primary school in a small village on the edge of Crocker Range National Park. 'About 70 children go to the primary school, but most of them live up to eight hours' walk away and have to stay in the community's homes during the week.' There are some compelling participant blogs on RI's website.

Impressed by the breadth and depth of Raleigh's action, I asked if I could reproduce one of their Borneo projects in the book as an example of focused, full of life, constructive volunteer work which is aiding communities and conservation.

KAMPUNG MANGKUWAGU TONGOD

Tongod District is situated in the centre of Sabah and takes several hours of driving off-road to reach. Communities in this area are predominantly of Sungai Makiang (river people from the Makiang River) origin, Christian and living in traditional-style housing of bamboo and leaf roofing. Some of the *kampungs* [villages] are extremely poor and lack a basic water supply, pre-school facilities and other amenities. Raleigh International has worked in the Tongod District for several years now, repairing and installing water systems and building a kindergarten, with funding from HSBC and Nestlé. Our latest undertaking with the grassroots community organisation PACOS [see below] was the construction of a kindergarten, this time in Kampung Mangkuwagu. The remote village suffers from a shortage of teachers and suitable buildings for schooling. Raleigh volunteers also taught English to children aged from four to twelve and helped organise community activities such as a sports day for the village, volleyball, football matches and swims in the river. The locals showed their appreciation by inviting us to their houses for meals, bringing fresh food to the team to cook and making gifts.

PACOS (Partners of Community Organisations) (✆ *088 712518;* **e** *pacos@ tm.net.my*) is a community-based volunteer organisation in Sabah that supports indigenous communities.

STUFF YOUR RUCKSACK – AND MAKE A DIFFERENCE

www.stuffyourrucksack.com is a website set up by television's Kate Humble which enables travellers to give direct help to small charities, schools or other organisations in the country they are visiting. Maybe a local school needs books, a map or pencils, or an orphanage needs children's clothes or toys – all things that can easily be 'stuffed in a rucksack' before departure. The charities get exactly what they need and travellers have the chance to meet local people and see how and where their gifts will be used.

The website describes organisations that need your help and lists the items they most need. Check what's needed in Borneo, contact the organisation to say you're coming and bring not only the much-needed goods but an extra dimension to your travels and the knowledge that in a small way you have made a difference.

BEGGING Giving money to children is not encouraged. Begging is uncommon in Sabah and Sarawak. The main exceptions are some coastal towns with a lot of poor Filipino and Indonesian migrants. Children might cheekily extend their hands for money when parents are not looking.

3

Natural History

'Life on Earth is not evenly spread around our planet. Borneo – the world's third largest island – is one of its richest treasure-houses, full of an immense variety of wild animals and plants, all living in a magnificent tropical forest.'

Sir David Attenborough, backing the WWF's Heart of Borneo project in 2007

BIODIVERSITY

Despite extensive destruction of its natural environment through forestry and agriculture, large areas of Borneo remain a paradise of tropical forests filled with a staggering array of plants and animals. The world's 'biodiversity hotspots' cover less than 1% of the earth's surface, and Borneo is home to over half of all the world's plant and animal species, bringing it on par with the Amazon and equatorial Africa for species diversity.

Many of these are endemic – not found anywhere else – and it's estimated there are over 5,000 flowering plants unique to Borneo, as well as some 500 mammals, birds, reptiles and fish. Indeed the island is just one of two places where the orang-utan, Asia's only great ape, has survived. The island's flora is also rich and varied. Just 10ha of Bornean rainforest can contain up to 700 tree species – more than are found in the whole of North America – whilst total flora species estimates are at least 15,000, including 3,000 different trees and over 2,000 orchids, with new species being discovered every year. The last 13 years of research alone have yielded 260 insects, 50 plants, 30 freshwater fish, seven frogs, five crabs, two snakes and one toad, to name a few. It's thought these new-found wonders are just the tip of the iceberg. As researchers penetrate deeper into the pristine forests at the centre of the island, known as the 'Heart of Borneo', (see page 117) more unknown species are expected to be unearthed.

GEOLOGY

Like all other islands, Borneo owes its isolation to tectonic plate movement and rising sea levels. Along with the Peninsular Malay and the islands of Java and Sumatra, the island is part of the Sunda Shelf, a stable continental shelf which runs below the shallow South China and Java Seas, as an extension of mainland Asia. Youthful on a geological scale, Borneo's foundations were set in place with the buckling of the earth's crusts around 15 million years ago. Over the next three million years, these underwater landmasses were forced above sea level by tectonic plate movement. When sea levels rose at the end of the last Ice Age, 12,000 years ago, Borneo was separated from Sundaland and the other territories with which it shares much common fauna.

Even today, most of Borneo's landmass lies at less than 150m above sea level and a marshy coastal belt – composed partly of rich alluvial (deposited by water) soils

While travelling around the Malay Archipelago from 1854 to 1862, pioneering explorer and naturalist Alfred Russel Wallace made two important discoveries central to biological science.

After completing his travels around the Amazon Basin, Wallace set sail for southeast Asia, documenting his travels and collecting species he found along the way. In the eight years he spent travelling around the region he collected a staggering 125,660 specimens, 1,000 of which were new to science. Through his observations of the region's flora and fauna, Wallace formulated ground-breaking theories about the environment and the evolution of species, similar to those of Charles Darwin. However, unlike Darwin, Wallace failed to elaborate on his ideas and did not work out a mechanism as to how evolution might occur. As a result, Darwin received much more credit and fame for his work and is often quoted as the sole author of the revolutionary theory in history books.

This was not the only breakthrough that Wallace made during his time in the Malay Archipelago. Whilst travelling around the islands, he noticed a striking pattern of distribution of animals across the archipelago and identified a distinct line that separated two groups of fauna with different origins. On one side they showed similarities to species found in southeast Asia, whilst on the other side species were clearly affiliated to Australasian fauna. Wallace had discovered the fault-line boundary separating two vast continental plates that had drifted together over time effectively bring two significantly different stocks of wildlife into close proximity. 'Wallace's Line' was consequently named in his honour.

washed down from the mountains – girths much of the island, and extends inland towards some hills and valleys. The centre of the island, however, is dominated by significant mountain ranges. These are concentrated in the north of Sabah, but extend southwest and northeast, with a few isolated peaks of 1,500–2,000m standing tall along the Sabah–Sarawak and Sarawak–Kalimantan borders.

SABAH Separating the low-lying coast from the rest of Sabah is the 100km-long Crocker Range, formed 35 million years ago as ocean sediments were compressed into sandstone and shale and later brought to the surface by geological uplift. Most of the range lies 500–900m above the sea, though it does features southeast Asia's highest mountain, Mount Kinabalu (4,100m) and Malaysia's second-highest peak, Gunung Trus Madi (2,643m). Several rivers rise from this mountainous core, including Sungai Kinabatangan, Malaysia's second-longest river, which flows east to the Sulu Sea.

Rearing high over the Crocker Range, Mount Kinabalu is Borneo's highest point – and, in fact, the highest point between the Himalayas and New Guinea. The mountain was formed from a ball of molten granite beneath the earth's surface 10–15 million years ago, later hardening to form a granite mound (known as a 'pluton'). This mound was then forced upwards, bursting through the Crocker Range relatively recently – one million years ago – making it one of the earth's youngest non-volcanic mountains. These forces are still at work, and Mount Kinabalu continues to grow by more than half a centimetre each year. Glaciers from recent ice ages have shorn the sandstone and shale that once covered the granite core and carved the summit into the stunning form of sharp peaks, vertical cliffs and valleys seen today.

Another geomorphologic wonder of Sabah is Maliau Basin, a spectacular crater-like hollow with a diameter of over 20km and rugged rims reaching up to 2km in height. Formation of the basin began around 15–20 million years ago, when much of Sabah was still submerged. Through a series of deposition and deformation events, Maliau and other basins were formed, further shaped through progressive elevation and buckling of the earth's crust.

SARAWAK Inland Sarawak hosts a spectacular array of limestone features, including pinnacles, protrusions, and record-breaking caves. The world's largest cave chamber and cave passage, and southeast Asia's longest cave, are all found within Gunung Mulu National Park. Sculpted by the corrosive action of flowing water through limestone and sandstone mountains, the immense subterranean system is continually being reformed; dripping water creates new features and rock is worn away by underground rivers.

BRUNEI Much of Brunei is low-lying coastal plains of alluvial soils, marked by mangrove-fringed river estuaries. The interior is dominated by hills composed of sandstone and shale that form, along with clay and mudstone, most of Brunei and west Sarawak's bedrock. The Temburong district in eastern Brunei is more mountainous, with Bukit Pagon peaking at 1,843m. Brunei Bay, which is shared with Sabah and Sarawak, is heavily indented and features marine terraces cut by waves of the South China Sea.

ECOSYSTEMS AND FLORA

Though Borneo is often perceived as the archetypal jungle-covered island, it actually hosts a variety of other equally important habitats. Though definitions differ, major ecosystem types can be divided into the following categories: tropical rainforest, montane forest, limestone forest, sub alpine and summit forest, heath forest, coastal forests and wetlands.

TROPICAL RAINFOREST Tropical rainforest covers 3% of the earth's surface and lies exclusively between the tropics, in a belt around the Equator. At one time as much as 90% of Borneo was under forest cover, but today that figure is much smaller – 50–60% in Malaysian Borneo. Much of this has been logged or left to regenerate as secondary forest and only pockets of primary 'old growth' rainforest remain. In Sabah, these can be found in the central Danum Valley and Imbak Canyon region, Sepilok Forest and Tabin wildlife reserves on the east coast, and lower elevations of Mount Kinabalu Park. In Sarawak, there is primary rainforest in some of the national parks in the south – Kubah, Bako and Tanjung Datu – and on the central and north coast, Similajau, Niah and Lambir Hills parks.

EMINENT BOTANIST'S VIEWPOINT

Sir Peter Crane
Climbing up into the rainforest canopy in Borneo at dawn is a terrifying experience: straight up the tall, ghostly grey trunk of a massive Koompassia tree to a platform 40m above the ground. And still you're not at the top. But from here, as the mist clears, the true grandeur of the lowland forest emerges. This is a precious place and home to some of the world's most charismatic animals.

Sir Peter Crane is a former Director of the Royal Botanic Gardens, Kew, England. He has been at the University of Chicago since 2006, and is a frequent visitor to Borneo's forests.

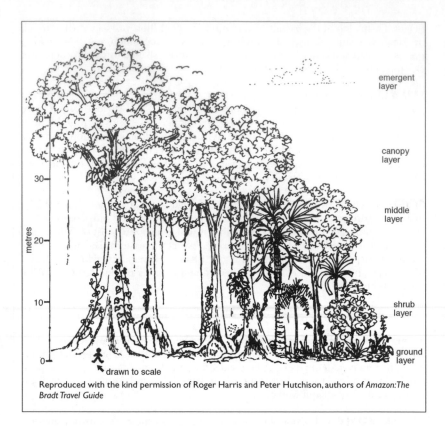

emergent
layer

canopy
layer

middle
layer

shrub
layer

ground
layer

40

30

20

metres

10

0

drawn to scale

Reproduced with the kind permission of Roger Harris and Peter Hutchison, authors of *Amazon: The Bradt Travel Guide*

Life in the forest's layers Despite the apparent chaos of growth, tropical rainforest is actually organised into at least three overlapping vertical layers.

Emergent (or overstorey) layer These forest giants tower over the canopy layer, projecting through at heights of up to 90m. The towering slivery-grey Menggaris (*Koompassia excelsa*), is one such species with trunks that grow up to 3m in diameter. The commonly named 'honeybee trees' are crowned by a mesh of horizontal branches where the giant bees (*Apis dorsata*) make their nests, safely out of reach of the honey-loving sun bear.

Canopy layer Most of the productivity in a tropical rainforest occurs in the canopy. At a height of 25–45m, sunlight and rain are most available for exploitation by trees and plants.

Dipterocarp forest Trees from the *Dipterocarpaceae* family dominate Borneo's rainforest canopy. The country is home to some 267 species – more than anywhere else in southeast Asia – and at the latest count 155 of those were endemic. Together these species account for up to 80% of tree species in Bornean forests. Sadly, they are also subject to the highest level of commercial logging activity: 80% of Borneo was once covered in lowland dipterocarp forest, but this has now been seriously whittled away.

Understorey and lower layers Below the canopy, the understorey contains younger trees patiently waiting for a gap to appear in the canopy. When this happens, they suddenly burst into rapid growth to claim the prized position in the canopy. Smaller trees and flowering bushes are also found here, and in Borneo the understorey features many species of the *Euphorbiaceae* and *Rubiaceae* families as well as Dipterocarpaceae. Euphorbiaceae is the second most common floral family in Borneo, with over 150 species from shrubs to creepers and wild fruiting plants. In some places such as the Danum Valley, Euphorbiaceae and Rubiaceae species dominate the understorey. Other common families are *Lauraceae* (laurels), *Ericaceae* (heaths and heathers) and *Annonaceae* (custard apple).

Lauraceae Borneo 'ironwood' (*Eusideroxylon zwageri*), locally known as *belian*, is a species of laurel that has been used by indigenous people for centuries to make roofs and a whole range of other things. Belian trees can reach heights of up to 40m and live for several hundred years (and take almost as long to decay). They are a common (non-dipterocarp) species in undisturbed forest canopies, though they have become less prevalent in many areas due to over-exploitation for their high commercial value. Belian timber is extremely durable, and is in great demand for heavy construction, roofing, agriculture and other uses.

As is sadly the case with many tree species, *belian* is more threatened in Indonesian Borneo – the species is now considered endangered in Kalimantan. When traditional agriculture became more industrial, larger trees began to disappear at a faster rate. When farmers started using *belian* as support stakes in pepper crops in the 1970s, numbers began to decline at very high rate indeed.

Fruit trees and palms Hundreds of tree species with edible fruit and nuts are found in the rainforest and have provided indigenous people with a bountiful and varied diet for centuries. Commonly used species include durian (*Bombacaceae*), mango (*Anacardiaceae*), and pawpaw. Several fruiting trees belong to the *Moraceae* family

READY FOR TAKE-OFF

Dipterocarp trunks emerging from their huge buttress roots 'look like rockets on the launch pad'. This fitting description was made in *Natural History* magazine in 1999. 'Their spreading limbs provide platforms and runways more than a hundred feet in the air, enabling many kinds of animals to eat, sleep, and give birth without ever descending to the ground.'

The name "dipterocarp" comes from the Greek meaning "two-winged seed" and describes the helicopter-style method with which the seeds are dispersed. The cyclical, sporadic and sudden flowering of *dipterocarpaceae* trees, known as masting, determines the reproductive rhythm of the entire forest. Species from orang-utans and gibbons, to hornbills and bats are entirely dependent on this flowering and subsequent fruiting and the manner in which dipterocarps 'dictate bounty and scarcity in the rainforest'. 'Dipterocarps do not depend on animals or the wind to disperse their seeds. Flanked by two winglike sepals, the seeds are heavy and gyrate to the ground close to the parent tree. Mature trees may not reproduce for three to ten years and then suddenly blanket the forest floor with their pea- to walnut-sized seeds. Masting is not unique to dipterocarps, but nothing compares with what takes place here: a long hiatus in reproduction throughout the forest canopy, followed by a sudden and simultaneous fructifying.'

'Flowering of the Forest – Dipterocarp trees of Borneo', by Art Blundell was published in Natural History *magazine (US) in July 1999*

including the jack-fruit-like *tarap* (*Artocarpus odoratissimus*), figs (*Ficus sp*) and many lesser-known fruits such as *peruput* (*Artocarpus rigidus*) and *timakon* (*Artocarpus lanceifolia*). One custard apple variety is used in a green, tangy drink called *sour sop*. Sago palms, *Eugeissona sp*, are a source of starchy energy, notably for the nomadic Penan who extract its fibrous pulp and turn it into flour.

Creepers and climbers The understorey is a dense, delightful world bedecked with rich entangles of lianas, lichens, orchids and epiphytic plants. The last are among the shade-tolerant species which thrive in the rainforest understorey, having developed ingenious ways of surviving. **Epiphytes** grow on the surface of other plants without needing to embed their roots in the ground and include many kinds of lichens, liverworts, orchids, mosses and ferns. **Lianas**, woody climbers, are organic ladders – they start on the forest floor but use trees, and one another, to climb towards the forest-canopy light to reproduce.

MONTANE FOREST Montane forest occurs at altitudes above 900m. This is sometimes further divided into lower montane forest (900–1,500m) and upper montane forest (1,500–3,300m).

Lower montane forest In lower montane forest the density of trees thins out, forest canopies drop as low as 20m, and oak-chestnut trees (*Fagaceae*) gradually take precedence over rainforest trees. Many orchids, both epiphytic and terrestrial varieties, flourish in these cooler conditions, as well as climbers such as rattan palm. In Sabah, lower montane environments exist in the Crocker Range, the Tawau Hills Park and lower elevations of Kinabalu Park around the park headquarters. There are over 1,000 orchid species on Mount Kinabalu, – 40% of all orchid species found on Borneo.

Upper montane forest In upper montane or **cloud forest** the spread of oak-chestnut trees are replaced by mossy forests rich in conifers, tea trees and pitcher plants. As altitudes rise, the vegetation becomes shrubbier in appearance

BORNEO FOREST & VEGETATION TYPES

KEY

- Evergreen Lowland Forest
- Forest Regrowth
- Peat Swamp Forest
- Mangrove

N

Bradt

and more stunted, the soils are thin and the canopy drops to 10m or less. Frequent cloud cover brings cool mists which shower the understorey and propagate luxurious undergrowths of numerous species of lichens, mosses, ferns, and orchids. Colourful rhododendrons thrive particularly well in the upper reaches (3,300m).

Within Sabah, this upper montane habitat type is restricted to Mount Kinabalu and the Trus Madi mountains and the unique habitat supports many rare and restricted-range species. Studies of floristic diversity in the area have shown Mount Kinabalu's species density is greatest at altitudes of 2,500–3,000m rather than at lower elevations, as may be expected. Nine species of pitcher plant dwell on Mount Kinabalu, in the crossover of lower and upper montane forest and in the rare **ultramafic forest**, where the dark, metallic soils are rich in nutrients thanks to the presence of mineral-rich ultramafic rocks.

LIMESTONE FOREST Composed of mostly small trees and shrubs, this type of forest can be found growing on limestone hills and formations, including the Gomantong and Madai caves in Sabah, and Niah and Mulu caves in Sarawak.

Rafflesias, orchids, pitcher plants and other unusual blooms have come to symbolise the extraordinary beauty of Borneo's forests and the botanical wonders which exist in them. Some feature on the endangered species list, but one hopes the awe and attention they attract as 'power flowers' will help to save them.

RAFFLESIA With its cabbage-shaped, riotous ruby-coloured blooms the rafflesia is not only an icon but an obsession in Malaysian Borneo. Also known as the 'corpse flower' for the rotting-flesh smell it emits when in bloom, the foul odour of this lowland rainforest and hill forest species has done little to dampen its popularity. Indeed, challenging smells in the botanical world (durian fruits are just as malodorous) seem to heighten interest. In 1928 Swedish entomologist Eric Georg Mjöberg described the smell as 'a penetrating odour more repulsive than any buffalo carcass in an advanced stage of decomposition'. The carcass smell attracts carrion flies in what has been described as 'pollination by deception'. Far from being a carnivore, the rafflesia is a parasitic plant that embeds and spreads its roots among *Tetrastigma* vines. The largest species in the rafflesia family is *Rafflesia arnoldii* (also known as the corpse lily in the US), which can produce flowers up to 90cm wide and weighing over 7kg – it is the largest known flower on the planet!

The first European to report it was surgeon and lay-naturalist Joseph Arnold, who discovered it during an expedition to the depths of Sumatra in 1818 with Sir Stamford Raffles. 'To tell you the truth, had I been alone with no witnesses I should have been fearful of mentioning the dimensions of this flower,' wrote Arnold. The giant flowers had long been admired by indigenous people, who reportedly use it for labour pains and post-natal fatigue, and as an aphrodisiac and fertility charm. Anglicised in Raffles's honour, the Rafflesiaceae family consists of 17 species, five of which are found in Malaysian Borneo: *R keithii* and *R tengku-adlinii* are only found in Sabah, while *R arnoldii*, *R pricei*, and *R tuan-mudae* can be seen in both Sabah and Sarawak. The rafflesia's strongholds in Sabah include the Crocker Range, Kinabalu Park and Maliau Basin, and Gunung Gading National Park in Sarawak. Known collectively as *Bunga pakma,* they generally grow in hill rainforest but also lower montane forests at elevations between 400–1,300m.

The rafflesia bud – a darkish brown lump the size of a large grapefruit – lies on the host vine for around nine months as it slowly swells in size. Upon its sudden opening, the giant flower heads have no leaves and virtually no stem, but five mammoth petals. Blossoming occurs over several days; during this time alerts are issued by national parks, wildlife departments and tourism offices, prompting a mad rush to see the flowers. They are at their most beautiful during their first day or two of blossoming. They then become covered in brown blemishes, and the flesh darkens and rots, to reveal a 15cm-wide fruit full of thousands of tiny, hard-coated seeds. It still isn't known whether elephants, ants, squirrels or other animals disperse the seeds – a theory hypothesised by Arnold – or why the flowers are so large.

The need for protection of the rare rafflesia is high; the flowers are threatened by spreading urbanisation, trampling by animals and people, and damage caused by egg-laying wasps. As many as nine out of every ten buds never open, apparently shrivelling and dying for inexplicable reasons.

With no specific breeding season, rafflesia can appear at any time, though blooms tend to be slightly more frequent between November and January. There are a number of hotlines you can call to check on the rafflesia status of the area you are in – check with national park or tourism offices, though you may be as likely to smell the blooms before you hear about them!

For more information see the illustrated *Rafflesia of the World* (Natural History Publications, Malaysia, 2001) by Dr Jamili Nais, Assistant Director of Research and Education for Sabah Parks.

PITCHER PLANTS Few plants capture the imagination more than the carnivorous pitcher plants (genus: *Nepenthes*). With an incredible diversity of designs, these jug-shaped, open-mouthed pitchers are modified petioles (stalks) that grow along herbaceous vines and specialise in luring, trapping, and devouring insects and small animals. The insects are attracted to the anthocyanin pigments (the colourful cups are often flushed with maroon and pink) or lures of nectar around the rim. But when they venture inside the trap, they slip on the mucus-lined walls and fall into the pool of liquid at the bottom, where they are dissolved by bacteria or enzymes secreted by the plant. Because the meat-eating plants derive their nutrients in this unlikely manner, they can survive in very poor soil.

Of the 30 species of *Nepenthes* found in Borneo, around half occur in Malaysian territory. The huge *Nepenthes rajah* is the largest of the genus, and is found only in Kinabalu Park and near Gunung Tambuyukon. The largest-ever pitcher recorded contained a staggering four litres of liquid and a half digested rat! Other species are endemic to the upper reaches of Mount Kinabalu, including *N burbidgeae*, *N villosa*, and *N edwarsiana*. Also known as 'monkey cups', the pitchers are used by some tribes to cook rice or carry water.

Prime pitcher-plant locations include the Kinabalu Park and Maliau Basin in Sabah, and Bako, Gunung Mulu and Lampir Hill national parks in Sarawak. They are far less elusive than *Rafflesia*, though you often have to climb to see them – most occur at 1,500–2,600m. Tham Yau Kong (e thamyaukong@thamyaukong.com, www.thamyaukong.com) runs one day two week *Nepenthes*-spotting tours in Sabah.

ORCHIDS Exquisitely delicate and intensely colourful, Borneo is said to house around one tenth of the world's orchid species: that's 2,500 out of a documented 25,000 species in the Orchidaceae family. About 1,200 of these (including several endemic species) are found in Kinabalu Park. The Rothschild's slipper (*Paphiopedilum rothschildianum*) exists only on Mount Kinabalu and is so rare that its specific location on the mountain was for many years kept secret because of repeated attempts of smuggling. Now protected by law, its close relatives include four other 'slipper' orchid species, two of which (*P dayanum* and *P rothschildianum*) are classed as endangered.

Other orchid treasures, says Dr Jamili Nais of Sabah Parks, include 'an amazing gigantic elephant-ear orchid (*Phalaenopsis gigantean*); peculiar species like the snake orchid (*Paraphalaenopsis labukensis*), which has rounded, cylindrical leaves looking like a snake; and the giant or tiger orchid (*Grammatophyllum speciosum*). About 120 Bornean orchids were on the IUCN's Red List in 2006 – at least 70 of which were listed as critically endangered.

RHODODENDRONS Adding resplendent colour to rainforest and mountain environments, Borneo's 50 or so species of rhododendron range from ground-hugging shrubs to hanging epiphytes, with pink and red tubular flowers. Around 30 are found in Sabah, including 12 endemic species. Kinabalu Park is a good place to see them.

LIPSTICK FLOWERS Various species of extravagant, multi-coloured 'lipstick flowers' (genus: *Aeschynanthus*, family: *Gesneriaceae*) are found in both Sabah and Sarawak. These Old World epiphytes flourish in temperate, montane forest environments such as Mount Kinabalu. According to Anthony Lamb, British botanist and author of *The Lipstick Flowers of Sabah* and *The Lipstick Flowers of Sabah and Sarawak* (Singapore Botanic Gardens, 2003/2005) the name was originally applied to *Aeschynanthus pulcher* from Java, because the flower buds emerging from the cylindrical calyx tube look like ladies' lipsticks. Former director of Sabah's Agricultural Park, Lamb has catalogued some of the most rare and unusual species including *A magnificus*, *A speciosus*, *A tricolour* and *A siphananthus*. Sabah has over 25 types alone, ten of which are found on Mount Kinabalu.

SUB-ALPINE AND SUMMIT FOREST Once you rise above 3,200m on Mount Kinabalu, the upper montane forest is replaced with scrubby sub-alpine vegetation made up of gnarled, stunted, wind-blown and bare trees. These trees and small shrubs rarely grow more than 50cm and are often confined to rock crevices which contain small patches of soil and protect them from the elements. These plant species are often referred to as **granite boulder** flora.

HEATH ('KERANGAS') FOREST Though relatively rare today, heath forest consists of small, poorly nourished trees growing in highly leached (nutrients washed away by rainwater) sandy soils. Found at the same altitude as lowland rainforest, they are concentrated around Sabah and Sarawak's coastal and inland areas. In estuarine areas of Sarawak the Iban call it *padang kerangas* ('land where padi can not be grown'), because rainwater cannot be retained to flood the land for planting rice paddy fields. Rain falling on the open vegetation and poor soils encourages the growth of acid-loving plants such as rhododendron and the tropical she-oak *Gymnostoma*. Heath forest is low in diversity but rich in endemic plants adapted to nutrient-poor soils such as pitcher plants, climbing epiphytes and, in the Bako National Park, ant plants (*Clerodendrum*). *Kerangas* forest is also found in the Lambir Hills and Similajau national parks on northern Sarawak's coast.

COASTAL FORESTS AND WETLANDS Sarawak, Sabah and Brunei contain a variety of wetland habitats. Wide coastal plains and marshy areas almost completely surround the island, stretching for up to 70km inland along the river system. Sabah's Wildlife Department groups beach vegetation and mangroves, freshwater swamp forest and riparian riverine forest, all under the umbrella of 'coastal forest'. These types of habitat are found 0–30m above sea level.

Beach forests Commonly consisting of coarse **casuarinas** coastal grass and **pandanus** (a genus of tropical palm trees), beach forest accounts for just a few per cent of total vegetation on Borneo. Due to coastal development schemes these habitats are on their way out, now often seen as a 'decorative remnant in developed areas'. Casuarinas are colonising species seen in strips along the coast in certain areas. *Casuarina equisetifolia* is the most common variety, seen swaying in the wind at heights of 30–60m. It is joined by other, mostly herbaceous, plants and shrubs with waterborne seeds.

Only plant species that can cope with the harsh saline environment survive, and as a result plant diversity in beach forest is relatively low. Some species – known as 'strand flora' – have moved back from the water line and occur behind a casuarinas fringe and a thin strip of mangroves. One such species is seashore screw pine (*Pandanus odoratissimus*), which is regularly sighted by the coast and features in many Sabah food dishes – the flesh of its huge fruits is used to make green cakes, green coconut paste (*kaya*) and even green bread.

Mangrove forests At the frontier where the worlds of sea and land meet, mangrove trees dominate. Their success in such a hostile environment is attributed to special adaptations to cope with the high salt and low oxygen levels. As the tide subsides, the trees' secrets are revealed – arching, tangled roots protrude above the surface, allowing the trees to absorb oxygen from the air when exposed and nutrients from the water when submerged.

Mangroves form important barriers from the sea, protecting coastal lands from the erosive actions of the tides and holding together unstable sandy soils. Many species of wildlife depend on mangroves for nesting and breeding grounds, exploiting the sheltered, tangled root system to lay eggs and raise young. In Sabah, Sarawak and Brunei mangroves are important breeding grounds for leaf monkeys, crocodiles, fish, large colonies of flying foxes, and wetland birds such as herons and egrets.

Mangroves usually grow in pure stands, and can often be found adjacent to lowland rainforest and coastal heath – a prime example is the Bako National Park in Sarawak. Mangrove forests were once widespread in low-lying coastal regions and along saline river estuaries, but now account for a tiny per cent of the state. Having been harvested for firewood, building and crafts for centuries by tribal peoples, the real damage was done with extensive clearing of mangrove-covered state land for industrial and urban developments, as well as for the mangrove timbers and the woodchip industry. More mangroves are under threat with growing urbanisation. Already a big belt of Kota Kinabalu city lies on what were once mangroves, and more are set to be swallowed up with the construction of shopping malls, apartment complexes and hotels. Though large-scale harvesting of mangroves for export has now been all but phased out, they are still used locally for firewood and other uses.

Brunei has slightly more remaining, with around 4% of its territory containing intact mangrove forest. Brunei Bay has one of southeast Asia's largest (relatively) undisturbed tracts of mangrove forest.

Nipah forests Nibong (*Oncosperma*) and nipah (*Nypa fructitans*) palms are found mingling with mangroves; the former in the dryer parts of mangrove forest, the latter in tidal reaches of rivers, such as along the Kinabatangan estuary. Nipah palms are less salt tolerant than mangroves and often occur in pure stands of 'nipah forest'. Nipah leaves are used by coastal communities – Malay, Bajau and Melenau – for roofing known as *atap,* and for basketry and other crafts. Nipah sap was once used as a form of fuel. Certain areas in Sandakan were once known as 'energy plantations' because of the large tracts of nipah forest. A lot of those areas are now planted with palm oil, used (controversially) as an alternative 'green' energy source. Brunei's riverbanks and estuaries are a good place to see nipah and nibong forest.

Transitional forest The crossover area between mangrove, nipah or swamp wetlands and dry land is sometimes referred to as 'transitional forest'. This belt of vegetation is characterised by thorny nibong palms, rattan (*Palmae*) and brown-reddish tinged merbau trees (*Intsia palembanica*), a durable hardwood.

Swamp forest According to the Sabah Forestry Department, swamp forest can be broadly separated into freshwater swamp and peat swamp. Freshwater swamps receive their water supply from streams and rivers, while peat swamps receive moisture solely from rainfall.

Freshwater swamp forest (Riparian riverine forest) When lowland rainforest is intersected by rivers, with an absence of tidal influences, specific riverine species of trees and plants flourish along the light-filled, water-lapped riverbanks: shrubs, creepers and climbing plants such as rattan, bamboo, begonias, ginger and bright yellow simpoh (*Dillenia excelsa*) grow in the fertile alluvial soils. Riverine forest plays an important role in absorbing floodwaters, protecting riverbanks and reducing soil erosion from hill slopes into rivers.

Peat swamp forests Mostly seen in Sarawak, peat swamp forests lie further inland from the mangroves and nipah, woven within river deltas. Acidic peat swamp forms as deposits of organic matter build up behind the mangroves and rivers drain towards the coast. These mires – the likes of which exist in the Maludam National Park in southern Sarawak – are habitats for proboscis monkeys and langurs; Sarawak's rare reptile; the false gharial; and aquatic species, including numerous wetland birds some of which will be on long continental migrations. Peat swamp forest covers 15,000km^2 of Sarawak's coastline, but the forests have been so extensively exploited to feed Sarawak's sawmills that they are almost depleted of timber trees.

MARINE ECOSYSTEMS Coral reefs and seagrass beds are the two most important marine ecosystems around Borneo. The latter are important grazing grounds for dugongs (sea cows) and sea turtles and provide vital nurseries for many species of fish; coral reefs are equally vibrant ecosystems. Indeed, much of Sabah's east coast and surrounding islands touch on an area dubbed the 'Coral Triangle', which encompasses the Sulu and Sulawesi seas. Here over 1,800 species of fish have been recorded, including 400 species of algae, five of the world's eight species of sea turtle, 22 marine mammal species and over 450 types of coral.

However, the reefs also face several challenges: the large rivers of Sarawak deposit sediment around the coast hindering coral formation and many of Sabah's reefs have been damaged by the practice of dynamite fishing – using explosives to surface dead fish en masse – as well as coral bleaching, sedimentation, coastal development and over-fishing. Serious conservation issues are being faced in the border-crossing area shared by Malaysia, the Philippines and Indonesia. Soaring populations and subsequent urban waste and pressure on resources, poaching and fishing piracy are all stressing the fragile ecosystem.

Enormous efforts are being made by Malaysian grassroots organisations and international NGOs to work with local communities and help them protect the seas around Borneo. WWF Malaysia has several conservation programmes in the region, and many efforts are under way to expand the protected marine zones – one of those is a proposed Semporna Islands Park. This has been in the pipeline since 2004 and may receive some European Union backing.

FAUNA

MAMMALS Logging and development have shrunk Bornean forests to half their original size, and with it the habitat of an estimated 222 mammals, including elephants, rhinos, apes, monkeys, wildcats and 44 (known) endemic mammals like the famous orang-utan, which only lives in Borneo and neighbouring Sumatra, and lesser-known wonders such as the odd-nosed proboscis monkey, banded langurs, tree-climbing sun bears, giant squirrels and the Borneo clouded leopard. Smaller mammals to be found include otters (hairy-nosed, oriental and small-clawed), porcupines, tree shrews, rats, bats and scaly pangolins. Nocturnal creatures include the 'flying lemur' or *colugo* (see box page 108), bearded pig, the sambar deer and the world's smallest hoofed mammal – the lesser mouse deer.

The total mammal count rises sporadically with exciting new discoveries and new 'mystery mammals' that baffle scientists. However, the depletion of Borneo's forests does not bode well for the survival of its mammals, especially endangered species like the Sumatran rhinoceros and pygmy elephant, which are only sighted occasionally.

Primates Some of the world's most interesting primate species are found on Borneo, and are relatively easy to see in the island's 'open' forests. Primates are characterised by their grasping hands with fingers rather than paws; fingernails rather than claws; and eyes on the front of the face, enabling stereoscopic colour vision.

Borneo is home to two types of ape – not including humans – orang-utans and gibbons; eight Old World monkeys (family: *Cercopithecidae*), including macaques, langurs (leaf monkeys) and the peculiar proboscis monkey; the slow loris, and the extraordinary tarsier, a primate so strange that taxonomists still cannot agree on which group it should be classified in. The prosimian (suborder that most closely represents ancestral primates) lorises and tarsiers are strictly nocturnal, but Borneo's monkeys and apes are active mostly during the day.

Apes

Orang-utan (*Pongo pygmaeus*) With its innate magnetism and undeniable appeal, the 'man of the forest' – from the Malay *orang* for person and *hutan* for forest – has become a mascot of Borneo, which is home to 90% of the world's orang-utans (the other 10% are located in Sumatra). Asia's only great ape exists exclusively in the tropical rainforest of the islands of Borneo and neighbouring Sumatra. Actually of African origin, they are thought to have dispersed to Asia during the Miocene period.

Orang-utans are almost entirely arboreal, spending more time in the trees than any of the other great apes. Males may reach up to 100kg, making them the largest arboreal animal on the planet, though the largest males may descend to the ground to cross gaps in the trees, travelling on all fours on the forest floor. Due to their large size, orang-utans use a form of locomotion known as quadrumanual climbing rather than the brachiating technique used by many other primates (see *Gibbons*, below). This involves clambering through the trees grasping firmly with both hands and feet. They are surprisingly agile considering their size, a feat aided by their extremely long arms, which may reach up to 2m long in males. As they do not swing or jump, 'orangs' will cross gaps in trees by rocking branches back and forth until they reach the other side.

Females may be up to 50% smaller than males; sexual dimorphism is so extreme it led early European explorers to believe they were entirely different species. Dominant males grow huge pads on their cheeks, and exhibit their superior rank by 'long calling', a booming grunt which can be heard up to 2km away and may be accompanied by violent branch shaking. Unlike other apes, orang-utans are largely solitary, spending much of their time travelling alone looking for food. A mother will be accompanied by her offspring until it becomes independent at around eight to ten years. Orangs have a long childhood, and may be suckled for up to six years. During this time they will watch their mother closely, learning which foods are good to eat and how to process them. Wild orang-utans enjoy a long life, some living up to an estimated age of 70 years.

Orang-utans will eat a diet of 100% fruit when it is available, but more usually this constitutes 60% of their dietary intake. They move around the forest based on

WHY ARE ORANG-UTANS ORANGE?

The long, shaggy bright orange body hair of the orang-utan is immediately striking and unmistakable. Variation between individuals is great and may change with age, from bright orange in infants to auburn and deep burgundy in adults. But why is the 'red ape' so vividly coloured?

Whilst the fiery colours blaze in the sunlight, they virtually disappear in the shadows of the forest canopy. The dark skin underneath absorbs the light so it is this you see rather than the hair on top, making the ape functionally black and virtually invisible. This 'trick of the light' may help orang-utans to blend into their scenery, whilst enabling them to be seen by other members of the species – another explanation for their bright colouring is to announce their presence to other orang-utans.

the availability of fruits, building a mental map of the forest to remember where and when trees are fruiting. A variety of other foods are eaten, including leaves, fungi, eggs, honey termites and small vertebrates. Orang-utans have a predilection for figs, and will stay in a laden tree for days on end, gorging themselves on the sweet fruits. They are the only species other than elephants which can crack open the sugar-rich durian fruit. As such, they are important dispersers of seeds through the forest.

Orang-utans are mostly active during the daytime. Each evening, an individual will construct a sophisticated nest high in the trees, weaving thin branches together to make a flat sleeping platform complete with a 'roof' to provide shelter from the rain. As well as being a flagship species, orang-utans are also an 'indicator species'

USELESS, DIRTY AND DUMB OR DIGNIFIED AND INTELLIGENT?

Adorable and endangered, orang-utans tug at many people's heart strings for the plight they have endured and have become a flagship for Malaysian tourism – but it hasn't always been that way. Orang-utans were once depicted as useless, dirty and dumb by 19th-century explorers and scientists, write Gisela Kaplan and Lesely J Rogers in The Orang-utans (Allen and Unwin, Australia 1999).

Stories were told of orang-utan males who abducted fragile English ladies and raped them in trees. The orang-utan was said to grow too large and strong for a pet, and to be of only limited use as a domestic helper. The ape was said to compare poorly in entertainment value to the chimpanzee and, overall, was not perceived as having any immediate medical or research value. It was further alleged that the orang-utan was difficult to observe, boring to watch because of its 'sluggish' behaviour and difficult to keep confined.

Based on their experiences with orang-utans in Sabah, the authors saw just how far from dumb these animals were, particularly in the extent to which they are adapted to their rainforest environment.

The fact that the orang-utan's habitat is shrinking seems all the more cruel when we understand how resourceful and flexible orang-utans are. In everything they do they are master generalists, just as humans are said to be. They are perhaps the fastest of the great apes in problem solving, have excellent memories and are superb imitators. They are also very skilled trapeze artists – as the largest mammal in the canopy, negotiating this habitat requires developed cognitive abilities.

Orang-utans are accomplished and innovative tool users, using leaves as hats or umbrellas when it rains, or as gloves to climb spiky-trunked trees. Sumatran orang-utans craft termite-capturing 'fishing rods' from twigs, poking them into termite nests to collect the insects as chimpanzees do. This intelligence goes beyond the confines of life in the rainforest. Orang-utans fall within a cognitive circle which was once thought to only include humans: they can make fires, learn to play a guitar, wash clothes, use tools and imitate whatever they see humans do, by simply observing rather than by being taught. 'In some areas a five-year-old orang-utan may perform at about the same level as a four-year old human child.' They are in fact 97% genetically similar to us, sharing a common ancestor 10–12 million years ago.

Orang-utans are gentle, intelligent, complex and contemplative, often sitting for hours just gazing. As Willie Smits told The Age newspaper in 2004, 'The world would be a better place if humans were a bit more like orang-utans.'

ORANG-UTAN DISTRIBUTION DECLINE

Orang-utan distribution
1930

Orang-utan distribution
1999

Orang-utan distribution
2004

Orang-utan distribution
2020

– barometers for the well-being of the forest. If orang-utan populations are declining, it is a sign that the forest and all that lives within it are in trouble too.

Orang-utan conservation The orang-utan's dependence on trees for food and shelter, slow breeding rate, and need for large amounts of space, makes it extremely vulnerable to hunting and habitat loss. Females may not breed until they reach 17 years of age, and with an inter-birth period of eight to nine years – the longest of any mammal – populations struggle to recover from losses. Around 40,000–50,000 wild orang-utans are thought to be left today – a figure half what it was 20 years ago – and the remaining population is suffering dramatic declines greater than ever before. At current rates, the orang-utan could be the first great ape to be made extinct in modern times.

The two habitat countries of the orang-utan, Malaysia and Indonesia, established protection for the species over 30 years ago, at a time when the 'red ape' and its plight was relatively unknown; they endured capturing, poaching and trade for pets and other markets. Things seemed to be looking hopeful as hunting and trading began to let up, national parks were established and laws began to be enforced. The first orang-utan rehabilitation centre was opened in Sarawak in 1961 by pioneering Barbara Harrison, and killing the apes was forbidden by law two years later in Sabah.

However, things changed as Indonesia and Malaysia entered the global economy in the 1980s and '90s. Indiscriminate logging and the conversion of forests to plantations for cash crops such as palm oil soon superseded any previous willingness to protect the species. Fires raged in Kalimantan as companies cleared forests to make way for crops, releasing huge amounts of carbon dioxide into the atmosphere, contributing to global climate change and increasing the El Niño effect of drought in the tropics – fuelling further fires and destroying more of the orang-utan's habitat. Around 80% of orang-utan habitat has been radically degraded or totally destroyed, and orang-utans without rainforest are like fish without a sea.

The 1990s saw numerous campaigns and documentaries, bringing the orang-utan into the spotlight as they captured the hearts of the world. Reports of cruelty and illegal transportation of orang-utan babies made international headlines. One famous case was that of the 'Bangkok Six' in 1990. Six orang-utans were transported from Borneo to Bangkok in wooden crates, one of which was upside down for whole trip, without food and water. Photos of the frightened, exhausted babies shocked and saddened readers worldwide. Though things have improved, the occasional case crops up that makes me question whether things have really changed at all. In July 2007, I opened a local newspaper in Sabah to read headlines of attempted smuggling of dozens of orang-utans, including babies. They were found packed into a cage ready to be taken to the Netherlands for scientific tests, excreting on each other and even cannibalising each other. The sheer unconcerned cruelty was simply heartbreaking.

In 2004 Dr Willie Smits, founder of the Borneo Orang-utan Survival Foundation, said: 'The rate of loss of orang-utans has never been greater than in the last three years, and oil palm plantations take the brunt of the blame.' Illegal logging, conversion of the forest to plantations and the illegal pet trade are the main continuing threats. In some previously densely forested regions of Sabah and Sarawak which have given over to large plantations, the orang-utan is considered to be a complete pest, one which must be disposed of to save crops. The fact that hunting orang-utans is illegal has not eliminated the practice.

What can be done to help? Increasing foreign investment will allow Malaysia and Indonesia to rely less on their raw natural resources and manage them more efficiently. Introducing certification of ethically sourced (sustainable) palm oil and labelling of products on supermarket shelves, will allow consumers to avoid palm oil that has not been produced from sustainable sources. The Malaysian government needs to ensure that laws are enforced and the orang-utans – and the forests on which they depend – are protected.

Gibbons Gibbons are the smallest of the ape family (indeed they are often referred to as 'lesser apes') and Borneo is home to two species – the **Bornean** or **Muller's gibbon** (*Hylobates muelleri*), whose distribution extends throughout much of the island, and the **agile gibbon** (*Hylobates agilis*), found only in Indonesian Borneo. Both species inhabit dipterocarp forests, swinging with admirable ease through the high canopy using a form of locomotion known as 'brachiation'. This involves the gibbon hooking its long fingers over a branch and using a hand-over-hand, under-branch motion to effortlessly and gracefully swing through the trees at high speed like arboreal acrobats.

Gibbons live in family units consisting of two monogamous adults and two to three offspring. These pairs were thought to be faithful until studies revealed that

THE PROBOSCIS MONKEY

Nasalis larvatus

The peculiar proboscis monkey, which features on the cover of this book, is an endemic species to Borneo and a few small islands very close to its shores. Its most distinguishing feature is its nose, huge and fleshy in males, and upturned and pixie-like in females. The male's pendulous nasal feature grows continuously and may reach a quarter of the length of his body! The function of this strange facial appendage remains to be determined, though it is thought to act as both an 'organ of resonance', amplifying the male's strange *kee-honk* vocalisation, and a thermoregulatory device. Females also seem to prefer males with larger noses.

Together with their pot belly and swaggering gait, the proboscis monkey's large nose led locals to nickname them *Kera Belanda* ('Dutch monkeys') – a rather unkind reference to the Dutch plantation owners of colonial times. The pot belly contains bacteria that help to digest the monkey's diet of toxin-containing leaves. The spindly legs that dangle from beneath these strange-looking primates as they rest also once earned them the description of looking like they are wearing 'a bomber jacket over ballet tights'.

Proboscis monkeys live near the waterways and coasts of Borneo, in mangrove, nipah, peat swamp and riverine forests. They can be seen catapulting themselves across expanses of water by swaying branches back and forth to gain momentum or, when a gap is too large, diving into the water and swimming across single file. With partially webbed feet, proboscis monkeys are accomplished swimmers. On land they will sometimes walk bipedally, swaggering and swaying from side to side on their hind legs.

Proboscis monkeys are threatened by habitat loss and fragmentation – the monkeys cannot cross plantations, which effectively isolate remaining populations.

Some of the best places to observe proboscis monkeys include Brunei's mangrove forests and riverbanks, Sarawak's Bako and Kuching Wetlands national parks, and Sabah's Kinabatangan river area and the Klias Wetlands. Proboscis monkeys are now rivalling orang-utans as the most popular primates to see in Borneo – it seems their striking appearance may help to save them from extinction. If they continue to draw in economy-boosting tourists, they may prove to be a viable alternative to cash crops.

mating with neighbours was common during inter-group encounters and some pairs will allow an extra adult to join them for short periods! Pairs do still mate for life though, and sing powerful duets at dawn to both strengthen the bond between them and announce their presence to the neighbours. The whooping song of the gibbon is one of the most evocative sounds of forest, and can be heard up to 2km away.

Old World monkeys These fall into two distinct groups: the generalist *Cercopithecinae* sub-family, and the specialist *Colobinae* sub-family. The *Cercopithecinae*, or 'cheek-pouch monkeys' have evolved pockets in their mouths to store food in, which they fill with food and retire to a safer place to eat. They also have 'ischial callosities', fleshy pads on their rear ends that act as built-in cushions. The only *Cercopithecines* outside of Africa are the macaques, of which Borneo is home to two species. In contrast, the *Colobinae* are selective in what they eat, choosing only leaves. These are digested in bacteria-inhabited, sacculated stomachs which process the toxins found in the leaves. Borneo's five langur species (also known as 'leaf monkeys'), and the bizarre proboscis monkey are all members of the *Colobinae*.

Langurs Langurs, or leaf monkeys as they are also known, are nimble primate lightweights at just 5–7kg in weight and 200–600cm in length. 'Langur' means 'long tail', and they certainly live up to their name – their tails are often longer than their bodies. Langurs are a diverse group found across Asia, and Borneo is home to five species.

The most widespread is the **maroon langur** (*Presbytis rubicunda*). Also known as the red langur, its fur is actually a fiery orange, with a ghostly blue-tinged face. Maroon langurs can be seen in lowland rainforest in Sabah and Sarawak, and in hill and mountain forests including those in the Kelabit Highlands. **Hose's langurs** (*Presbytis hosei*) are found in the northwest of the island, and have a grey upper and cream lower body with black hands and feet. Their pale pink faces have distinct black bands across the cheeks and a prominent black crest on top of the head. Hose's langurs (also known as gray langurs) live in the canopy of lowland and hill forests. Found exclusively in Sarawak, the inky **banded langur** (*Presbytis melalophos*) is so called due to its distinctive black cheek bands. Colouring varies between black and white, black, red and white, and (in *Presbytis melalophos cruciger* – one of several recently-identified types) burgundy with black markings. Adult males make a distinctive, loud *ke-ke-ke* call. Banded langurs live in lowland and hill forest including those in the Tanjung Datu and Maludam national parks. The **silvered langur** *(Presbytis cristata)* bears a physical resemblance to the banded variety, but it lacks the bands on its face – instead it is entirely charcoal coloured.

Macaques Macaques are one of the most successful primate genera, with a wider geographical range than any other primate except *Homo*. Unlike most other monkeys, macaques spend a lot of their time on the forest floor and lower canopy levels, where they feed on a variety of foods from fruit, leaves and seeds to insects eggs, lizards and other small invertebrates. The **pig-tailed macaques** *(Macaca nemestrina)* of Borneo have a short tail that is carried half-erect, resembling that of a pig – hence the name. They are mostly olive-brown in colour, with whitish underparts and brunette patches on the head and neck. Males can reach up to 9kg and measure 500cm and can be quite intimidating with their stocky stature and bold nature.

Long-tailed macaques (*Macaca fascicularis*) are varying shades of grey and reddish-grey with fairer hair underneath. Many have prominent cheek whiskers and facial hair. Travelling in large troops of 20–30, they can cover up to 1.5km between dawn and dusk and can be very noisy!

Both of Borneo's macaque species live in lowland rainforest and hill forest as high as 1,300m; the long-tailed macaque is also found on coastal wetlands, small islands, mangroves and beach forest. Macaques will raid plantations and sometimes tourist lodges, so beware! I have had my fair share of run-ins, including one in the forest while pointing a camera lens too close at a pig-tailed macaque – not advisable! In my experience, the pig-tailed variety is more menacing.

Prosimians These are the forerunners of the monkeys and apes, 'prosimian' literally meaning 'before monkeys'. Of the two sub-orders of primates, prosimians make up the Strepshirhini, or wet-nosed primates. Primates within this sub-order, which include the lemurs of Madagascar, bushbabies of Africa and lorises of Asia, rely more heavily on olfactory (smell) communication and possess several anatomical differences from the other, more visually oriented Haplorhini primates which include monkeys, apes and humans.

Slow loris In contrast to the other fast-moving agile primates of Borneo, the nocturnal **slow loris** (*Nycticebus menagensis*) takes things at a much slower pace, creeping and clambering through the forests at night with slow, deliberate movements. Lorises can cling to branches for hours on end with their powerful grip, and communicate through the forest using olfactory and auditory – including ultra-sonic – communication. Grey-brown to reddish brown in colour, with a dark strip down the spine towards the base of the short tail, lorises are among the least-studied of all primates. Their diet consists of slow-moving, often toxic invertebrates. Lorises produce toxic secretions themselves, exuded from their underarms which they lick to numb prey when biting into them. These prosimians can reach up to 28cm in length and weigh around 2kg. Protected under Sabah's 1963 Fauna Conservation Ordinance, these endangered primates are threatened with habitat destruction and hunting.

Western tarsier (*Tarsius bancanus*) Tarsiers are something of a bone of contention in primate taxonomy (and they take their name from their extended tarsus leg bone). Scientists cannot agree on which of the two primate sub-orders they should belong to, with compelling evidence for their inclusion in either group. This bizarre looking nocturnal primate looks like it could be an extra from *The Lord of the Rings*, its extraordinarily large eyes are the biggest of any mammal in relation to body size, with each eyeball weighing more than its brain! Their long, powerful hind legs fold thrice into a zigzag at rest but spring into action as the diminutive creature makes spectacular leaps of up to 40 times its body length between the trees. Tarsiers live in lowland rainforests across Borneo, though they are rarely seen. Nocturnal species are often located by shining torches into the darkness and looking for the reflected torchlight from the animals' eyes. However, tarsiers lack such reflective eyes, enabling them to remain elusive in the dark forests at night. More often they are heard, making distinctive high-pitched shrieks. Tarsiers are among the smallest primates in the world, 70–150cm in length and weighing around 1kg. Their diet is entirely carnivorous, consisting of large insects and lizards, and even bats and birds. The best place to see them in Borneo is the Danum Valley in Sabah.

Large mammals
Borneo pygmy elephant Despite being known as a 'pygmy' species, the Borneo pygmy elephant is still among the largest land mammals in Asia, with males reaching over 2m in height. However they are still much smaller than their mainland Asian counterparts, who can stand at over 3m tall, whilst their African cousins are even larger. Their compactness gives them an endearing charisma, and their tolerant nature allows onlookers to get up fairly close to them. The herbivorous pachyderms are an important part of the forest ecosystem, trimming vegetation and dispersing seeds throughout the forests. They are also lovers of durian, swallowing the fruits whole – spikes and all.

Recent genetic and archaeological evidence appears to have solved the riddle of the Borneo pygmy elephant's origins. Thought for many years to have been introduced from mainland southeast Asia or Sumatra, genetic evidence recently revealed the species to be genetically distinct from other southeast Asian elephants, strengthening the case for their protection as a distinct species. Whilst some scientists immediately heralded Borneo's elephants as an endemic species ('*Elephas maximus borneensis*'), more recent research has shown that there is no archaeological evidence of a long-term elephant presence on Borneo. So where *did* they come from? It appears that the 'Borneo' pygmy elephant is in fact the last vestiges of a subspecies that has long been extinct on its native island – Java. The last of the Javan elephants disappeared shortly after Europeans arrived in southeast Asia, and the 1,500 or so remaining in Borneo are most likely the descendants of two individuals introduced to Borneo 300 years ago as a gift from the Sultan of Sulu (present-day

The WWF considers the three Asian rhino species as 'flagships' – 'charismatic representatives of the biodiversity of the complex ecosystems they inhabit'. By protecting them and their habitat, many other species benefit. WWF teams have been working on rhino conservation for decades. In 1998 WWF created the Asian Rhino and Elephant Action Strategy (AREAS), aimed at not only protecting specific areas but at reviewing land-use practices, strengthening anti-poaching efforts, monitoring trade of rhino horns and raising public awareness. The Sumatran rhino – *Badak Sumatra* in Malay – is a protected species within Sabah's national parks and reserves.

Only two areas in Sabah – Tabin and the Ulu Segama-Kuamut area – contain rhino populations with prospects of long-term survival, if adequate protection and management is allowed,' says the WWF. 'The Tabin rhino population was under pressure from forest loss and was afforded protection by the Sabah government in 1984 through the establishment of the 1,225km^2 Tabin Wildlife Reserve. The second population – the Ulu Segama-Kuamut area – is scattered through a vast area of several contiguous forest reserves, but probably centred within an area of less than 4,000km^2 in the catchment areas of the upper Segama and upper Kuamut Rivers. The latter area includes the Danum Valley and Maliau Basin Conservation areas in the Sabah Foundation's 100-year logging concession.

In 2003, WWF and Columbia University researchers proved that Borneo's elephants are genetically distinct from other Asian elephants. Together with Sabah's Wildlife Department, surveys have been carried out on elephant populations, tracking them with satellite radio collars. Despite being endangered, they are not a protected species in Sabah and are very vulnerable to being hunted, shot at or electrocuted for 'trespassing' on oil palm plantations. The WWF calls them 'the least-understood elephants in the world'. What is known is that they rely on having large open areas to live – but their habitat is shrinking more and more.

Philippines). These findings make it even more crucial to protect them from the habitat destruction, poaching and persecution that threatens them today.

Many of the elephants' traditional migratory routes have been converted to plantations, bringing them into conflict with humans when they continue to travel through them.

Elephants can cause considerable damage as they walk through, and forage in, farmers' crops. Their range is fairly small, restricted to lowland rainforest of eastern and central Sabah (Danum Valley and surrounding areas), and into Kalimantan. This range is being further eaten into by conversion of forests to plantations, bringing the elephants into more conflict with people.

Sumatran (Asian two-horned) rhinoceros (*Dicerorhinus sumatrensis*) The Sumatran rhinoceros, also known as the Asian two-horned or hairy rhinoceros, is the smallest of the five extant species of rhino today – at around 2.5m long, just over one metre tall and weighing in at around 800kg. The Sumatran rhino is a tropical forest ungulate (hoofed, grazing animal), classified along with horses, zebras and tapirs as 'perissodactyls' – odd-toed ungulates – as they have three toes.

There are two subspecies, only one of which (*Dicerorhinus sumatrensis harrissoni*) is found on Borneo. The other (*Dicerorhinus sumatrensis sumatrensis*) is native to Sumatra and Peninsular Malaysia. Their reddish-brown hide has patches of stiff, dark hair which keeps mud caked to the body, helping to cool the animal and protect it from insects. Regular mud-wallowing keeps the protective layer intact. Despite their thick skin, the Sumatran rhino is critically endangered– teetering on the edge of extinction after years of heavy poaching and habitat destruction.

'Rhinoceros' means *nose-horn*, and the animals have been hunted for decades for their keratin-rich horns, which are used in Asian medicine. 'The creation of forestry access roads deep into the forest home of the rhino led to an influx of poachers who target rhinos, especially in the Tabin Wildlife Reserve and several areas adjacent to the Danum Valley Forest Reserve,' says the WWF. It is in these areas that conservation efforts are being focused.

The Sumatran rhino is classified as 'Critically Endangered' on the IUCN Red List, though the WWF worryingly claim it to be 'possibly extinct' in Sarawak and Kalimantan, with 'fewer than 25 surviving in Sabah'. Once widespread throughout Borneo, numbers have plummeted in recent times, dropping by half in the last 15 years. The original threats of poaching and deforestation, are now joined by the palm oil industry as more and more forest is converted to plantations.

Bornean clouded leopard (*Neofelis nebulosa diardi*) In 2007, Borneo's largest predator was recognised as a unique subspecies. Based on DNA research, scientists at the US National Cancer Institute concluded that the one metre long wildcat – one of Asia's largest – differed from mainland species it had previously been lumped with, to a similar extent that other large cat species such as leopards and snow leopards differ. The species diverged around 1.4 million years ago, around the time Borneo separated from the mainland.

Separate studies of fur patterns also provided a key. Mainland leopards have large cloud-like markings on their skin – swirls of black around big tawny patches; their Bornean cousins are the inverse: thin tawny cloud-linings, around many more speckled dark clouds and with much more black overall. The clouded spots provide effective camouflage, allowing the leopard to hide from its prey in the forest, pouncing on unsuspecting deer, wild pigs and monkeys. Their presence is an indication of forest health – the fact that they are rarely sighted today shows not

CLOUDED CONSERVATION

The clouded leopard, or *Harimau Dahan* in Malay, is a 'totally protected species' in Sarawak, and protected in Sabah's parks and reserves. It is listed as endangered by CITES and vulnerable by the IUCN. The WWF maintains an extensive leopard conservation operation, and puts Borneo's clouded leopard population at somewhere between 5,000 and 11,000. Their 'last great forest home' is the Heart of Borneo, in both Sabah and Kalimantan.

Extensive conservation and research work on this species is being carried out by the American Clouded Leopard Project, which provides this insight on the leopard's behaviour:

Clouded leopards are one of the best climbers in the cat family. They are able to climb upside down underneath tree branches and hang from branches with their hind feet. Several adaptations allow the leopards to achieve these amazing arboreal skills: their legs are short and stout, providing excellent leverage and a low centre of gravity while climbing; large paws with sharp claws allow them to gain a good grip on tree branches; and the tail is extremely long – up to three feet, the same length as its body – and is extremely important as a balancing aid.

Natural History **FAUNA**

3

only the effects that habitat loss and over-hunting have had on their populations, but also how degraded the forests themselves have become.

Civets Of the several kinds of cat-like civets, the largely tree-dwelling, usually nocturnal binturong *(Arctictis binturong)* is perhaps the most fascinating, known as the 'bear-cat' because its stocky, dark-furred body gives it a bear-like appearance. Other civets include the masked palm civet *(Paguma larvata)* and common palm civet *(Paradoxurus hermaphroditus)*, Malay civet *(Viverra tangalunga)* and Sunda otter-civet *(Cynogale bennettii)*.

Sun bear *(Helarctos malayanus)* Averaging one metre in length, the sun bear, or honey bear as it is also known, is the world's smallest bear species. Endemic to Borneo, the sun bear is largely arboreal and primarily nocturnal, feeding on insects in the rainforests at night. As their alternative name suggests, they also have a taste for honey, using their long, sharp claws to reach beehives at the top of tall trees. Their dark fur makes them difficult to spot in the dark, though the V-shaped patch of lighter fur on its chest is a giveaway. Its intimidating 'bark' and hoarse grunts drive off potential threats – Sarawak Forestry classifies it, along with the pygmy elephant, as one of the few potentially dangerous animals on the island, because of the 'unpredictability of its behaviour'. The *beurang*, as it is known in Malay, is threatened by habitat loss and poaching, both for meat and medicinal purposes, and is listed by the IUCN as endangered.

Giant squirrel *(Ratufa affinis)* This dark-furred squirrel with a white underbelly and luxurious brush tail is one of the world's largest tree-dwelling rodents, growing up to 50cm in length to the tip of the tail, and weighing up to 1.5kg. It feeds on leaves, shoots, birds' eggs, bark and insects during the day when it is most active and can make leaps of up to 6m between trees. It is fiercely territorial, defending its home patch with raspy chattering sounds.

Bearded pig *(Sus barbatus)* This surprisingly large creature, looking much like a wild boar but with far more facial hair, can be rather formidable in appearance but is actually quite shy by nature. Their long, over-sized heads are covered with a coarse beard of bristles all the way along the lower jaw, made even more ungainly by upward-pointing incisors that protrude from either side. Though they are primarily nocturnal, I have sighted them during the day lolling around muddy

THE FLYING LEMUR

The 'flying lemur' is a double misnomer, for it is neither a lemur nor does it truly fly. Though it is not a primate like a lemur, recent research suggests that it may be the closest living relative of the primate group. Previous studies had indicated it was more closely related to the *Scandentia* group which includes tree shrews.

Flying lemurs (also known locally as *colugos* or *kubungs*) belong to the *Dermoptera* group. *Dermoptera* literally means 'skin wings' and refers to the patagium, a flap of skin between its limbs and tail, which is used to glide (rather than fly) between the trees of Borneo's forests. The strange squirrel-like animal can reach distances of up to 70m using its 'wings', though is much less adept at climbing trees. During the daytime, colugos hang upside down much like bats, or cling to tree trunks. They come out at dusk and feed throughout the night on leaves, flowers and sap, which they scrape from tree trunks using a 'comb' formed by the fusion of lower teeth.

environs of the Bako National Park in Sarawak, foraging for earthworms, fallen fruits and seeds. The bearded pig's thick skin and lightly fuzzy coat colouration varies from grey to reddish brown, depending on how much wallowing it has been doing. The females make large nests on higher flood-free ground, out of piles of torn-off shrubs, saplings and plants.

BIRDS Borneo's forests are alive with birdsong. Of the island's 620 listed birds, 420 are known to breed there and 41 are endemic; the rest are found throughout the Malay Archipelago. The Bornean endemics include large birds such as eagles, pheasants and partridges through to much smaller wren-babblers, flycatchers, flower-peckers and thrushes.

The wonderfully named chestnut-crested yuhina, Bornean treepie, blue-banded pitta, black-browed babbler and white-crowned shama are all mountain birds, occurring above 1,000m, and are high on the list of must-sees of ardent birdwatchers. Two-thirds of Borneo's endemic birds only live in montane areas, which makes Sabah in particular a birdwatchers' paradise. Lowland forest endemics of particular interest include the blue-headed pitta, Bornean wren babbler, Bornean blue flycatcher, yellow-rumped flower-pecker, Bornean bristlehead and dusky munia. There are also endemic eagles, falcons, cuckoos, partridges and pheasants.

Buwler's pheasant (*Lophura bulweri*) The male Buwler's pheasant is, as Sarawak National Parks puts it, 'spectacularly handsome, with splendid blue facial wattles and a long, spreading, curved white tail'. Bulwer's pheasant is only found in tropical hill forests of central and northern Borneo, where it nests and forages on the ground and roosts in trees. It is a poor flier but a fast and nimble runner, using a combination of darting runs and flurried bursts of flight to avoid predators. During the mating season the male produces a shrill, piercing cry and performs a tail-spreading, wattle-raising dance for females. Though widespread in central Borneo, it has a low population density and is threatened by illegal hunting and habitat loss.

Hornbills Sarawak's list of 'totally protected species' contains 26 birds including various egrets, eagles, pigeons and terns – but the most coveted are the hornbills which earn their name from the large horn-like casques which crown their colourful beaks. There are eight species of hornbill – all of them protected and all with delightful names, from the white-crowned to the bushy-crested, wreathed, wrinkled and oriental pied varieties to the two largest species: the helmeted hornbill (*Buceros vigil*) and the rhinoceros hornbill (*Buceros rhinoceros*).

Though not endemic to Borneo, the rhinoceros hornbill is the symbol of Sarawak, believed by the Iban people, who call them *kenyalang,* to be messengers from the spirit world. Their huge wings, which have a span of over 1m, make a distinctive whooshing sound overhead as they fly past. Like most hornbills, the female builds her nest in the cavities of large trees and seals up the hole with mud, leaving just enough room for the male to pass fruit through as she broods. When the young hatch, the female leaves the nest and feeds her offspring through the hole with her partner, with whom she will mate for life. The hornbill is dependent on large trees for nesting places, but selective logging practices have limited their options. Sabah's diverse forests support an extraordinarily varied avifauna, and have been a magnet for ornithologists for over a century. A comprehensive reference guide is *The Birds of Borneo* by B E Smythies, but a more up-to-date and manageable field guide is the *Pocket Guide to the Birds of Borneo* compiled by Charles M Francis (see *Appendix 2*, page 294).

Top birdwatching spots To see the various Asian and Bornean riverine, lowland or montane birds, top birdwatching areas are Kinabalu Park, Danum Valley and the Kinabatangan river area. The 200 species in the Kinabatangan floodplain include all eight species of hornbills.

AMPHIBIANS AND REPTILES There are some 150 known endemic frog and reptile species across Borneo, but new discoveries happen regularly. Prominent reptiles include several rainforest and mangrove snakes, the bizarre-looking monitor lizard (*Varanus salvator*), geckos, giant turtles, painted terrapins, and a couple of crocodiles including the little-known Malayan false gharial and the notorious freshwater gharial.

Frogs According to WWF figures, Borneo is home to 150 known frog species. Within the past decade or so, at least seven frogs and a giant river toad have been discovered. A *Field Guide to the Frogs of Borneo* (see *Appendix 2* page 294) is available, describing such gems as the Bornean horned frog, green paddy frog, jade tree frog, blue-spotted tree frog, greater swamp frog and Mjoberg's dwarf litter frog.

Snakes Borneo's snakes number more than 150, of which a few are venomous. Among the several pythons is the reticulated python with its diagonal beadwork-like decoration in black, white and mustard. Others include the king cobra, common cobra and black spitting cobra, the Sarawak water snake and mangrove snakes.

Crocodiles Saltwater crocodiles (*Crocodylus porosus*), which live in the coastal swamps and rivers of Sarawak are nicknamed *bujang senang* ('happy bachelor') after one infamous 6m individual that went on a killing rampage in the Sungai Batang Lupar River in southeast Sarawak in 1993, before being shot dead. A lot more can be learnt about this bloodthirsty bachelor at Jong's Crocodile Farm near Kuching, where his skull is on display in a museum.

Care should be taken when visiting areas where there are crocodiles. You would be very ill-advised to swim in the rivers where they dwell. The warning from Sarawak Forestry says: 'Adult crocodiles have a largely fishy diet, though sometimes develop a taste for dead or dying prey. Prey are taken alive and, unless they are very small, are generally left to rot before being eaten. They tend to be aggressive during mating season or when guarding nesting areas. They are territorial and will attack if you come on to their territory.'

Malayan false gharial crocodile (*Tomistoma schlegelli*) These crocodiles have long, narrow noses tipped by a bulbous form. They are residents of Sarawak's rivers, peat swamps and mangroves, normally nesting by the riverbank. Despite being described by the state as a 'taxonomically unique and harmless crocodilian species', human parts were found in the stomach of a 3m female in the 1990s. They feed primarily on fish, but it is thought that this particular croc might have enjoyed some of the happy bachelor's leftovers.

Monitor lizards (*Varanus salvator*) Monitor lizards are decidedly antediluvian and reptilian in appearance. They live in all sorts of water habitats – even urban puddles – and can be seen lurking in tropical forests, mangroves, swamps, farmland and towns. Predatory and unfussy, monitor lizards will eat anything from young monkeys, snakes, lizards, birds, crabs, domestic chickens, carrion, human faeces and food waste. One species, the earless monitor lizard known as *cicak purba*, is a particularly bizarre, ancient- looking lizard.

FRESHWATER FISH Some of the most important recent discoveries have been freshwater fish, catfish in particular, which display amazing adaptations to their environment. The WWF recently announced the discovery of a 'forest-walking catfish' in Borneo, so-called because it can travel short distances over land. They are also named Labyrinth catfishes after the 'labyrinth organ', a specialist gill adaptation that allows a special suborder of fish to take in oxygen from the air. Another species of catfish secretes poisonous mucus that causes instant death to other fish in the vicinity.' Since the mid 1990s, 30 new freshwater fish have been identified in Borneo, but one of the most fascinating is one that has been known for a while. The green arowana, or dragon fish (*Scleropages formosus*), is a primitive 'living fossil' of a fish, representing an ancient lineage of fish species. Known locally as *kelesa*, it is a large freshwater fish found in Sarawak's rivers and lakes, preying on smaller fish, insects, worms, spiders, small lizards, small snakes and frogs.

INVERTEBRATES

Insects Lowland tropical rainforest harbours the greatest diversity of insect life on the planet, and the Bornean rainforest teems with insect life. There are over 100,000 species of beetles, hundreds of butterflies, stick and leaf insects, cicadas, cockroaches, dragonflies, termites, ants and mosquitoes on Borneo. At Kinabalu Park, insects are said to represent 'the bulk of the fauna' with thousands of different species. Like much of Borneo's natural history, insects are understudied, but Sabah Parks has been collaborating with the German Society for Tropical Ecology to increase understanding of the insect world. Kinabalu Park has some 300 butterflies, mostly around the lowland rainforest and foothills areas but also on lower montane slopes. Over 50 are endemic to Sabah – the stunning Rajah Brooke's birdwing (*Trogonoptera brookiana*) wears a cloak of black with a jagged frill of metallic emerald green triangles all along its wings. It was first catalogued by Alfred Russel Wallace in 1854 who collected hundreds of insect specimens in Borneo – he named it after Rajah James Brooke who presented him with the specimen. Many butterfly specimens are contained in the 'Borneensis' collection, which is housed within the University Malaysia in Sabah.

The website of the ASEAN Review of Biodiversity and Environmental Conservation (ARBEC) (*www.arbec.com.my*) provides good links to studies and findings in entomology and other areas. One such link is to Dr J Holloway's *Moths of Borneo* (*www.mothsofborneo.com*), an 18-volume work documenting the larger moths of Borneo – currently estimated at some 4,500 species, and all of which are illustrated in colour. The Universiti Sarawak Malaysia, Natural History Museum in London and ARBEC are responsible for making the entire work available online.

Crustaceans There is a great variety of freshwater crustaceans in Borneo such as lobsters, giant river prawns (*udang*) and crabs, all of which are important food sources to *Orang sungai* (river-dwelling populations). Mangroves especially have many interesting clawed critters such as hermit crabs and fiddler crabs which burrow into the mudflats among the mangroves. Male fiddlers are equipped with one overgrown, vividly coloured claw, which serves to attract females during the mating season and ward off male competitors trespassing on his mudpatch territory. The claw – called a *cheliped* – grows so big it can constitute 65% of his total body weight. The horseshoe crab, known in Sarawak as the *belangkas,* is not actually a crab but a descendant of an extinct marine arthropod lineage, the trilobites.

MARINE LIFE The coral reefs on the west and east coasts, particularly around the east coast's islands, support a huge variety of extravagantly coloured fish: lion fish with their 'mane' of chocolate brown and white frills, giant frogfish, hump head parrotfish, red and white clown fish, mandarin fish, snake eels and garden eels and many kinds of small colourful sand-dwelling gobies. Besides fish, there are molluscs and crustaceans including crabs, shrimps, giant clams, squid, blue-ringed octopus and sea urchins, sea cucumber, sea moths, cuttlefish, sea horses and other tubular-nosed pipefish. One of the fish to watch out for when diving is the clown triggerfish which can bite, charge at you or chase you to the top of the water in mating season.

Corals Used as a barometer of marine biodiversity and coral health, the reefs of Sabah and Sarawak are home to hundreds of species of bright-banded and flecked butterfly fish. The corals themselves are kaleidoscopic in colour and variety – fern, stag horn, mushroom, cabbage and brain varieties are all common. All hard and soft corals are protected species in Sarawak, but sadly many reefs are suffering from the effects of dynamite fishing.

Sharks There are quite a few sharks in Borneo's waters, though no deadly ones. It is common to see white-tip reef sharks when diving. In mid 2007 the Borneo shark (*Carcharhinus borneensis*) – a species of which no sightings were reported for over a century, and was thought to be extinct – was declared 'rediscovered' by Universiti Malaysia Sabah researchers. The shark can reach up to 20m in length and is brown on top with a white underside. The university's Borneo Marine Research Institute warned at the time sharks could soon be extinct in Sabah because of the over-harvesting of fins.

Dolphins All dolphins, porpoises and whales are protected in Sarawak and sightings of several species are commonplace: the Irrawaddy, bottlenose, Indopacific humpback, finless porpoise and pantropic spotted dolphin are all frequently seen, especially between March and September.

Sea turtles I have been lucky enough to experience the wonder of swimming among sea turtles – *penyu* – several times in Borneo, in the aquamarine waters off Sabah's east coast. They seem such solid, wise creatures, but several species are seriously threatened due to poaching (of both adults and eggs), habitat loss, pollution and accidental catch in fishing nets. Even without these extra pressures, life as a turtle is tough, with low reproduction rates and slim chances of survival of babies. Witnessing the plight of the youngsters trying to make their first journey to the sea (see *Chapter 7, Northeast Sabah*, page 204) can be heartbreaking.

The Turtle Islands in Sabah have the world's largest remaining populations of **hawksbill turtles** (*Eretmochelys imbricata*). The species is critically endangered, partly due to the enduring market for tortoiseshell jewellery and curios – the black and brown shell with splashes of yellow is unfortunately very popular. The name comes from their narrow pointed beak, reminiscent of a bird of prey, though locals know them as *penyu sisik* – 'scaled turtle', which refers to their attractive shells.

Larger **green turtles** (*Chelonia mydas*) are a protected species in Sabah and Sarawak, though Sarawak's population of green turtles has halved since 1970s. They are still one of the most widely seen and the biggest of the marine turtles, reaching over 1m in length. Despite weighing over 150kg they can they can swim at speeds of 15–20 km/h. Their name comes not from their carapace – this is olive or darker grey with swirled motifs – but from the colour of their meat. Like all marine turtles, they are a traditional food source for local people.

Whether indigenous people have the right to continue traditional practices of eating species now at risk of extinction is a controversial issue. Suluk people and the Bajau Laut ('sea gypsies') eat marine algae, sea grass, large fish including barracuda, grouper and red carp of deeper waters. Some also eat dolphins and

dugong. This tusked 'sea-cow' is a protected species and ocean heavyweight, reaching lengths of over 3m and touching on 600kg.

Ocean dangers This warning is issued to visitors of the Tanjung Datu National Park in western Sarawak, but applies to many other coral reefs around Borneo:

The reefs are home to several venomous creatures, including sea snakes, coral snakes, stonefish and cone shells. Marine snakes are generally harmless if undisturbed. Stonefish may conceal themselves in mud or sand around coral, especially at low tide, so do not walk or swim barefoot around coral reefs. Cone shells are highly venomous and should not be handled under any circumstances.

DEFORESTATION

Borneo is at the epicentre of deforestation worldwide. Half of all tropical timber used on the planet comes from this one island. Peat swamp forests like Sungai Putri are among the most important carbon sinks on the planet, yet vast areas of them have been drained in recent years for conversion to agricultural land, releasing millions of tons of CO2 into the atmosphere.

The Independent (online edition), December 2007

Just a few centuries ago, over 90% of Borneo was carpeted in thick, luscious forests. Since the age of discovery and exploration, humans have voraciously spread across the island exploiting natural resources. In the mid 1980s, 75% of the natural forest cover remained, but by the early 1990s, Sabah had only 66% of its original forest left and today, only 50% of Borneo's natural forest remains – a mere 7% of which is virgin lowland forest. The situation is most grave in Kalimantan (Indonesian Borneo), but Sabah and Sarawak too have been seriously affected by excessive forest exploitation.

Since the 1960s half of Sabah and Sarawak's primary forest has been logged, either selectively or intensively. Massive destruction was wreaked in the two Malaysian states for three decades, reaching a crescendo in the 1980s when an unrestrained timber industry raged, producing large-scale tropical hardwood exports, and exploitation of the forest for agriculture was rife and unchecked. Between 1963 and 1985, 2.8 million hectares of primary forest was logged in Sarawak alone, and deforestation rates doubled from 1980 to 1990. Things have slowed somewhat today, but 850,000 hectares are still estimated to be lost each year.

Decades of intensive logging for timber products, and the later extensive conversion of forests to rubber, palm oil and cocoa plantations, have been accompanied by huge losses of biodiversity and indigenous people's homes. Many timber licences issued by the Sarawak government cover the traditional lands of natives. Since early 1987, native people have been protesting about this encroachment on their homeland, putting up blockades across timber roads in a desperate attempt to stop logging activities (see *Indigenous land rights* box, *Chapter 1*, page 13). Logging in dipterocarp forest has been shown to be excessive, with poor management of water catchments and poorly controlled logging operations.

THE SAWMILLS OF MALAYSIA Sabah and Sarawak have been described as the 'sawmills of Malaysia'. More than 70% of Malaysia's plywood mills are in the two states, and they produce nearly all of the country's exported timber. Almost all trees felled are for export. Forestry underpins the economy and provides thousands of jobs – 40% of people in Sarawak are employed in the timber industry. The dipterocarp forests are the sites of most hardwood exploitation. Dipterocarp timber is not of very

BORNEO FOREST COVER 1950–2005

high quality though, and most is used to produce plywood and sawn timber for construction – door and window frames, flooring, decking and other such uses.

Ninety per cent of logging licences ('forest concessions') were supposedly terminated in Sabah in 2000. The industry says cutting forests has been reduced to a trickle but many logging operations are still carried out in government reserves, on large concessions which are still valid for decades to come. The woodchip industry in Malaysia apparently stopped in 1995, but hardwood exploitation has not ceased.

Critics say that palm oil has simply taken up where logging left off, wreaking just as much, if not more, environmental damage in its path. The industry took over as Sabah's biggest employer in the 1990s, and is now its biggest exporter, reaping 37% of total revenue – over a quarter of Malaysia's palm oil.

Forestry remains the biggest industry in Sarawak, though palm oil is hot on its heels. The round-the-clock forestry practices which were rife in Sarawak in the 1990s have apparently eased, but there are still large timber-harvesting operations. Amid international criticism from NGOs of continuing bad forestry practice, misinformation in the local media is common. News reports in Sarawak talk of the state's 'green gold' – lush tropical rainforest cover of 70% – with no mention of the extent of logging and losses. Such reports are used to let the forestry industry justify their activities, while turning the blame onto traditional shifting cultivation practices: 'As soon as we open a forestry road the natives come running in to clear the land', one timber company said in a report in 2007.

FACING UP TO THE CONSEQUENCES

If the forests become too fragmented, their ability to function efficiently is compromised. Half a rainforest does not contain half the number of original species. It contains far fewer.

From *Wild Borneo* by Nick Garbutt and Cede Prudente

As forest cover drops below 20%, many species are lost or become endangered. Scientific studies have shown logging in Sabah and Sarawak to have serious effects on the extent and intensity of reproduction of plant species including dipterocarp trees. An international symposium on biodiversity conservation in tropical rainforests (held in Japan in 2006) heard that the continuing deforestation in Malaysian Borneo was threatening 200 orchid species, 35 bird species, all rafflesia flowers and over 80% of primate species to the point of extinction.

In 2007, UNESCO joined the battle for Borneo's forests, saying that through illegal logging, the island's rainforests would soon be decimated. If forest depletion continues at the current rate, all lowland forest of Kalimantan is estimated to have disappeared by 2010, and by 2020 no undisturbed habitat outside of protected areas will remain in upland Borneo. Based on current estimated extinction rates, 13–42% of species inhabiting the region at the beginning of the 19th century could be gone by 2100.

CONSERVATION

The riches of Borneo's forests were one of the first things to attract outside interest to the island. As early as the 10th century, Borneo's Asian neighbours wanted a share in its natural bounties. The Chinese traded ceramic jars in exchange for Borneo's jungle treasures. 'Luxury goods' were produced for the Asian market, using Borneo's turtles, birds, bark and wood.

The magnitude of Borneo's natural riches is not yet reflected in sufficient levels of protection. However, things are changing. Revisions of Malaysia's (1972) Protection of Wildlife Act should enable a more solid legal framework to safeguard flora and fauna at a national level. In 2003, the Sarawak Forestry Corporation was created to manage the forests and national parks of the state. The concept of sustainable forest management was virtually non-existent until the late 1990s. The Corporation has adopted the International Union for the Conservation of Nature (IUCN) recommended action that at least 10% of its land area should be in totally protected areas.

SARAWAK One area in which Sarawak appears to be setting a precedent, at least relatively, is the legal protection of its wildlife and flora. Commercial sale and capture of wildlife is outlawed under its 1998 Wildlife Protection Ordinance, which imposes severe penalties – 50,000MYR and imprisonment is the going rate for killing a rhino. Hunting however, was not banned, as 'it was recognised that rural communities depend on wild meat'. The ordinance safeguards 52 of Sarawak's rare and endangered mammals, birds and reptiles as 'Totally Protected Species' and another 40 as 'Protected Animals'. Only two plants are 'Totally Protected' – the various rafflesia species and the dipterocarp tree species *D obloglofolius*. Another 46 plants, including many other dipterocarps and other tree species, are simply 'Protected'.

Sir Peter Crane

The rainforest of Borneo has been high on the international conservation agenda for decades. The reason is simple – Borneo is one of the world's most important centres of biological diversity and there is still time to make a difference. Over the past decade, significant help for conservation in the Borneo rainforest has come from many national and international initiatives, including the Darwin Initiative of the UK government. A key aim has been to help countries that are rich in biodiversity but relatively poor financially and in human resources, to develop innovative approaches to conservation and sustainability through international partnerships. An encouraging sign has been the 'Heart of Borneo' initiative that is supported by the governments of Brunei, Indonesia and Malaysia.

A primary target of national and international efforts in Borneo has been the conservation and sustainable management of the forests in Sabah, which has involved improving means to assess and manage plant diversity. A key partner in Borneo is Yayasan Sabah ('The Sabah Foundation'), a charitable foundation set up in the mid-1960s with the aim of improving education, health, welfare and other social services for the people of Sabah. Yayasan Sabah's income derives mainly from managing around a million hectares of tropical forest, of which about 15% is already devoted to primary forest reserves. These include the Danum Valley and Maliau Basin conservation areas, which are of global conservation importance.

The **Danum Valley Conservation Area** preserves some of the last remaining lowland rainforest in the whole island of Borneo. It is a pristine and more or less intact ecosystem of almost 450km², dominated by giant dipterocarp trees, legumes and other trees. It is also home to globally significant populations of large mammals, such as the Bornean pygmy elephant, the binturong (a type of arboreal civet), the sun bear and the Sumatran rhino. Danum and surrounding areas also support more than 4,000 orang-utans – the largest population of this primate in the world. First set aside by Yayasan Sabah, Danum is now designated as a Class I Protection Forest Reserve by the Sabah state government. As a result of a long-term partnership with the UK's Royal Society, it is well monitored from one of the most active of all research stations in southeast Asia.

These latest moves are the first signs of Sarawak moving towards adhering to international conventions in forest policy. The Protected Areas and Biodiversity Conservation Unit, a section of the Sarawak Forestry Corporation, is the 'custodian of Sarawak's national parks', responsible for environmental protection and conservation activities throughout the state. Its vision is to be 'globally recognized as a leader in management of totally protected areas'.

SABAH In some ways, Sabah is lagging behind in the modernity of its approach and extent of its parks, though it does have a dedicated Wildlife Department in which its conservation goals and strategies are vested. However, this department falls within the Ministry for Tourism Development, Environment, Science and Technology – not exactly a major government portfolio.

Only 13 mammals, reptiles and plants make it to Sabah's 'Totally Protected Species' list and, under the state's 1963 Fauna Conservation Ordinance, species are only protected if they are within a national park or other protected area. Since the late 1990s, the state is showing a more concerted effort to implement CITES and other international agreements on biodiversity. The Sabah Wildlife Conservation Enactment of 1997 was the first to seriously set aside and manage protected areas, and regulate wildlife exploitation.

In contrast to Danum, the **Maliau Basin Conservation Area** contains relatively little lowland rainforest, but it is nevertheless of great conservation importance. Covering nearly 600km², it is a remarkable block of tropical forest – virtually the entire catchment of the Maliau River – almost encircled by a dramatic escarpment that rises to over 1,600m in places. The basin includes spectacular waterfalls and vast tracts of forest. Again, this area was originally set aside by Yayasan Sabah and then formally upgraded to a Class I Reserve.

Perhaps the most exciting recent development for conservation on the whole island of Borneo has been the voluntary designation by Yayasan Sabah of a new and very significant conservation area. Recent exploratory expeditions to the **Imbak Canyon**, which included scientists from the UK and other countries, together with partners from Sabah and elsewhere in Malaysia, confirmed its truly exceptional conservation value. It is the last remaining significant area of unprotected lowland dipterocarp rainforest in Sabah and a crucial link between Danum to the southeast and Maliau to the southwest.

The conservation reserves at Danum Valley, the Maliau Basin and now the Imbak Canyon are a testament to the foresight of Yayasan Sabah in preserving large tracts of forest – for the people of Sabah, and also for the unique animals and plants that these areas sustain. It would be all too easy to harvest the timber and clear the land for oil palm plantations. Instead, watersheds are protected and key parts of the unique natural heritage of one of the world's most remarkable tropical islands have been secured for the future. The challenge now is how to manage the forest matrix in which the reserves are embedded in the best possible way. Well developed buffer zones, and forest management systems that encourage the free movement of plants and animals among the three protected areas, will be crucial. If implemented effectively they will ensure that the outstanding conservation values of Maliau, Imbak and Danum are secure, and that the global significance of these remarkable places will continue to increase – rather than diminish – for many, many years into the future.

Sir Peter Crane is a former Director of the Royal Botanic Gardens, Kew, England. He has been at the University of Chicago since 2006, and is a frequent visitor to Borneo's forests

THE FUTURE FOR BORNEO Since it hit world headlines and the US supplied major funding, there's been a lot of talk of the 'Heart of Borneo' conservation project agreement between the island's three nations. But even this large core of remaining rainforest is threatened says the WWF: 'Logging, land-clearing and conversion activities are considered to be the greatest threats to the Heart of Borneo. Today the conversion to oil palm plantations can be considered one of the biggest threats for the remaining rainforests in Borneo and the species that inhabit them.'

With such an apparently bleak outlook, can things be turned around? Experts in forest rehabilitation say the effects of selective logging on biodiversity are not necessarily irreversible. Dr Glen Reynolds, senior scientist at the Danum Valley Field Centre, says 'even lowland rainforests which have been selectively logged still support the highest levels of biodiversity …. It is the conversion of forests to plantations – particularly oil palm – that has the really disastrous impacts on biodiversity.'

THE HEART OF BORNEO – NOW OR NEVER As the forests of Borneo rapidly disappear, it is becoming apparent that the current fragmented network of protected areas does not have long-term viability. For forests to survive they must be within in a connected network to prevent isolated pockets of forest being doomed to failure.

Expanses of pristine rainforest teeming with life still exist in Borneo's hilly interior, but only parts are protected. As logging companies and plantation owners set their sights on the next lucrative schemes, WWF has stepped in with an ambitious project to save what is left.

The 'Heart of Borneo' refers to a region the size of the United Kingdom – 220,000km^2 – in the central northern region of the island, encompassing parts of Malaysian, Bruneian and Indonesian Borneo. This region is of undeniable biological importance, harbouring up to 6% of the world's biodiversity, a figure expected to rise with new discoveries; three new species have been found here every month for the past ten years. In January 2007 the governments of Malaysia, Brunei and Indonesia officially endorsed the project, an unprecedented multi-national commitment to conservation of biodiversity.

Conserving the Heart of Borneo area will preserve the integrity of watersheds that supply the entire island, maintain global climate-regulating forests and safeguard indigenous communities from loss of their homes and cultures – not to mention preserving the thousands of species that inhabit the region. There are challenges to be faced – the greatest threats are commercial (and illegal) logging and clearing for plantations, particularly oil palm. But WWF's vision is realistic. Recognising the increasing global demand for oil palm, and that more plantations are needed to meet this demand, it is attempting to identify areas where such developments would have the least devastating environmental effects.

The multi-national commitment to the Heart of Borneo project was a huge triumph for the WWF, but the real test will be time. Whilst none of the current advances have come too early, most agree they are not too late – and Borneo has a chance to turn things around. Mubariq Ahmad, WWF's executive director in Indonesia said: 'If someone had tried something like a "Heart of Sumatra" project 20 years ago, what we see today would be very different. This is why these three governments have committed to save whatever remains in Borneo, after realising that if they do not do something now, the future of Borneo's forests will be much like Sumatra today – most of them are gone.'

PROTECTED AREAS

Sarawak Sarawak claims to have one of the most extensive protected-area networks in Malaysia, encompassing 18 national parks, four wildlife sanctuaries and five nature reserves, covering a total area of 512,387ha. In a state nearly the size of England, this constitutes less than 5% of the land. Nearly half of the state is 'Permanent Forest Estate', apparently for 'sustainable forestry', though critics would say this is simply logging. Currently 15 protected areas are open to the public.

The 18 **national parks**, covering a total of nearly 300,000ha, are as follows:

Name	Area (ha)	Division	Date gazetted
Bako	2,727	Kuching	4 May 1957
Gunung Gading	4,196	Kuching	3 May 1988
Kubah	2,230	Kuching	11 May 1989
Tanjung Datu	1,379	Kuching	19 May 1994
Talang Satang	19,414	Kuching	4 November 1999
Kuching Wetland	6,610	Kuching	10 October 2002
Batang Ai	24,040	Sri Aman	11 May 1989
Maludam	43,147	Sri Aman	31 May 2000
Similajau	7,064	Bintulu	20 April 1978
(Similajau Extension	1,932	Bintulu	2 June 2000)

Bukit Tiban	8,000	Bintulu	31 May 2000
Gunong Mulu	52,865	Miri	3 October 1974
Niah	3,138	Miri	2 January 1975
Lambir Hills	6,949	Miri	26 June 1975
Loagan Bunut	10,736	Miri	29 August 1991
Usun Apau	49,355	Miri	29 September 2005
Gunung Buda	6,235	Limbang	18 January 2001
Pulong Tau	59,817	Limbang, Miri	24 March 2005
Rajang Mangroves	9,373	Sibu	3 August 2000

The five **nature reserves** are:

Name	Area (ha)	Division	Date gazetted
Wind Cave	6.16	Kuching	4 November 1999
Sama Jaya	37.92	Kuching	23 March 2000
Semenggoh	653	Kuching	20 April 2000
Bukit Hitam	147	Limbang	22 June 2000
Bukit Sembiling	101	Limbang	22 June 2000

The four **wildlife sanctuaries** are not open to visitors – they exist to 'preserve and conserve vulnerable ecosystems or endangered wildlife'.

Name	Area (ha)	Division	Date gazetted
Samunsam	6,092	Kuching	1 July 1978
(Samunsam Extension	16,706	Kuching	29 May 2000)
Pulau Tukong Ara Tukong	1.4	Kuching	28 February 1985
Lanjak Entimau	168,758	Sarikei, Sibu, Kapit	2 February 1983
Sibuti Bird Sanctuary	678	Miri	29 May 2000

Sabah Things are very different in Sabah, where there are just six national parks, gazetted under the 1984 Parks Enactment and managed by Sabah Parks. Three of these are terrestrial parks: Mount Kinabalu, the Crocker Range and

PROTECTED AREAS OF SARAWAK

KEY

1 Samunsan WS	10 Lanjak Entimau WS
2 Gunung Gading NP	11 Simalajau NP
3 Kubah NP	12 Bukit Tiban NP
4 Semenggoh NR	13 Niah NP
5 Sama Jaya NR	14 Sibuti NP
6 Bako NP	15 Lambir Hills NP
7 Maludam	16 Loagan Bunut NP
8 Rajang Mangrove NP	17 Gunung Mulu NP
9 Batang Ai	18 Pulung Tau NP

WS = Wildlife Sanctuary NP = National Park
NR = Nature Reserve

SOUTH CHINA SEA

Sabah

KALIMANTAN (INDONESIA)

Tawau Hills; and three are marine parks: Turtle Island, Tunku Abdul Rahman and Pulau Tiga. In total, this approximates 266,000ha. Under the 1968 Forest Enactment (revised in 1984) there are seven classes of 'Protected Forest Reserves' ranging from 'Class I Protection Forest Reserve' to 'Class VI Virgin Jungle Reserve' and 'Class VII Wildlife Reserve'. Class II forest – commercial forest – is not listed on Sabah Forestry's website and amounts for the bulk of these reserves – 2,685,199ha.

According to *Discovering Sabah* (Natural History Publications, Borneo), of the seven classifications, only

four of these may be regarded as protected areas. The main function of Class I Protection Forests is to safeguard water supplies, soil fertility and environmental quality. Danum Valley and Maliau Basin, managed by Sabah Foundation, are two such reserves. Class VI, Virgin Jungle Reserves, comprise some 50 relatively small areas intended to provide undisturbed forest for research purposes and the preservation of gene pools. The fourth conservation class is Class VII, Wildlife Reserves, which are for the protection of wildlife. The core of the large Tabin wildlife reserve today falls under Forest Class VII.

In 1997 the Wildlife Conservation Enactment enabled the creation of more protected areas. There are projects in the pipelines for gazetting more areas.

Wildlife/bird/marine sanctuaries	Size (ha)
Lower Kinabatangan	27,800
Sipadan	12
Kota Belud	12,200
Mantanani Kecil	61
Kota Kinabalu	24
Lankayan Billean Tegapil Marine Conservation Area	30,000

PROTECTED AREAS OF SABAH

KEY
1 Maligan FR
2 Gunung Lumaku FR
3 Klias FR
4 Sungai Binsuluk FR
5 Taman Negara Banjaran Crocker Park
6 Crocker Range FR
7 Kinabalu Park
8 Mandamai FR
9 Bidu-Bidu FR
10 Bukit Kuamas FR
11 Bukit Taviu FR
12 Ulu Telupid FR
13 Tawai FR
14 Lungmanis FR
15 Kabili Sepilok FR
16 Kinabatangan WS
17 Kulamba WR
18 Tabin WR
19 Mount Hatton FR
20 Silabukan FR
21 Danum Valley FR
22 Sungai Imbak FR
23 Maliau Basin FR
24 Tawau Hills Park-Ulu Kalumpang
25 Mount Pock PFR
26 Pulau Timbun Mata FR

FR = Forest Reserve WS = Wildlife Sanctuary
WR = Wildlife Reserve PFR = Protection Forest Reserve

SOUTH CHINA SEA

SULU SEA

BRUNEI

Sarawak

KALIMANTAN (INDONESIA)

CELEBES SEA

Habitats
Dense undergrowth is a key
characteristic of secondary forest.
(NG) page 89

above left At a towering 4,095m Mount Kinabalu is the fourth tallest mountain in Southeast Asia. It sits within the World-Heritage Gunung Kinabalu National Park (LIT/TIPS) page 179

above right Upper montane forest covers the slopes of Mount Kinabalu — in the distance you can see the mountain's distinctive 'Donkey's Ear' peak (NG) page 92

below Mangroves at high tide, Bako National Park (NG) page 96 right **The mist filled canopy of Ulu Temburong National Park, Brunei** (BT) page 90

below **The reefs surrounding the idyllic outer-lying islands support extensive marine ecosystems** (ST) page 98

Deforestation

above   Illegal logging is devasting
Borneo's rainforests. In the
1980s 75% of Malaysian
Borneo was covered in
primary forest; today that
has been reduced to 50%
(GAR/TIPS) page 113

left   NGOs and passionate locals
do what they can to
replace cleared areas (TT)
page 115

Forest Flowers

below   Borneo is said to house one tenth of the world's orchid species. They favour upper montane forest (NG) page 95

right   The brilliantly named lipstick flower (BR/NV) page 95

bottom left   A cluster of fungi near the forest floor (NG)

bottom right   Spider lily (TT)

Rafflesia

There are 17 different species of the Rafflesia or 'corpse flower' — so called for the whiff of rotting flesh it gives off when in bloom — all of them are endemic to Borneo. The one featured above left is a 3—4 day-old *Rafflesia pricei* (NG) page 94

The giant bloom of a *Rafflesia keithei* on the forest floor — indigenous tribes believe the species have aphrodisiac powers (NG)

The bloom only lasts for a week. This specimen is 8—10 days old (NG)

Pitcher plants

above   Two varieties of aerial pitcher plant, *Nepenthes rafflesiana*. These carnivorous plants lure flies and insects to the slippery mucus-lined rim where they fall into the pool of liquid within and are dissolved by enzymes and bacteria secreted by the plant (NG) page 95

below   These ground pitcher plants, *Nepenthes ampullaria,* have adapted to survive on the forest floor (NG) page 95

Aerial view of the jungle. Borneo is a
biodiversity hotspot and contains more than
half of all world's plant and animal species

Mammals

above   **The orang-utan — 'man of the forest' in Malaysian — is endemic to Borneo** (NG) page 99

left   **Male silvered langurs live in groups with 9—30 other individuals around mangrove and riverine forest** (NG) page 104 *above left* The male proboscis monkey is easily recognisable thanks to its shlong-shaped nose (NG) page 103

above right Thankfully, the female has a more modest nose! (NG)

below Naturalists have been unable to classify the adorable tarsier — it's relegated to its own taxonomic group (NG) page 105 *above* Male Bornean pygmy elephants at Kinabatangan River, Sabah (NG) page 105

left Due to poaching, the sumatran rhino is listed as critically endangered on the **WWF IUCN** Red List (CT) page 106

below left Despite being Borneo's largest predator, the one-metre long clouded leopard is relatively small (DP) page 107 *above* The leopard cat, *Felis begalensis,* sleeps in hollow trees, caves and root cavities during the day, emerging at night to hunt bats, birds and rodents (NG)

below A nocturnal Malay civet foraging, *Viverra Tangalunga* (NG) page 108 *above* **The tree-dwelling sun bear is the world's smallest bear and endemic to Borneo** (MJ) page 108

below **The comical bearded pig is incredibly shy. It forages for earthworms and fallen fruits** (NG) page 108 *above*　The lesser mouse deer is the world's smallest hoofed animal — weighing in at just 2kg (SS/NV) page 90

below　The *pangolin* — the Malay word for 'something that rolls up' — or scaly anteater is nocturnal　(RK) page 98

The bizarre looking colugo, or flying lemur, glides (not flies) using the patagium membrane between its limbs (NG) page 108

Get eye-to-eye with canopy-dwelling species: a tree-top walk at Ulu Temburong National Park, Brunei

(TT) page 145

Birds

above   The large stork-billed kingfisher is highly territorial and has been known to chase away eagles (NG)

left   The majestic harpy eagle. Standing at half the height of an average man, it's the world's largest eagle (BT) page 109

below left   Lesser fish eagle, *Ichthyophaga humilis*, scanning the water for prey (NG) page 205

opposite page

top   The rhinocerous hornbill is the second-largest hornbill and Sarawak's national bird (BT) page 109

middle   The oriental pied-hornbill is found throughout Asia and particularly fond of lowland rainforest (NG) page 109

bottom   The orange-bellied flowerpecker prefers lowland rainforest and mangroves (RP)

above left The endemic Bornean treepie can mimic the calls of other birds (RP)

above right, The chestnut-crested yuhina (above right) and white-crowned shama (below left) both favour
below left, montane habitats, whilst the dusky munia (featured below right) — an Old World finch species
below right — favours lowland forest (RP)

Frogs

right Wallace's flying frog is named after influential biologist, Alfred Russel Wallace, who collected the first specimen for identification in the 19th century (NG) page 110

below right Spotted stream frog (NG)

bottom right Harlequin treefrog (NG)

below Wallace's flying frog mid glide (NG)

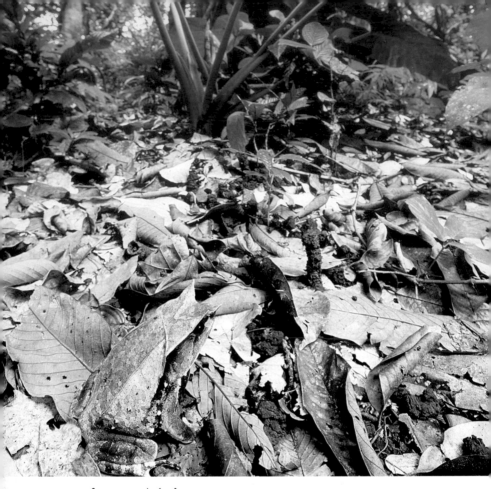

above	**Can you spot the frog?** (NG)
below right	**The Bornean horned frog is perfectly camouflaged among the leaf litter** (NG)
below left	**Female file-eared frog laying eggs and mating with two males** (NG)

Reptiles

right   Misleadingly, the black spitting cobra doesn't spit; it sprays its venom. A gust of air is expelled from the lung which aerosolises the venom ejected from the fangs (SK) page 110

below   The venomous yellow-ringed cat snake in threat posture, it hunts among mangroves and is an adept swimmer (NG)

bottom   Juvenile Wagler's pit viper on Asam Paya palm (NG)

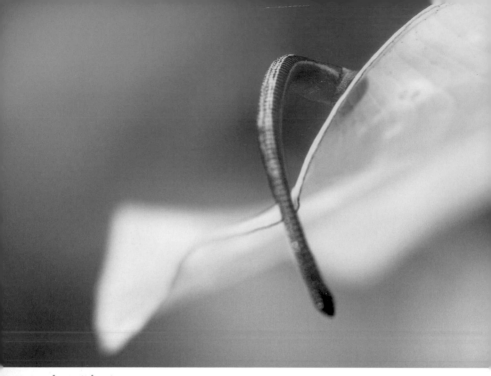

Invertebrates

above   Tiger leech waiting for a host. Despite their blood-thirsty reputation some leeches take great care to nuture their young — a highly unusual trait among invertebrates (NG)

below   Did you know the adult emperor scorpion has a fluorescent mineral in its outer shell that makes it glow under UV light? (NG)

above Male three-horned rhino beetle: he uses his horn in mating battles against other males. Relative to size, these beetle are the strongest creatures on the planet, they can lift up to 850 times their own bodyweight (NG)

right Giant stag beetle — their distinctive mandibles are named after a stag's antler and are used for fighting (NG)

above   Thorn spiders construct new webs every night (NG)

above right   Dead-leaf mimic mantis lying in ambush (NG)

right   Chinese lantern bug — all varieties attract prey by lighting the appendage on their head (NG)

below   Female leaf insect (NG)

left   **Sunrise and mist over lowland dipterocarp rainforest, Danum Valley** (NG) page 90

below   **Male Rajah Brooke birdwing; females are browner and have white flashes on the tips of the wings. It was named after Sir James Brooke, the Rajah of Sarawak, by naturalist Alfred Russel Wallace in 1855** (NG) page 111

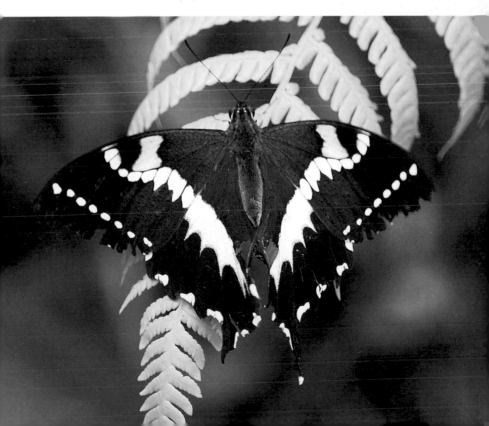

Aerial view of Semporna — the jumping-off point for diving trips to Sipadan (GAR/TIPS) page 217

Marine Life

top **Due to the presence of symbiotic algae (zooxanthellae), mushroom coral fluoresceses under light** (RD/WF) page 112

above **Brain coral grows slowly but can reach 6ft high and live for hundreds of years** (FB/WF) page 112

right **Cabbage coral** (MS/WF) page 112

The pristine waters around Sipadan allow fragile soft coral colonies to flourish. (FBWF)

right The endangered green
turtle — so-called
because of the fat
underneath its shell
(ANMA) page 112

below The critically
endangered hawksbill
turtle feeds on sea
sponges and jellyfish
(JC/NV) page 112

above   Unlike the manatee, the herbivorous dugong has a fluked, dolphin-like tail and feeds almost exclusively on sea grass (MB/WF) page 113

above left   Until March 2007, the Borneo shark hadn't been seen since 1859 and was thought to be extinct. Photographs of it are very rare; this dead specimen is the only image we could find (UWT) page 112

left   The endangered Irrawaddy dolphin is found near coasts and estuaries, but is notoriously shy. This picture was taken in captivity, to allow the reader to see what the species looks like (PK) page 248

opposite

top   The saltwater crocodile is the the largest of the *Crocodylus* species and can grow up to 6m long (PT/W) page 110

bottom   Rare for crocodiles, the Malayan false gharial does not care for its young after birth (W) page 110

Bumphead parrotfish often grow to 1.2 metres in length and can live for up to 40 years. The bulbous forehead and exposed teeth plate are used to break off and gnaw at coral containing the algae they feed on (KS)

left Named after the rob[e]
of an Imperial Chine[se]
mandarin
(bureaucrat), the
mandarinfish sticks
closely to reefs
(QW) page 111

below The first dorsal spin[e]
of the giant frogfish[,]
modified as a fishin[g]
lure to attract prey
(WM) page 111

bottom The halimeda ghost
pipefish can float
upside-down feeding
on crustaceans safel[y]
because it is perfect[ly]
camouflaged to look
like seaweed
(JPT) page 112

opposite

above Only the male fiddle[r]
crab possesses an
over-sized claw; it'[s]
used during courtsh[ip]
to attract females a[nd]
ward off competing
males (BR/NV) page 111

below The horseshoe crab [is]
more closely related [to]
scorpions and spide[rs]
than other crabs
(HA/NV) page 111

above Between April and July scalloped hammerhead sharks gather in their hundreds off Layang Layang – a manmade atoll 300km northwest of Kota Kinabulu (E) page 179

left Hammerhead sharks are endangered and the sale of pups in fish markets like this seriously threatens the regeneration of stocks (NKP)

below Fishing for sharks fins – used in soup and Chinese medicine – is illegal, but covertly continues in Malaysian Borneo because the financial reward for fishermen is often hard to resist (NKP)

Protected forest reserve	Size (ha)
Class I Protection	342,216
Class II Commercial	2,685,119
Class III Domestic	7,350
Class IV Amenity	20,767
Class V Mangrove	316,024
Class VI Virgin Jungle	90,386
Class VII Wildlife Reserve	132,653

Marine parks (including coral reef)	Size (ha)
Kinabalu	75,370
Tungku Abdul Rahman	4,020
Turtle Islands	1,740
Pulau Tiga	15,864
Tawau Hills	27,927
Crocker Range	139,919

Source: *Discovering Sabah*, Natural History Publications, Borneo

BRUNEI The government of Brunei Darussalam claims that 'primary tropical jungle' covers about 75% of the country, though also cites forestry as a major activity. Thanks to oil, Brunei has had little need to cut down its forests for export to the extent its Malaysian neighbours have, so the country's rainforests, peat swamp and mangrove environments are among the better preserved in the region. However, its record is not entirely clean – forestry is a major economic activity; mangrove woods have been culled to make charcoal, and mangroves are continually being cleared for urban and industrial developments. Urban pollution is a major environmental issue, with sewage from the huge water village in its capital running directly into the river and its ecosystems. Sustainable forest management is a new concept, but the country is aware of the need to preserve everything it has left and is setting itself up to be a beacon of sustainability and ecotourism.

The Forest Act categorises forest reserve into five types: Protection Forest; Conservation Area; Recreational Area, Production Forest and National Park. There is just one national park, the 50,000ha Ulu Temburong National Park, created in 1988 within a huge forestry reserve. A further 32,000ha of reserves are classified for conservation purposes, and there are many urban and rural recreational areas. A respectable 15% of Brunei's total land area is fully protected. The Forestry Department manages the reserves and has started to carry out some early-day greening activities such as rehabilitating degraded lands and raising public awareness. There has been talk of bolstering the Wildlife Protection Act, established in 1978, to give it more scope to create national parks and sanctuaries.

Natural History CONSERVATION

3

Part Two

BRUNEI

International telephone code +673
Currency Brunei dollar (BND)
Exchange rate US$1 = 1.47BND, €1 = 2.00BND, £1 = 2.53BND (October 2008)
Climate Humid, average daily temperature 28°C
Geography 5,765km², situated on Borneo's northwest coast
Population 372,000; 73% Malay, 15% Chinese, 12% various indigenous tribes
Capital Bandar Seri Begawan (BSB)
Visa requirements 3-day transit (5BND) or 3-week (20BND) on arrival; see
Chapter 2, page 45
Language Official language Malay; Chinese and English also widely spoken.
Emergency numbers Police ☎ 993; Fire ☎ 995; Ambulance ☎ 991
Banking/business hours 08.00/9.00–16.00/17.00 Mon–Fri,
08.00/9.00–11.00/12.00 Sat
Shopping centre hours 10.00–22.00 daily
Government website www.brunei.gov.bn
Tourist board ☎ +673 238 2822; **e** info@tourismbrunei.com;
www.tourismbrunei.com

4

Brunei Darussalam

Being an inkblot of a nation has bruised neither Brunei's self-image nor its prosperity. The Islamic pride and sovereign swishness are embodied in the flag – regal, striking and strict all at once – the yellow banner with white and black diagonal stripes bears a red insignia of wings, umbrellas and masts signifying justice, peace and prosperity. A lofty sense of all three permeates the watery ambience of Brunei, along with the sounds of Muslim prayer time emanating from its golden-domed mosques. Brunei is the most strong-spirited Muslim place in Borneo – nearly two-thirds of its population are of Islamic faith, and the foundations of the national philosophy *Melayu Islam Beraja* – 'Malay Islam Monarchy' – are deeply entrenched. While it describes itself as a moderate Muslim country, there are signs of severity: the death penalty for drug possession, imprisonment for drinking alcohol, fines for not fasting, corporal punishment with rattan canes, and less individual freedom than in Malaysia. Women are 'strongly encouraged' by state authorities to cover their hair with a *tudung* and men wear the traditional Malay cap, the *songkok*. This clothing is not necessarily a sign of oppression; it is cultural, and the people of Brunei are smiling, warm people, washed over by gentle Malay-ness, if a little socially straightjacketed.

For their reverence to the monarchy and Muslim ideology there are many rewards. People get free education and health care, tax-free salaries, cheap housing loans and lots of other incentives to comply There's virtually no crime, unemployment is below 5% and inflation hovers at around 0.5%. Brunei is also a youthful nation – 90% of its population are under 50. Duty-free imports account for the majority of goods consumed, from food to electronics, and most people have two modern imported cars – driving around is a breeze on the uncongested roads. A high quality of life is also accorded by gardens and space: Brunei is ten times the size of Singapore with one-tenth of the population, and green spaces are spread generously between settlements.

The modern face of Brunei is still in the making. The sultan-owned national carrier Royal Brunei Airlines only started to promote its realm to the world in the mid 1990s and promotes Brunei as a 'stop-over' to Sabah and Sarawak. The country is aware of its size limitations, yet Bruneians love their quality of life and boast that they have jungle, sea, mosques and malls on their back doorstep. In the Brunei insider's guide, *BiG Magazine*, local DJ and television presenter Jenny Malai Ali aptly describes Brunei as 'a magical little place that offers the luxuries of the new world against a rich and beautiful historical backdrop'.

HISTORY

Historical archives tell of trading between the Chinese and a region invariably called Puni, Poli and Bun Lai as far back as the 6th century, which thrived from

Once the world's richest man, Hassanal Bolkiah has had to settle for being the world's second-wealthiest ruler, with US$20 billion to his sultanate. Inside his palace there are purportedly stables, a concert hall, helipads, several swimming pools, 200 bathrooms, a priceless art collection and many luxury 'toys' including Boeing airplanes, helicopters (the sultan is a licensed pilot and did his military training at Sandhurst in England), 200 ponies and an automobile empire of some 2,000 cars including Rolls-Royces, Ferraris, McLaren F1s, Porsches and Bentleys. The perennially handsome polo-playing sultan is revered by his subjects who call him Sultan Kitani, 'our sultan', and he is seen to share his riches around and have a genuine interest in the people. Despite the seemingly down-to-earth manner with which he deals with the public, nothing can hide the lavish lifestyle he leads, and the privileged halo of friends that surrounds him. A list of honorary titles such as *Dato* and *Pehin* are handed out on his birthday. Vast amounts of media space are given over to every detail of the royal family's official life, but never his private one.

In 2005, the sultan's third marriage was to a woman 32 years his junior – then 26-year-old Azrinaz Mazhar Hakim. The queen, or raja, of Brunei is his first wife (and first cousin) Anak Saleha whom he married in 1965. His two wives (he divorced his second wife in 2003), appear with him on all official occasions. Islam allows men to have up to 4 wives. The sultan's birthday is celebrated each July with three weeks of public 'partying' in which the palace dons a large shawl of fairy lights and big (booze-free) festivities take place.

the 10th century. In the 14th century, a Malay–Hindu–Buddhist settlement developed on the banks of the Sungai Brunei River. Folklore dictates that on discovering the area the newcomers exclaimed '*barunah!*' – Malay for 'this is it!' Barunah later changed to *Barunai*, derived from the Sanskrit word *varuna*: a nation of seafarers. The name of the small trading post endured countless variations by Chinese, European and other merchants, explorers and passers-by, cited as Bornei, Borney, Borneo, Bruneo, Burne and Bruni. The first Malay king to seriously entertain Islam was Raja Awang Alak Betatar. He changed his name and became the first sultan of Brunei, Muhammad Shah, completely altering the course of history and cultural following in Brunei. He ruled from 1363 to 1402. The line-up of sultans ever since represents the longest-lasting – though colonially interrupted – dynasty in the world, now into its 29th sultanship.

The signing of the 1906 Brunei Treaty paved the way for a strong period of British influence in Brunei which has left a permanent mark on its royalist Islamic make-up. Executive powers were handed over to Britain through a British Residential System, by which a Brunei-dwelling British diplomat advised the sultan on all state matters excluding Malay customs and religion. In 1929 Brunei's fortunes took a positive turn when the only major onshore oilfield was discovered in the southern Seria District. Before the outbreak of World War II, British-administered Brunei was already enjoying a lot of oil-export profits. At the end of Japanese occupation (1945), retreating British troops sabotaged all oil infrastructure in Brunei and Sarawak to prevent them falling into enemy hands. Brunei Town was also bombed when allies repossessed it. After the war the British era in Brunei began to wane, and in 1959 a constitutional agreement handed back more domestic rule to the sultanate. At around the same time, the Brunei Shell Petroleum Company started offshore drilling, striking oil for the first time in 1963, off the coast of Belait.

The 28th sultan, Haji Omar Ali Saiffuddien III (the father of the current sultan), is widely regarded as the architect of modern Brunei. From his ascendancy in 1950 he used Brunei's oil revenues to finance a five-year development plan to bring some modernity and infrastructure to the town.

A DEMOCRATIC BRUNEI? The British Gurkhas army of Nepalese troops are revered in Brunei today for helping bring to an end Brunei's last brush with democracy – a 1962 coup by the pro-democratic Brunei People's Party (PRB). It, and other political parties, have been outlawed ever since. Brunei was the only Malay state to snub the Malaysian Federation in 1963 through fear of losing the absolute monarchy's regal hold and oil wealth. It remained a British Protectorate until 1 January 1984, when it attained full independence.

In late 2007, the new 62 million BND Legislative Council was christened after being fast-tracked towards construction in two years. It's said to be part of some slow intentional steps towards more democracy by the sultan. Whether that process will also be fast-tracked remains to be seen, but the sultan is apparently all too aware that his kingdom is something of a relic, with the clock of a changing world ticking overhead. He even hosted a conference on royalty in 2006 at which there were many predictions – among them those of his majesty himself – of the eventual demise of absolute monarchies.

GETTING THERE AND AWAY

Brunei is divided into four administrative divisions. **Brunei Muara** which includes the capital Bandar Seri Begawan, **Tutong, Belait** and **Temburong**. At an eighth of the size of Switzerland, the country's longest trip by car takes little more than three hours.

BY AIR

Brunei International Airport The only airport in Brunei is 11km from the capital, Bandar Seri Begawan. The airport is connected to worldwide destinations with services by Singapore Airlines, Thai Airways, Philippines Airlines, Malaysia Airlines, and Dragonair through their hubs in Singapore, Bangkok, Kuala Lumpur and Hong Kong.

National carrier Royal Brunei Airlines (RBA) fly from Bandar Seri Begawan to 20 major cities in the Asian Pacific, the Middle East and Europe. RBA have direct flights several times weekly between Sydney (suspended at time of going to press), Brisbane, Perth, Darwin and Auckland and Bandar Seri Begawan. They fly from London to Bandar Seri Begawan (via Dubai) three times a week.

Within Borneo, RBA have several daily flights between Bandar Seri Begawan and both Kota Kinabalu and Kuching.

Airline offices All are in Bandar Seri Begawan city centre.

✈ **Royal Brunei Airlines** RBA Plaza, Jln Sultan; ☏ 2212222/2240500
✈ **MAS** ☏ 2224141/2

✈ **Air Asia** ☏ 2333045
✈ **Singapore Airlines** ☏ 2244901/2
✈ **Thai Airways** ☏ 2242991/2.

For flight information at the airport ☏ 2331747.

Getting to/from the airport The Central Line buses stop at the airport every 15 minutes and make several stops in the city district before arriving at the city bus terminal. Some hotels have airport transfers. Average taxi fares to the city are

If you have already travelled in Sabah or Sarawak, you start out feeling you are paying the same price in Brunei – about 1BND for most market produce, a bus fare or a bottle of water, until you realise that the dollar is double the value of the Malaysian ringgit so you are effectively paying twice as much for most food items, transport and in some cases accommodation. If you are on a tight budget, eat mostly at food stalls and coffee shops, and take buses or walk rather than taking taxis. You may be limited with accommodation, though good deals can be struck in budget hotels. In the words of one budget traveller: 'Brunei may be a wealthy country but it is certainly affordable.' One thing that does drop by almost half in price between Malaysia and Brunei is petrol – it costs just 53 cents a litre. A litre of mineral water costs 1BND.

15BND. The website of Brunei Tourism (*www.tourismbrunei.com/info/ground.html*) has a useful list of fares to dozens of destinations – hotels, city landmarks and attractions – with the airport taxi service.

BY CAR Bound on all sides by the Malaysian state of Sarawak, the 'Pan-Borneo' Highway – a network of federal roads – connects Brunei with Miri in Sarawak and Kota Kinabalu in Sabah. It takes about 12 hours to drive between Brunei and Kuching, and about half that to Kota Kinabalu. The immigration post when travelling to or from Miri is at the Sungai Tujoh River between Sarawak and Kampong Sungai Teraban in the Belait District of Brunei. Travelling to or from Limbang in Sarawak, the trip to Bandar Seri Begawan is 45 minutes and the immigration control post is Kuala Lurah. From Limbang it is also possible to travel on to Kota Kinabalu.

BY BOAT

To and from Sarawak Limbang in northern Sarawak is a 30-minute express boat ride away from Brunei's capital. Regular water taxis and express boat services to Limbang as well as neighbouring Lawas (in Sarawak) leave from the riverside Temburong Ferry Terminal on Jalan Residency in Bandar Seri Begawan city.

To and from Pulau Labuan Car and passenger ferry services link Brunei with the Malaysian island of Labuan. The ferries operate from the new Serasa Terminal in the Muara District, about 20km from the capital. Take the blue Eastern Line bus (No 33).

Boats leave six times a day, at 07.30, 08.30, 09.00, 13.00, 15.30 and 16.40. From Labuan to Brunei the departure times are 08.00, 11.00, 12.15, 14.00, 16.00 and 16.30. The journey takes around an hour and a half. Ferries to Lawas also leave from here, but at the time of writing had been temporarily suspended. Ferry schedules are subject to change and it is best to check the boat schedule either online (*www.marine.gov.bn*) or by calling the **Shipping Office of the Marine Department** (\ *02 773071 for services to Labuan & Lawas;* \ *02 244251 for services to Temburong & Limbang*) ahead of a trip.

BY BUS The bus journey between Sarawak and Brunei is circuitous: almost five hours, three different buses and a ferry to cover 120km. Even within Brunei a change of bus is required between Seria and Kuala Belait. The journey will cost around 20BND, depending on how you tackle the trip.

LOCAL TOUR OPERATORS

Continental Yachting Tours ✆ 2233200;
✉ continentaltour@brunet.bn; www.onebrunei.com
Freme Travel Services ✆ 2234277;
✉ fremebsb@brunet.com; www.freme.com. An
established company said to be good with British
clients.
Intrepid Tours ✆ 2221685; ✉ tours@bruneibay.net;
www.bruneibay.net
Mega Borneo Marketing Services ✆ 2224026;

✉ megaborneo@brunet.bn. Relatively new, but
recommended. Familiar with British, Australian &
continental clients.
Sunshine Borneo Tours and Travel No 2 Simpang 146,
Jln Kiarong, Kampung Kiulap, (BSB); ✆ 2446509,
after hours ✆ 8715863; ✉ sales@
exploreborneo.com; www.exploreborneo.com. Highly
efficient for day trips & excursions. A second branch
is found in the lobby arcade of the Empire Hotel &
Country Club in Jerudong (✆ 2610578)

BANDAR SERI BEGAWAN

Few people have even heard of Brunei's capital city before visiting, and it's hardly the most easily remembered name. Fortunately, everyone calls it BSB. Known as Brunei Town (*Pekan Brunei*) up until 1970, the idyllic-sounding replacement of *Bandar Seri Begawan* (roughly translated as 'city of the glorious retiree') honours the 28th sultan who took the title Seri Begawan Sultan when he abdicated from the throne in 1967. It is a fascinating place – on the one hand you feel you are in a place entrenched in trading history and Islamic exoticism; on the other, the 'modernised capital' image is increasingly apparent. The much publicised 'lavish adornments, gold towers, sparkling fountains and colourful mosaic tiles' exist at particular sites rather than throughout the city. There is no historic mass of buildings; early settlements and colonial buildings were bombed before the end of World War II.

The city spreads out over 16km from the downtown area. The rest of the riverfront is largely state-owned land, lined with vast recreational parklands, museums and ministries.

When the lights go out, so does most of the action. At 18.00 all public transport stops, and Bruneians head for their favourite evening spot. As the sun sets over Bandar Seri Begawan, and the chants and the cicadas resonate through the city, the full name of the country seems very fitting: *Negara Brunei Darussalam*, 'state of Brunei, abode of peace'. Once you get past the logistical challenges and locate the *tamu* (markets), museums and mosques, the gorgeous green spaces and nearby beaches, you can join the locals and enjoy a high quality of life for a few days as well as some rich cultural experiences.

ORIENTATION Bandar Seri Begawan itself has three districts: **Bandar** – the city centre or central business district (CBD) – hedged around the riverfront, and **Gadong** and **Kiulap**, two neighbouring commercial districts just west of Bandar and separated from it by a couple of kilometres across a narrow estuary of the river. Unless you intend to stay longer than the standard couple of stopover days, you will probably base yourself in either the CBD or in Gadong where there are a few hotels. Vibey Gadong is home to markets, malls, shoplots, restaurants and cafés. Kiulap is a new up-and-coming urban precinct, growing out of an older village area. The upmarket beachside suburb of Jerudong is some 13km northwest of the city. It is part of the Brunei Muara District (the Jerudong Playground theme park is located here). The northern part of Muara, known as Berakas, is the administrative and government zone which also has many sports facilities (stadiums, swimming pools, sports

4

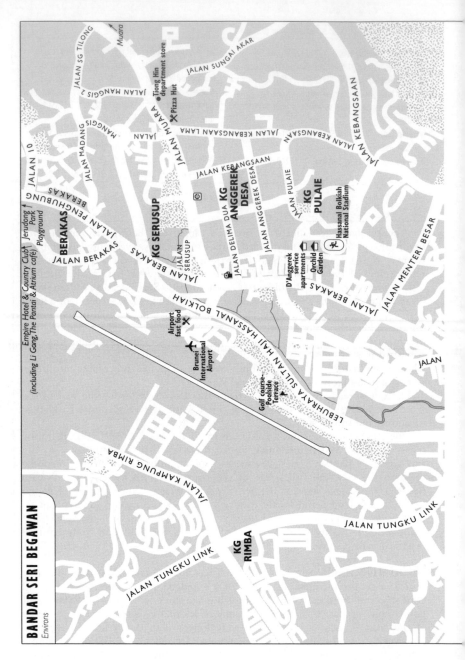

BANDAR SERI BEGAWAN
Environs

Map labels:
Muara
JALAN SG TILONG
JALAN MANGGIS 2
JALAN SUNGAI AKAR
Tiong Hin department store
Pizza Hut
JALAN MANGGIS
JALAN MADANG
JALAN MANGGIS
JALAN MUARA
JALAN KEBANGSAAN LAMA
JALAN
JALAN KEBANGSAAN
JALAN KEBANGSAAN
JALAN 10
JALAN KEBANGSAAN
JALAN PENGHUBUNG
BERAKAS
JALAN KEBANGSAAN
KG ANGGEREK DESA
JALAN PULAIE
KG PULAIE
Empire Hotel & Country Club Jerudong Park Playground
(including Li Gong, The Pantai & Atrium café)
JALAN BERAKAS
JALAN PULAIE
Hassanal Bolkiah National Stadium
KG SERUSUP
JALAN BERAKAS
JALAN DELIMA DUA
JALAN ANGGEREK DESASAN
JALAN MENTERI BESAR
JALAN SERUSUP
D'Anggerek service apartments
Orchid Garden
JALAN BERAKAS
Airport fast food
LEBUHRAYA SULTAN HAJI HASSANAL BOLKIAH
Brunei International Airport
Golf course
Poolside Terrace
JALAN
JALAN KAMPUNG RIMBA
JALAN TUNGKU LINK
KG RIMBA
JALAN TUNGKU LINK
JALAN TUNGKU LINK

complexes, etc) and a couple of hotels. The Muara area beaches lie north of the capital on Brunei Bay.

GETTING AROUND

By car Brunei's capital is not the easiest place to get around by public transport. The infrastructure is there, to an extent, but the last buses run at

18.00 so if you plan to be out after dark, you must either walk or travel by car. The city sites are spread out over several kilometres, so the best option if you want to see as much as possible in a couple of days is to have your own car, or combine a hire car in the city area with day or overnight tours to other places of interest. A litre of petrol costs around 53 cents – a tank is filled for around 20BND. Diesel is 31 cents a litre.

Car hire

🚗 **Avis Rent A Car** ☎ 2426345. Avis have an airport counter & a branch at the Sheraton Utama Hotel (☎ 2227100).

🚗 **Azizah Car Rental** ☎ 2229388
🚗 **Budget-U-Drive** 5th Floor, D'Anggerek hotel, near the Convention Centre; ☎ 2345573

By taxi Metered taxis can be hailed from most hotels, shopping centres and the airport. In the capital, taxis are located at the Jalan Cator car park. Considering the

Meragang Beach

Nakhoda Ragam
Lambak Kanan
Vocational

Perpindahan
Lambak Kanan

Kg. Madang

Pantai
Muara

Muara Flotilla

Kg. Delima Satu

Kg. Sg. Tilong

Kg. Sungai Hanching

Kg. Salambigar

Kg. Tanah Jambu

Kg. Kapok

Kg. Sabun

33

Department of Ports

38
36

38
37

33, 37
38, 39

Muara
Town

36

37

39

Kg. Pance
Delima

Kg. Anggerek
Desa

Kg. Sungai
Buloh

33

Kg. Pulaie

Kg. Sutat Dakiar

Gurkha Reserve Unit
(Sungai Akar)

Immigration &
Labour Dept.

Pantai Mentiri
Golf Club

Kg. Serasa

33 Ferry Terminal

Serasa Beach

01
34

Kg. Mentiri

Kg. Belimbing

23, 24
38

MIPR

37

Perpindahan
Serasa

Jln Kebangsaan
Mabohai

Kg. Subok

Kg. Sungai Besar

Tasek Lama Kg.

Kg. Batu Klanggeh

Kg. Sg. Belukut

37

Kg. Pelambaian

Kg. Serdang

Kg. Kota Batu

Kg. Dato Gandi

Kg. Sg. Matan

39

Brunei Museum

39

KEY TO DISTRICT BUS LINES

Northern Line	
Circle Line	
Southern Line	
Central Line	
Western Line	
Eastern Line	
Bus Stop Interchange	o-o
Bus Terminal	
Bus Interchange Station	

low cost of petrol taxis are expensive, about 1BND per kilometre (3BND for the first kilometre, 20 cents per subsequent kilometre).

By bus The Bandar Seri Begawan Bus Terminal is also located in the Jalan Cator car park. There are six bus routes (with names such as **Northern Line**, **Western Line**, etc) serving Bandar Seri Begawan and the wider Muara District, departing every 15–20 minutes during 06.30–18.00. Average fares are 1BND. The two routes which stop at the CBD, museums and other sites of interest are the **Central Line** and the **Circle Line**. The widely available Brunei Tourism map includes the essential public bus transport network map. Longer-distance buses leave from here too.

By boat

Water taxis For the city area, these can be hailed from numerous docking ports and jetties along the banks of the river. They are the most common form of transport for the *Kampung Ayer* (water village) area and prices are usually negotiable. The standard one-way fare for the river crossing to *Kampung Ayer* for residents is 1BND. You can also negotiate for longer trips with the water taxis for anything from 10BND to 30BND for a half to full hour, either to tour the river area or to get to the Malaysian towns of Limbang and Lawas.

Longboats These are used in rural areas. Be aware that when the waters are low, you might be required to get out and push!

TOURIST INFORMATION There is a visitor's information centre on Jalan Cator in the city centre.

WHERE TO STAY There are limited accommodation choices in Brunei. What is available includes one–five-star hotels, serviced apartments, guesthouses and hostels. Nearly 90% of this accommodation is in the capital. Given the spread-out nature of the city and its sights, it is best to pick your accommodation according to what you most want to be near: the CBD which is also the riverfront and transport hub; the main retail district which thrives at night, Gadong; or among the groomed greenery and beaches out of the city in Jerudong. The limited budget establishments aimed at leisure travellers are in Bandar. It is possible to upgrade by staying in a hotel out of the CBD. The Brunei Association of Hotels website (*www.hotelsofbrunei.com*) links to its members which count about two-thirds of the country's hotels.

Luxury

Empire Hotel & Country Club (423 rooms) Muara Tutong Highway, Jerudong (13km north of town); ☎ 2418888; e sales@theempirehotel.com; www.theempirehotel.com. Fit for a sultan (or sultaness), the 6-winged hotel has swirled marble floors, stairway railings plated in 21-karat gold & wool carpets interwoven with gold thread. The stunning open-tiered lobby is actually on the 5th floor overlooking the sea; most rooms have ocean-facing balconies & the smallest suites are 30m². The swimming pools are Olympic-sized, fluid-formed & sand based. Within the majestic grounds of the Country Club there are amazing sport & spa facilities. The dining alternatives rival those of a luxury shopping galleria & entertainment includes 3 cinemas. $$$$$

Rizqun International Hotel (168 rooms, inc non/s floor) Abdul Razak Complex Gadong; ☎ 2423000; e info@rizquninternational.com; www.rizquninternational.com. An uplifting Muslim-Malay feel to this hotel, with its touch of palatial, huge marble & granite lobby, classical comfort & gracious staff. Deluxe rooms come with luxurious marble bathrooms, high-tech touches, lots of lounge furnishings & work spaces. Excellent location close to city centre but in the heart of Gadong. Good Chinese/Malay/Indian/Western b/fast. Premier Club floor has benefits inc a club lounge (⏱ 06.30–23.00), complimentary b/fast & free 24hr internet access in rooms. Terrace swimming pool & fitness centre. $$$$$

Upmarket

The Centrepoint (216 rooms) Abdul Razak Complex, Km4 Jln Gadong; ☎ 2430430;

e centrepoint@arhbrunei.com; www.arhbrunei.com. Rooms & furnishings far less appealing than the

Sheraton, but still comfortable with good facilities (AC, writing desk, minibar, sat TV, kettle, swimming pool, gym). Very service oriented & well staffed. Deluxe rooms, junior/executive/business suites & non/s floor. Dining choices in the hotel are plentiful & frequented by locals, especially Dynasty Restaurant (see *Where to eat*, page 137). $$$$

🏠 **Sheraton Utama** (142 rooms) Jln Tasek; 🕿 2244272; e sheraton @ brunet.bn; www.sheraton.com/utama. Best-situated of all the top

hotels if you want to be city centre. Actually the only luxury hotel close to the CBD – 10 mins' walk from the river. Some standard rooms are a bit dated, but Superior/Executive Deluxe rooms are spacious & well furnished. Ask for pool-facing if you don't want traffic noise. Overall a very smart hotel with helpful staff, good in-house eating, lobby, private 'bar' (BYO), a small pool & jogging tracks at the back door. $$$$

Mid-range

🏠 **Orchid Garden Hotel** (155 rooms) Lot 31954, Simpang 9, Kampung Anggerek Desa (3km from CBD), Jln Berakas; 🕿 2335544; e ogh@brunet.bn; www.orchidgardenbrunei.com. Chinese pagoda-style cream building in Berakas District; swimming pool, fitness centre & restaurants, rather floral but quality décor & furnishings, spacious rooms, nice lobby, Western & Chinese (*Vanda*) restaurants with dim sum Sun buffet. $$$

🏠 **Riverview Hotel** (130 rooms) Km1, Jln Gadong (1km from CBD); 🕿 2238238; e rivview@ brunet.bn. Halfway between Bandar & Gadong on an estuary of the Sungai, big 3-star leisure hotel, not for peace-seekers but family fun, poolside BBQ & steamboats, business centre, jacuzzi & gym, kids' playground, 24hr café. Shuttle service to both Gadong & CBD. $$$

Budget

🏠 **Brunei Hotel** (63 rooms) 95 Jln Pemancha; ☏ 2242 2372; e bruhot@brunet.br; www.bruneihotel.com.bn. The best budget hotel in the city centre for standard rooms, with some mid-range (more spacious) deluxe rooms. AC, sat TV, tea & coffee making & safe in rooms. 10–15min walk to riverfront & Jln Residency. $$

🏠 **Jubilee Hotel** (41 rooms) Jubilee Plaza, Jln Kampung Kianggeh; ☏ 2228070; e jubilee@brunei.bn; www.jubileehotelbrunei.com. Another to try which gets good reports for its reasonable rates, city centre, TV, AC, self-catering facilities, family suites. $$

🏠 **Terrace Hotel** (80 rooms) Jln Tasek Lama; ☏ 224 3554; e terrahtl@brunet.bn; www.terracebrunei.com. Good location in northern part of Bandar near the Tasek Recreational Park, yet still within 20 mins' walk from town. Outdoor pool, fitness centre, Cempaka Café serving steamboats & Malay *nonya kueh* cakes. Rather boxy but well-appointed rooms for price. TV, AC & safes. $$

🏠 **Traders Inn** (84 rooms) Block D, Lot 11620 Jln Gadong (3km from CBD); ☏ 2442828; e traders@brunet.bn; www.tradersinn-bn.com. Budget business hotel, very nice atmosphere & management, on industrial edges of Gadong area with market & coffee shops close by. Spacious, simple, freshly decorated & well-appointed rooms, business centre, free Wi-Fi, in-house coffee lounge (🕐 06.30–23.00) plus foot reflexology centre; great value. Cheapest of the budget hotels. $$

Shoestring

The only two shoestring accommodations are both in Bandar city centre.

🏠 **KH Soon Resthouse** Jln Sungai Kianggeh; ☏ 2222052; e khsoon_resthouse_brunei@hotmail.com; http://khsoon-resthouse.tripod.com. Spartan but clean, for those seeking a sgl/dbl room rather than dorm bed, & prepared to pay more than for a hostel. Reportedly clean, calm & well kept, close to coffee shops & bus transport, good for solo travellers. 35–40BND/US$15–18 for sgl/dbl with attached bathrooms. $

🏠 **Pusat Belia Youth Hostel** Jln Sungai Kianggeh; ☏ 2223936; e jbsbelia@brunet.bn. AC, 4-bed dorms. Approx 10BND/US$6. $

Serviced apartments

🏠 **D'Anggerek Service Apartments** (30 rooms) Lot 11044 Kampung Luagan Pulaie, Jln Berakas (3km from CBD); ☏ 2345222; e inquiry@danggerek.com; www.danggerek.com. In the government Berakas District, near Convention Centre & Brunei National Stadium, rooms & suites; the building has its own library, cyber-lounge, games room & mini-gym, restaurant & coffee house. $$–$$$

🏠 **Le Gallery Suites Hotel** Km2.5 Jln Tutong, Seri Complex, Kiulap; ☏ 2221228; e rooms@legallerysuiteshotel.com; www.legallerysuiteshotel.com. Budget-chic rooms & apts, 5km from town. Even budget rooms have Wi-Fi, TV, business-centre access. Good for business travellers wanting minimalist sleek. Not so central for leisure traveller. $$–$$$

🏠 **Abdul Razak Hotel Apartments** (96 rooms & suites) Jln Laksamana Abdul Razak, Km2, Jln Tutong (5km from CBD, 7km from airport near Supreme Court); ☏ 2241536; e dmarp@arhbrunei.com; www.arhbrunei.com. 24 deluxe rooms, 56 1-bed suites & 16 2-bed suites all with fully equipped kitchenettes, central AC, daily room-cleaning services, writing desk, fridge & minibar, sat TV & room service until 21.30. A good choice if you have your own car, though buses do run this way. Described by one friend as 'apartments for the flashpacker'. $$

✗ **WHERE TO EAT** Street food in Brunei is among the most delicious and immaculately presented in Borneo. Indoors, there are many good coffee shops and casual restaurants; more sophisticated and/or international dining is mostly found in four–five-star hotels, though Brunei lacks much of a fine dining scene. Gadong is the best place for multi-ethnic, well-priced food at small family-run businesses. New-wave cafés in the Kiulap District are the focus of East-meets-West flavours and décor for a young, affluent crowd. Restaurants are not open as late as they are in Malaysian Borneo with last orders around 21.00–22.00, but there are some all-night cafés and food stalls. It is best to reserve for hotel restaurants on weekends.

Market and street food Two of the most spirited markets for food are the Pasar Kianggeh (Kianggeh market) and the Pasar Gadong (Gadong night market). Held near the riverside along Jalan Residency, the **Pasar Kianggeh** market is a vestige of rural life in the city centre. Many of the *gerai makan* (food stalls) here are family-run, opening from around 15.30 and running through until late; a couple remain open all night. They serve satays and soups, noodle and rice dishes, fresh coconut juice and *ketupat* – origami like pouches of rice wrapped in coconut palm or *padan* leaves, served with peanut satay sauce.

Pasar Gadong (Gadong Market) is also a night-time affair – an outdoor eating theatre with the best range of food stalls in the city. The several dozen stalls are open from around 17.00 to midnight. Held in a vast parking lot near the 'wet market' in the Gadong District, it is one of the best *pasar malam* (night markets) in the whole of Sarawak, Sabah and Brunei. Meticulously packaged portions of rice wrapped in banana leaves are a market mainstay: the trays of pyramid and finger-shaped *nasi lemak* contain rice filled with chicken, beef or anchovies and topped with spicy *sambal* sauce and *nasi katok*.

For those staying in the city centre, the **Taman Selera** (⏱ *17.00–as late as 02.00*) is an excellent night-time food stall area. Set in a large car park zone between Jalan Tasek Lama and Jalan Kumbang Pasang, north of the CBD and opposite the Sheraton Utama Hotel, the name literally means 'appetite park'. While it lacks the overall ambience of the Gadong market, some of the food is still very good, and a godsend in this rather uneventful and dining-deprived zone. The **Bob U Me** stall is recommended for fresh seafood, cooked before your eyes whichever way you like it.

As far as shopping-centre food courts go, there is the **Padian Food Court** in the city centre area – in the riverfront Yayasan complex – serving chicken, rice, *laksa*, Indian and Western food. In Gadong, there are two food courts – the ground-floor **Centrepoint Food Court**, and one on the top floor of the more upmarket the **Mall Shopping Arcades.**

Fast food is on the rise – and the big international names and domestic all have outlets in the city and at Jerudong Park, including KFC, Pizza Hut and McDonald's, Sugar Bun and Jollibee. But why eat foreign fast food, when you can have *nasi katok* around the clock from many coffee shops and stalls?

Malay/Bruneian

✗ **Aminah Arif** Unit 2–3, Block B, Bangunan Haji Abdul Rahman; ☎ 2236198. An institution among locals for the *ambuyat*. In the Kiulap District, **$$$**

✗ **Restoran Seri Balai** Unit 3, Bangunan Haji Menudin, Block A, Kampung Pengkalan Gadong; ☎ 2456447. *Ambuyat*, but with quality Malay dishes, snacks & cakes also on the menu, this is a place for the adventurous. Found in the village of

Kampung Pengkalan Gadong opposite the Gadong commercial centre. **$$**

✗ **Seri Kiantan Restaurant** 5 Bangunan Menglait, Gadong; ☎ 2444848; ⏱ Mon–Sat. Casual place for Malay staples such as *nasi lemak*, *cucur udang* (prawn fritters) *kelupis* (glutinous rice rolls) & lots of Malay *kueh* (cakes). **$–$$**

Chinese

✗ **Dynasty Restaurant** Ground Floor, Centrepoint Hotel, Abdul Razak Complex, Gadong; ☎ 2430430; ⏱ 08.30–14.00 &18.00–22.00 daily. The most popular & established Chinese eatery in Brunei, famed for introducing halal dim sum & more recently for its rock melon *sago* dessert. Alongside the Centrepoint shopping mall in Gadong. **$$–$$$**

✗ **Li Gong Chinese Restaurant** Empire Hotel & Country Club, Tutong Muara Highway, Jerudong; ☎ 2418888; ⏱ 11.00–14.00 & 18.00–22.00 daily. Favourite local haunt for Sun brunches of dim sum & Cantonese roast duck. Chic modernised Chinese glass temple in form. **$$$–$$$$**

✗ **Four Sea Hut** or **Shikai Restaurant** Unit 1, Block E, Sempurna Complex, Jln Batu Bersurat, Gadong;

JERUDONG
Environs
Sketch map (not to scale)

N

Bradt

South China Sea

Pantai
Jerudong

Fish
market

Hospital   Jerudong

Jerudong Park
Playground

Istana
Nurul Izzah

Tutong

The Empire
Hotel &
Country Club

Pantai
Tungku

Muara

TUTONG MUARA HIGHWAY

JALAN TUNGKU LINK

Bukit
Shahbandar

BT SHAHBANDAR

JALAN JERUDONG

2456222. ☻ lunch/dinner High on rustic ambience, décor & food quality, this little place among suburban shop-lots serves Hong Kong-style roast duck & chicken dishes, plus a mix of Malay & Chinese noodle & soup staples. **$$–$$$**

Seafood
✕ **RMS Portview** Block H, Yayasan Shopping Complex; ☎ 231465. Mix of Western (burgers) & seafood, River-lapping location. **$$$**

Indian
✕ **Zaika** G24 Block C, Yayasan Sultan Haji Hassanal Bolkiah Complex; ☎ 2231155; ☻ 11.00–14.00 & 18.00–22.00 daily. For Indian delicacies in the city centre, reputedly excellent, stylishly antiquated décor. **$$–$$$**

Japanese
✕ **Takara** Ground Floor, Centrepoint, Gadong; ☎ 2450180; ☻ 11.00–14.00 & 18.00–22.00 daily. Established Japanese restaurant with a Teppanyaki kitchen – seafood, meat & vegetables grilled by the chef on large steel hotplate before you. **$$$**

Thai
✕ **Lemongrass Thai Food** 7 Bangunan Urairah, Kiulap; ☎ 2230316. **$$–$$$**

✕ **Vanda Restaurant** A popular suburban Chinese at the Orchid Garden Hotel, 3km from CBD. **$$–$$$**

✕ **The Pantai** Empire Hotel & Country Club, Muara Tutong Highway, Jerudong; ☎ 2418888; ☻ evenings only. Very popular, breezy beachside seafood buffet & BBQ, 20mins from BSB. **$$$–$$$$**

✕ **Popular Restaurant** Ground Floor, Seri Complex, Mile 1, Jln Tutong; ☎ 2221375; ☻ 08.00–22.00 daily. Quality Indian savouries & sweets, samosa, *vadai* & many vegetarian dishes. Finish with the Indian twist on Malaysia's favourite tea, *the-tarek halia* (ginger-pulled tea). Cash only. **$$**

✕ **Escapade Sushi** Ground Floor, Block A, Q-lap Complex, Kiulap; ☎ 2234012; ☻ 11.00–22.00 daily. Sushi-train restaurant – fast but high-quality Japanese food. **$$**

Italian

✗ **Fratini's Italian Restaurant** 1st Floor, Jln Pemancha, BSB; ☎ 2231466; ⊕ 10.30–22.30 daily. Brunei does very average Italian food, but the upper balcony of this franchise Italian restaurant overlooks the Sungai Brunei, offering river-soaked ambience. **$$$**

✗ **Spaghettini's** Empire Hotel & Country Club, 6th Floor, Lobby Building, Jerudong; ☎ 2418888; ⊕ 18.00–22.00 daily. A tiny place serving Italian food. **$$$**

Western

✗ **Deals** Sheraton Utama; ⊕ 12.00–14.00 & 19.30–21.30 daily, 19.30–21.30 public holidays. The Sheraton's 'fine dining' restaurant with soft lights, nice décor, business lunch or formal dinner. **$$$$**

✗ **Atrium Café** Empire Hotel & Country Club, Tutong Muara Highway, Jerudong; ☎ 2418858; ⊕ 06.30–22.30 daily. An impressive buffet spread & sublime location with ceiling-to-floor glass windows looking over the sea from up high. The buffet switches themes around international, Malay & Indian specialities, & there is also an à la carte menu with local & Western dishes. **$$$–$$$$**

✗ **Manjaro** Bl, Shakirin Complex, Kililap; ☎ 2236493. A chic, banqueted restaurant with an eclectic lounge-lit atmosphere. Western & fusion food of the likes of 'Jumbo Combo's' with buffalo wings, fish fillets & coconut prawn fritters, deep-fried chicken wantons, & aromatic peppered tenderloins. Late-evening crowd move towards the boudoir-style upstairs salon for house music. **$$$–$$$$**

✗ **Charcoal** Ground Floor, Le Gallery Suites Hotel, Seri Complex, 1.5 Mile Jln Tutong; ☎ 2221171; ⊕ 10.00–late daily. Very popular American grill. Burgers & ribs, chicken & lamb. **$$$**

✗ **Tasek Brasserie** Sheraton Utama Hotel, Jln Tasek; ☎ 2244272; ⊕ 18.30–22.00 daily. Warm, woody setting & poolside eating. Excellent range of seafood & meals. DDQ evenings & good salad buffet **$$$**

Cafés There is a **Coffee Bean & Tea Leaf** on the ground floor of the Bangunan Maya Puri Building, in central Bandar Seri Begawan. A 24-hour meeting place is **de Royalle Café** run by a veteran journalist. In Gadong, **Chill's** is at The Mall, and **Coffee Zone** near Centrepoint serves coffee and decent light food.

ENTERTAINMENT AND NIGHTLIFE In a place where there are no bars, alcohol is banned and public transport ends at 18.00, you could be forgiven for assuming there may not be much nightlife to seek out. However, Brunei's capital does

---

BRUNEIAN FEAST

Some Malay specialities are still sold from people's homes – you knock on the door to place your order, which is where *nasi katok* – 'knock rice' – takes its name from. Served in a cone of waxed brown paper and topped with a bit of fried chicken, beef or egg, and spicy sauce – take-away food à la Brunei. The famous *ambuyat* is a bowl of *sago* paste served with a variety of foods including beef jerky strips, fried fish, vegetable pickles, bamboo shoots, mango and chilli preserves. You can also eat these side dishes with rice if you prefer. For dessert, *kuch wajid* (pounded Temburong hill rice) is slow-cooked in palm sugar and coconut cream then wrapped in banana leaves and steamed until the sugar almost caramelises. Bruneians love their biscuits and cakes, collectively known as *kueh* or *kuih*. Green pandan-flavoured crêpes *kueh gulung* are filled with coconut and palm sugar. Every morning at Jing Chew, Bandar's oldest coffee shop, they serve fresh-baked egg buns, toasted and spread with coconut jam (*kaya*). Each district of Brunei has its specialities, closely linked with agriculture. Tutong's savoury signature is grilled rolls of glutinous rice filled with shrimp or beef *pulut panggang*. *Chendol Temburong*, is a dessert-drink made from droplets of green bean flour mixed with palm sugar, with or without coconut milk.

have plenty to offer. For family fun and theme-park entertainment, the sultanate's take on Disney is the **Jerudong Park Playground and Gardens** (*Muara-Tutong Highway, 20 mins from BSB;* ☉ *17.00–24.00 Wed–Fri, 17.00–2.00 Sat, 16.00–24.00 Sun & pub hols; 1BND, day ticket 15BND adults, 5BND children; bus No 55*), 57 acres of gilt-lined roller coasters and marbled fun for everyone – 'including members of the Royal Family!' states the brochure. Reports are that the playground is a bit lacklustre, despite being full of marble, making it no different from many other faded urban theme parks. The night-time atmosphere is still lots of fun though.

FESTIVALS Food plays the leading role in Brunei's festivals. Celebrated festivals include the **Chinese Lunar New Year** in late January and the month-long **Ramadan** (mid-September to mid-October) when government offices close for the day at 14.00 and food markets spring into action all over the city (See *Chapter 2*, page 73).

SHOPPING It may not be obvious that you are in a tax-free country, as the savings are pretty much offset by higher living costs compared with most of Asia. Still, there are savings to be had, with zero tax on clothes, food and (non-alcoholic) beverages; 5% tax on watches, jewellery, cosmetics, cameras, electrical equipment, furniture, photographic materials and electronics; and 20% tax on vehicles and car accessories.

Cultural buys Brunei's riches are revealed in its 'handicrafts' – not just beads and basketry but silverware, brass artefacts (such as cannons), silk and gold-threaded fabrics, gold brocade – *kain tenun*. The gold or silver thread for *kain songket*, is imported from Japan but woven in Brunei. The gold fabric costs 500–600BND a yard – making for quite an expensive sarong! The riverside **Arts and Handicrafts Centre** on Jalan Residency may be an expensive place to purchase artefacts and fine handicraft items, but it is well worth a visit. For more affordable handicrafts and traditional souvenirs, head to the markets. At the **Tamu Kianggeh** (city centre), you can buy a keepsake *tudung dulang* – the decorative rattan food covers – or take home machete-like *pemarang* (though you may have trouble getting this through your own country's customs). Many traditional handicrafts are made from bamboo, rattan and leaves, and are woven, waved and plaited. The best place to buy them is at city and rural *tamu* (markets). For fabrics, shop around the Gadong commercial zone – there are a couple of shops selling batiks, silk and sarongs near the Mall Shopping Arcades. Plant lovers shouldn't miss the **Horticulture Centre** in Kampung Rimba (Gadong). In the further-flung area of Serusop, ('little India') (*Jln Muara, in the Berakas District*), you will find shops with *songkets* in multi-gilded tones and bolts of bright silks. Serusop in general is an off-the-beaten-track shopping paradise, where many foreign workers shop.

Markets The **Kianggeh Tamu** is an open-air market held in the village of Kampung Kianggeh, adjacent to Bandar Seri Begawan city centre. The market unfurls every day, with stalls spread out over 0.5km along on the banks of the Sungai Kianggeh (*off Jln Residency*). Water taxis ply the river waiting for a catch (to take tourists to the *Kampung Ayer* and around). Here you can buy fresh and cooked food, handicrafts, baskets – all the usual things of a *tamu* – every day from morning to evening. A 24-hour weekend market is held along Jalan Sultan (☉ *18.00 Sat–18.00 Sun*). On Friday and Sunday mornings, the Gadong market place blooms into a **flower market**, *pasar bunga* (☉ *07.00–12.00*). A new market was also being developed as part of a new cultural village.

Shopping centres The largest shopping complex in Bandar Seri Begawan is the **Yayasan** (*CBD, riverfront*), another sultan-owned business, billed as an 'upmarket array of shops and boutiques'. Most serious retail is found in the Gadong and the Kiulap commercial districts. **The Mall** in Gadong (*buses Nos 55 & 01*) is one which has a bit more ritz than glitz. It houses over 150 shops, including some brands and boutiques. The neighbouring **Jaya Centrepoint Hypermarket** is lacklustre in presentation but has lots of cheap buys in jewellery and clothing and food.

Food/supermarkets The **Utama Grand** superstore on the ground floor of the Gadong Mall is the best supermarket for variety with a smattering of cool international products (Californian teas, Italian coffee, French cheese). **SupaSave** in Gadong has a huge range. The supermarket of the **Hua Ho** department store has branches in the Yayasan complex and in Gadong and Kiulap, with fewer imports than the Utama Grand but loads of local and Asian produce. A chain store for food and other goods around Brunei is the **Milimewah**.

OTHER PRACTICALITIES

Post office Located in the CBD on the corner of Jalan Sungai Kianggeh and Dua (☉ *07.45–16.30 Mon–Thu & Sat, 08.00–11 & 14.00–16.00 Fri*). There is also a post office in Muara town. The General Post Office is on Jalan Sultan.

Internet Internet cafés are not as common in Brunei as they are in Malaysian Borneo. There are a couple of cafés in the city centre (see map), at the Yayasan complex and the RBA Plaza. There are more around the main shops of the Gadong district, and one in Muara town centre.

Money There are many licensed money exchanges in Bandar Seri Begawan city centre (see map), one at the airport, and one in Gadong, but there are very few elsewhere so make sure you have enough money on you for excursions. The same goes for ATM machines – you will find them in towns, but they are few and far between in rural areas.

Hospital The The Raja Isteri Pengiran Anak Saleha (RIPAS) hospital (☎ *2242424*) is on the corner of Jln Tutong and Haji Hassanal Boliah.

WHAT TO SEE AND DO A full day (six-hour) city tour, offered by many tour companies, usually takes in three or four museums, mosques, markets and a river trip to *kampung ayer*. Brunei Tourism have a good list of tour operators on their website, but to get a good idea of tours available look at the website of Freme Holidays (*www.freme.com*).

Palaces and parliaments Built in 1984 at a cost of US$400 million, the **Istana Nurul Iman** – the sultan's home – has 1,788 rooms and stretches over 0.5km along the riverbank, making it the largest residential palace in the world. The Istana (palace) opens once a year to the public, at the end of Ramadan during the Hari Raya Aidilfitri celebrations. Thousand of Bruneians and foreigners queue for hours at its gates to peek inside. The open-house times are published in local newspapers, including the *Borneo Bulletin* (English language) and *Media Permata* (Malay). At other times, the best exterior view of the palace, in its 300-acre groomed grounds, is from a boat on the Sungai Brunei. On a night cruise you will see it lit up – with some 55,000 light bulbs (the electricity is apparently very cheap, powered by gas turbines!) Failing that, you can gaze at it from a parking lot just opposite on Jalan Tutong, or in the adjacent park **Persiaran Damuan**

(*Jln Tutong;* ☉ *daily; free*). The 1km-long riverbank jogging haven has paved
walkways and a series of sculptures by artists from the original six members of
the Association of Southeast Asian Nations (referred to as the Asean-6) –
Indonesia, Malaysia, the Philippines, Thailand, Singapore and Brunei
Darrusalam.

On a river tour, you can see a rather different kind of palace. The **Istana
Darussalam** is a modest, mint-coloured wooden home in Kampung Sumbiling
(one of the *kampung ayer* villages), and was where the sultan's father, the 28th
sultan, was born – and where he returned to die.

If Brunei does one day become a democracy, the doors of the **Lapau** (Royal
Ceremonial Hall) will probably be thrown open as a monarchial museum-piece.
For now though, official permission is required to enter the gold-lined chamber
where his majesty was crowned on 1 August 1968. In the same neighbourhood, on
Jalan Sungai Kianggeh, is the old **Dewan Majilis** (Legislative Council). The new
one is well removed from these city centre landmarks, on Jalan Mabohai in the
Berakas governmental district.

Mosques The most beautiful night-time views in Brunei come from the lights and
bulbous forms thrown from its two very distinct mosques. The cream and gold
Sultan Omar Ali Saifuddien Mosque (*in the CBD, nr the Central Bus Station;*
☉ *08.00–12.00, 14.00–15.00 & 17.00–18.00 Sun–Wed*) is the older city mosque,
built in 1958. It is a magical apparition of stained glass, Shanghai granite,
chandeliers and Italian marble, surrounded by a lagoon on which a replica of the
royal barge floats. The mesmerising gold dome contains 3.3 million fragments of
Venetian mosaic, over a surface of 520m².

Despite it lacking any historic awe-factor, you will be struck by the opulence and
strong sense of Islamic faith at the **Masjid Jame'Asr Hassanal Bolkiah Mosque**
(☉ *08.00–12.00, 14.00–15.00 & 17.00–18.00 Sun–Wed, & Sat if no official ceremonies;
Bus No 1 & 22*). Gloriously ornamental, the edifice is a solid statement of the place
of Islam in Bruneian life: architectural elements come in 29s. There are 29 golden
domes, 29 steps and 29 pillars – the magic number represents the number of
sultans that have ruled to date. Built to commemorate the 25th year of the current
sultan's reign, it is familiarly known as the Kiarong Mosque.

Kampung ayer (Water village) With 30,000 residents, the 'village' is a watery
suburbia actually made up of 28 villages, interconnected over 8km of stilted
walkways. One of the largest floating communities in the world, it has mosques,
schools, markets and a fire station. The government has been trying to relocate the
people onto land, but they refuse to give up their spiritual home. Though it has
burnt down several times, its origins date back to at least the 16th century when
Italian historian Antonio Pigafetta described it as the 'Venice of the East'. The latest
village addition, Kampung Bolkiah, is a high-tech set-up built with fireproof
materials, with an eco-sewage system and houses spaced nearly 10m apart.

Residents of 'KA' commute to work on a flotilla of water taxis, leaving their cars parked along Jalan Residency in town. To visit Kampung Ayer, you can take a water taxi from several points along Jalan McArthur and Jalan Residency to any location in the village and walk around; the one-way fare is around 1BND. Alternatively, you can take a tour. I still feel that the water village is best gazed at from afar at night, from the riverfront area, with water taxis whizzing past in trails of coloured lights taking people home.

River cruises Most operators offer 30-minute to two-hour trips, taking in the river sights, water village and proboscis monkey sightings. There are also night-time cruises.

Museums All are in the Muara District, though none of Bandar Seri Begawan's museums are right in the CBD. Note that during Ramadan, museum opening hours are usually shorter, closing at around 15.00 rather than 17.00.

The most interesting historically is the **Brunei Museum** (*Jln Kota Batu;* \ *2244545; www.museums.gov.bn/bangunan.htm;* ⊕ *09.30–17.00 Sat–Thu, 09.00–11.30 & 14.30–17.00 Fri; free; bus No 39*) with its bronze and brass artefacts, Chinese ceramics, jewellery and natural history displays, plus the story of the oil industry. A real highlight is the Islamic art gallery – exquisite jewellery and tapestries from around the world, dating to the 10th and 11th centuries, and belonging to the sultan's private collection. In a lovely, leafy riverside location just out of town, the museum is situated on an archaeological site in **Kota Batu** where Brunei's former settlements are still being unearthed. Ceramics and coins from the Tang dynasty have been found here. Nearby is the tomb of Brunei's fifth Islamic monarch, Sultan Bolkiah, who ruled from 1473–1521.

The **Malay Technology Museum** (*Jln Kota Batu, opposite the Brunei Museum;* \ *2244545;* ⊕ *09.30–17.00 Sat–Thu, 09.00–11.30 & 14.30–17.00 Fri; free; bus No 39*) is 'peopled' by rather unrealistic, doll-like dummy-natives in their primitive *Kampung Ayer* stilt houses and Iban people in their longhouses. Nevertheless, this is an interesting documentation of ancient housing and water-village cottage industries, including boatmaking technology, goldsmiths and fishing.

Celebrity attracts, and the **Royal Regalia Museum** (*Jln Sultan;* \ *2238358;* ⊕ *09.30–16.30 Sat–Thu, 09.00–11.30 & 14.30–16.30 Fri; free*) is Bandar Seri Begawan's most visited museum. It exudes all the insignia and privileges fitting to such a stronghold sultanate, from royal artefacts to photos, with most of the attention centred on the coronation of the present sultan in 1968. There are royal family photographs old and new, a replica of the throne from the royal palace, ceremonial armoury, the crown jewels, costumes and gold and silver chariots.

It's name literally means the 'House of Twelve Roofs' – the oldest surviving

KAMPUNG OR KAMPONG?

Expect endless variations in the spelling of *kampung* and *kampong* (both meaning 'village') in Brunei and Malaysian Borneo, and within states or even single documents: it's one of the maddeningly erratic things about Borneo. Spelling discrepancies come down to more than different dialects. The spelling of an administrative entity, food or cultural dance can vary three times within as many pages of the same brochure and it is difficult to tell which is the correct version. Is it *kueh* (cakes) or *kuih*? *Chendol* or *chendul*? Once you get used to the variations in spelling you stop noticing them and can appreciate the charm of such a fluid language.

colonial building in Brunei, **Bubongan Duabelas** *(Jln Residency;* ✆ *2244181;* ⊕ *09.00–16.30 Mon-Thu, 09.00–11.30 & 14.30–16.30 Fri)* is a timber house with a dozen peaked canopies, balustraded porches and wide roof overhangs. Built in 1906, it was once home to the British Resident and British High Commissioner of Brunei.

Back closer to town is the **Arts and Handicrafts Centre** *(Jln Residency;* ✆ *2240676;* ⊕ *08.00–17.00 daily; free)*, which conducts classes in making *songkoks* (traditional caps), weaving, woodwork, basketry and other age-old local skills, whilst revealing some of the cultural history of Brunei.

Urban reserves The nature reserve in the city is the **Tasek Lama Recreational Park** *(Jln Tasek Lama, about 2km north of the riverfront; Bus Circle Line)*, a protected pocket of rainforest with waterfall and lakes. On Jalan Residency, another green oasis in the city with views of the river and *Kampung Ayer* is the hilly **Bukit Subok Recreational Park** (⊕ *07.45–18.00 daily; free)*. It is more centrally located than the former if you are staying river-side.

EXCURSIONS FROM BANDAR SERI BEGAWAN

For leisure tourists, most other destinations in Brunei (and there are only two or three!) are best done as day trips (or at the most, overnight trips) from Bandar Seri Begawan, or as you pass through if you are driving. Outside of the capital, the number of accommodations can be counted on one hand. Thankfully, the short distances involved make day trips possible, but don't rule out immersing yourself in Ulu Temburong National Park or the oil district for a night or two.

RESERVES If you want to go green for the day, or even just a morning or afternoon, there are several reserves within an hour (driving or boating) of Bandar Seri Begawan, with nature trails for hiking and biking and places for picnicking.

Bukit Shahbandar *(15km from Bandar, along the Muara–Tutong Highway;* ⊕ *07.45–18.00 daily; free entry)* A 70ha hilly recreational park with a good network of well-signed trekking paths, a mountain-bike trail, observation towers with views over Bandar Seri Begawan and the Jerudong area, and long-tailed macaque monkeys. This is where the Brunei Marathon is held every December.

Wasai Kendal *(off Jln Tutong, the road which runs by the palace)* This waterfall area is a favourite forest retreat for family outings with its picnic facilities, trails, tropical flora and easy trekking. It is within 20 minutes' drive south of the capital, still in Brunei Muara.

Hassanal Bolkiah National Stadium *(5km from city centre;* ⊕ *08.00–12.00 & 13.30–16.30 daily)* The Hassanal Bolkiah sports stadium in Berakas was built in 1999 for the SEA Games. It includes a high-tech sports medicine and research centre, indoor and outdoor stadium, an international swimming complex and practice track and field complex. Public facilities include the swimming pool, squash courts and a tennis complex.

Pulau Selirong (Mosquito Island) A small mangrove-forested island with a plank walk through tropical forest (a half-day tour). It's a 45-minute boat ride away from Bandar Seri Begawan off Brunei Bay.

BEACHES AND WATERSPORTS Situated to the north of Bandar Seri Begawan, the Muara District is the most popular urban beach escape.

Pantai Serasa Beach (*off Jln Serasa; bus No 33, Eastern Line*) A ten-minute drive from central Bandar Seri Begawan, Pantai Serasa is home to the Royal Brunei Yacht Club, the Royal Brunei National Windsurfing Association and the Serasa Water Sports Complex, where you can sail, windsurf, kayak and water-ski, or just hang out. It's also frequented by those who like fishing – not just fishermen, but women.

Pantai Muara Beach (*off Jln Serasa; bus No 33, Eastern Line*) Some 27km from Bandar Seri Begawan, the beach has a long waterfront esplanade, basic picnic, playground and toilet facilities, and there are lots of food and drink stalls around the headland area on the weekends. Bus No 57 heads northwest to Pantai Jerudong Beach, where there are watersports, as well as seafood and other food stalls.

ULU TEMBURONG NATIONAL PARK Brunei's 'green jewel' is Ulu Temburong National Park – the 50,000ha of rainforest constitute Brunei's first and only national park, lying within the huge Batu Apoi Forest Reserve. The Temburong District – at the base of one of the two inland juts which make up the shape of Brunei – is a major rice-growing area, producing nearly half the country's rice. It is also the area which protrudes into the 'Heart of Borneo' deep forest region bordering Sabah, Sarawak and Kalimantan. The journey to get there is more than half of the fun, on a boat trip through wide bays and narrow rivers, through mangrove forests full of proboscis monkeys, and trespassing briefly on Malaysian territory before swinging back into Temburong – Iban, Murut and Malay territory.

Getting there and away
By boat From Bandar Seri Begawan, the journey through to the national park (the destination for most visitors) requires a mix of speedboat, longboat and road transport: the first part is by express boats to Bangar, the main town in Temburong. Boats leave regularly from the jetty on Jalan Residency between approximately 07.00–17.00. The 45-minute journey costs 7MYR.

From Bangar you require a vehicle transfer to **Kampung Batang Duri** where local Ibans take you in a *temuai* (longboat) to the park, a 30–40-minute trip. The whole trip, if things flow smoothly over more than a dozen rapids, can be done in about two hours. The easiest thing may be to book the trip through a tour operator in Bandar Seri Begawan or in Temburong, including park accommodation if you require it, as the longboat trip alone costs about 100BND.

By car If you are driving yourself, you can drive in as far as Batang Duri and then go up river from there to the park.

Tours to Temburong A day tour from Bandar Seri Begawan to the park including all transport, a longhouse visit and lunch costs about 136BND with **Sunshine Borneo Travel and Tours**, and with **Freme**. Double that for an overnight stay at a park chalet. **Intrepid Travel** are good for groups and adventure and do specialised rafting trips to Temburong, and say the Grade 1/2 rapids are good for beginners. Some of the operators offer student discounts.

Where to stay and eat Park lodgings and the information centre are operated by the Forestry Department, and consist of a 'hostel' (a few bunk rooms), some self-contained chalets (sleeping two to four people, with basic cooking facilities and shower), and a campsite. Connected by a boardwalk through the forest, and along the riverbank, some rooms are over 500m from the arrival jetty. Lights (generator-powered) go off at 22.00. There is a canteen but it is not always open, so pack some food. The insect sounds and isolation at night are an incredible experience. There is no online booking system in place; it is best to either go through a tour operator in Bandar Seri Begawan or contact the Tourist Information Centre Temburong (*13/14 Kedai Rakyat Jati;* \ *5221439*) for further information on how to get to the park, general lodgings and touring. **Outward Bound Brunei Darussalam** (OBBD) (*www.outward-bound.org*) operate in the Temburong National Park rainforest and there are opportunities for education groups and activities. There are several *kedai* and coffee shops along the main street of Bangar – Chinese, Malay and Indian. If you are heading for the park, stock up here as it's your last chance.

What to see and do Bangar consists of the river jetty area and two or three streets. There is a daily market with fruit and other fresh produce, from wild ferns and bamboo shoots to handicrafts. There are some Iban longhouses in the area – if you want to visit for a traditional dance show, book ahead through the Temburong tourist information centre or request it as part of a day tour through an operator in Bandar Seri Begawan.

The **Bukit Patoi Recreational Park** is 15km from Bangar in Kampung Labu. There is a two-and-a-half-hour trek with rainforest and waterfall, and every September the hilly area is the site of an International Challenge Run (15km).

Only reached by a river trip, the headquarters of the park are situated in a big rainforest buffer zone at the confluence of the Sungai Temburong and Sungai Belalong rivers. The Heart of Borneo jungle is an extremely peaceful place where the evening conversation of cicadas and insects will permeate through your hut walls. The variety of life is incredible; one entomologist discovered over 400 species of beetle on a single tree here.

By day you can bathe in the river, kayak and hike. It has 7km of well-marked elevated boardwalks, with in-depth, intelligent and finely illustrated botanical interpretation. The canopy walk is a 250m-high stainless steel pathway in the sky. Reached after a 2km upwards trek from park HQ, the structure has five ladders which you climb progressively up and along on interconnecting metal bridges. It was built with funds from sultan-owned Shell. It is worth pushing yourself the extra mile if you are flagging near the top – the view over the jungle canopy at the top is awesome. Usually done early morning, possible wildlife encounters on this walk include the Bornean gibbon, macaques, civets, sun bears, pit vipers, hornbills and Rajah Brooke's birdwing butterflies. On the return journey, take the standard jungle trail for an off-boardwalk real forest experience.

The Kuala Belalong Field Studies Centre A rainforest research base is run by the Universiti Brunei Darussalam. On the way up the river to park HQ, you will pass by an attractive building set into the rainforest – a series of dark timber houses, with pike roofs and swerving balustrades At night it glows like a beetle on stilts. It is an important centre for rainforest studies and it is not uncommon to bump into visiting scientists at night at park HQ further upstream. Not for ecotourists or recreation, but researchers and students can enquire about studying here via the university's biology department (↘ 2463001; e kbfsc@ubd.edu.bn).

TUTONG AND BELAIT DISTRICTS The Tutong District is largely rural with hillier rainforest and lake reserves inland, with some longhouse territory bringing together people from the Dusun, Iban, Kedayan and Tutong tribes. Further south is the Belait District and Brunei's oil coast, centring on the towns of Seria and Kuala Belait.

Getting there and away
By car There are two roads heading to Tutong and Belait districts – the coastal Muara Tutong Highway and an inland route along the old road Jalan Tutong. From Seria to Kuala Belait (17km), the fast route is via the Seria bypass. The longer coastal road passes the Istana Manggalela, the sultan's residence during his visits to town. The road leads to the Sungai Belait River, where there is a ferry to the village of Kampung Sungai Teraban. Coming from Sarawak you can arrive in Kuala Belait via the Sungai Tujuh checkpoint. Kuala Belait is about 90km from the capital, and 30km from Miri in Sarawak.

By bus There are buses to Seria and Kuala Belait from Bandar Seri Begawan and from Miri in Sarawak.

Where to stay

🏠 **Plaza Sutera Biru** Lot 73, Jln Sungai, Kuala Belait; ↘ 3347268; e info@psb.com.bn; www.psb.com.bn. This new 'boutique' hotel opened in Kuala Belait at the end of 2007. It's a new enough concept for Brunei, let alone Kuala Belait, where it's aimed at the empty upmarket niche with its spacious, expensive & possibly overpriced rooms & suites. Lots of high-resolution photos on the website. $$$$–$$$$$

🏠 **Riviera Hotel** (30 rooms) Lot 106, Jln Sungai, Kuala Belait; ↘ 3335252. Well-fitted standard & deluxe rooms, AC, sat TV, Shahryza Restaurant (⊕ 07.00–23.00), 3–4 star. Both this & the following hotel send clients on to nearby Harun's Gym for a workout (in DBB Bank). Recommended. $$$

🏠 **Seaview Hotel** (87 rooms/apts) 2.6 km Jln Maulana, Kuala Belait; ↘ 3332651. I have heard some bad reports of this 'resort style' hotel, more expensive than its mid-range competitors for apparently less service & dowdy rooms. $$$

🏠 **Sentosa Hotel** (36 rooms) 92–93 Jln McKerron, Kuala Belait. AC, sat TV, broadband internet, non/s rooms, mini fridge & safe deposit box. The Syazana Café has good Malay & Indian food (⊕ 06.00–23.00). Recommended. $$$

🏠 **Halim Plaza Hotel** Lot 9003, Kampung Petani, Mukim Pekan Tutong; ↘ 4260688; e info@halimplazabrunei.com; www.halimplazabrunei.com. Around 30 mins from BSB, a riverside plaza hotel in small town, bit of a wedding & banquet place, well furnished though frilly-decorated rooms & suites, serviced apartments, café, restaurant & shops. $$

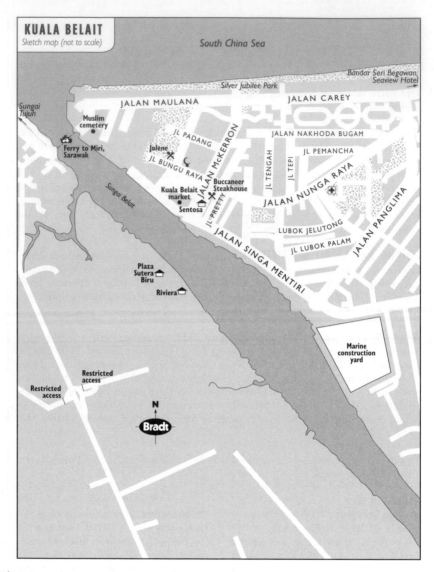

KUALA BELAIT
Sketch map (not to scale)

South China Sea

Bandar Seri Begawan,
Seaview Hotel

Silver Jubilee Park

Sungai Tujuh

JALAN MAULANA

JALAN CAREY

Muslim cemetery

JL PADADG

JALAN NAKHODA BUGAM

Ferry to Miri, Sarawak

Jolene

JL BUNGU RAYA

JALAN McKERRON

JL PEMANCHA

JL TENGAH

JL TEPI

Buccaneer Steakhouse

Sungai Belait

Kuala Belait market

JALAN NUNGA RAYA

Sentosa

JL PRETTY

JALAN PANGLIMA

JALAN NUNGA RAYA

LUBOK JELUTONG

JL LUBOK PALAM

JALAN SINGA MENTIRI

Plaza Sutera Biru

Riviera

Marine construction yard

Restricted access

Restricted access

N

Bradt

✕ **Where to eat** For a district population of just 60,000, there is a good selection of restaurants in Kuala Belait. There are daily fish, fruit and vegetable markets with many food stalls set up along the riverbanks and around town, as well as the usual Malay and Chinese dishes – noodles, *laksa* and spicy prawns – served in several coffee shops. The **Buccaneer Steakhouse** (*Lot 94 Jln McKerron;* ☎ *3334553*) is recommended by Western meat-eaters and **Jolene Restaurant** (*Lot 83, 1st Floor, Jln Bunga Raya*) has good, though relatively expensive, Chinese food – clay-pot dishes, prawns and noodles.

What to see and do The following interesting locations are listed in approximate ascending order as though you were driving from Bandar Seri Begawan to Kuala Belait:

Tutong District Barely 40km from Bandar Seri Begawan the town of Tutong, also known as Kuala Tutong, lies among coconut palms near the Tutong River. *Kuala* means 'river mouth' (and has nothing to do with Australian marsupials!); there are several *kampung* named Kuala along Brunei's estuary-specked coast. The **Tamu Tutong Kampung Serambagun** is a daily open-air market held 1km from the town centre, with lots of local foods, including fruits and vegetables, and handicrafts. Many vendors come from the hinterland to buy and sell produce.

Pantai Seri Kenangan – 'the unforgettable beach' – is a popular recreation spot (fishing, swimming, picnics) five minutes' drive from Kuala Tutong town, lying on a narrow spit of land between the South China Sea and the Tutong River. It has beach chalets, picnic pavilions, restaurant and food stalls. You can also take a trip on the Sungai Tutong.

Situated 27km inland, **Tasek Merimbun** – a serpentine, freshwater lake surrounded by peat swamp and grass marsh – is a wildlife sanctuary, research station and recreational centre. Proclaimed an Asean (Association of Southeast Asian Nations) Heritage Park in 1984, some say it is the de facto first national park, though it is not a gazetted one. There is an island in the centre of the lake for picnics, and a trail through the forest. Resident fauna includes the clouded leopard, white-collared fruit bat, Bornean gibbon, giant squirrel, silver leaf monkey, pig-tailed macaque, sambar deer, honey bear, western tarsier, argus pheasant, hornbill, purple heron, pangolin and reticulated python.

Belait District Driving through Brunei you are never short of recreational and picnic spots and places to stretch the legs. On the coast side of the Muara Tutong Highway is the **Sungai Liang Forest Reserve**, some 70km south of Bandar Seri Begawan (turn left at the Sungai Liang junction and proceed 450m along the Jalan Labi road to the park's entrance on the right). There's a canopy walk, and several other well-marked trails of varying grades through lowland rainforest. Another 25km or so, along Jalan Labi, there is an alluvial freshwater swamp in the **Luagan Lalak Forest Recreational Park** which fills up like a lake in the wet season. From here, a steep 2km trek leads to the **Wasai Wong Kadir** waterfall. The Labi District is home to Iban people and there are chances to visit their longhouses along the way.

Oil littoral starts in Seria: there is an **Oil and Gas Discovery Centre**, an interactive museum of oil history and technology; and the hard-to-miss **Billionth Barrel Monument** – a blend of Islamic tiles with industrial architecture. Kuala Belait is a town grown up on oil and a foreign workers' community, which has added a cosmopolitan touch to the place. Loved by expats, and with a bit of an R&B edge – someone even wrote a love song about Kuala Belait. There's not a whole lot to do, though more than anywhere else outside of Bandar Seri Begawan, and locals have a good quality of life. For jogging and family recreation they head to **Pantai Lumut**, a secluded beach 10km from Seria off the coastal highway. Those looking for a really good time should cross the border to the lively town of Miri for the weekend (see *Chapter 12, Northern Sarawak*, page 275).

Part Three

SABAH

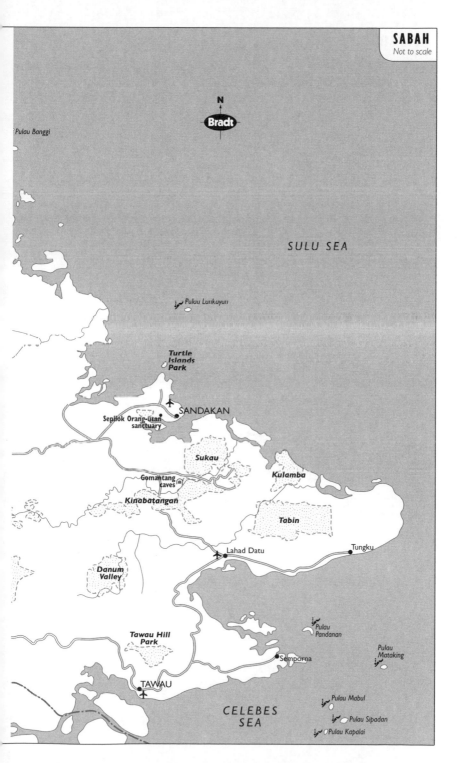

SABAH
Not to scale

N

Bradt

Pulau Banggi

SULU SEA

Pulau Lankayan

**Turtle
Islands
Park**

SANDAKAN

**Sepilok Orang-utan
sanctuary**

Sukau

**Gomantang
caves**

Kulamba

Kinabatangan

Tabin

Lahad Datu

Tungku

**Danum
Valley**

*Pulau
Pandanan*

*Pulau
Mataking*

**Tawau Hill
Park**

Semporna

TAWAU

Pulau Mabul

**CELEBES
SEA**

Pulau Sipadan

Pulau Kapalai

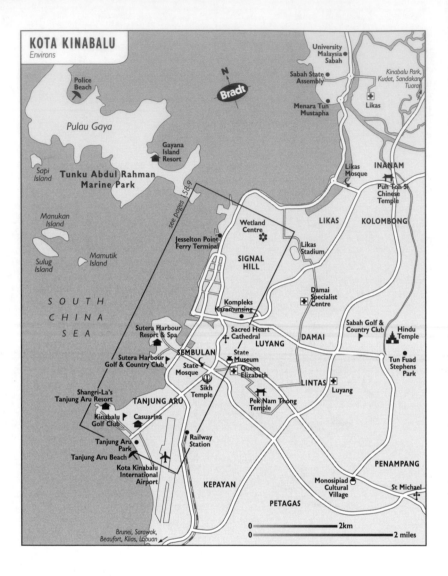

KOTA KINABALU
Environs

Police
Beach

Pulau Gaya

Sapi
Island

Tunku Abdul Rahman
Marine Park

Gayana
Island
Resort

University
Malaysia
Sabah

Sabah State
Assembly

Kinabalu Park,
Kudat, Sandakan,
Tuaran

Menara Tun
Mustapha

Likas

Manukan
Island

Sulug
Island

Mamutik
Island

SOUTH
CHINA
SEA

see pages 58–9

Jesselton Point
Ferry Terminal

Wetland
Centre

SIGNAL
HILL

Likas
Stadium

Likas
Mosque

LIKAS

INANAM

Puh Toh Si
Chinese
Temple

KOLOMBONG

Damai
Specialist
Centre

Kompleks
Karamunsing

Sutera Harbour
Resort & Spa

Sutera Harbour
Golf & Country Club

Shangri-La's
Tanjung Aru Resort

Kinabalu
Golf Club

Casuarina

Tanjung Aru
Park

Tanjung Aru Beach

Kota Kinabalu
International
Airport

Brunei, Sarawak,
Beaufort, Klias, Labuan

SEMBULAN

State
Mosque

Sikh
Temple

Sacred Heart
Cathedral

State
Museum

Queen
Elizabeth

TANJUNG ARU

Railway
Station

Pek Nam Thong
Temple

LUYANG

DAMAI

Sabah Golf &
Country Club

Hindu
Temple

Tun Fuad
Stephens
Park

LINTAS

Luyang

KEPAYAN

PETAGAS

Monosipiad
Cultural
Village

PENAMPANG

St Michael

0 _____ 2km
0 _____ 2 miles

5

Kota Kinabalu

With emerald bays and islands, and a backdrop of lush, low-lying hills, the coastal city of Kota ('fort') Kinabalu has rather ramshackle architecture but a sublime sea setting. Among all the shop-lots and small-city chaos, 'KK' has a discernable holiday-resort atmosphere – many locals take to the water after work and on weekends, enjoying the beach location to the full. Levelled during World War II, some of its shabbier buildings are being revamped as part of a small development spurt. From up on Signal Hill, you can see how 70% of the town centre lies on a narrow belt of land reclaimed from the sea in the 1920s.

Today, mangroves are ceding to waterfront shopping centres. The Waterfront Esplanade runs for about 1km along the city's façade, a mix of markets, five-star hotels and dilapidated buildings, with cargo vessels floating about the bay. Of the 350,000 residents, 60% are Malay, Kadazandusun and Bajau, 35% are Chinese; Murut represent a few per cent; and about 1% are Indian. The remainder are largely Filipino and Indonesian immigrants. The city appears to be reaching to the futuristic vision of the Malaysian capital, though on a much smaller scale. It cannot really compete in the competition for 'biggest is best'; there is a seven-storey limit on buildings due to air traffic.

HISTORY

Like the stilted water villages still found on the fringes of Kota Kinabalu today, the earliest coastal settlements were those of indigenous people. The first British presence came when the British North Borneo Chartered Company (BNBCC) set up a trading settlement in 1882 on Pulau Gaya, the largest of the five islands across the bay from Kota Kinabalu. Before Europeans arrived, the island was inhabited by the Bajau people. Not everyone approved of the foreign authority. The BNBCC was insensitive to local customs and imposed taxes everywhere.

KOTA KINABALU – REVERED PLACE OF THE CHINESE WIDOW?

The city being named after the mountain which looms high on the city's horizon, folklore holds that *Kinabalu* means 'Chinese widow' – *kina* being the Dusunic word for Chinese and *balu* Malay for widow. A story is told of a Chinese prince who came to the mountain in search of a pearl guarded by a dragon at its summit. During his quest, he married a local woman, but ended up returning to China, leaving her heartbroken.

A more spiritual explanation comes from the Kadazandusun people, for whom the name means 'revered place of the dead', derived from the term *Aki Nabalu* – *Aki* meaning ancestors or grandfather, and *Nabalu* the mountain's name in the Dusun language.

Rebel Muhammad Salleh – popularised as Mat Salleh – was a Bajau trader who virulently opposed a controversial tax on rice. In 1897, he and his supporters raided the British settlement on Pulau Gaya and burnt it to the ground. Salleh and some 1,000 followers were killed in a gun battle with the British police a few years later. By then, the BNBCC had restored its headquarters with a small mainland settlement – named Jesselton, in honour of the company's vice chairman Sir Charles Jessel. The town was known to locals as *Api-Api*, – 'fire-fire' – apparently because of the frequent fires which blazed water villages during firecracker-filled celebrations. A less politically correct version says it came from the sight of the BNBCC trading base on Pulau Gaya going up in flames. As is the case with many questions on the history of Malaysian Borneo, answers are few and far between, shedding little light on the plausibility of either side of the story. Jesselton was renamed Kota Kinabalu in 1968.

GETTING THERE AND AWAY

BY AIR Kota Kinabalu International Airport (Kota KinabaluIA) (\ *088 238555*) is the major hub for those arriving in or leaving Sabah for overseas and domestic destinations. Perched over the water, the airport commands a stunning view over a blue horizon dotted with green islands. The airport is in the throes of a major five-year renovation due for completion in 2009, which will hopefully add better banking facilities to its already decent range of duty-free shops and food outlets. Terminal 1 serves international flights as well as **Malaysia Airlines** domestic flights, while Terminal 2 is used mainly by the low-cost carrier **AirAsia**. There are direct international flights to and from Bandar Seri Begawan, Singapore, Manila, Cebu, Hong Kong, Taipei, Kaoshiung, Seoul and Tokyo. **MAS** and AirAsia come and go between other Borneo towns including Sandakan, Tawau and Lahad Datu in Sabah, and Kuching, Sibu and Miri in Sarawak, as well as to the island of Labuan.

The airport is 7km from the city centre. Many of the hotels have their own transport; if you have booked a package, ensure transits are included. For taxis, buy a coupon in the arrival hall (around 20–25MYR) before heading out front to catch a cab. You can also catch a minibus to the city from the main road. On returning to the airport from a city centre hotel, taxis generally ask for 30MYR.

Airlines Many of the airlines have an office in both Kota Kinabalu International Airport (most on Level 2) and in the city. Several of the city offices are located in the Kompleks Kuwasa (*Jln Karamunsing*) and Kompleks Karamunsing commercial centres, in the southern zone.

✈ **AirAsia** Ground Floor, KKIA, Terminal 2; \ 088 538 756/341; www.airasia.com. Book online for the best fares.
✈ **Cathay Pacific** Ground Floor, Kompleks Kuwasa; www.cathypacific.com
✈ **DragonAir** Level 2, KKIA; \ 088 237306. Also Ground Floor, Kompleks Kuwasa; \ 088 254733. Hong Kong airline.

✈ **Malaysia Airlines** Level 2 KKIA; \ 088 260106; first-class check-in \ 088 243617. Also in Kompleks Karamunsing; \ 088 213555
✈ **Royal Brunei Airlines** Ground Floor, Kompleks Kuwasa; \ 088 242193
✈ **Singapore Airlines** Level 2, KKIA; \ 088 219940. Also Ground Floor, Block C, Lot GC 12–13, Kompleks Kuwasa; \ 088 255444
✈ **Thai Airways** Ground Floor, Kompleks Kuwasa; www.thaiair.com

Visas If you have already passed through Malaysian customs *en route* in Kuala Lumpur, it seems a bit bizarre to have to again pass through foreign passport control, and customs, and have a visa issued in Malaysian Borneo. One of the conditions on which Sabah and Sarawak entered the Malaysian Federation in 1963 was that they kept control of their own immigrations. Thirty-day visas are issued automatically to citizens of Commonwealth countries, the USA and most western European nations. These can be extended for another 60 days at the Immigration Department in Kota Kinabalu.

BY CAR There are four main highways to and from Kota Kinabalu. The Kota Kinabalu–Sandakan Highway (A4) connects the capital to the east-coast cities of Sandakan, Lahad Datu, Semporna and Tawau (via Tuaran, Tamparuli, Kundasang, Ranau and Telupid). Although it is only 335km, the entire cross-state trip from Kota Kinabalu to Sandakan takes six or seven hours. The Kota Kinabalu–Kudat Highway (A1) heads north up the west coast to the Kudat Peninsula, via Tuaran, Tamparuli, Kota Belud, Kota Marudu and Pitas. The Kota Kinabalu–Sindumin Highway (A2) heads south towards the Brunei border, and Sarawak, via Penampang, Papar, Beaufort and Sipitang. The Kota Kinabalu–Nabawan Highway (A3) heads southeast into the hinterland, via Penampang, Tambunan, Keningau and Tenom.

Inter-city distances Kota Kinabalu to Mount Kinabalu Park 88km; Kota Kinabalu to Kota Belud 75km; Kota Kinabalu to Kota Marudu 131km; Kota Kinabalu to Kudat 190km; Kota Kinabalu to Sandakan 335km; Kota Kinabalu to Semporna 565km; Kota Kinabalu to Sindumin 158km.

BY BOAT There are daily ferry services between Kota Kinabalu and Labuan, and on to Brunei – see *Chapter 4, Getting there and away*, page 127.

GETTING AROUND

ON FOOT The city centre is reasonably compact, though not particularly pedestrian-friendly. The traffic is quite chaotic, and watch out at crossings: cars tend to fly through them. Poorly lit, lowly-frequented areas behind the waterfront are best avoided at night.

BY CAR It is not convenient to have a car in the city centre, as it is rather confusing to drive around, and parking is not easy. For seeing the Kota Kinabalu area and heading further afield however, a car can be very useful.

Car rental

🚗 **Adaras Rent A Car** Counter at KK International Airport (KKIA); ☎ 088 218798. Also at Wisma Merdeka commercial centre (city centre), Jln Tun Fuad Stephens, Lot G03 Ground Floor; ☎ 088 222137

🚗 **Extra Rent A Car** Beverly Hotel, Lrg Kemajuan, 2nd Floor; ☎ 088 218160; e admin@ e-erac-online.com; www.e-erac-online.com

🚗 **Kinabalu Rent A Car** 1st Floor, Kompleks Karamunsing; ☎ 088 232602; e jose_loh@ kinabalurac.com.my; www.kinabalurac.com.my

🚗 **KMT Global Rent A Car** Wisma Merdeka, Lot G02 Ground Floor; ☎ 088 223022

🚗 **Mayflower Car Rental** Discovery Tours counter, KKIA; e carhire@mayflower.com.my; www.mayflowercarrental.com.my. Also at Wisma Merdeka, Lot 128 1st Floor; ☎ 088 221244

BY TAXI Taxis are generally cheap and plentiful, though fares vary. Some fares are set, such as the journey from the airport to the city. Expect to pay around 5–10MYR for inner-city trips, and double that at night. Fares can be shared by up to four people in a cab. There are several ranks in the city: opposite the Hyatt Hotel on Jalan Datuk Salleh Sulong; at the post office on Jalan Tun Razak; and outside Centre Point shopping centre on Lebuh Raya Pantai Baru. A long-distance taxi station with taxis to places such as Mount Kinabalu is located near the long-distance bus station by Padang Merdeka (Merdeka Field).

BY BUS Buses come and go from all over the place. As Kota Kinabalu is undergoing a big overhaul of the bus system, temporary terminals are currently set up and it's not always clear where to catch certain buses. The best thing to do is to check with your hotel or hostel; they are the most likely to be aware of the latest changes. Sabah Tourism Board's postings on how to get to key destinations are often confusing.

Bas Mini (minibuses) Small buses and vans serve the inner city and suburbs, but also make longer journeys, as far as the east coast. They leave from several different locations, when (and only when) they are full. Buses are usually marked with a route number, with corresponding destinations posted at the station and key bus stops.

Wawasan Plaza Minibus Station The main minibus depot is at the south end of the waterfront, at the junction of Jalan Tun Fuad Stephens and Jalan Kemajuan, near Wawasan Plaza. Buses from here serve the city and outskirts. City and suburban trips cost around 1–2MYR.

City Hall Minibus Station The buses to and from Wawasan Plaza make several stops along the waterfront or the main stretch of Jalan Tun Razak, near the City Park and the Court House Post Office. There is a second minibus station in front of City Hall – though it is often referred to as temporary.

Long-Distance Bus Station (Bandaran Berjaya) The station area is on Jalan Padang, near Padang Merdeka (Merdeka sports field). Air-conditioned express buses, minibuses and vans for longer journeys leave from here. Bigger buses head south for Papar, Beaufort, Tenom, Keningau and Tambunan. Various kinds of buses head

KOTA KINABALU
City Centre

KEY
1 Wah May
2 High Street Inn
3 Trekkers Lodge
4 Ang's
5 Hotel Holiday

northeast to Kundasang/Ranau – this is the direction to take for Kinabalu Park. Expect Bandaran Berjaya to be quite chaotic!

City North Bus Station This is in Inanam, a suburb of Kota Kinabalu, from which long-distance express buses head north and northeast to Tuaran, Kota Belud, Kudat, Ranau, Sandakan, Lahad Datu and all the way to Tawau and Semporna. It takes about eight hours to reach Sandakan. You can get to Kinabalu Park on the Ranau and Sandakan buses, but if travelling from Kota Kinabalu you must first take a minibus from downtown to reach Inanam: it's easier to just take a van straight from Kota Kinabalu to Mount Kinabalu.

BY RAIL Sabah State Railway operates the only railway in Borneo, a 134km line from Tanjung Aru (just south of Kota Kinabalu) to Tenom. Known by locals as 'the slowest train in the world' – it takes four hours to cover 93km – the journey via Papar and Beaufort is more a scenic tourist attraction than a viable means of public transport. Schedules plus a distance/fare grid are available online (*www.sabah.gov.my/railway*). The station is near the airport on Jalan Kepayan and there are four trains each day.

BY BOAT The jetty and ferry terminals are both at Jesselton Point, to the northern edge of the waterfront. Boats leave here to the islands of the Tunku Abdul Rahman Marine Park, as well as to Labuan.

TOURIST INFORMATION

i **Sabah Tourism Board & Tourism Information Office** 51 Jln Gaya; 🕾 088 212121
i **Sabah Tourist Guide Association** (STGA) Lot 128, 1st Floor, Wisma Sabah; 🕾 088 242990;
e sabah_stga@hotmail.com; www.stga.com.my

i **Tourism Malaysia** Sabah office, Lot 107, Ground Floor, Block 1, Lorong Api-Api 1 (in the Api-Api Centre); 🕾 088 248698; e enquiries@ tourism.gov.my; www.tourism.gov.my

Jalan Tun Fuad Stephens along the waterfront is the domain of luxury and upmarket hotels. Shoestring hotels and hostels are concentrated around Jalan Pantai and Jalan Haji Saman. A new precinct of shopping centres and hotels is being developed at the eastern end of the waterfront (at the time of writing, a 262-room 'Novotel 1 Borneo' was planned for Kota Kinabalu by the end of 2008 and this was thought to be its proposed location). For those who prefer not to stay in the city, but remain within its easy reach, see the accommodation listings under *Excursions from Kota Kinabalu,* page 171.

LUXURY

⌂ **Le Meridien** (306 rooms) Sinsuran Complex, Jln Tun Fuad Stephens; ☏ 088 322222; e reservations.kk@lemeridien.com; www.starwoodhotels.com/lemeridien. Smart, black-uniformed staff, though service can swing from personal to poor. A happening & central location, some rooms have views over the bay & market. There are great deals to be had on the Club Floor; high-speed internet access & Wi-Fi in public areas, if you don't mind the cigarette smoke. The b/fast content is excellent, but it's a rather rushed & crammed affair. $$$$$

⌂ **Shangri-La's Tanjung Aru Resort** (500 rooms) No 20 Jln Aru, Tanjung Aru (3km south of city centre); ☏ 088 225800; e tah@shangri-la.com; www.shangri-la.com. Expansive coastal resort with beaches & island views, flourishing gardens & golf course. Sublime ambience, location & food; top-notch facilities & service. Even at b/fast you can eat Malay, Indian, Chinese or European, though from some rooms it takes 10mins to get there! Lovely breezy lobby area & bar, chic deluxe rooms with balconies over sea. Excellent gym & entertainment. The Shang Palace Restaurant is recommended for fine Cantonese dining. $$$$$

⌂ **Sutera Harbour Resort** (956 rooms) 1 Sutera Harbour Boulevard; ☏ 088 318 888; e sutera@suteraharbour.com.my; www.suteraharbour.com.my. Resort facilities here are second to none in Borneo: a marina, Olympic-size swimming pool, golf course, several restaurants, live entertainment, suites with marble-lined bathrooms & balconies; though it might not be your cup of tea if you don't think size is everything. Sprawled out along a new harbour area adjacent to the city, over 384 acres (150ha), the resort has two distinct sections – the Pacific Wing & Magellan Wing – the first more business-class, the second luxury leisure. For such a big place, some of the standard rooms are small. Main criticism is the rather aloof reception & atmosphere. $$$$$

⌂ **Hyatt Regency Kinabalu** (288 rooms) Jln Datuk Salleh Sulong; ☏ 088 221234; e reservation.hrkinabalu@hyattintl.com; www.kinabalu.regency.hyatt.com. Best location on waterfront, next door to Wisma Merdeka. Large, luxurious rooms, business & restaurant zone, close to markets & Jesselton Point ferries, pool, business centre, popular entertainment outlets. $$$$–$$$$$

MID-RANGE

⌂ **Hotel Shangri-La** (121 rooms) 75 Bandaran Berjaya; ☏ 088 212800; e enquiries@kkshang.com; www.kkshang.com.my. Higher priced mid-range but with presentation & services to match. Spacious, well-furnished, bright AC rooms, sat TV, fridge & minibar. Not part of the international chain of same name, nor is it prime waterfront location, but close to shopping *kompleks*, banks, long-distance bus terminal, & good local restaurants of the SEDCO Square area. Good-value deals inc B&B for two. Round-trip airport transfer for 20MYR (07.00–17.00) to 40MYR pp (17.00–07.00) $$$–$$$$

⌂ **Promenade Hotel** (451 rooms) Lorong Api-Api 3, Api-Api Centre; ☏ 088 265555; e enquiry@

promenade.com.my; www.promenade.com.my. Right in the thick of things, this is considered the best 4-star hotel in town centre, with good service & dining. The slightly small rooms can come at budget prices. Larger superior rooms or deluxe suites have city or sea views. Internet specials regularly available. Gym & pool. $$–$$$$

⌂ **Imperial International Hotel** (formerly **Mercure Waterfront**) (208 rooms), Block D, Warisan Square; ☏ 088 522888. Flagged to open as a Hotel Mercure in the chic Warisan Square waterfront area, all of a sudden this 4-star hotel instead appeared under a different name, with about a quarter of its rooms open when I visited. Still no website. Swimming pool,

'Sun' & 'Moon' bars, Restaurants, fitness centre, meeting rooms. $$$
⌂ **Jesselton Hotel** (32 rooms) 69 Jln Gaya; ✆ 088 223333; e jesshtl@po.jaring.my; www.jaring.my/jess. The oldest hotel, opened in 1954 when Sabah was still British North Borneo. 'Guests can rest assured that they will still be afforded the personalised service & impeccable attention to detail that delighted such illustrious colonial-era guests as Lady Mountbatten', the hotel promises. For those who like a bit of yesteryear atmosphere. Held in high esteem among business clientele, it has good service & a good location in the heart of the banking & financial district of KK. Rates inc b/fast & airport transfer. $$–$$$
⌂ **Tang Dynasty Hotel** (203 rooms) 1–1 Lorong Plaza Wawasan, Coastal Highway; ✆ 088 263389; e tdhhotel@tm.net.my; www.hoteltangdynasty.com. Near southern side of waterfront area in the Wawasan Plaza shopping centre, a big 3-star buzzing & bright business hotel, with banquet halls, business centre, swimming pool, & *Taipan* coffee house. Good rates inc b/fast. $$–$$$

⌂ **Radius International Hotel** (96 rooms) 7th Floor, Warisan Square; ✆ 088 525969; e reservations@radius-waterfrontkk.com; www.radius-waterfrontkk.com. A new minimalist-sleek hotel, describing itself as 'Boutech'. The rooms are bright & furnishings fun. AC, sat TV, deluxe & non/s rooms & suites. Seems like a switched-on 3-star, business centre; complimentary broadband internet, internet promotional rates seem incredibly budget priced, yet it is low on other hotel facilities (no pool, gym, etc). $$–$$$
⌂ **Beverly Hotel** (formerly **Hotel Karamunsing**) (200 rooms) Lorong Kemajuan; ✆ 088 258998. Not the best for location (southern-side of CBD), but still within walking distance of everything. Very spacious rooms, terrace pool, gym, babysitting. Good facilities & dining. $$–$$$
⌂ **Berjaya Palace Hotel** (160 rooms) 1 Jln Tangki Karamunsing; ✆ 088 211911; e bhr@berjaya.com.my. A bit of a faded old dame – 3-star – desperately needs a lift in décor & service. Not recommended. $$ $$$

BUDGET Kota Kinabalu has many budget-priced hotels, usually classified locally as one-star. There is so much variation in the price and the quality it is very hard to classify them. Some quite ordinary places have suites at budget prices, and very ordinary rooms at shoestring prices. Other overall better establishments have deluxe rooms at budget prices even though they are more mid-range in services and facilities with coffee shops and restaurants.

⌂ **D'Borneo Hotel** (24 rooms) 6 Blk L Sinsuran; ✆ 088 266999; e info@dborneohotel.com; www.dborneohotel.com. Another newcomer. Bright & business-oriented budget hotel on waterfront. Very personal presentation & welcome for such a small no-frills hotel. Good services non/s floor; café serves Malay & Western food. $$
⌂ **Hotel Deleeton** (47 rooms) Lot 45–45 Block E Asia City, Jln Coastal (just off Lebuh Raya Pantai Baru); ✆ 088 252222. Good CBD location for Centre Point & Sedco Square area, 5min walk from waterfront. Small smart hotel for 1-star category, with AC, minibar, air transfers, non/s floor. $$
⌂ **King Park Hotel** Jln Masjid Lama, Bandaran Berjaya; ✆ 088 270500. This is near the long-distance bus station, not waterfront but not cut off. Close to commercial centres, 24hr reception, internet. Seems like an efficient, budget-priced business with all the mod cons. $$
⌂ **Winner Hotel** (36 rooms) 9-10 Jln Pasar Baru; ✆ 088 243222; e www.winnerhotel.com. Newish & really priding itself on budget brilliance. Though rooms look very boxy, they are clean & cheap. The

suite rooms are not much more stylish but are bigger, with sofa beds, kitchenettes & lots of furniture. All rooms have AC, Wi-Fi, TV & phone. Standard rooms not much bigger than the king-sized bed, but cheap. Option to add a table to superior rooms, or coffee table & chairs to deluxe rooms, all still at very low prices. $–$$ (suites)
⌂ **Wah May Hotel** (24 rooms) 36 Jln Haji Saman; ✆ 088 266118; e wahmayhtl@pd.jaring.my; www.wahmayhotel.com. In an area rather crammed with no-star budget hotels, the 1-star grading of Wah May is reflected in its presentation, but not its prices. AC, TV, fridge in deluxe rooms. Standard rooms less impressive. $$
⌂ **Casuarina Hotel** (44 rooms) Lorong Ilan Lais (off Jln Mat Salleh) in Tanjung Aru (3km from CBD); ✆ 088 221000. Peaceful beach area with free hourly shuttle transport to KK centre. Comfortable rooms, business centre, 24hr reception, coffee house. Rooms & suites. $–$$
⌂ **Kinabalu Daya Hotel** Lot 3–4, Block 9, Jln Pantai; ✆ 088 240000; e info@kkdayahotel.com. Reputedly an efficient 2-star near Wisma Merdeka. $$

SHOESTRING HOTELS Locally classed as no-star 'budget hotels', the best of this category will be clean, modern and security-wise, with friendly staff, air conditioning, satellite television, hot showers, a fridge and rooms you can (just about!) move around in. The worst will have cramped, windowless rooms, tepid showers, a fan rather than air conditioning, and be borderline clean, or just pretty shabby. Price-wise they mostly come under 100MYR, some as low as 50MYR for a single/double. Some will offer family rooms for 100–150MYR and there is usually the choice of 'upgrading' to a superior room, which may just mean the addition of a bathtub, and a piece of furniture or two.

🏠 **Ang's Hotel** (35 rooms) 28 Lorong Bakau (off Jln Pantai); ☎ 088 234999; e angshotel@asi.com.my. A clean, partly windowless box with AC & (non sat) TV, dble bed & toilet/shower. Falls in the no-star budget category & great value for this price. 'A bargain with clean sheets' was one tourist's comment. Good location & many coffee shops in the area, inc at the hotel itself. $

🏠 **High Street Inn** 38 Jln Pantai; ☎ 088 218111. In the charm-free budget category but clean with AC & TV. In the street behind Ang's Hotel. $
🏠 **Hotel Holiday** Lot 1-2, Block F, Segama Shopping Complex; ☎ 088 213116. On all accounts a bit rough around the edges; showers aren't always hot, some taps are faulty, but the rooms are clean, with TV, AC, and good enough value for this price. It has family rooms for around 100MYR. In the CBD/waterfront area. $

HOSTELS There is a growing pack of budget hostels and lodges, where tariffs often include breakfast. I can't possibly list them all – so have listed the ones I know and/or come highly recommended by other travellers. (See links to another 15 or so backpacker places on www.hostelworld.com.) They are generally priced between 20MYR (dorm room) and 50MYR (twin room). Some have family rooms. There is a beehive of hostels centrally located in the streets between Jalan Gaya where the Sunday tamu market is held, and further back between Jalan Balai Polis, Australia Place and the base of Signal Hill.

🏠 **Trekkers Lodge** 30 Jln Haji Saman; ☎ 088 252263; e sales@trekkerslodge.com; www.trekkerslodge.com. A central, reputable, B&B hostel among an age-varied clientele. Dorm, twin & family rooms with shared bathroom facilities, & homely common room facilities, a balcony, & Wi-Fi. All prices inc b/fast. $
🏠 **Borneo Backpackers** Jln Balai Polis; ☎ 088 234009; www.borneobackpackers.com. Run by Borneo Eco Tours (of Sukau Rainforest Lodge fame); accolades of being clean, cosy, friendly & well run. 4/6/10-bed dorms, plus private rooms, free Wi-Fi, laundry, lounge & roof garden deck, fan & AC. The

hostel's basement café-cum-wartime museum has already become a bit of a landmark, loved for its yesteryear ambience. Styled as a traditional post-war coffee shop, the **Borneo 1945 Museum Kopitiam** is decked with copies of war memorial plaques, photos of 'unsung' wartime heroes — Australian & British — & antique furniture $
🏠 **Borneo Global Backpackers** e Borneogb@ streamyx.com; www.bgbackpackers.com. South of the CBD towards Tanjung Aru Beach & the airport, gets good reviews for cleanliness & good management. Buses run out front so transport is easy. $

SERVICED APARTMENTS
🏠 **Penthouse KK** Marina Court; e noel@ penthousekk.com; www.penthousekk.com. A New Zealand couple lease this fully equipped, 2-level 5-bed penthouse with views over KK bay, for 500MYR/night. $$$$
🏠 **Marina Court Resort Condominium** Lorong Api-Api 3, Api-Api Centre; ☎ 088 260003; e mcrc@ promenade.com.my. 3-bedroom luxury condominium

apts managed by the Promenade Hotel group. $$$–$$$$
🏠 **Likas Square Business Suites** 1 Lorong Likas Sq, Jln Istiadat Likas (2km north of city); ☎ 088 252233; e likassq@tm.net.my; www.likassquare.com. 1–3-bedroom suites for nightly/weekly/monthly lease, overlooking Likas Bay or Mount Kinabalu. Living & dining rooms, fully equipped kitchens, AC, sat TV,

phone, fridge, etc. Within Likas shopping & business centre, many restaurants & its own De Square Café $$$

🏠 **Promenade Hotel** Api-Api Centre; ☎ 088 260888; e apartments@promenade.com.my. More budget to mid-range apts for weekly/monthly leases. $$–$$$

✖ WHERE TO EAT

Whilst there are some quality hotspots to discover in Kota Kinabalu, there are also some pitfalls to avoid. Flashy décor doesn't always mean good food, so don't look for shiny counters and dozens of Western faces as signs of a good place to eat. It is often the less polished places that serve the best food, and at the best value. You can get a good meal of noodles with meat or seafood for as little as 6MYR

STREET FOOD/FOOD COURTS For quality food on the go, there are food stalls at several places in the city. At the southern end of the waterfront they are found in the area of Anjung Senja ('sunset deck').

Pasar malam (night markets) There is a *pasar malam* on the waterfront, near the Handicraft Centre. Among fresh fruit, fish and vegetable stalls, many **gerai makan** stalls set up here from late afternoon until about midnight, serving grilled fish, satays, Malay and Indo Malay fast (but good!) food. Try the Murtabak. There is another night market with loads of food stalls along Jalan Kampung Air, back from the waterfront, behind City Park. Further east towards the museum district, the **Kompleks Karamunsing** commercial zone has outdoor evening food stalls serving Malay and Indonesian food.

Tanjung Aru Beach Three kilometres south of the city (in the direction of the airport). Head here for beachy night atmosphere. There are some food stalls and open-air seafood restaurants along the beachfront and through the parkland (Anjung Perdana). At **First Beach** Tanjung Aru, there is also a nightly (more Western) beach BBQ where you can select a platter of seafood or meat and have it cooked then served with different sauces.

Wisma Merdeka Food Court On the second floor of the shopping centre, with at least a dozen different stalls serving Malay, Chinese and Indian food, noodles, curries and *laksas*, and one vegetarian stall (**Healthy Vegetarian**). Here you will find a fantastic range and quality, with all you can eat and drink for under 10MYR. For the stalls which serve prepared dishes from *bains-marie* it is best to arrive between 11.00 and 14.00 when it is fresh and hot. For dishes cooked on the spot, any time in shopping centre hours is fine. At one entrance, the cake shop **Tea Time Express** has pork-free pastries and buns (English-style cakes, Chinese buns, avocado cake, mango puddings, etc).

Segama Complex This is opposite Wisma Merdeka, with dozens of rather ordinary shop-lots – small shops, coffee shops and fast-food chains such as KFC, descended on by Western tourist masses and beer drinkers alike.

Warisan Square More upmarket food (though less interesting than authentic Malaysian food court grub), cafés and restaurants – including Asian and international chains – spread over several floors. On the ground floor, you will find **Fish & Co** for 'Seafood in a Pan'. **Starbucks** and **San Francisco Coffee** are both on the first floor, as is **Yoshima Japanese Restaurant**.

Kota Kinabalu **WHERE TO EAT**

5

COFFEE SHOPS There are coffee and food shops scattered all around Kota Kinabalu's streets and between its shop-lots, serving from breakfast through to dinner. At many of these places you can enjoy good-quality food and drink for 5–10MYR. I have eaten excellent *kway teow* noodle dishes with prawns for 3–4MYR from coffee shops with no names in the district of Kampung Air and the night markets.

✕ **Kedai Kopi Yuan Li** 28 Jln Pantai; ✆ 088 255864; ⏱ 06.00–15.30. Cheap curry noodles, noodles with seafood and plenty of other noodle dishes.

✕ **Yu Kee** 74 Jln Gaya; ⏱ 16.30–23.00. Famous for its *bak kut*, the herb and meat hotpot soup (about 5MYR a bowl), which has a variety of meats in it. Apparently this dish 'attracts lots of ex-Hong Kong film stars' to the place!

RESTAURANTS **Sri Selera** (formerly known as **Sedco Square** food court) Jln Haji Saman, Kampung Air (next door to Golden Screen Cinemas), is a large courtyard in which you can dine al fresco (with a rolling roof in case of wet weather) at a few seafood restaurants or kitchens. **Suang Tain Seafood**, **Sri Mutiara** and others display an array of seafood in tanks, so you can choose by weight from the lobster, elephant tusk clams, squid, crab and fish. There's also an à la carte menu and plenty of vegetables – jungle ferns, spinach, cauliflower, broccoli. The place has plenty of atmosphere – it seats up to 1,200 people, so it can be noisy. Prices average around 30MYR per person, though there are also many *gerai* food stalls in the area for cheaper options.

✕ **Ocean Seafood** Jln Tun Fuad Stephens, waterfront (next to Promenade Hotel); ✆ 088 264701; ⏱ lunch & dinner. This place is Malaysia-renowned – like a theme park of seafood dining. So if you don't mind the tour buses rolling into its car park the food experience is excellent. Crabs, prawns, scallops, oyster & lobster by the kilo (min 300g) cooked however you choose; pick straight from the eel-filled aquarium at the entrance & eat in a nice watery, partly open-air (no AC) atmosphere. **$$$**
✕ **Port View Seafood Restaurant** Jln Tun Fuad Stephens (opposite Warisan Sq shopping mall); ✆ 088 221753; www.portview.com.my; ⏱ 11.00–23.00 daily. Another waterfront seafood-world, but this one's halal. Big Chinese pergola-palazzo-style place serving many Chinese-style fish dishes: steamed fish & lobster in lemon butter sauce, crabs with black pepper, prawns 'Cantonese fisherman style', mussels with green pepper & soybean sauce. **$$$**
✕ **Grand Port View** Jln Tun Fuad Stephens (between the Customs Department & Marine Police, by Jesselton Point ferry terminal); ✆ 088 538 178. Open lunch and dinner. Further along the waterfront, an AC, more upmarket version of the other two on this stretch; largely a business clientele. **$$$**
✕ **Kampung Nelayan Restaurant** Taman Tun Fuad (15 mins' drive east of town); ✆ 088 231003/5; ⏱ 11.30–14.00/18.30–23.00; dance performance

19.45–20.45. It may well be a tour-group place but it can be an incredible evening on this antiquated floating 'seafood market restaurant' with its cultural dance performance, seafood, Chinese, Malay (and ample vegetarian) dishes. The main restaurant is open air but they offer private VIP rooms with AC, karaoke, couch, washroom, etc – which seems to bypass the best of the atmosphere. **$$$**
✕ **Beijing** Also at Kampung Nelayan, Taman Tun Fuad (15 mins' drive east of town); ✆ 088 231003. Open 6.30–11pm. Open-air buffet, BBQ & steamboat, from 25MYR pp – it's a very child-friendly place, which promises 'Below 3ft height = FOC [free of charge], & below 4ft height = half price'! **$$$**
✕ **Garden Seafood Restaurant** Jln Mat Salleh; ✆ 088 215555. Evenings. Back in Tanjung Aru, another eat-with-the-locals seafood diner. Very popular for good-quality & value seafood. **$$$**
✕ **Restoran Rasa Nyonya** 50 Jln Gaya; ✆ 218 092. Lunch through to late. Tasty, budget-priced & authentic Nyonya food – spicy chicken & fish, Penang *laksa*, noodles. Halal. **$$**
✕ **Restoran Sir Melaka** 9 Jln Laiman Diki (in Kampung Air zone). Another place for Nyonya & wider Malay food, more chic yet inexpensive. **$$**
✕ **@mosphere Restaurant** 18th Floor, Menara Tun Mustapha; ✆ 088 425100; e info@ atmosphererestaurant.com; www.atmosphererestaurant.com. Best views in town. Lots of Westerners go there. It is all lights & glitch

& colour, with pastel-coloured couches & shutters. The same décor in the cocktail bar. **$$**
✗ **Luna Rossa** Bulatan Perdana, along Jln Sulaman; ↘ 088 266882; ⏱ 11.00–14.00/18.00–24.00, later on w/ends. A new, stylish-looking restaurant & bar run by an Italian, quite a way from the waterfront. The décor looks like Borneo meets Bali. **$$**

In addition, the **Waterfront Esplanade** is a lively new area opposite Warisan Square. Highlights include **Shiraz** on Sedco Square, **Kohinoor North Indian Restaurant** (↘ *235160*), and **Jothy's Banana Leaf** (*ground floor, Api-Api Centre*) is popular for cheap but good Indian grub.

COFFEE AND CAKE For local baked goods sniff out the **Southern Cake Shop** – there's one on Jalan Pantai, near the Sunday market area. The **Coffee Bean & Tea Leaf** have four outlets about town: in Wisma Merdeka, along the Waterfront Esplanade, in Kompleks Damai shopping centre and in Kompleks Karamunsing. It's totally Westernised and standardised in its sandwiches, salads and sweets but makes a nice peaceful place to sit and have good (non-Sabah) coffee if you are craving Arabica's, espressos and lattes (or waffles and scones) while stocking up on coffee beans or ground coffee and speciality teas or enjoying the free Wi-Fi. Prices on the vast drinks menu average 7–10MYR, while snacks, sandwiches and pastas range from 10 to 15MYR.

ENTERTAINMENT AND NIGHTLIFE

Most of the action, from bars to nightclubs, exists along the waterfront stretch from south to north. For a medium-sized city, Kota Kinabalu has a lively nightlife and thriving gay and lesbian scene. If you prefer musical and cultural events to clubbing the best thing is to check with Sabah Tourism Board (↘ *088 212121; www.sabahtourism.com*) for current shows and festivities. During major cultural celebrations, hotels will put on music and dance performances on a daily basis. Drinks prices vary between venues (as does the quality of mixed drinks and cocktails), from 10–15MYR for a beer, whilst a shot of spirits or glass of wine can be up to double that. Many places have happy hours and some have 'ladies' nights', serving free drinks to female customers.

♀ **Upper Star** Segama Complex, opposite the Hyatt Hotel, Jln Datuk Salleh Sulong. A multi-decked venue, with a good cocktail bar-lounge. People swear by this bar for its good atmosphere, affordable drinks & good snack food. Mixed venue, but popular with the gay crowd.

♀ **Shenanigans** Hyatt Hotel, Jln Datuk Salleh Sulong. Bar/disco where locals spend their savings on extravagantly priced drinks. It's an old-timer on the local night scene but is still going strong (locals refer to it as Sheni'). Mixed venue, but popular with the gay crowd.

♀ **Q Bar** 50 Jln Gaya. Many gay clubbers rave about the decor and friendly staff here.

♀ **Mosaic** Jln Datuk Salleh Sulong. A sleek wine bar, with modern AC restaurant & café (said to be 'the perfect place to cruise').

♀ **Cocoon Bar & Restaurant** Jln Tun Fuad Stephens; ↘ 088 0211252; ⏱ 11.00–01.00/02.00; bar opens 17.00. The name aptly describes the low lights & modern décor. Far from cosy however, it's a big place – primarily a lounge club with live bands, inexpensive bar food & a garden restaurant serving light food by day (from *laksa* to Western) & more serious eating at night (when the main bar is crowded & bands are noisy). There's also inexpensive bar food.

♀ **Rumba** Ground floor Le Meridien hotel, Jln Tun Fuad Stephens. Latin grill & bar comes complete with Filipino male dancers happy to give ladies free salsa lessons. The bouncers try & woo you in the back door as you are walking past.

Despite its pleasant name, the Waterfront Esplanade is not the most picturesque zone – it's a raffish mix of souvenir shops, bars and cafés. It does have some hot clubbing spots for the in-crowd though. At twilight the temporary shop-lot look fades into the watery setting and often resplendent Kota Kinabalu sunsets. **Bed** (I believe it stands for 'Best Entertainment Destination') is good for live bands, live dance and international DJs. If you make it out before 23.00 you can head next door to the waterfront food stalls before going back to the other places on the waterfront. European beers flow freely at **The Loft**, and trendy crowds frequently stay to see the sunrise. Drinks average 15MYR.

The lobby wine bar **Blue Note** at Shangri La's Tanjung Aru is far more low-key and low-light, and one of the few places with a range of wines by the glass. Things can liven up here too – it is also the dance floor and venue for live band and DJ nights.

For a traditional British theme, Irish bar **The Shamrock** and the **Cock 'n' Bull** have beer, pool tables and live music on tap (if a Filipino band doing Phil Collins renditions is your thing!).

FESTIVALS AND EVENTS

For further details on the following or other cultural celebrations and events, contact Sabah Tourism (**e** info@sabahtourism.com). Also pick up a copy of the bi-monthly *Discover Sabah* magazine.

TADAU KA'AMATAN (Harvest festival) Celebrations of the Kadazandusun and Murut communities happen during the month of May so look out for dance and other cultural performances at your hotel, or in the streets. See *Chapter 1, People*, page 151, for more information.

SABAH ART GALLERY During the month of May, watch out for the Patterns and Colours of Sabah, an annual month-long exhibition where craftspeople from Sabah's multi-ethnic communities show new samples of their intricate combinations of pattern and colours in their designs.

THE SABAH DRAGON BOAT RACE A traditional Chinese festival which attracts dragon boat teams from China, Japan, Brunei and Australia during the month of June. It is held at Likas Bay (also the site of Merdeka Month – a month-long celebration to celebrate Malaysian independence, from mid-August).

MOONCAKE FESTIVAL Usually held in late September, and known as the mid-autumn festival, it marks the rebellion against the Mongols in 14th century China and is celebrated with the eating of many moon cakes and with lantern parades.

RAMADHAN BAZAAR (spelt Ramadhan in Malay, as opposed to Ramadan in other societies). Sometime around mid-September to mid-October, Muslims fast for a month. Ironically, amazing food is served at the sundown Ramadhan bazaars held at various locations in Kota Kinabalu and organised by the Kota Kinabalu City Hall.

SHOPPING

HANDICRAFTS SRI PELANCONGAN (*Lot 4, Ground Floor, Block L, Sinsuran Complex, off Jln Chong Thian Vun;* **e** *kadaiku@sabathtourism.com*) This is owned by Sabah Tourism and has a handicraft shop selling woven items, tapestries, paintings, books, musical instruments, T-shirts, beads, baskets, bookmarks, souvenirs and locally produced products such as Sabah tea and Tenom coffee. **The Waterfront** precinct (*Jln Tun Fuad Stephens*) houses the outlet for the Borneo Trading Post (e *www.borneotradingpost.com*) – an upmarket, ethnic online distributor with a Monsopiad warrior mascot called 'Borneo Bob'.

SHOPPING CENTRES Kota Kinabalu is not yet major high-street territory, but signs of the slow arrival over coming years of some luxury flagships are there. **Warisan Square** has more upmarket brands – international, casual couture labels and Asian natural cosmetic brands. Overall, it's a chic shopping mall in a partly glass-roofed pavilion, with arcades of shops to each side (rather than the predominant wall-to-wall, sometimes unattractive and cramped, style of other shopping centres). The **Wisma Merdeka** is far more down to earth – the second-biggest shopping centre in Sabah has plenty of shops, restaurants and a food court. It's good for electronics and clothes, and lots of 'buy-one-free-one' offers. **Centrepoint** has good entertainment, electronics and photographic stores. **KK Plaza** is quite stuffy and dowdy, but it has a good supermarket, some very cheap phone/electronic and clothing stores, and is open late in the basement level.

The best supermarket if you want imports, foreign wines and liquor, or if you are craving brands such as Lindt, McVitie's or Walkers Highland Oatcakes, is the **Tong Hing Supermarket** (*Jln Gaya; ⊕ 08.00–22.00*). It has a nice little Chinese bakery too. Nearby, on Jalan Pantai, is **Milimewa**, the oldest supermarket chain in the state.

MARKETS The main foreshore area of the CBD along Jalan Tun Fuad Stephens is market row. Stretching over half a kilometre, side by side are the handicraft market, central market (*pasar besar*) and fish markets for loads of fresh *ikan*. A fresh fruit and fish market, interspersed with tables and chairs, is set up on the water's edge each afternoon opposite Le Meridien Hotel. By evening it transforms into a *pasar malam* (night market), full of food stalls. The main night market is held around the streets south of City Park. The handicraft market seems to be a new, anglicised name aimed at concealing the real name of *pasar Filipino* (Filipino market), which is viewed a bit disdainfully at times for the Filipino produce that floods it. The large undercover market has few genuine Sabahan crafts, but is still a very vivid place to mingle. **Pesta Jalan Gaya** also known as the **Gaya Street Fair** or Sunday market is held along Jalan Gaya every Sunday (⊕ *06.00–13.00*) and is described as Kota Kinabalu's particular interpretation of the *tamu*. Remedial herbs, aquarium fish, baskets, bric-a-brac, crafts, potted plants and food of many flavours and forms (*nasi lemak*, all kinds of *kuih* cakes, coconut juice) are among the things you can buy here.

OTHER PRACTICALITIES

WHAT TO SEE AND DO

Between the ocean in front and the green belt of hills behind, the city exists around three main parallel streets, spanning just a few hundred metres.

The waterfront is rimmed by Jalan Tun Fuad Stephens. The hub of three–five-star hotels, shopping plaza and markets, it runs for about 1.5km from the Sutera

Harbour area in the south to the Jesselton Point ferry terminal in the north. Parallel to this is Jalan Tun Razak, which runs through lots of shop-lots and several shopping complexes. The name of the road changes a few times too. Hugging closer to the foothills of Signal Hill, Jalan Gaya is a neighbourhood on its own, with smaller boutique and budget hotels, hostels, banks, restaurants and the Sunday *tamu* market.

LOOKOUTS AND LANDMARKS

Signal Hill This is the green belt which swathes Kota Kinabalu for its entire length, and forms a leafy backdrop to the city. The view from the observatory takes in the entire city, coast and islands. Below, at Jalan Gaya 51, you can see the **Sabah Tourism building**, dating to 1916, which is one of just three buildings which withstood World War II bombings. After minor restoration work, it was gazetted as a heritage structure and held many hallowed roles including Government Printing Office, Treasury, Audit Office, District Office and Attorney General's Office, before the Sabah Tourism Board moved in in 1991. At the other end of Signal Hill Road on Bukit Brace (Brace Hill) is another war survivor, the **Atkinson Clock Tower**, a quaint, white, wooden structure. It was built in 1905 by an English woman, Mary Edith Atkinson, in memory of her son, Francis George Atkinson, the first District Officer of Jesselton, who died of malaria aged 28.

Sabah's State Mosque (Masjid Negeri Sabah) Lying south of the city centre in Sembulan, its towering minaret and pewter-coloured bulbous dome bear striking gold inlay motifs. Visitors must report to the information officer on duty prior to entering, and are asked to dress appropriately. Visiting hours change according to prayer times, but generally are mornings and afternoons, never around midday and after 16.00, with shorter visiting hours Friday.

Likas Bay The coast road from the city around Likas Bay offers a strip of the best edge-of-city nature and leisure, passing through parklands and mangroves – a favourite area for picnics and evening jogs. On one side is the ocean, with the Crocker Range foothills in the background, capped by Mount Kinabalu.

Wetland Centre (❧ *088 246955;* ⊕ *08.00–18.00 Tue–Sun, closed Mon; adult 10MYR, student 5MYR, under 6s free*) Nestled among some remaining mangrove forest, the centre used to be the Kota Kinabalu City Bird Sanctuary but reoriented itself to become more educational and recreational, with 24ha of parklands, tree planting and other activities. Binoculars can be bought for 5MYR to view the 80 different types of birds. To get there by bus take the bus No 1, direction Likas from city hall or Wawasan Plaza stations, and get off at Likas Square.

Menara Tun Mustapah The biggest contrast to the colonial relics, the tower sits out over the foreshore of Likas Bay, 3km north of the city. From the outside, it looks like a glass-windowed kaleidoscope. Despite appearing cylindrical in form, it is actually a 72-sided polygon. With walls of 2,160 special reflective panels, it can withstand winds of up to 272km/h. The 30-storey building must have been très avant-garde for Kota Kinabalu in the 1970s when it was built. It still makes quite a statement, with its glass panes reflecting the silhouettes of mountains, mosques and sea in a stunning way. Although it is mostly occupied by offices, the public can enjoy the best part from the top-floor revolving restaurant and cocktail bar.

City Mosque Perched over the water village of Kampung Likas, at one end of a small lake, are the shimmering white walls and blue bulbous dome of the City

Mosque, which simply radiates in the sunlight over the river. A fine example of contemporary Islamic architecture, built in 1997, the prayer floor can accommodate 10,000–12,000 people, and houses three *madrasahs* (Islamic religious schools). Take bus No 5A or a taxi for around 12–15MYR. Visiting hours as above for Sabah's State Mosque.

MUSEUMS

Sabah Museum Complex *(Jln Bukit Istana Lama;* ✆ *088 253199;* e *muzium.sabah@ sabah.gov.my; www.mzm.sabah.gov.my;* ☉ *09.00–17.00 daily; 15MYR)* It is very refreshing, and so very Sabah, to find most of the city's museums located together in a kind of urban jungle. A 4km journey from the city, up on Bukit Istana Lama (Old Palace Hill) where British North Borneo's colonial governor once resided, the complex brings together the **State Museum**, a **Science and Education Centre**, **Sabah Art Gallery**, the **Museum of Islamic Civilisation** and a reconstructed 'heritage village' with traditional tribal houses and ethno-botanical gardens. Take bus No 13 (direction Penampang) and get off at the bottom of the hill and walk up, or take a taxi for 12–15MYR. Photos can only be taken outside, not within the museum buildings.

The State Museum This has an exhibition hall on its ground floor with changing expos and six permanent galleries: the Islamic Civilisation Gallery, the Archaeology and History Gallery, Natural History Gallery, Art Gallery, Ceramic and Brassware Gallery, and Traditional Costumes Gallery.

The Science and Education Centre The centre houses the Geology Gallery, permanent exhibitions on the petroleum industry and copper mining in Sabah and other, temporary exhibitions.

BEACHES Located 3km south of the city centre, **Tanjung (Cape) Aru** gets its name from the rows of casuarina trees (*aru*) along the shoreline of its long, beach-rimmed headland. It's a peaceful, sand-lovers escape from the city centre of Kota Kinabalu, but still with quite a bit of nightlife, dining (see *Where to eat*, page 163) and conveniences, including a new shopping plaza. If you are staying here, most resorts offer bus-shuttle services to and from Kota Kinabalu city centre. If not, take the bus marked Tanjung Aru Beach from the City Hall terminal. Join the locals in running or walking along the shoreline through Tanjung Aru Park (formerly known as Prince Philip Park), which also has a good children's playground.

WELL-BEING

Cres Moment *(Warisan Square, Block A)* A relatively upmarket southeast Asian chain, offering foot reflexology, shiatsu back massage, body massages, milk baths and steam baths. Treatments cost 48–128MYR.

D'Bor Neobayu Spa *(Wisma HCS, Jln Kolam, Luyang;* ✆ *088 216648;* e *neobayu1@ streamyx.com)* For a more traditional treatment, take a taxi to Luyang. Situated 15km from the CBD, this family-run business of traditional Kadazandusun healers has been operating under the guidance of 'Auntie Rosie' for almost three decades. The Kadazandusuns use lemon grass (*sogumau*) in healing as well as cooking. It's one of the main detox ingredients used here in massages, scrubs, steams, compresses and exfoliations. The two-hour Neobayu Sirih Pinang treatment won an award as Best Traditional Treatment during the 2006 Malaysia Spa & Wellness Awards in Kota Kinabalu. If you have children, they are taken good care of while you have a treatment – they may even come away having learnt the *sumazu*, the Kadazandusun traditional dance.

Jari Jari (*Lot 2.1, Block B, 2nd Floor, Tanjung Aru Plaza;* \ *088 272606;* e *sales@jarijari.com.my; www.jarijari.com.my*) This place offers traditional Dusun massage.

WALKS There is a heritage walk on Tuesday and Thursday mornings operated by KK Heritage Walk (e *info@kkheritagewalk.com; www.kkheritagewalk.com*). Take a look at their itinerary.

EXCURSIONS FROM KOTA KINABALU

Some places in the following chapter, *West Coast Sabah*, are possible day trips. The following are much closer to the capital (30–35km) and can easily be half-day trips or used as an alternative accommodation base.

SOUTHEAST OF KOTA KINABALU – PENAMPANG The Penampang District is the nerve-centre of Kadazandusun culture. Fringed by rice paddy and the Sungai Babujong/Penampang River, the region was once deep hinterland, but is now virtually Kota Kinabalu city limits. **Kampung Dongonggon** is the heart of the district and the place to be every Thursday and Friday morning for the *tamu*. Starting from about 06.00 and continuing through to early afternoon, you will find everything from *lihing* (rice wine) to *butod* (sago worms) – the witchetty grubs of Borneo. There are a couple of places in town serving typical Kadazandusun food.

For a taste of mythical Kadazandusun culture, tribal warriors and headhunting, visit **Monsopiad Cultural Village** (MCV) (\ *088 774337;* e *info@monsopiad.com; www.monsopiad.com;* ⊕ *09.00–17.00 daily; adult 60MYR, children 12 & under 25MYR*). It's a tourist attraction with a capital 'T' and ghoulishness galore. The thing which pulls the crowds is the House of Skulls (Siou Do Mohoing), where all 42 'trophies' of the Dusun warrior Monsopiad hang from the rafters. There are other traditional houses in the village – the *tangkob*, or granary, where the *padi* is housed, and a small Monsopiad museum housing artefacts such as ceramic jars, *padi* grinders, bamboo items and *bobohizan* (high priestess) costumes. Admission includes welcome drink, performance (three daily) and guided tour (three daily).

Getting there and away
By car Take Jalan Penampang from near the State Mosque just south of downtown Kota Kinabalu (in Sembulan), and head about 13km southeast to Donggongon. MCV is another 2km from here

By taxi 35MYR one-way from Kota Kinabalu.

By bus Take the No 13 bus to Donggongon town from either the City Hall or Wawasan Plaza station. The fare is around 1.5MYR for MCV transfer to a minibus bound for Terawi; indicate your stop to the driver. Fare is 1MYR.

NORTH OF KOTA KINABALU – TUARAN Rivers and rural markets meet headland silhouettes and wispy beaches in the Tuaran District. While the coast is starting to build up, it is still far from a riviera – to reach it you will pass roadside food stalls selling *kelapa* (coconut pudding), mangrove swamps, lagoons and water buffalo in rice *padi*. The sprinkling of luxury and mid-range resorts in the area offer an alternative to the rush of Kota Kinabalu for families, beach and nature lovers, with the city still in easy enough reach. From the Karumbunai Peninsula in Meggatal the beach continues 6km through to Pantai Dalit Beach in Tuaran interrupted by a few lagoons.

Getting there and away

By car Drive approximately 35km north of Kota Kinabalu, and 42km from Kota Kinabalu Airport. Take the Kota Kinabalu–Kudat highway north.

By bus From Wawasan Plaza, buses leave for Tuaran between 07.30 and 17.00. Make sure to indicate to the driver where you want to get off.

Where to stay

Rasa Ria Resort (420 rooms) Jln Pantai Dalit, Tuaran; ☎ 088 792888; e rrr@shangri-la.com; www.shangri-la.com. An enchanting beach & bay setting – 400 acres of gardens on the edge of a 64-acre nature reserve & orang-utan sanctuary. Spacious, nicely furnished deluxe rooms (with rainforest or garden & sea views), fitness centre, jacuzzi, steam room & massage. Lots of outdoor & children's activities, watersports & fishing, horseriding, cycling, nature walks & nature interpretation centre. Good dining & entertainment. Shuttle service into KK for about 28MYR return. $$$$–$$$$$

Nexus Resort Karambunai (485 rooms) Off Jln Sepangar Bay (30km from KK), Meggatal, ☎ 088 411222; e info@nexusresort.com; www.nexusresort.com. The luxury resort describes its lawns as 'manicured' & it's spot-on, all through the ocean-fronted gardens; villa-looking rooms have rather heavy Chinese-inspired furniture. Lovely lobby area, lounges, clubs, pool bars & dining galore. Multiple pools & good swimming beach (when the jellyfish are absent). Special kids' care & activities. $$$$–$$$$$

Tuaran Beach Resort Off Jln Pantai Dalit, Jln Sabandar; ☎ 088 793593; e info@ tuaranbeachresort.com; www.tuaranbeachresort.com. Formerly the Sabandar Bay Resort this reopened after a makeover in 2007. On a 5km beach, large rooms & suites (25m² upwards), chalet style, many with sea-facing balconies. Local tour guides highly recommend it. Chinese, Malay & Western food; activities & child-oriented Health centre, big pool, shuttle service to & from KK. $$$$

Where to eat

Coast Restaurant & Bar Pantai Dalit, at the Rasa Ria Resort; ⏰ 17.30–24.00, last order 22.30. If you are craving Mediterranean food the stunning glass-walled place through which the sun sets has décor extravagance, lights like neon octopus tentacles hanging over tables, Italian cooking, and a chef from Norwich. Average 80MYR main course. $$$$

Gayang Jln Sulaman Tuaran; ☎ 088 229066. A seafood restaurant in mesmerising setting among mangrove forest & inlets, with fish straight from the aquariums if you wish. $$$

Salut Seafood Restaurant Jln Sulaman Tuaran; ☎ 088 301300. Just next door to Gayang & said to be good for its fresh seafood, crab & grilled fish. $$$

What to see and do The district township of **Pekan Tuaran** has a wistful river setting at which you will see people fishing from longboats. Smoke from the daytime *gerai makan* food stalls billows around its banks and you can get excellent cheap Malay food – grilled fish and meats and Murtabak – and try the local noodle dish, *Tuaranmee*, in the village coffee shops. Home of the Lotud tribe – part of the Kadazandusun – there is also a lively Sunday *tamu* market here (⏰ 06.00–14.00). There's a *tamu* in neighbouring **Tamparuli**, about 5km further north, on Wednesdays. The *bambangan* condiment, made from a sour mango-like fruit, is delicious.

Dalit Bay Golf Club & Spa (e *sales@karambunaigolf.com*; ⏰ 07.00–20.00 daily) Situated in Tuaran, the club has an 18-hole course, designed by golf architect Ronald Fream, sculpted from a former mangrove swamp. There is also white-water rafting on the Kiulu River, and there are equestrian centres for horseriding.

Kampung Mengkabong (*4km from Tuaran*) This is a satellite-dish-decked, yet dilapidated, Bajau village perched on the river. Perhaps a little over-rated as a tourist attraction. Some locals welcome tourists and have crafts ready, others do not. The Mengkabong River estuary has many mangroves, and there are river cruises to go on. For watersports enthusiasts, the beach resorts offer them all, while **Lagoon Park** near Karambunai has skiing, jet skiing, kayaking and windsurfing (and river cruises start from here too).

Rasa Ria Nature Reserve Established by Shangri-La's Rasa Ria Resort in collaboration with the Sabah Wildlife Department in 1996 as an orang-utan sanctuary, the babies proceed to Sepilok when they reach a certain age. The reserve runs nature activities, birdwatching and nocturnal animal trips. Treks range from 20 minutes to a two-hour 'climb' to an observation tower (just 95m altitude) which gives good views over the Tuaran District.

WEST OF KOTA KINABALU – TUNKU ABDUL RAHMAN (TAR) PARK
Off the coast of Kota Kinabalu, the five islands of the TAR will accompany you through your journey in Kota Kinabalu and in coastal areas north and south of the capital. Pulau Gaya, Pulau Manukan, Pulau Sapi, Pulau Mamutik and Pulau Sulug make up a marine park, created in 1974 and named after Malaysia's first prime minister, the fiercely pro-independence (*merdeka, merdeka!*) Tunku Abdul.

Overseen by Sabah Parks the TAR park takes in about 50km² of islands, coral reefs and ocean. The largest and most handsome, **Pulau Gaya**, is home to several *kampong ayer,* or water villages, with hundreds of houses precariously perched on stilts over the water looking back over to the shores of Kota Kinabalu. The Bajau people were allowed to remain living in the park under native customary land rights. The original trading settlement of the British North Borneo Chartered Company was established here. The tiny (10ha) outcrop of **Pulau Sapi** was once connected to Pulau Gaya and you can still cross between the two by foot at low tide.

The state of the waters of this marine park are not always in keeping with a marine reserve. Too many tourists could be one problem. Where there's a water village (*kampung ayer*) there's usually a fair bit of rubbish, though education is hoped to slowly improve things here. The TAR, and all the islands within it, have a fringe of reefs – more so on the sheltered southern and eastern fronts facing the mainland. The beaches of **Pulau Manukan** and **Pulau Sapi** descend gradually into the reef drop-off, and you can see the line quite clearly unless the winds are up. The ocean-facing western and northern coasts of the islands are more remote and marked by rocky cliffs and coral debris.

A shattered chain of lumps of sandstone and sedimentary rock, the islands broke off from the mainland during the last Ice Age. They are marked by honeycombed cliffs, caves, and a mix of coastal and strand flora including screw pines (*Pandanus dubius*), casuarinas, coconuts, big (really big!) monitor lizards and long-tailed macaque monkeys are among the terrestrial animals most commonly encountered. Along the trails, you may sight the weird, scaly anteater, or pangolin, or even a bearded pig.

Getting there and away Speedboats leave from Jesselton Point wharf in town about every half-hour from early morning until late evening. Local tour companies will arrange transfers, lunch, park entry fees, etc. If you are staying at one of the resorts on the islands, transfers are included. The trip takes 10–20 minutes. The conservation fees to Sabah Parks are 10MYR for adults, or 6MYR for visitors below 18 years. Divers pay 50MYR per person per day.

⌂ Where to stay and eat

⌂ **Manukan Island Resort** (20 chalets) Pulau Manukan; ☏ 088 302399; e info@ suterasanctuarylodges.com; www.suterasanctuarylodges.com. The hilltop & beachfront chalets & lodges all have a 'back to nature' feel about them, with chunky wood & big windows onto forest greenery & ocean blue, yet they have many nice comfort & aesthetic touches. As the island gets invaded by day-tripping hordes it is still easy to escape the crowds & go trekking, boating or make your way to a private cove & beach. By night it is bliss, as the crowds retreat to the mainland by early afternoon. The cosy yet spacious single- & double-storey chalets feature nice traditional building materials & decorations, have AC, a living area, TV & 1–2 bedrooms. Food-wise there are a couple of resort restaurants but you will be a captive audience to higher resort prices – don't expect street food & markets. All-inclusive prices for chalets, transfers, b/fast, park fees are expensive for the accommodation style. $$$–$$$$

Gayana Island EcoResort (44 rooms) Malohom Bay, Gaya Island; ℡ 088 245158; e info@gayana-ecoresort.com; www.gayana-ecoresort.com. Built in semi-water village style, the landing, main pavilion, bars & restaurants are all on stilts & duckboards. The resort & rooms are built in natural materials, with some swish exotic design details. Rooms have AC & ceiling fan, coffee/tea-making facilities, mini fridge, TV, lounge furnishings, & en-suite bathrooms. The resort has its own marine ecology research centre. Luxury & eco go in hand a lot these days: there is a vast 'Nature Pool', a private 162ft luxury motor yacht for cruising, & a mix of Western–Malaysian cuisine at the Island Seafood Restaurant & Waterfront Bistro. $$$

Ⲗ Camping There are campsites operated by Sabah Parks (www.sabahparks.org) on Mamutik, Sapi and Gaya islands. 5MYR pp per night (2MYR under 18s).

What to see and do Many people don't see beyond the somewhat cattle-driven barbecue buffet lunches offered by Sutera Sanctuary Lodge on **Pulau Manukan** – which is fine for a quick taste of the islands, but there are many other marvellous things to do. If you are after seclusion, then seek it out! In peak season, dozens of people are descending on these islands a day, so you can escape the crowds by planning to do a less prescribed activity, sailing around and choosing a secluded cove, doing a hike into one of the island interiors, or staying out on one of them at night with just a handful of people. Manukan has the most facilities.

Trekking Pulau Gaya This is the largest island, covered in primary rainforest which rolls its way voluptuously through creases and indents in the landscape. The forest is said to be one of the few undisturbed coastal dipterocarp forests left in Sabah. There are several trekking paths you can follow which criss-cross the island, ranging from 20 minutes' duration to several hours. One plank walk leads inland to a mangrove forest. Pulau Manukan also has several treks and there is a nice trail on Pulau Mamutik with cliff-views over the sea.

Yachting and private boat charter There are numerous secluded beaches and bays which are reachable only by boat, including **Police Beach** on the northern end of Gaya. This is the place for snorkelling, diving and swimming in clear 15m-deep waters of the bay. Its western cove is a popular resting point for sailboats. For island or cove hopping you can charter boats from the **Sutera Harbour Marina** in Kota Kinabalu.

Diving and snorkelling

The fish are almost as numerous and even more colourful than the corals, spotted, striped and patterned in a variety of rainbow colours. Pink-and-green parrot fish, the turquoise moon wrasse, clown fish, sea cucumbers and star fish are all common. If you are very lucky, you might spot an ever-friendly whale shark!

Sabah Travel Guide.com

Pulau Mamutik The smallest island (just 6ha across) has the best reefs and coral, with clear deep waters. It is Borneo Divers' dive station and frequently used for both novice and advanced PADI courses. It is also an access point to the more vibrant corals of the TAR marine park. The beaches, white sand and reefs start almost

5

immediately in the shallows. The waters descend quickly on the eastern side facing Tanjung Aru on the mainland. Basic facilities include toilets, picnic shelters, tables and barbecue pits. Contact **Borneo Divers** to arrange diving trips (*9th Floor, Menara Jubili, 53 Jln Gaya;* \ *088 222226;* e *information@borneodivers.info*).

Pulau Sapi ('Cow Island') The deep crystal aquamarine channel between Pulau Gaya and Pulau Sapi has many reef patches for snorkelling and diving. Pulau Sapi has far more facilities than Pulau Mamutik, and far more tourists. It has a watersports centre and is also a big barbecue day spot, indented with gorgeous deep blue pool coves. Its marine life is said to be good, towards the reef drop-off, on its sheltered eastern and southern sides.

'Sapi is famous for its resident monkeys, but take note, they are cunning thieves and will take just about anything they can get their paws on!' warns the Sutera Harbour Marina. 'During the migration season, the resident bird life is enriched by a large number of migrant waders, which arrive from Europe and Japan around August and September, escaping the northern winter, and returning home in April and March.'

Pulau Manukan I was very disappointed with the snorkelling off the main beach in Pulau Manukan which obviously gets very disturbed by the crowds, and is also subject at times to strong currents and winds (though not as strong as on the exposed north and western sides of the islands). With more time on the island, you can wander off and find the other long sandy strips and isolated bays.

Pulau Sulug At 8ha, Pulau Sulug is an island-beach, formed from large sandbar and rimmed by coral reefs. It is the most remote and least-visited of the islands. The rocky northwestern side of the island provides interesting diving with many sightings of sea turtles and rays, and there is watersport equipment for hire on the island as well as decent facilities.

SOUTH OF KOTA KINABALU – KINARUT The rural Papar District begins around Kinarut, and this area is another option for coastal accommodation, about 20km from Kota Kinabalu. A car or taxi from the airport will have you at your lodging within 15 minutes. The taxi fare will be about 40MYR. Between visits to Kota Kinabalu you can take catamaran trips to nearby islands, go fishing or picnicking or head further south into Papar's *padi* fields, sago palms and Kadazan culture.

Where to stay

Beringgis Beach Resort (74 rooms, 10 units, 2 chalets) Km 26 Jln Papar, Kampung Beringgis (26km from KK); \ 088 752333; e bbrpapar@ tm.net.my; www.beringgis.com.my. Clean, tasteful rooms & units with garden/sea views & Wi-Fi. Next to a fishing village on a 3km stretch of beach. $$–$$$

Langkah Syabas' Beach Resort (18 chalets) \ 088 752000; e langkahsyabas@myjaring.net. A leisurely 100m from the beach, chalets with swimming pool, appeases budget travellers & families who want it leisurely & laid-back. Food mostly Western. Australian managed, pool, leafy surrounds. $

Seaside Travellers Inn (24 rooms) Km 20 Jln Papar (Papar-KK Highway); \ 088 750555; e stinnjo@tm.net.my; www.seasidetravellersinn.com. Basic but friendly, family-run, relaxed beach-house accommodation sipping up the Kinarut seashore & South China Sea. Gardens are idyllic, with swimming pool. From basic bungalows to clean 'deluxe' rooms with their own bathroom, plus family chalets. Cats everywhere. Simple Malay & Western food from its sea-balcony café. $

6

West Coast Sabah

Between Kota Kinabalu, hilly coastal plains and a range of mountains separating the coast from the interior is *Gunung* (Mount) Kinabalu. The mountain touches almost all parts of the west coast in some way. Two exceptions are the northern and southern extremes of the coast – the rocky coastline of the Kudat Peninsula and the wetlands environment of Kota Klias. The Kudat Peninsula enters the world of the Bajau and Rungus people, and a blend of forested and agricultural landscapes. Eventually you wind up on the headland, Tanjung Simpang Mengayau, popularised as the 'tip of Borneo'. South of Kota Kinabalu (KK), inland roads wind past the Crocker Range, lined with tapioca, rubber trees, wet *padi* (of rice cultivation) and water buffalo, given as dowry by the Kadazandusun.

KOTA BELUD AND KUDAT PENINSULA

Flagrantly promoted by Sabah Tourism as a day trip to 'Cowboy of the East' territory, Kota Belud is the stronghold of the Bajau who have a reputation for being expert horsemen and women. A predominantly Muslim town, the rural surrounds of Pekan Kota Belud are river-ribbed and picturesque, plaited with well-irrigated wet rice *padi*. Further north, the Kudat Peninsula is inhabited by the Rungus people and some of their *kampung* are involved in tourism through homestays and cottage industries. The woven fabrics, beadwork and basket-ware are being sustained partly for tourists. On the coast are some minority races originally from the Philippines including Irranun and Suluk. It is possible to continue touring towards the Bengkoka Peninsula via Kota Marudu, then Pitas through to Sandakan. The roads however are poor and there are almost no visitor facilities (though this could be an attraction in itself).

GETTING THERE AND AWAY

By car Kota Belud is 75km north of Kota Kinabalu, reached along the Kota Kinabalu–Kudat Highway; Kudat is 175km from Kota Kinabalu, the tip of Borneo is 215km. If you are continuing around the coast of Sabah, it takes another hour and a half to Kota Marudu from Kudat and about seven hours to Sandakan.

Car hire Sabah Tourism says: '4x4s and cars are stationed near the Indian Restaurant opposite the Health Clinic in Kampung Air Kota Kinabalu. 4x4s take seven or eight passengers at 20–25MYR per person return; the cars take up to four passengers and charge 240MYR for a return trip to the tip of Borneo'.

By bus Air-conditioned buses destined for Kudat, via Kota Belud, leave from Padang Merdeka at 06.30, 07.30, 12.00 and 13.00. Minibuses leave daily between Kota Kinabalu and Kota Belud.

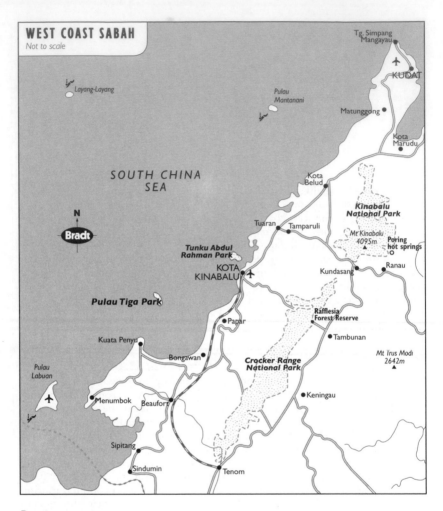

WEST COAST SABAH

SOUTH CHINA
SEA

By air MASWings (*www.maswings.com.my*) have three-weekly services (Mon, Wed and Sat) to Kudat from Kota Kinabalu in 19-seater Twin Otters. The 40-minute trip from Kota Kinabalu International Airport is quite bumpy.

WHERE TO STAY The only 3-star hotels are in Kudat town. Here there are also over a dozen small hotels and guesthouses for under 60MYR a double, but few are recommended on the basis of either cleanliness or safety standards.

Kudat town

Kudat Golf & Marina Reort (88 rooms) Jln Abdul Rahim; ☏ 088 611211; www.kudatgolfmarinaresort.com. Commanding position over Marudu Bay, a welcoming Chinese-run hotel with small fitness centre, a swimming pool, tennis court, sauna, 18-hole golf course, Wi-Fi in lobby & restaurant, excellent Chinese coffee house/restaurant. Poolside rooms can be noisy

during holiday periods. Rooms are spartan but bright, with kettle, fridge & TV. Spacious suites at mid-range prices. $$–$$$

Ria Hotel (24 rooms) Jln Marudu, Ground Flr, Lot No 3 Kudat; ☏ 088 622794. In a bright tangerine & yellow, cube-shaped building, it's the best budget hotel in town. With AC, TV, phone, minibar & kettle. The suites are even better value for money, spacious

& with a kitchenette. Next door there is a restaurant and 'Hawaii Internet Centre'. $–$$

⌂ **Upper Deck Hotel** (26) Jln Lintas Kudat; ☎ 088 622 272. On the top floor of a modern, but bland, city-centre building, above the Milimewa supermarket, some with views over Kudat Bay. Best shoestring option, AC, attached bathroom, phone, sat TV, kettle.

Tip of Borneo

⌂ **Kudat Karma** (15 villas) ☎ 088 249-276; e luxuryvillas@kudatriviera.com; www.kudat-riviera.com. A Balinese-style, eco-friendly, luxury time-share resort opened in 2008, overlooking Mosquito Net island. Managed by Touch Down Holidays. $$$$–$$$$$

⌂ **Misompuru Homestay** Kampung Minyak, 26km south of Kudat; ☎ 013 8721765 or 016 8155056; www.sabah-homestay.com. Co-ordinator Jeffry Yahya. A homestay network in the Kudat region, involving some 35 families who live in modern housing rather than longhouses, yet claim to offer a taste of traditional life through Rungus lifestyle & daily activities such as boat trips through mangrove

There are 2 suites with a few more fittings $–$$

⌂ **Kudat Rest House** (20 rooms) Jln Abdul Rahim (adjacent to the town sports field) Padang; ☎ 088 622708. Former government resthouse overlooking Kudat golf course. AC, TV, bathroom & balcony, VIP suites. Some reports of cleanliness not being up to scratch. $–$$

forest, cultural dances, gathering wild food & fishing. $

⌂ **Kampung Bavanggazo Rungus Longhouse** Also known as **Meranjak Longhouse** (10 rooms) ☎ 088 621971. Located in a valley a few kilometres off the main road to Kudat, signposted at the turn-off along Jln Tinangol. Family-run venture consisting of 2 purpose-built longhouses made traditionally with split bamboo, beaten bark & rough-hewn wood. 'Twin-bedrooms' means 2 mosquito-netted mattresses with an oil lamp & natural ventilation. Also dbl bedroom chalets. Approx 80MYR PP for dinner, bed, cultural dances & b/fast. Can be arranged through Sabah Tourism. $$

✖ WHERE TO EAT

Kota Belud There are many food stalls held by day and evening along the riverbank. **Kota Raya Restoran** is clean, bright and open-fronted with an excellent low-priced buffet. **Kudat** seafood is excellent – shellfish, fish, squid, prawns. A Hakka (northern Chinese) speciality is stuffed tofu with minced pork, *yong tau foo*. Adjacent to the *pasar ikan* fish market are a couple of shoebox-sized permanent food and drink stalls, opening onto a tree-lined car park used as extra seating space in the evenings. **Gerai Makan Dan Minum** (food and drink stall No 2899) is very good. 5–6MYR will get you a generous seafood noodle or rice dish and a drink – seaweed, coconut or sugar-cane juice. Its neighbour, **Gerai Makan Sing Wang**, is also good. In the new part of town, **Sungai Wang Restaurant** is a popular Chinese restaurant with air conditioning and outdoor dining, standard Chinese food choices but seafood-heavy, with beer and soft drinks. **Ah Foo Coffee Shop** at the Kudat Golf Club, is a Chinese seafood restaurant, good and open to public. A night market of Malay (halal) food stalls is held on Jalan Data near the Lembaga Bandaran, the open-air *gerai makan* stalls serve grilled meats and fish. No alcohol is served here. **Kedai Kopi Yu Hing** (*ground floor at the rear of the Hotel Ria*) has good, cheap breakfasts and lunch of *pau* (steamed buns), dim sum and noodles; also good for local coffee or Chinese tea. The one local place famous for its *yong tofu* is a small unnamed shop in a block of five old shop-houses along the main road into town, left of the Siew Lan tailor shop and Jaja Trading.

WHAT TO SEE AND DO

Kota Belud Acclaimed home of the *tamu* tradition, Kota Belud ('hill fort') grew up around the site of the original market, held every 20 days as a meeting place for people from all over the region. It still has that essential social flavour, the market is held every Sunday (⊕ 06.00–14.00) at Jalan Hasbollah near the town *padam* (sports field). Lots of handicrafts and good food can be found among the rather jumble-sale produce. The big annual **Tamu Besar**, where *tamu* meets beauty pageant, is in October – showground atmosphere, traditional dress and water-buffalo races.

Rungus Kampung (Kampung Gombizau) (*5min drive from main Kudat road along Jln Kampung Gombizau, 43km from Kudat town*) With a communal longhouse and locals involved in honey production, Rungus Kampung has come to be known as *Kampung Madu* or 'honeybee village'. The Rungus also gather wild plant matter for use in traditional herbal medicines, and make many useful and decorative things from coconut husks and fibre such as brooms, bowls and wooden poles. At neighbouring **Kampung Sumangkap**, the cottage industry is gong-making. There are 'nominal entry fees' to some of these villages. Many tour operators in Kota Kinabalu will organise day visits to longhouses here. A visit to **Kampung Bavanggazo** costs 35–40MYR for a welcome drink, cultural dance and handicraft item.

Tip of Borneo Kudat Peninsula, and Borneo, end at **Tanjung Simpang Mengayau** or 'lingering junction'. The cross-over point of the South China and Sulu seas, separated by Marudu Bay. The 11km unsealed road is due to be sealed by 2009. Off the coast are the islands **Pulau Balambangan** and **Pulau Banggi**. The first-ever British settlement in southeast Asia was a quickly thwarted effort to establish a trading post on Pulau Balambangan in 1773 to further the empire's developing trade with China. All signs on the peninsula lead here – at the end of a long gravel stretch penned-in by Chinese plantation houses and coconut palms is a rocky headland with its stone-scaped pathways and giant pewter globe and promontory boarded by glorious long beaches such as **Pantai Kalampunian**. The lighthouse here came too late for the numerous ships which lie wrecked under this sometimes treacherous stretch. Tour operators do day trips from Kota Kinabalu to the Kudat Peninsula, taking in some of the longhouse cottage industries, lunch and Tip of Borneo, from 250MYR to 300MYR.

Kudat Kudat is named after the coarse *lalang* grass which grows between the coconut and sago palms. Until the 1970s, the only way in was by boat along the river from Sikuati, 20km west – and it still feels marvellously isolated today. Despite its isolated location, Kudat was British North Borneo's 'capital' from 1882 until 1884. In 1882, the chartered company wooed Christian Hakka families to Kudat from southern provinces of China to fill a labour shortage on farms and coconut plantations. Those immigrants – and the coconuts – have had a long-lasting impact on the town. The **Pesta Kelapa** coconut festival is held here every September. Declared the cleanest district in Sabah in 2003, Kudat town is seaside relaxed with a 2km waterfront esplanade, and an old and new town – the former lies along Jalan Lo Thien Chok, with its fan-cooled *kedai kopi* and mixed businesses, temples and mosques. A prime angling destination, here you can negotiate with local boat owners to hire fishing or cruising vessels – just head to the marina. From there an air-conditioned ferry leaves every day at 09.00 for **Pulau Banggi** (its main township Kerakit) and returns mid-afternoon. There are markets in Kudat new town – Pekan Tomburungus – on Tuesdays and Wednesdays, and a *tamu* in Kudat on Wednesday (⊕ *06.00–14.00*). **The Kudat Golf Club** – Sabah's first – boasts of its historic links with St Andrews in Scotland.

Beaches The beaches in Kudat District are much cleaner than anywhere else in Sabah, largely because of low population density. On the peninsula's west coast, the deeply indented, funnel-shaped bay of **Teluk Agal** – accessed via Kampung Bingolon – has a beach bookended by two rivers. Past Kampung Minyak – oil

LAYANG LAYANG – A DIVER'S PARADISE

Situated 300km northwest of KK, Layang Layang is a manmade atoll, built as a Malaysian navy base and later developed into a dive resort the Layang-Layang Island Resort (e *layang@pop.jaring.my; www.layanglayang.com*). Dive writer William Moss:

Layang Layang is the summit of a huge seamount rising 2,000m from the ocean's abyssal depths. The submerged atoll spans over seven kilometres, encircling a vast lagoon. Its steep walls are a magnet for pelagics. The most famous residents are the scalloped hammerhead sharks. Usually making an appearance from April to July, they gather in their dozens or even hundreds. Other frequent visitors include manta rays, schools of barracuda, dogtooth tuna, grey reef sharks, and leopard sharks. Spinner and bottlenose dolphins frequently follow the dive boats. Rarer sightings include whale sharks, orcas and melon headed whales. Isolation from the mainland keeps the reef pristine, and the small inhabitants are equally splendid. Dives at Layang Layang are often drifts and tend to be deep, so are best for experienced divers. There are sheltered waters in the lagoon, but divers with at least an advanced qualification will get the best of the atoll's pelagic majesty and 35–40m visibility. The resort is comfortable and has a great swimming pool. Layang Layang is reached by Twin Otters from Kota Kinabalu. The small aircraft have limited carrying capacity, so photographers or others carrying excess baggage should plan well ahead.

village – **Pantai Terongkongan** features a narrow cave carved into the rocky headland to the north. **Pantai Kelambu**, near the tip of Borneo, has a sand spit leading to two small islands, with bays on either side – nice for picnics and swimming. The closest beach to Kudat is **Pantai Bak Bak**, 7km north. It's rocky rather than sandy, but rimmed with a picnic area. A few more kilometres north is **Pasir Putih**, a good swimming beach with fine white sand true to its name.

Diving Kampung Kuala Abai, a fishing village 20km west of Kota Belud, is the departure point for Mantanani Island where there is one dive resort **Mantanani Island Resort** (✆ *088 230000; www.bornsea.com; AC cabins*) and 16 dive sites. Lots of boats went down on the northwest coast before a lighthouse went up on Pulau Kalampunian, so the region is popular for wreck-diving. Kota Kinabalu-based **Sipadan-Mabul Regal Tours** have one live-aboard going there, the *Scuba Explorer*, a 22m yacht with accommodation for 12 divers.

GUNUNG KINABALU NATIONAL PARK

Mount Kinabalu had been held sacred by local indigenous communities long before Kinabalu Park was granted World Heritage status by UNESCO in 2000. For the Kadazandusun, the mountain is the resting place of souls, so those who've climbed it have always made an offering to avoid being cursed by spirits. Lower zones of Kinabalu Park have been scarred by forestry, mining and slash-and-burn agriculture; UNESCO's decision could not have come too soon.

Spreading over 754km², an area larger than Singapore, the park encompasses several mountain environments and climate zones. The coolest place in Borneo, it is a botanical and ornithological paradise with over 300 bird species, 5,000 flowering plants and a multitude of mosses, ferns and fungi. The floral inventory includes 26 rhododendrons, nine pitcher plants, over 80 fig tree species and more than 60 species of oak and chestnut tree. The 1,200 orchid species range in size from as small as a pinhead to having 2m-long stems.

Ascending from 600m to 4,101m above sea level, Gunung Kinabalu passes through 12 climate zones. With this variety comes a wealth of biodiversity, with flora and fauna adapted to the varying local conditions; from conifers and lowland rainforest to alpine meadows. The massif is marked by 16 granite peaks of various heights, culminating at the 4,095m summit. The highest is called Low's Peak, after Sir Hugh Low who led the first official expedition to the summit on 7 March 1851, when he was colonial secretary of Labuan.

At Panar Laban hut – 6km up the 8.5km trail – Low and his local guides performed the ritual sacrifice of a chicken to appease the ancestral souls and seek safe passage. Two expeditions to explore the mountain's flora and fauna led by Professor John Corner on behalf of the Royal Society of London in 1961 and 1964 were also important steps to the creation of the national park in 1964. According to the UNESCO World Heritage Centre, a World War II prisoner of war also played an instrumental role. One of six survivors of the Sandakan to Ranau death march formed the Kinabalu Memorial Committee hoping to 'preserve the Kinabalu area for the decency of man and a facility for the enjoyment of all of Sabah'. The pride of Sabah, the park gets about 400,000 visitors a year. Most do not climb to the top, choosing instead to just soak up the sublime surroundings around the lower slopes of the mountain. Gradually, this tourism is hoped to provide more jobs in industry to locals, so they can rely less on agriculture.

GETTING THERE AND AWAY

By car About 88km from Kota Kinabalu, the journey to the park takes about two hours. The last hour's climb passes vegetable markets, food stalls and craft stalls. At Kampung Nabalu, a few kilometres before the park, there is a *tamu* market every Thursday.

By taxi Leave from the long-distance taxi rank near Merdeka Field. Taxis will charge around 160MYR for up to four passengers. The taxi fare from a hotel starts at 300MYR. Reserve taxis at the park reception counter for return journey.

By bus Take minibuses and vans heading to Kundasang-Ranau from the Merdeka Field station. Buses leave from 07.30 to 17.00, and a one-way fare will cost around 18MYR. Get off on the main road opposite the Kinabalu Park entrance. Air-conditioned express buses between Kota Kinabalu's city north terminal and Ranau or Sandakan also pass the turn-off 100m from park HQ. Fares are around 15MYR.

WHERE TO STAY Accommodation in the park consists of the lodges and chalets around park HQ, those at Mesilau Nature Resort and the mid-climb accommodation at Laban Rata. All are operated by **Sutera Sanctuary Lodges** who have a contract from Sabah Parks to manage accommodation and eateries in the park. The main office is in Kota Kinabalu (*G15, Ground Floor, Wisma Sabah;* ✆ *088 243629;* e *info@suterasanctuarylodges.com; www.suterasanctuarylodges.com*). It is always best to book ahead, especially in high season around June–September and school holidays. Major mountain-climbing events and festivities such as the Chinese New Year are also very busy times (see *Chapter 2, Public holidays and festivals*, page 73, for important dates). Consider staying outside of the park (see listings on page 187 for Kundasang and Ranau), where there are a few budget to mid-range hotels and guesthouses and more expensive resorts.

Park accommodation consists of lodges including both hostel accommodation and chalet units of one to three bedrooms, heated showers and fireplaces (the first lot of firewood is included in the price), and in some cases television, kitchen and

Whether you are planning to visit Kinabalu Park for a day trip, stay for a few days in the park or plan to climb the mountain, the following information is essential. More climbing-specific information is outlined below in the Climber's Essentials.

CLIMATE Do not underestimate the cooler temperatures you will encounter in the Kinabalu Park area, not only compared with the coast, but also with towns only half an hour away. Daytime averages around park headquarters (1,563m altitude) are 21°C, but can drop to 8°C overnight. Have a thermal layer ready and trousers instead of shorts. There are dense downpours rather than prolonged rain. From Poring Hot Springs on the southern edges of the park to the summit, temperatures shift from a humid 25–28°C to 4–8°C and colder.

ARRIVAL Kinabalu Park HQ is the nerve centre for all people arriving in the park. Just off the main road, and engulfed in a swirling mass of clouds, there can be too many coaches and coach fumes to really feel the wonder of the place here, but you don't have to venture far to see the beauty of the area.

ADMINISTRATION The park is very efficiently run. Well-informed Sabah Park naturalists staff the park, most of them locals with a passion for their culture and nature.

OPENING HOURS Offices, shops and restaurants are open for a minimum of 12 hours, restaurants up to 16 hours. The reception office is open 07.00–12.00, as most visitors have arrived in the park by then for day or overnight visits. Sabah Parks operation counter is open from 07.00–19.00, but it can be very hard to get assistance here, and you really have to insist on obtaining one of the scanty maps they provide. The Sutera Sanctuary reception has helpful staff, dressed in jungle greens. The souvenir shop is open 07.00–22.00.

PARK ENTRY (CONSERVATION FEES) Adult 15MYR, under 18 years 10MYR.
NB: If you plan to visit Poring Hot Springs, hold on to your ticket stub as it entitles you to entry at the springs as well.

living room. The omnipresence of fireplaces gives an idea of the temperature drop you might experience from the coast region – especially at night (and still 2,500m from the summit of Mount Kinabalu!).

Sutera Sanctuary Lodges, Kinabalu Park (✆ 088 889086) There are two hostels and eight lodges scattered through the forest near park HQ. The lodges are each made up of individual units of one to three bedrooms. The key differences are size – and thus suitability for individuals, couples or families – plus extra furnishings and fittings. All are fully detailed on the website.

🏠 **Liwagu Suite** (4 units) Split-level units plunging into the forest, 1 dbl bedroom upstairs, living room & balcony downstairs. Tea/coffee-making facilities, AC, TV. At busy times the beauty of this place can be marred by noise through thin walls & communal TV – the units are in the exhibition centre for the park, so there is quite a lot of traffic. $$$

🏠 **Nepenthes Lodge** (8 units) 2 bedrooms with 4 sgl beds, 1 queen, dining & living rooms. $$$

🏠 **Rajah Lodge** (3 bedrooms: 2 twin, 1 dbl) Dining & living areas, TV, kitchen, attached bathrooms. $$$

🏠 **The Hill Lodge** (10 units) 1 twin bedroom chalets. Pleasant rooms, with rattan furnishings, lamps, desk, sofa & armchair. $$

🏠 **Menggilan & Medang, The Rock Hostel** (28 beds in dormitories) & **Grace Hostel** (20 beds in

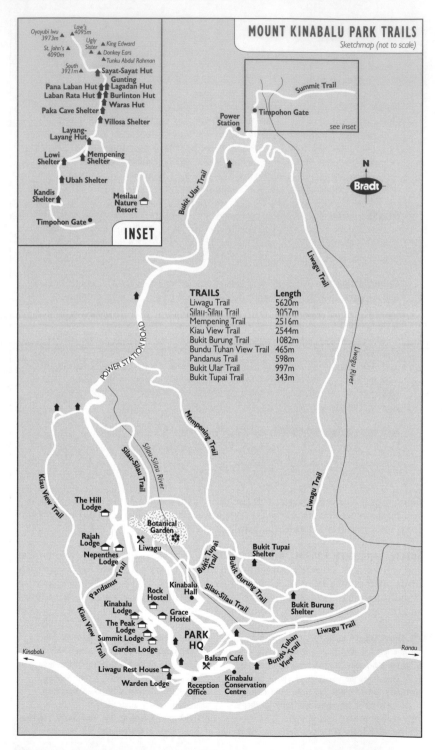

MOUNT KINABALU PARK TRAILS
Sketchmap (not to scale)

INSET

Oyayubi Iwu 3973m
Low's 4095m
St. John's 4090m
Ugly Sister
South 3921m
King Edward
Donkey Ears
Tunku Abdul Rahman
Sayat-Sayat Hut
Gunting
Lagadan Hut
Pana Laban Hut
Laban Rata Hut
Burlinton Hut
Waras Hut
Paka Cave Shelter
Villosa Shelter
Layang-Layang Hut
Lowi Shelter
Mempening Shelter
Ubah Shelter
Kandis Shelter
Mesilau Nature Resort
Timpohon Gate

Power Station
Timpohon Gate
Summit Trail
see inset

N
Bradt

Bukit Ular Trail
Liwagu Trail
Liwagu River
POWER STATION ROAD
Mempening Trail
Silau-Silau Trail
Silau-Silau River
Kiau View Trail

TRAILS	Length
Liwagu Trail	5620m
Silau-Silau Trail	3057m
Mempening Trail	2516m
Kiau View Trail	2544m
Bukit Burung Trail	1082m
Bundu Tuhan View Trail	465m
Pandanus Trail	598m
Bukit Ular Trail	997m
Bukit Tupai Trail	343m

The Hill Lodge
Botanical Garden
Rajah Lodge
Liwagu
Nepenthes Lodge
Bukit Tupai Trail
Bukit Tupai Shelter
Pandanus Trail
Rock Hostel
Kinabalu Hall
Silau-Silau Trail
Bukit Burung Trail
Kinabalu Lodge
Grace Hostel
Bukit Burung Shelter
The Peak Lodge
Summit Lodge
Garden Lodge
PARK HQ
Kiau View Trail
Kinabalu
Balsam Café
Liwagu Trail
Ranau
Liwagu Rest House
Bundu Tuhan View Trail
Warden Lodge
Reception Office
Kinabalu Conservation Centre

dormitories) have 48 beds between them in 4/6/8 bed dormitories. They provide a basic & clean place to sleep, in misty forested settings, with a communal lounge with TV, common bathroom & toilet facilities. $

Mesilau Nature Resort (☎ *088 871519*; $$–$$$) In the eastern part of Kinabalu Park on the Mesilau Plateau, this is 17km past park HQ. It's good for climbers taking the alternative Meislau Trail to the summit and anyone who prefers a less crowded, secluded forest environment. The venue is popular for scientific seminars and meditation retreats. From the turn-off at Kundasang, it is 11km to Mesilau. Lodgings include the 96-bed Bishop's Head Resthouse and nine other lodges with names such as Donkey's Ear Peak Lodge and Ugly Sister's Peak Lodge, broken up into 16 (three-bedroom) chalets with heating, living areas but no kitchen and six (two–three-bedroom) free-standing chalets with kitchens. They tend to be slightly more spacious than at park HQ and include several attractive cathedral-style ceilinged, split-level chalets.

Mid-Climb Lodgings (☎ *088 872907*) At 3,273m, Laban Rata is the acclimatisation spot for climbers that have started out from the Kinabalu Park or Mesilau Nature Resort that morning. There are several rustic accommodations where climbers and guides spend a few hours resting before resuming the climb to the peak the following morning at 03.00.

🏠 **Panar Laban Hut** (12 beds) at 3,314m, **Waras Hut** (12 beds) at 3,244m & the **Gunting Lagadan Hut** (60 beds) at 3,324m. All have basic cooking facilities, common bathroom & heated shower, though no room heater. $

🏠 **Laban Rata Resthouse** (76 bunk beds, 2 units) At 3,274m, dormitory accommodation, heated shower, room heater, restaurant area, & a common bathroom. Within the same building there is a heated unit **Laban Rata Buttercup 1**, a twin-share room & bathroom & the **Laban Rata Buttercup 2**, which has 2 twin-share rooms. There is also a restaurant. $

✗ **WHERE TO EAT** Whether you arrive at 07.00 or 17.00, getting quality food within the park is no trouble at several venues. The **Basalm Café** (⊕ *06.00–22.00 daily*), down among the ferns near park HQ, serves buffet breakfasts and à la carte lunches with plenty of Asian, Western and vegetarian options. The daily climber's briefing is held here at 18.00. At the **Liwagu Restaurant** a few hundred metres along from park HQ there is an à la carte menu and a set menu with higher (but still reasonable) prices. On the same site, there is a second **Basalm Café** (⊕ *06.00–22.00*) which has a menu-breakfast, buffet lunch and à la carte options. The **Kedamaian Restaurant**, at the Mesilau Nature Resort, is much the same style as the Liwagu.

WHAT TO SEE AND DO

Mountaineering The summit peaks of the mountain are divided between western and eastern plateaux along a 16km-long chasm, which plunges over a kilometre into Low's Gully. Most people who attempt the 17km-return **Summit Trail** do so overnight, and with an average trekking duration of some 15 hours. The record

6

THE GROWING MOUNTAIN

The official figure of the summit height of Gunung Kinabalu varies between 4,095.2m and 4,102m, perhaps explained by the fact that the massif is still growing – some clearly haven't caught up with the latest growth spurts!

PERMITS In high season (May–Sep), it is necessary to book ahead to climb Mount Kinabalu, otherwise you will arrive to be put on a waiting list, without any guarantee of making the ascent. Book at the **Sabah Parks Office** in Kota Kinabalu (*Lot 3, Block K, Sinsuran Complex;* ☏ *088 212719/088 211881;* e *info@sabahparks.org.my; www.sabahparks.org.my).* All climbers are legally bound to obtain a permit and pay insurance and guide's fees with Sabah Parks before the ascent. First- and second-class certificates include transport to and from Timpohon Gate (Power Station) or Mesilau Nature Resort. See below for a guide to prices.

MOUNTAIN GUIDES If you plan to climb the mountain, a guide is mandatory rather than optional, not only for the safety considerations and expertise of local guides on the hiking routes, but also because of the sacredness of the park to idiginous peoples and the need to oversee climbers in both their hiking practice and general comportment. See below for prices.

ACCOMMODATION For any accommodation in the park pre-, post- or mid-climb, you must book well ahead through Sutera Sanctuary Lodges.

TRAILS There are two trails to the summit, the Summit Trail (8.5km) and Mesilau Route (10.2km). They intersect at Layang Layang, at 2,740m, 4km from the start of the Summit Trail (Timpohon Gate), and 5.5km from the Mesilau Nature Resort. There are shelters along the way of both trails. The Meislau Trail started out in 1998 being used mostly by scientists and researchers. It is considered more rich in plant and wildlife, not just altitude gain. It is tougher in parts, with 2km of unrelenting steps leading to the Tikalod Shelter. If you want to taste both trails, pay the fees to ascend the Summit Trail and descend the Mesilau or vice versa.

DURATION Though the hike can be done in a day, it is not advised – I have heard of many people who have ended up with altitude sickness as a result. The best approach is a two-day overnight climb. On the Summit Trail it takes four to five hours to reach Laban Rata (at 6km mark); add an hour or two for the Mesilau Trail. The next morning the final stretch to the summit (2.5km) takes two to three hours. There are ladders, hand railings and ropes to help you on your way. After taking in the scenery at the top, climbers return to Laban Rata or Panar Laban for breakfast, before the final four- or five-hour descent to the park (the record slowest is 12hrs!).

ETIQUETTE This is a deeply sacred and special place. You should show the highest respect to the nature and to the local tribes who value it more than most. Shouting, fooling around and damaging the mountain environment should be avoided.

return time is two hours and 37 minutes, set in 2003 by an Italian during the annual (October) Climbathon up the mountain. Some tour operators tackle the mountain along different routes to avoid the crowds.

Hikes Other than the summit climb, there are relatively few trails around the park. If you want a good hike, consider paying for a guide for the first leg of the mountain-walk return in a day. There are nine walks of varying lengths near park HQ (see *Mount Kinabalu Park Trails* map on page 182) for which you do not require a guide, though you can hire the services of a resident naturalist if you wish. The **Bukit Tupai Trail** is the shortest at just 343m; The **Silau Silau** is a very pretty trail of just over 3km through the nearby forest and back to the botanical garden.

PEAK TO PEAK Other peaks on the mountain include Donkey's Ear Peak (4,054m), St John's Peak (4,091m) and Victoria's Peak (4,090m) on the western plateau and King Edward Peak (4,086m) and King George Peak (4,062m) on the eastern plateau. Special permits are required from Sabah Parks to do these more challenging climbs.

CLIMATE Be prepared for the cold. Temperatures at the top can drop to 0°C but average around 4–8°C in the morning. At Laban Rata and the other mountain resthouses (around 3,300m/10,800ft) the early-morning temperature hovers around 10°C (50°F). Wind, cloud and frequent rain (even when the whether is mild) must be expected, so waterproofs are essential to avoid a miserable ascent.

THINGS TO BRING
Clothing Suitable walking shoes, warm clothing, wind breaker, long-sleeved shirts, change of clothes, extra socks, hat, gloves.

Trail munchies Don't forget to bring some food. The canteens and lodges in the park organise packed lunches but they are pretty basic cheese sandwiches in a polystyerene container. It is best to bring your own trekking eats and drinks including drinking water, high-energy food (chocolates, nuts, raisins, glucose).

First-aid kit Headache tablets, sun block, lip balm, deep-heat lotion, plasters, insect repellent, mosquito oil.

Equipment Binoculars, camera, waterproof bag for camera, torchlight, towel/tissue paper, toilet roll.

Items available for rent Jackets, torchlights, blankets, sleeping bags and towels can be rented.

MEDICAL NOTE It is recommended that all climbers should have themselves medically checked before attempting any mountain climb. Sabah Parks advise people not to climb if you suffer any of the following ailments: heart disease, hypertension, diabetes, palpitations, arthritis, severe anaemia, peptic ulcers, epileptic fits, obesity, chronic asthma, muscular cramps, hepatitis (jaundice); or any other sickness which may either hamper your climb, or be triggered by severe cold, exertion and high altitude.

DEPARTURE For safety reasons all climbers must depart from the Kinabalu National Park HQ by or before noon. This is also the reason for the horrific 03.00 start from the Laban Ratu hut the following morning, to avoid cloud which quickly gathers at the peak.

The longest is the **Liwagu Trail**, over 5.5km. A daily guided walk also sets out from park HQ at 11.00.

Nature appreciation The parks run an **Interpretative Education Programme** – ask for a sheet with the current range of educational activities on offer (for both children and adults) at the Sabah Park Operation Counter or Sutera Sanctuaries desk. Activities include a Mount Kinabalu **Botanical Garden Tour** (*09.00, 12.00 & 15.00 daily; 4MYR*), daily screenings of the documentary *Kinabalu Park – A Beacon of Biodiversity* (2MYR) and the **Mount Kinabalu Natural History Gallery** at Liwagu (⊕ *09.00–15.00 daily; 2MYR*). Flora from all over the park has been planted at the **Mount Kinabalu Botanical Garden** or **Mountain Garden**

CLIMBING PERMIT (Timpohon Gate/Mesilau Gate) Adult 100MYR, under 18 40MYR

CLIMBING INSURANCE 7MYR per person

MOUNTAIN GUIDE FEE (for return overnight trip, half fee for day hike)

Timpohon Gate–Peak–Timpohon Gate
1–3 climbers – 70MYR   4–6 climbers – 74MYR   7–8 climbers – 80MYR

Mesilau–Peak–Timpohon or Timpohon–Peak–Mesilau
(starting and ending at different point)
1–3 climbers – 80MYR   4–6 climbers – 90MYR   7–8 climbers – 100MYR

Mesilau–Peak–Mesilau
1–3 climbers – 84MYR   4–6 climbers – 86MYR   7–8 climbers – 92MYR

PORTER FEE (optional) The prices below are all based on an overnight return trip, staying at Laban Rata climbers' lodge *en route* with 10kg. For a day trip halve the cost.

Timpohon Gate return
To Laban Rata – 66MYR   To Sayat-Sayat – 80MYR   To Mt Kinabalu Peak – 88MYR

Mesilau Trail return
To Laban Rata – 88MYR   To Sayat-Sayat – 100MYR   To Summit – 110MYR

Mesilau Trail to Timpohon Gate return
To Laban Rata – 76MYR   To Sayat-Sayat – 88MYR   To Summit – 100MYR

TRANSFER TO TIMPOHON GATE The trailhead is 4.5km from park HQ.
5 people or fewer 15MYR per person one-way
6 people or more 4MYR per person one-way

CERTIFICATE (optional)
10MYR per person (full colour) to reach Low's Peak
1MYR per person (black and white) before Low's Peak

(☉ *09.00–13.00, 14.30–16.00 daily*), not only beautiful ones, but those esteemed for their medicinal value by the local Dusun community.

The Liwagu conference and exhibition centre houses another small display on the park history and conservation, and there is a slide-show presentation held here (*14.00 & 19.00 daily except Wed & Sat*) that introduces you to the park and its splendour (days and times are subject to change however, so it is always best to check).

In the vicinity of the **Mesilau Nature Resort**, wild orchids and the world's largest pitcher plant – the *Nepenthes rajah*, or Emperor – grow in abundance and there are guided nature walks (*09.30, 11.00 & 14.00 Mon-Fri, 07.30, 10.30 & 14.00 Sat & Sun*). Whether you are staying in the area or not, try to do some strolling or trekking around the **Mesilau Plateau** as it provides a very different picture of mountain ecology from park HQ, due to the higher altitudes. At the Mesilau Gate, you will be welcomed by a rather loud sign on a plaque of wood: *GRANITY*

MESILAU: YOU ARE NOW STANDING 2,000m AND INHALE 100% FRESH AIR FROM OUR HIGHLAND TROPICAL RAINFOREST. In the vicinity are conifers, climbing bamboos, and Agathis trees, orchids and orange-coloured rhododendrons. Near the ridge crest, the forest becomes more stunted with rocks, tangled tree roots, spongy mosses and liverworts.

KUNDASANG AND RANAU

The first settlement after Kinabalu Park is Kundasang, a village surrounded by conical hills like Chinese hats, dropping into a knife-cut in the valley. Crops cover the hills from head to toe. Kundasang is famous for its cool-climate vegetables – asparagus, spinach, broccoli, cauliflower, cabbage and mushrooms – people come from Brunei and Sarawak to bulk-buy. The loss of forest habitat to intense cultivation has been high. There is still apparently no firm buffer zone between these communities and Kinabalu Park – private land continues right up to its borders. The slippery-slide Kundasang road is lined every morning with wooden market stalls, selling local produce, *lihing* (rice wine) and honey. Ranau, an industrious yet relaxed town, is the commercial centre of the district – its population of 50,000 is bloated every day by those who come to market to buy and sell. Sitting prettily in a surround of hills tipped with mountain mist, it's a nice place to absorb some atmosphere, eat and stock up at the market.

GETTING THERE AND AWAY Kundasang is 7km along the road from the Kinabalu Park HQ, Ranau another 15km. From Ranau there is a road through to Tambunan, the Crocker Range and Tenom.

⌂ WHERE TO STAY

⌂ **Perkasa Hotel Mount Kinabalu** Kampung Kundasang Ranau; ☎ 088 889511; f 088 889101; e hpmk@tm.net.my; www.perkasahotel.com.my. This red & white structure is up on the highest of Kundasang's conical hilltops with a commanding view from 1,500m over the valley. The décor is bit dated, but this 3-star hotel is efficient & comfortable with well-furnished AC rooms. The hotel's **Tinompok Restaurant** is considered among the best (mid-range) in the district (Chinese, Malaysian & Western menu). There's also a cocktail & karaoke lounge, Kouvangha. The Perkasa offers a lot of golfing packages inc accommodation, meals, golf fees & transfers. $$$

⌂ **Zen Garden Resort** (7 chalets, 120 rooms) Km2 Jln Mohimboyon (2km from Ranau); ☎ 088 889242; e info@zengardenresort.com; www.zengardenresort.com. Sprawling hillside resort, units with kitchenettes & living rooms, TV, coffee house, big restaurant, BBQ dinners, steamboats, Malaysian & Western food. $$–$$$

⌂ **Kinabalu Pine Resort** Kampung Kundasang (along Kundasang–Ranau road); ☎ 088 889388; e k_pine2002@yahoo.com.sg; www.kinabalupineresort.com. The very Dallas entry is just on the right after the Kundasang market. Gorgeous nature-lodge setting in the forest, attractive

hardwood cabins. A Malaysian Tourism Award for excellence (2-star winner in 2006), the site includes children's playground & BBQs. The **Pines Restaurant** has Western & local food & steamboats, & there's the ubiquitous karaoke lounge (⌚ 21:00–23.30). $$

⌂ **Sabah Tea plantation** (17km from Ranau, see details below) There is some purpose-built Rungus longhouse accommodation here. The longhouse sleeps about 25 & can be group booked. There are also twin-share bungalows (12 rooms) with ceiling fans. There's an on-site restaurant & tea garden serving Western & Asian dishes from pancakes to butter prawns. $$

⌂ **Kinabalu Rose Cabins** Km18 Jln Ranau-Tamparuli (4km from Park HQ); ☎ 088 889233; e maxcarry@tm.net.my; www.mtkinabaluhotels.com. Family & deluxe rooms & chalets & a 10-bed budget room. Plain but clean lodge with big hostel-like restaurant (⌚ 07.30–21.40 daily) with home-cooked, Western, local & vegetarian dishes. $–$$

⌂ **D'Villa Rina Ria Lodge** Km53 Jln Tinompok (500m from Kinabalu Park); ☎ 088 889282; e info@dvillalodge.com; www.dvillalodge.com. Family, twin & bunk rooms, unadorned but spotless, with bathroom, heating, TV; lodge has a leisure corner & restaurant. $–$$

Slagon Homestay (15 rooms) Kampung Silou, Ranau; ☎ 088 878187; e cruzellyn@yahoo.com; www.slagonhomestay.com. Guests at the Minudin family's home are told they can fruit-hunt & do mini jungle treks on this forest property. Twin/dbl bedrooms with & without bathroom & AC, chalets with kitchenettes. Meals served. Strangely enough, peak visitor season here is during the northeast monsoon, when Japanese people come & live for weeks to escape the cold at home. $–$$

✖ **WHERE TO EAT** Ranau's dearth of accommodations is countered by a smorgasbord of food outlets, all crammed within a couple of streets. There are dozens of *restoran* and *kedai makan dan minum* (food and drink shops), serving Islamic, Malay and Chinese food. At the bottom of Jalan Persiaran there is a market every evening. Nearly all the Chinese shops are good (even if some toilets are best avoided) such as **Sung Fun Tong** (*Jln Kibarambang*) which serves great food. Next door is a good cake shop, **Kedai Kek Delicious**. Opposite there is a **food corner** with some open-fronted *kedai kopi* serving noodle and rice dishes. **Selan Kembera** near the market has Malay food.

WHAT TO SEE AND DO
The Other Mountain
Obscured by its big sister, **Gunung Tambuyukon** (2,579m) also lies within the Kinabalu National Park. It's about a two-hour drive from Ranau by 4x4 to Kampung Manggis, a vegetable-, chilli- and pepper-farming area and the closest village to the mountain's base. You will still need a climbing permit and insurance from the Sabah Park Office at park HQ, though a guide is not compulsory. Local tour guides put the summit trek at three days and two nights, with two camps on the way up. There is a government-established homestay programme at Kampung Manggis, with a population of about 150. Some locals can be hired as porters for the trip. **TYK Adventure Tours** is an expert on this climb which takes in lowland dipterocarp and lower montane of oaks, laurels up to 30m tall, mossy forest, pitcher plants, bright rhododendrons and orchids.

Kundasang War Memorial (⊕ *09.00–17.00 daily*) At the Ranau end of the atrocious World War II 'death march' from Sandakan (see page 8), this memorial in landscaped gardens with ponds and pools and water features might look like a fort but is a stone-walled peace haven on the hilltop. The dichotomy of war and peace, horror and beauty couldn't be greater. There are four interlinking gardens representing the homelands of soldiers: an Australian garden, an English rose garden, a Borneo garden with wild flowers of the Kinabalu Park, and a Contemplation garden with a reflection pool and pergola. Having fallen into a state of degeneration as a hangout for local youths, the memorial and gardens were restored in 2005 – on the 60th anniversary of the end of World War II. Memorial services are often held here. Just a few metres from the memorial is the **Agro T Nursery** with flowers, fruit and vegetable plants – roses, orchids, hibiscus, tomatoes.

Nepenthes Garden The garden is within the Mesilau Nature Resort, on the eastern slopes of the Kinabalu Park, a mountain slope covered with pitcher plants including the giant *Nepenthes rajah*.

Mount Kinabalu Golf Course If you want to go golfing with your head in the swirling mists and massifs, this 18-hole course is nearby, at 1,500m above sea level in the Kundasang-Ranau area.

Pekan Ranau The undercover *pasar pekan* (town market) is at the bottom of Jalan Persiaran. This is a wet market with fish and meats. Alongside is the rainbow-coloured cultural and produce market, the *Pasar Terbuka Pekan Ranau*, an open-air market where Dusun and Murut people from the region sell myriad items, all fresh and fascinating. If you need supplies for the onward journey (or electrical items and car repairs), Ranau is the place. As well as fresh market produce, there is a 'Milimewa' supermarket on Jalan Kibarambang, and a 'Superstore' 2km past the town on the right-hand side of the road.

Roadside rafflesia There are several private plots of rafflesia on the lower slopes of Mount Kinabalu, near Ranau and Poring Hot Springs. Look out for roadside signs in English announcing 'rafflesias Blooming'. One such plot is found at Kokob Baru, 5km east of Ranau along the Ranau–Sandakan road.

Sabah Tea (*Km17, Jln Ranau-Sandakan Kampung Nalapak;* ↘ *088 889330;* e *info@ sabahtea.net; www.sabahtea.net*) Situated 17km east of Ranau on the Ranau–Sandkan road is the plantation and factory behind the prominent Sabah Tea label which you will find in just about every hotel room and guesthouse in Sabah. In a blanket of 800m-high hills, the plantations produce both standard and organic (certified by a Dutch association) tea. Following a factory visit, you can sit at the tea house/restaurant with its wonderful views. The venture won the Malaysia Tourism Award's 2004 Best Tour Programme for Educational Tourism. TYK Adventure Tours organise a Sabah Tea Adventure – a strange brew of tea education with jungle survival skills, night treks and traditional longhouse immersion. The tour (including transfers, accommodation, etc) costs about 550–650MYR per person for the package. They also run day tours to the plantation.

Hiking and biking The 2,500ha tea plantation is buffered by forest, and the trails through the tea bushels and surrounds of the Sapon Recreational Area are terrific terrain for mountain biking and hiking. Sabah Tea organise an Annual mountain-bike competition in August. There is an easy two–three-hour return trek to the top of the picturesque hill Bukit Kamunsu, through a small marvel of rivers, rafflesia, waterfalls and wild ginger.

Jungle survival camps Father and son Sadib and Maik Miki run 'Miki Survival Camp' near the foothill of Mount Kinabalu in Kampung Kiau. Both are highly experienced Bornean trekkers, licensed mountain and cycling guides. During the camp they pass on skills from their Dusun ancestors. It's a three-day, two-night adventure in tents, about two hours' walk from Kiau. Others choose to visit Kampung Kiau for a big rice-wine party, held every Sunday. Contact **Maik Miki** directly (↘ *019 8072814*) or via **TYK** (↘ *088 720826; www.thamyaukong.com/miki*). **Intrepid Tours** do a homestay in the Kinabalu foothills area, sleeping in hammocks and staying with locals.

PORING HOT SPRINGS

Many climbers end their walk and ease their tired limbs and muscles with a near-direct descent into the hot springs. *Poring* is a Kadazandusun word for the bamboo which grows here. The lowland forests of Poring are part of Kinabalu Park, located on its southern fringes at about 550m altitude in prime rafflesia territory. The park posts a notice if there is a rafflesia in bloom. Butterfly and birdwatchers are in for a treat. Both thrive among the mixed dipterocarp forest between the Menggaris 'bee trees' (*Koompasia excelsa*), durian, mango and fig, which are adorned with epiphytic lianas, ferns and orchids. The eastern flank of Mount Kinabalu bears the scars of the Mamut copper mine which was, interestingly, mined for decades after the creation of the national park through to 1997. The health of local communities

6

is still affected by pollution from the mine and its heavy metal run-offs. Plans have been mooted to convert the huge mining lease into an ecotourism resort, as the state tries, if a little tardily, to rectify errors of the past.

GETTING THERE AND AWAY The springs are 126km from Kota Kinabalu, 38km slightly northeast of Kinabalu Park HQ, 15km from Ranau along the Ranau–Sandakan road. There are several minibuses each day between Kinabalu Park HQ and Poring. There are also buses from Ranau. If you are coming or going to Kota Kinabalu by minibus you have to transfer in Ranau (buses leave from near the market). All long-distance buses plying the route between Kota Kinabalu and Sandakan pass the springs.

WHERE TO STAY AND EAT

⌂ **Sutera Sanctuary Lodges** ☎ 088 878801. Camping, hostel, lodges & chalets. Sutera Sanctuary again makes its mark in the park, though there are other choices beyond the springs' gates. The camping ground accommodates 100 people. There are 2 hostels, the **Serindit Hostel 1** (24 beds) & the **Serindit Hostel 2** (48 beds), with common bathrooms & a sitting room & pantry. (⑤) **The Tempua Cabin** has a dbl bedroom, lounge, TV, kettle, lovely with big bathroom, outdoor bath & harem-like bed. The cabin is lovely by night, but not ideal by day if you value your privacy & peace, as it's wedged between 2 car parks & the entry to the springs. (⑤⑤) **Enggang Cabin** has 3 bedrooms, a

ceiling fan, dining & living rooms, bathroom & kitchen. (⑤⑤) The **Rajawali Lodges** (2 units) have 3 bedroom chalets with AC, a dining & living area, bathroom & kitchen. (⑤⑤)
⌂ **Round Ine** (10 rooms) Main road at entry to the springs. Family-run, basic twin share, AC, cold showers, borderline clean rooms. There is an adjoining Chinese coffee shop with noodles & Western b/fasts, fish & chips & steak. ⑤
⌂ **Sungai Biru Guesthouse** A few kilometres before Poring Hot Springs, on Jln Ranau-Sandakan. ⑤
✗ **Rainforest Restaurant** ⏲ 07.00–22.00 daily. An under-cover wood pavilion by the springs. Serves Malaysian & Western dishes & drinks. ⑤–⑤⑤

WHAT TO SEE AND DO
Poring Hot Springs & Nature Reserve (*40km northeast of Kinabalu Park in Ranau;* ☎ *088 878801;* ⏲ *07.00–18.30 daily; entry adult 15MYR, under 18 10MYR*) Operated by Sabah Parks, this sulphuric wonder-world by the banks of the Sungai Mamut River combines a series of hot sulphur baths with the park's other natural attractions. Once used by Japanese troops, the baths are five minutes' walk from the entrance down a gully and over a suspension bridge. The surrounding gardens brim with hibiscus, palms and ferns. As well as hot and cold pools (temperature controlled from different sources), there are enclosed individual tubs and four indoor sulphur bathtubs (15–20MYR per hour) complete with living room, showers and toilet, and one with a Jacuzzi. The conservation (entrance) fee should be paid at the visitor centre and park administration building, and includes access to an open-air bath, a slide pool, rock pool and Kinabalu Park. Be warned that there are several add-on costs for additional activities around the springs, including camera and video fees. The springs are very busy during holidays and festivities.

Walks There are several treks starting from the springs. The jungle-walk attraction is the 150m-long **canopy walkway** (⏲ *09.00–16.00; adult 5MYR, under 18 2.50MYR*). Strung above the forest floor in 40m-high Menggaris trees, it provides an adrenalin-rushing view of the forest floor. A 1km hike leads to the small **Kipungit Waterfall**, a pretty picnic spot. The 3.3km Lanangan Trail leads to the highest waterfall in the Poring area, 120m-high **Langanan Waterfall**. Along the way, about 30 minutes from the entrance, is **Bat Cave** and a boon for botanists with frequent sightings of *Rhizanthes* – a parasitic flower and cousin of the rafflesia. The grounds also include a **butterfly farm** and **tropical garden** (2–10MYR).

The **Orchid Conservation Centre** has the largest collection of endemic wild orchids with all 1,200 species found in Kinabalu Park represented.

TAMBUNAN TO TENOM

The Crocker Range – the backbone of Sabah – runs south from near Kinabalu Park towards Tenom, skirting the townships of Tambunan and its large bamboo plantations and the industrial little town of Keningau, across the Padas River and down towards the swamp forests on the Sarawak border. The journey is a wonderful one, through changing landscapes of lowlands and highlands, mossy forests and mountain mist, gorged river valleys, Kadazandusun communities and coffee crops. The Taman Banjaran Crocker – the **Crocker Range National Park** – is the biggest park in Sabah. The mountain has been an integral part of the ethnographic history of the interior and continues through an era where native land titles and conservation values both count. Many locals are still hunter-gatherers, collecting forest vegetables and plants for food and medicine.

GETTING THERE AND AWAY

By car Tambunan is 65km southeast of Kota Kinabalu in the direction of Penampang. The Crocker Range National Park is 144km, 13km from Keningau on the Keningau–Papar Highway (Jalan Raya Keningau-Papar). Kota Kinabalu–Tenom is 200km. This whole circuit can make a very nice round trip from Kota Kinabalu, up over the Sinsuran Pass at 1,670m and back, with a slight deviation to Tenom. If you are coming from Kinabalu Park, there is a road from Ranau.

By bus Take the Keningau bus from the long-distance bus station, Padang Merdeka. For Tenom, take the Tenom bus (Nui Luk bus).

By train The Kota Kinabalu–Beaufort train (*07.45 departure Mon–Sun Tanjung Aru; Station Master Tanjung Aru,* ↘ *088 262536; Sabah State Rail,* ↘ *088 254611*) is particularly scenic as it passes the Padas Gorge between Tenom and Beaufort

WHERE TO STAY AND EAT Food is always available at coffee shops in the small centres of Keningau and Tenom (such as **Storkbill Kingfisher** cafe in the latter), but accommodation is thinner on the ground. There are a couple of decent two–three-star hotels with very competitive rates and internet promotions offering a 40% discount, including breakfast.

⌂ **Pesona Hotel Tenom** (formerly Perkasa Hotel) (63 rooms) ↘ 087 735881; e pesona_tm@ hotmail.com. Chinese hotel on top of a forested hill above the town of Tenom, with rafflesia jungle & jogging tracks adjacent. The rooms are comfortable, though not highly fashionable. TV & AC. The hotel has 2 good eateries, the Kemabong Garden Terrace (coffee house) & Sapong Restaurant

PLANTS FOR LIFE

Over 70% of the local populations in the Crocker-Range districts harvest wild plants and vegetables, mostly for their own consumption. The rest gather wild vegetables to sell at the market place. Studies have shown that the rate of harvest of these plants is not an environmental threat, with the exception of wild palms (many are used to make crafts for tourists). The Kadazandusun people around the Crocker Range use over 50 plant species for treating minor wounds, skin diseases, diarrhoea, fever, coughs, malaria, hypertension and rheumatism.

The Crocker Range extends over more than 120km, separating Sabah's coastal region from the interior. Often nestled in rain cloud, its peaks undulate between 800–1,800m, covered in mixed lowland and hill dipterocarp, montane forest, primary and secondary forest. Indraneil Das from the Institute of Biodiversity and Environmental Conservation at the Universiti Malaysia Sarawak says the Crocker Range is 'geologically and floristically' part of the same range as Mount Kinabalu. 'The altitudinal variation of this Park is remarkable, in rising from near sea level to 1,670m and extending from the base of Gunung Alab to the town of Tenom. The higher slopes are dominated by moss forests and by a profusion of rhododendrons and orchids.' The largest protected area in Eastern Malaysia, the 139,919ha national park was established in 1984, taking its name from William Maunder Crocker, a British administrator in the late 1800s under Rajah Brooke's Sarawak Civil Service.

The Crocker Range is bisected by the Padas Gorge – a conduit for the rapid-rippled Padas River. As it's a large remaining slice of montane forest, dozens of different studies are being carried out on its plant diversity: the many species of fish fauna in its upper rivers and mountain streams; on its bats, birds, insects and small mammals; and amphibian and reptile fauna. Over 200 kinds of vascular plants, 30 birds, 250 moths, 15 cicadas and 40 bat species have been found here, and high levels of deforestation of surrounding regions, particularly lowland rainforests, have sharpened the urgency to protect its primary forests. On its eastern side, the range falls towards the most densely mountainous parts of Borneo – the 'Heart of Borneo', see *Chapter 3, Natural history*, page 117 – towards Gunung Trusmadi (2,642m) and thickets of highland montane forest. Many rivers have their source in this area, including the mighty Kinabatangan.

(Malaysian/Chinese/Western). Standard rooms a bit gloomy, best to opt for a spacious deluxe suite with views. Even executive suites are affordable. $–$$$

🏠 **Perkasa Hotel Keningau** (63 rooms) Jln Kampong Keningau; ✆ 087 331045; e phkgau@tm.net.my; www.perkasahotel.com.my. Established 3-star on the edge of town, with coffee house (Top Corner), Full Moon Restaurant, Peppermint karaoke lounge & a health centre. $$

🏠 **Hotel Juta Keningau** (91 rooms) Peti Surat 25 ✆ 087 337888; e hjuta@tm.net.my; www.sabah.com.my/juta. A flashy tower for this part of the woods, marble lobby, heavy tropical wood panelling in rooms, AC, TV, safe deposit, internet, room service. Restaurant & bar. $$

🏠 **Hillview Gardens Resort** (20 rooms) 1 Jln Menawo, Keningau; ✆ 087 338500; e hillview@alfons.com; www.hillviewgardens.com. A 3-Orchid homestay in a pretty tropical garden setting, the resort is run by a family, their friends & some amateur radio enthusiasts. Very good at local tours (& massages) & there are mountain bikes, Wi-Fi, cultural shows & karaoke by the pool-bar. All flower-named rooms have TV, AC & phones & include a couple of deluxe & a family room. $–$$

🏠 **Tambunan Village Resort Centre** (TVRC) Jln Tvrc, Kampung Keranaan, Pegalan Riverside, Tambunan; ✆ 087 774076. Split bamboo chalets & longhouse hostel. A hostel for activities – rafting, hiking, kayaking, mountain biking & buffalo riding, though not held in high esteem by travel industry. $

Shoestring inns A few un-tested hotels in Keningau where rooms will cost 50–100MYR include the **Kristal Keningau Hotel** (*Block E, Pengalan Shopping Complex;* ✆ *087 338888*), **Tai Wah Hotel** (*Jln Besar;* ✆ *087 332092*) and **Paramount Hotel** (*Lot 1 Jln Masak Spur;* ✆ *087 333084*). In Tenom, recommended by the nearby Sabah Agricultural Park, are the **Orchid Hotel** (*Blok K Jln Mustapha;* ✆ *087 737600; 50–80MYR*) and **Sri Jaya Hotel** (*Lot 78, Blok L, Jln Datuk Hj Yassin;* ✆ *087 736000; 40–50MYR*). The Agricultural Park itself has an 88-bed **Hostel & Camping Ground** (*hostel 25MYR, tent 10MYR*).

WHAT TO SEE AND DO

Matt Salleh Memorial (*Kampung Tibabar, Tambunan;* ◊ *088 253199;* ⊕ *09.00–17.00 daily; free*) Opened in 1999, this concrete igloo-like structure is a tribute to Sabah's rebel son and freedom fighter on the place where he lived and died. Quite a local hero, his bronze plaque outside the government-funded memorial reads: 'This plaque marks the site of Mat Salleh's Fort which was captured by the North Borneo Armed Constabulary on the 1st February 1900. During this engagement, Mat Salleh, who for six years led a rebellion against the British Charted Company administration, met his death'. Under the umbrella of the Sabah Museum, the memorial contains some photographs, weapons and other paraphernalia. The Sabah Museum provides tour guides to this area on request.

Rafflesia Information Centre (*KK–Tambunan Rd;* ◊ *087 774691;* ⊕ *08.00–15.00 daily*) This is an education and conservation centre, set up in a forest reserve along the main road, and there's a host of plots of potential rafflesias planted all over the reserve between 1,000 and 2,500m altitude which can be reached within 15–90 minutes. Mandatory ranger-guides charge 30MYR for a maximum of six people. Phone ahead to check if you have your hopes pinned on blooming buds.

Crocker Range National Park (*Taman Banjaran Crocker Park HQ, Keningau–Papar Rd;* ⊕ *08.00–07.00; adult 10MYR, under 18 6MYR*) The facility opened in 2004 and is a small set-up. It is a very peaceful park to visit, especially after the masses of Kinabalu Park. There are just a couple of short walking trails including the 2km Crocker Trail, some rafflesia sites and educational facilities. Accommodation comprises a camping ground (*5MYR per person*), a 16-bed hostel (*adult 20MYR, under 18 10MYR*) and a hut with two double rooms (*50MYR each*). It is easiest to book through Sabah Parks in Kota Kinabalu, or online.

Trekking, cycling, rafting The 40km **Salt Trail** traversing the Crocker Range has been used by locals for decades, originally to get to the *tamu* markets on the coast where salt was among the prized produce. The walk can be done in either direction, between Inobong in the Penampang District to Tikolod in Tambunan in two to three days. The Sabah Parks **trail permit** (*adult 80MYR, under 18 40MYR*) is compulsory, guides and porters optional. TYK Adventure Tours and Borneo Eco Tours are both old hands at organising this trek, as well as trips to *Gunung* (Mount) Trusmadi. They, and other specialists listed in *Chapter 2*, page 41, do cycling, hiking, camping and white-water rafting trips throughout the Crocker Range, Tenom and Padas region.

Keningau Some 13km from the Crocker Range Park HQ, squatted down among the timber factories, this is the largest town in Sabah's hinterland and home of the Murut peoples. The surrounding mountains and cultural colour are the attraction rather than the town itself. As the owners of Hillview Gardens resort say, the area has built its fame on the timber industry – high-quality plywood and sawn timber – which is now in a state of transition, and being replaced by oil palm plantations and 'more sustainable agriculture and economic activities'.

Tenom This is a pretty area, interlaid with gorges, rivers, mountains and coffee crops. The 'local' coffee you will drink in hotels and coffee shops in Sabah is from the factories around here, and some of them are open for visits. They are usually Chinese managed – at the **Fatt Choi Coffee Factory** (*Jln Tenom-Kemabong*) you will not only sample the coffee, but also iced coffee with Durian ice cream. Tenom Kopi is mostly

MAT SALLEH – REBEL, WARRIOR

As Joseph Binkasan and Paskalis Alban Akim wrote in the *New Straits Times* after the opening of the Matt Salleh Memorial in 1999

> The locals were unhappy due to alleged exploitation, and one man that stood up and led a rebellion against British rule was Datu Paduka Muhammad Salleh better known as Mat Salleh. To the British, he was a rebel but to locals, he was a warrior. He was killed in a gun battle with the British police on Feb 1, 1900 ... Also killed in the gun battle were about 1,000 of Mat Salleh's followers who fought from the neighbouring villages of Lotud, Tondulu, Piasau, Timbou, Kitutud, Kepayan and Sunsuron.

Mat Salleh and his followers were fed up with the British North Borneo Company's meddling in local law, especially the imposition of taxes on rice. Salleh was a voice for many angry people, but contrary to misconceptions he was neither a lone crusader, nor the sole voice of dissent. Many others tried to throw off foreign rule in Sabah – each district seemed to have its warriors – and there is a spattering of memorials to them around the state including the Ontoros Antanom statue, of a Murut hero killed in a battle with the British in the Tenom District in 1915.

LOCAL HERO, LOCAL HISTORY In the British-tainted history of North Borneo it's not very often you get to read what you feel are truly objective (or at least non-British) local accounts of Sabah's history. There is so little written history (in English at least), by other than outsiders. So it's refreshing to fall upon a fresh slant on the rather top-heavy pro-colonial accounts. In the story on the new Mat Salleh memorial in the *New Straits Times* (9 March 2000) Sabah Museum director and a Tambunan local, Joseph Pounis Guntavid, suggested the British had long bragged of downing Mat Salleh's rebellion to their rule. 'But a search and study on Mat Salleh's actions strongly indicated that he was not a rebel but a warrior who went against foreign rule, fighting for North Borneo's self-government,' he said. 'Mat Salleh initiated patriotism that led the people to fight for self-rule until Sabah gained her independence through Malaysia on Sept 16 1963.'

made from lower-altitude Robusta beans and is powder-fine, with a dark and muddy taste. It sells from the factories for about 10MYR per kilogram. There are several short forest trails in the area of Tenom passing along streams and by waterfalls.

Markets Keningau's *tamu* on Sundays is a great place to see Kadazandusun traders from the region selling fresh produce and handicrafts.

Murut Cultural Centre (*Tenom;* ☏ *087 734506;* ⊕ *09.00-17.00 daily*) Here is a showcase of Murut culture, with dance, tattoo and handcraft demonstrations. The annual Murut festival, Tenom Pesta Kalimaran, is held here at the beginning of April with two days of dance performances. The Murut have many dances but the most famous is the *magunatip* warrior dance.

Sabah Agricultural Park (*Taman Pertanian Sabah, 15km from Tenom;* ☏ *087 737952;* e *agripark@sabah.net.my*) Within vast gardens, set among lakes, this is an agri-world with permanent living crop museums, bee centres, a native orchid centre, ornamental garden, agro-forestry and ethno-botany displays, as well as temporary expositions and events. A good family attraction, it is set in lovely grounds, with some forest trails, an animal park, picnic areas and a restaurant.

The **Klias Wetlands** region has recently become a top destination for nature lovers. Relatively secluded on the table-shaped cape, with tidal areas, rivers and swamps, mangrove and nipah forest intersected by the Sungai Klias, the wetlands area has a large population of proboscis monkeys. The area is one of just a few remaining dabs of mangrove forest – which has largely been swallowed up by forestry, agriculture and coastal development. You will see a lot of sago palm (*Matroxylon sagus* or *M. rumphii*) on the way to the Klias area through Papar and Beaufort. Known locally as *rumbia*, the Kadazandusun and Bisayas use it for roofing, floor mats and baskets, and also produce the starchy food *ambuyut* from it as Bruneians do. On the tip of the peninsula, Kuala Penyu is the launching point for the **Pulau Tiga Park**, a marine-and-reef park of more than 15,000ha, taking in three small islands about 10km offshore.

GETTING THERE

By car Beaufort is 95km from Kota Kinabalu, the Klias Peninsula around 110km.

By bus Take a minibus to Beaufort, then a connecting bus to Kuala Penyu. Contact the lodges below to arrange transport, or do the whole trip – transfers, accommodation and tours. It is possible to do it as a day trip though.

By train Kota Kinabalu to Beaufort.

By boat Pulau Tiga Island is a 30-minute trip from the Kuala Penyu jetty. Boats leave at 10.00 and 15.00 and return 09.00 and 16.00.

WHERE TO STAY AND EAT
Klias Wetlands/Kuala Penyu

🏠 **Borneo Proboscis River Lodge** Kota Klias (1km from the bridge over Klias River); 📞 087 209221; e lyndatang@pd.jaring.my; http://borneowildlife.org. Beautiful riverbank & traditional village setting, the nicest place to stay in Klias & a very good operator. Rungus longhouses on stilts with bamboo walls & thatched-palm roofs & AC terrace-house room with attached bathroom. Also has good food and riverside dining. Excellent value. Overnight package with 5 meals, accommodation & 3 river cruises for 300MYR. $$–$$$

Pulau Tiga Island

🏠 **Borneo Survivor Resort** 📞 088 230806; e neubay@tm.net.my; www.borneosurvivor.com.my. Robinson Crusoe-type adventure stuff of TV series,

🏠 **Tempurung Seaside Lodge** (11 rooms) Putatan Point (off JKR Rd), Kuala Penyu; 📞 088 773066; e info@borneo-authentic.com. Stunning seaside location, on a forested hill above beach, homestay style, bathrooms, AC. $$–$$$

🏠 **Bukit Naga Aman Puri Beach Retreat** (8 rooms) 1 Jln Bukit Naga, Kampun, Tempurung, Kuala Penyu; 📞 087 884929; e mail@nagapuri.com; www.nagapuri.com. A hip & homely place but shared bathrooms & no AC. Just bed & beach. Owner-operated, above the beach with volleyball, archery & a small library. $

staying in longhouse & tents. Various tour/ accommodation/food packages, from KK & Kuala Penyu, inc island, golfing, rafting & river cruises. $$–$$$

RESPONSIBLE TOURISM

Whilst visiting the Park in 2003, youth volunteers from the aid organisation Raleigh International upgraded several trails in the Crocker Range, including the Salt Trail. They also helped local communities in the region repair water piping and paint buildings, while experiencing true village life; a good example of responsible tourism.

🏠 **Pulau Tiga Resort** 11th Floor, Wisma Shopping Centre, KK; ☎ 088 240584; www.pulau-tiga.com. Operated by Sipadan Divers, with PADI diving centre, chalet accommodation, standard & superior rooms, AC, good buffet meals & casual friendly atmosphere. Games room & watersports. $$–$$$

🏠 **Sabah Parks** ☎ 088 243629. Accommodation on the island, includes hostel rooms, 2-person cabins & a campsite. $

🏠 **Weston Wetland** ☎ 088 239476; e tayweelet@westonwetland.com; www.westonwetland.com. Operated by Borneo Eco Stay. In the mouth of the Padas River, longhouse dormitory with common bathrooms. $

A few no-star, no-frills hotels in Beaufort about 20km away are the **Mandarin Inn** (*Lot 38 Jln Beaufort Jaya;* ☎ *087 212800*), the **Beaufort Inn** (*Lot 21–22 Lochung Park;* ☎ *087 211232*) and the **Beaufort Hotel** (*Lot 19–21;* ☎ *087 211911*).

WHAT TO SEE AND DO For visits of the Klias Wetlands, boats leave the Kota Klias jetty late afternoon on river wildlife safaris. Other residents which may be spotted are macaques, crocodiles, monitor lizards, tree snakes and eagles. The night-time spectacle comes with a glowing performance by thousands of fireflies having a good feed out on the mangrove tree enzymes to impress their female friends. It is really worth doing this trip with an experienced wetlands guide such as Chris Lo (☎ *019 8957968;* e *lo_christ2003@yahoo.com; www.chrislotour.com*), either from Kota Kinabalu or meet up in Klias – he will be your guide, but also organise lodgings and a package.

Pulau Tiga (*adult 10MYR, under 18 6MYR*) The crêpe-shaped island is 4.5km long and 1.5km wide, upholstered in old-growth rainforests, some palms and volcanic outcrops. It shot to minor fame as a location for the popular US television series *Survivor*. In Kuala Penyu, there is a **Rumbia Information Centre** (*Kampung Kasugira;* ☎ *087 897078;* ⊕ *Mon–Fri (closed lunchtimes), Sat am*) with handcraft displays on things made with sago palm, and sago cooking demonstrations. Padas River white-water rafting trips set out from Panggi station near Beaufort.

WEST COAST ISLANDS

PULAU LABUAN (*www.labuantourism.com.my*) Situated 10km off the coast of Sabah at the entrance to Brunei Bay, Labuan is a Federal Territory of Malaysia, a duty-free island and Brunei's main import–export hub. Its capital, Victoria, is a deep-sheltered harbour and a centuries-old maritime crossroad. Part of British North Borneo, the township suffered grievous damage in World War II. In 1990, it was declared a tax haven to boost its development as an offshore finance centre. Historic landmarks include the War Memorial Cemetery and Surrender Point where the Japanese surrendered to Australia in 1945. The 98km² isle has a population of 55,000, made up mostly of Malay and Kadazandusun. An increasing pack of international retirees are also settling here, attracted by its relaxed lifestyle and safe-haven environment with Brunei and Malaysia in easy reach. With all those flunked ocean passages beneath it, Labuan has become one of Malaysia's wreck-diving hubs, and Borneo Divers have a PADI dive centre here.

Getting there and away

By air MAS have four flights daily each way between Kota Kinabalu and Labuan, and two between Kuala Lumpur and Labuan. AirAsia have a daily flight between Kuala Lumpur and Labuan. MASWings operate Twin Otter flights between Kota Kinabalu and Labuan and Miri in Sarawak.

By boat High-speed, air-conditioned ferries ply daily between Kota Kinabalu and Labuan. There is also a passenger and vehicle ferry from Menumbok – just across from Labuan on the south coast of Sabah.

Where to stay There are many hotels; the top for service and facilities is the Grand Dorsett Hotel Labuan (*462 Jln Merdeka;* ☏ *+60 87 422000;* e *s_labuan@tm.net.my; www.dorsetthotels.com/labuan*), which has three restaurants, a fitness centre and a pool.

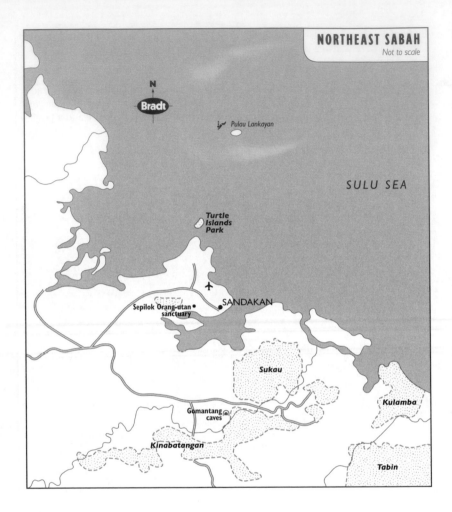

7

Northeast Sabah

SANDAKAN

Overlooking a huge belly of water, dotted with islands, rickety fishing vessels and cargo boats, Sandakan has an old-world trading flavour about it. The beautiful harbour carries winds of other lands and people: the sea border with the Philippines, just 28km away, is visible across the water, and the hundreds of Filipino migrants are just the latest in many exotic waves of immigration which have populated the town. From the port area up, there is a very Chinese flavour to Sandakan. Known as 'Little Hong Kong', its charm lies in the creaky water villages which throw rich hues and reflections over Sandakan Bay. Capital of British North Borneo from 1883 until 1899, Sandakan was nearly flattened by bombings at the end of World War II. Now Sabah's second-largest town with a population of around 350,000 people, its economy is increasingly being strengthened by the palm oil industry after its port's past as a major tropical wood exporter from the 1930s. Crowned by a swathe of lush – though secondary forested – hills, the name *Sandakan* means 'the land that was pawned' in Suluk tongue (Suluk are Filipino people who settled in the area). The town's foundations were set in the 1870s when the Sultan of Sulu forfeited some land on adjacent Pulau Timbang Island to Scottish adventurer and engineer William Clarke-Cowie, in return for ammunition and protection from Spanish conquerors. The area was subsequently leased by the BNBCC. Curious colonial dregs include Edinburgh-style streets, English tea houses, Anglican churches and an Old Rex Theatre. The modern sobriquet is 'nature city' because of Sandakan's strategic position as a gateway to many of Sabah's natural wonders: the Kinabatangan River, the Sepilok Forest Reserve and Orang-utan Rehabilitation Centre. However it is a slogan which will soon ring hollow if that nature is swallowed by expanding industrial crops. A lot of people come to Sandakan just to see the orang-utans and the river, but failing to spend at least one night in this fascinating anchorage of maritime and migratory history would be a shame.

GETTING THERE AND AWAY

By air Both MAS and AirAsia operate daily flights between Sandakan and both Kota Kinabalu and Kuala Lumpur. MAS flights also link Sandakan to Lahad Datu and Tawau. The airport is 12km from the central business district (CBD), a 20–30-minute taxi ride (around 20MYR). There are no buses to town.

By car By road, Sandakan is 227km from Kota Kinabalu (a five–six-hour drive), 91km from Lahad Datu. Tawau and Semporna are 177km away.

By taxi Taxis are relied upon a lot in Sandakan. The **Sandakan Taxi Association** (*Jln Leila, Hsiang Garden;* ✆ *089 222439*) charges about 6MYR for around-town trips, 20MYR to the airport, 35MYR to Sepilok and 80MYR to Labuk Bay.

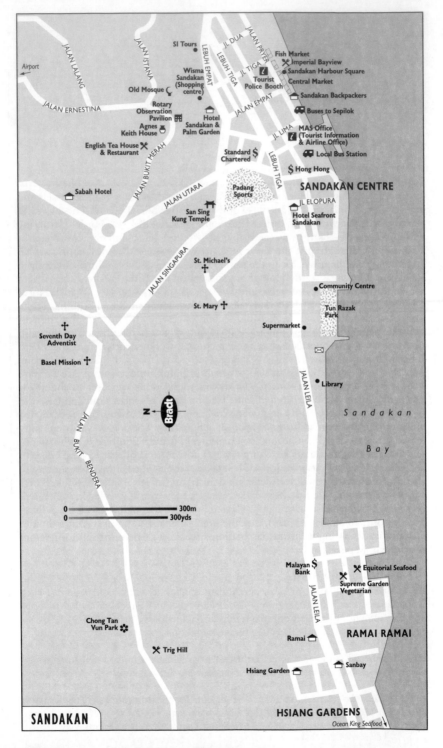

SANDAKAN

By bus There are air-conditioned long-distance buses to and from Kota Kinabalu, Tawau and Lahad Datu. The long-distance bus station is 4km from town (a 10MYR taxi fare). There are also minibuses from the local bus station on Coastal Road near Centrepoint Mall. Further along on Jalan Pryer, towards the Central Market, buses come and go all day, to Sepilok and Labuk Bay.

By boat Various companies operate boat trips from the jetty on Sandakan Bay to islands and the lower Kinabatangan area. Other than established trips, there are not

MONOCULTURE?

Travelling around the east coast of Sabah, you will be struck by the huge expanses of oil palm crops along the coast, inland, down hillsides, and deep into areas which were once covered by forest or jungle. Soaring global demand for palm oil products has seen Malaysia and Indonesia become the world's two leading producers, supplying over 80% of the market – using their Bornean states for large-scale monocultures of the high-yielding, thick-fronded palms *Elaeis guineensis*.

The reddish-brown oil, extracted from crushed fruit of the palm, is riding high on the international commodities charts after coming into demand as a cheap and quickly produced ingredient in a huge range of modern products. You will see 'palm oil' as an ingredient in a range of products from foodstuffs to cosmetics, including chocolate, biscuits, ice cream and bread, toothpaste, soap and body lotions. It's also being looked at as a source of biofuel. Meant to be a green fuel, critics now knock it as 'deforestation diesel' because of the widespread forest clearing carried out by the industry.

Oil palm plantations contribute about 5% of Malaysia's national GDP, and provide nearly 1.5 million jobs. Sabah is the biggest producer, though Sarawak is quickly catching up. Since the end of the 1990s, production in Sabah has multiplied and the amount of land under plantation has doubled from 700,000 to 1.4 million hectares – that's a staggering 20% of the total state area!

Sabah's favourable climate yields the highest palm oil crops per hectare, attracting a swarm of potential investors. The majority of palm oil plantations are found in the east of the state where, according to the Sabah Institute of Development Studies, 'suitable agricultural land is available'. However, much of what is claimed to be 'suitable agricultural land' is actually destroyed forest, ruined by logging or oil palm practices.

In precious natural areas such as the Kinabatangan River, it is deeply troubling to see just how much of the habitat of endangered species has been swallowed up by the industry. Orang-utans who once lived in the jungle now live in plantations, where they are considered pests. The Palm Oil Council says these environmental encroachments are errors of the past, and that it is seeking greater yields through seed technology rather than through land clearing. But as the voracious appetite for palm oil and plantation space continues, they are accused of 'the genocide of the orang-utan' – many animals are killed during forest clearing and many more lose their habitat – doomed to nibble away at plantations for the rest of their life instead of living freely in their once-dense forest home.

The increasingly common large-scale plantations in Sarawak are now said to be encroaching on the land of native people as well – there have been many confrontations between indigenous people and the police called in by contractors. Instead of palm oil production being an answer to rural poverty, as the government claim it to be, critics see it as a gateway to misery as indigenous people are forced to abandon their homes and work for pittance on plantations.

a lot of boat services, but that does not stop the adventurous chartering a speedboat (or even a fishing boat!) as a water taxi and heading off to an island in the bay. The **Sandakan Yacht Club** is on the marina.

⌂ **WHERE TO STAY** Sandakan has just a handful of hotel choices, ranging from deluxe to shoestring. A new boutique hotel and five-star international chain are on the drawing board for the Harbour Square waterfront precinct. Several budget and shoestring hotels are located about 1.5km along the waterfront in the adjacent Ramai Ramai and Hsiang Garden districts.

⌂ **Sabah Hotel** (120 rooms) Km1, Jln Utara (1km from city centre); ☎ 089 213299; www.sabahhotel.com.my. Sandakan's top leisure hotel in 5ha of garden overflowing into the rainforest (with jogging trail), big & bright deluxe rooms, business centre, swimming pool fed by a waterfall, fitness club & spa. Great buffet b/fasts & lunches, fun dining themes, warm layout, ambience & staff. $$$–$$$$

⌂ **Hotel Sandakan** (105 Rooms) Block 83, 4th Av; ☎ 089 221122; e info@hotelsandakan.com.my; www.hotelsandakan.com.my. Excellent range of rooms & suites, switched-on service & technology. It has more of a business beat about it than the Sabah. Save 30–40% on internet bookings. $$–$$$

⌂ **Hsiang Garden** Mile 1.5, 8 Block C, Jln Leila, Hsiang Gardens; ☎ 089 273122. $$

⌂ **Hotel Seafront Sandakan** (23 rooms) Lot 1 Blk 43, 4th Lane, Jln Leila; ☎ 089 222233; e seafront@streamyx.com; http://seafront.com.my. In the CBD, this new hotel looks good value for standard & deluxe rooms all under 100MYR with split-unit AC, sat TV & seafront café. $

Sandakan Backpackers (11 rooms) Lot 108, Block SH-11, Sandakan Harbour Sq; ☎ 089 221104; e enquiries@sandakanbackpackers.com; www.sandakanbackpackers.com. Dorm, sgl/dbl rooms & 1 family room. No curfew; lounge & sundeck, internet, complimentary b/fast. Good for backpacker tours in the area. $

✕ **WHERE TO EAT** Sandakan has fantastic fresh seafood and you don't have to go to a seafood restaurant to enjoy it – food stalls and coffee shops sell it at a fraction of the price. Some good Malay, Chinese and Western eateries are found in hotels of all price brackets, usually with the choice of sitting outdoors or inside with air conditioning.

✕ **English Tea House & Restaurant** 2002 Jln Istana, adj to Agnes Keith Hse Museum; ☎ 089 222544; e info@englishteahouse.com. Very British, with its Bermuda grass & croquet lawns. The food is a rather bland fusion of Western & Asian, sandwiches & *laksa*, but the gorgeous breezy hilltop location & viewpoint over the sea & city make it worth it for a cup of tea at least. Relatively expensive. $$$–$$$$

✕ **Imperial Bayview Restaurant** The Rotunda, 1st Floor, Central Market, Sandakan Harbour Sq; ☎ 089 246888; ⏲ 09.30–14.00/18.00–22.00 Mon–Fri, from 08.00 Sat & 07.00 Sun. B/fasts of dim sum, lotus buns & prawn dumplings; lunch & dinner lots of seafood, steamed fish, clams with garlic & vermicelli. Views over Sandakan Bay from waterside location. Large restaurant – can be noisy. $$$–$$$$

✕ **Ming Restaurant** In Sabah Hotel, Km1, Jln Utara; ☎ 089 213299. Large menu of Cantonese & Szechuan dishes including some interesting vegetarian 'chicken' & 'pork' meals (ie: 'sweet & sour tofu' or

'honeyed soy'). In the same hotel, the poolside **Plantation Café** has excellent lunch & dinner buffets, inc steamboats & BBQs. In-house breads (Chinese & European, white & sourdough) & pastries are sold in the lobby delicatessen. $$$–$$$$

✕ **Ocean King Seafood Parlour** Pasir Putih (White Sand). A 20min drive from town centre on the coast – out of town but worth the trip. Full & fresh seafood platter menu at very reasonable prices. Loved by locals. Recommended. $$$

✕ **Palm Garden** In Hotel Sandakan, Block 83, 4th Av; ☎ 089 221122. Chinese restaurant specialises in Cantonese & dim sum delicacies. There is also a halal coffee shop – the **Palm Café**. $$$

✕ **Equatorial Seafood Restaurant** 6-10 Block K, 1st Floor Ramai-Ramai Centre, Jln Leila; ☎ 089 272303. Another good seafood restaurant. The **Lee Kong Restaurant** is also based here. $$–$$$

✕ **Supreme Garden Vegetarian** Block 30, Lot 3, Ground Floor, Ramai Ramai Centre, Jln Leila; ☎ 089 213292. Vegetarian steamboat & menu. $$–$$$

Street food Head to the Central Market, and adjacent Open Market where you will find lots of fresh and cooked food, stalls and coffee shops. Malay food stalls are always set up between the waterfront Jalan Coastal, and the Sandakan Community Centre.

ENTERTAINMENT AND NIGHTLIFE At Mile 4, about 5km from town towards Sepilok, **Bandar Indah** is a young, nouveau-riche suburb. A happening place with lots of bars and pubs, happy hours run from 17.00 to 18.00. Live performances often follow, and things really start heating up at around 22.00 with karaoke and disco action. There is also some local nightlife for those staying in the **Ramai-Ramai** area, in the form of discos, bars and hotel entertainment.

SHOPPING The main city shopping centre is a multi-levelled mall at the back of town, **Wisma Sandakan**. Here you will find plenty of fast food, electronics, clothing and internet cafés. The state-owned souvenir and crafts-shop chain, **Sabakraf**, is just behind this plaza. For books, the **South East Asia Bookstore** is off Jalan Empat in the CBD. The **Milimewa Superstore** is in the Centrepoint just off Jalan Pryer, along the waterfront.

PRACTICALITIES
Tour operators Three of the best operators for excursions in the region are SI Tours, Borneo Eco Tours and Wildlife Expeditions (see *Tour operators, Chapter 2*, page 41, for contact details). All three can facilitate the excursions outlined below, including day and overnight trips to the Kinabatangan River and the Turtle Islands. Other lodges organise their own transport and tours, including Uncle Tan Wildlife Adventures (listed below).

Airlines The MAS office is between Jalan Lima and Jalan Pelabuhan.

Banking The banks district revolves around the visitors' information centre – HSBC, Bumiputera Commerce and Standard Chartered Bank.

Miscellaneous The post office and library are both on the southwest edge of town, near Tunku Razak Park.

WHAT TO SEE AND DO
Waterfront Sandakan is a port city and can be enjoyably explored on foot. The **Sandakan Harbour Square** is a new shoreline development linking with the 1.5km-long **Esplanade**, a nice stretch for strolling. Right in the middle of Harbour Square are the **Fish Market** and **Central Market**, situated in a modern three-storey market complex, with the 'wet' and 'dry' markets on the ground level and clothing stores and shop-lots on the upper levels. A *tamu* is held here on Sundays – a cultural bouillabaisse of all the flavours ocean migrations have brought to Sandakan. Around the harbour, water villages are strung out on stilts – residents of the creaky, colourful, flower-potted Kampung Buli Sim Sim simply throw the fishing line out their window to catch their dinner and enjoy views of Sandakan's cargo boats and islands.

Temples and mosques Sandakan's velvety hills are covered with places of worship. **Sam Sing Kung** ('Three Saints Temple') is the city's oldest building, completed in 1887 – its three deities uphold righteousness, safety of fishermen and success in exams. A high spiritual, architectural and panoramic experience is the **Puu Jih Shih Buddhist Temple**, a red-shingled, white-walled spectacle of writhing dragons and gilded Buddhas. Perched on a hilltop a few kilometres north of the town centre, the temple was built in 1987 at a cost of 7 million MYR. Other holy places lie along the **Sandakan Heritage Trail**, including the **Masjid Jamek Mosque** and **St Michael's & All Angels' Church**. One of the only pre-war buildings to survive, St Michael's was built in 1893 from local granite. Pick up a map of this trail from the **Visitor Information Centre** (*between Lebuh Empat & Lebuh Tiga avenues*) – it lists 14 places linked together over a 90-minute to two-hour loop from waterfront to hilltop. The walk also takes in the **Chinese World War II memorial** and some more temples, up to the **English Tea House** via forested parkland and the **Stairs with a Hundred Steps** (warning: there have been reports of muggings in this area despite it being alongside a police station).

Museums Agnes Keith's book on life in pre-war Sandakan popularised the use of the old seafarer's name for Sabah - 'Land Below the Wind'. The American writer lived in a colonial wooden bungalow overlooking Sandakan Bay with her husband Henry Keith, the first forestry chief of British North Borneo. **Agnes Keith's House** (*Jln Istana*; ☏ 089 222679; ☉ 09.00–17.00 daily; 15MYR) is along the heritage trail, as is the more interesting local history depot, the **Sandakan Heritage Museum** (*Wisma Warisan Centre;* ☏ 089 222679; ☉ 09.00-17.00 daily).

Memorials Within the Sibuga Forest Reserve, 12km north of the city, is the **Sandakan Memorial Park** (*Mile 7 Jln Labuk Utara;* ☏ 016 8221616; ☉ 09.00–17.00 daily), just opposite the site of the original Sandakan prisoners of war camp. The 2,700 Australian and British POWs brought here in 1942 were used as labour force to build a military airstrip – later destroyed by the Japanese. This is also where the dreadful Sandakan to Ranau 'death marches' set out from (see *History* in *Chapter 1*, page 8). The memorial park's Commemorative Pavilion has a graphic display with an excellent, though heart-rending, interpretation of this appalling period. See also the **Chinese World War II memorial**.

EXCURSIONS FROM SANDAKAN

ISLANDS For diving and turtle-watching (or just playing Robinson Crusoe!), there are several islands within and beyond Sandakan's beautiful harbour.

Pulau Berhala Right in Sandakan Bay, the soaring red cliffs and dark forested clusters of Berhala Island are stunning. It was used as a POW camp during the war – and prior to that, a leper colony. Some Australian POWs used the old leper settlement as an escape route, swimming to the cliffs where they were helped by natives to freedom. Reached by charter boat or tour.

Turtle Islands Marine Park Situated 40km north of Sandakan in the Sulu Sea, the Turtle Islands Marine Park lies within a major nesting ground for green and hawksbill turtles. The turtle sanctuary, established in 1977 to protect the two species, encompasses three small islands: Pulau Selingan, Pulau Bakungan Kecil and Pulau Gulisan. Pulau Selingan is the main nesting area for hundreds of green turtles, while the hawksbills are more attracted to the shores of Pulau Gulisan. Shaped like a musical note with a sandy rim and green core, it is less than 9ha in size.

Green turtles usually spend their time in shallow seagrass beds, but come ashore to lay their eggs. Each night during the nesting season, hordes of turtles drag themselves up the beach to deposit their unhatched offspring. An individual may spend hours choosing the right spot, before she commences digging a hole in the sand with her flippers. The best time to visit is between March and September

Flowing 560km from its source near the Crocker Range of Sabah through to the Sulu Sea in the east, the Sungai Kinabatangan – Kinabatangan River – is Sabah's longest (and Malaysia's second-longest) waterway. The watery journey deep into jungled hinterland, home to proboscis monkeys and river people, is one of my most memorable experiences in Borneo.

The boat journey starts from Sandakan Bay, heading out into the Sulu Sea before swerving back up the river estuary, through gaping floodplains and narrow straits. Much of the deeper river area is protected as the Lower Kinabatangan Sanctuary – a 28,000ha reserve created in 1999. The huge, serpentine bends that the route follows meander through the floodplain and swell to bursting during the rainy season. The area provides a variety of habitats for flora and fauna: freshwater swamp, mangrove, palms, bamboo. The area is one of only two places in the world inhabited by ten species of primates. Four are endemic to Borneo: silvered, maroon and Hose's langurs, and the distinctive proboscis monkey. The area boasts the highest concentration of proboscis monkeys, as well as orang-utans, in Malaysian Borneo. Other wildlife encounters may include long-tailed and pig-tailed macaques, Bornean gibbons, the rare slow loris, pygmy elephants and Sumatran rhinoceros. Over 200 species of birds are also found here – eight types of hornbill (including the rare wrinkled hornbill), lesser fish eagles, stork-billed kingfishers, black and yellow broadbills, pitas and bulbuls.

The name *Kinabatangan* comes from a combination of the words *Kina* – China – and *Batang* – large river. Evidence suggests there was a Chinese settlement on the banks of the river as far back as the 7th century, trading in birds' nests, beeswax, rattan and ivory. The Orang Sungai Kinabatangan – river people who live along the riverbanks today – are of mixed ancestry including Dusun, Suluk, Bugis, Bajaus and Chinese. It was a Chinese princess from the Kinabatangan that married the first sultan of Brunei in the 15th century.

Worryingly, oil palm plantations are encroaching on this beautiful area at an alarming rate. Decades of logging have cleared the area, opening it up for more exploitation. Electric fences shock pygmy elephants who try to feed on the plantations that lie on the once-forested land they used to roam free through. Local villages that once looked out onto forests and orang-utans now see only agricultural estates. Despite the state government dubbing it a 'Corridor of Life' in 2002, and gazetting it as a Wildlife Sanctuary, the Kinabatangan is a continually shrinking and disturbed habitat that remains vulnerable until it is declared a national park. As you join rush hour on the river for dusk wildlife tours, you can't help but wonder whether the tourist traffic is also upsetting the balance of nature. See the section on responsible travel (page 81) for ways to minimise the negative impacts on the environment as you travel.

(peak laying season and calm seas). Personally, I found the overcrowded spectacle quite upsetting. Rangers illuminate the scene with torches, revealing not only the egg-laying but the newly hatched youngsters making their way to the sea. One can't help but feel that these beautiful natural moments would be better left to take place in private.

Getting there A boat leaves Sabah Parks' jetty on Jalan Buli Buli daily at 09.30. The trip to Selingan takes an hour. Sabah Parks has enlisted **Crystal Quest** (\ *089 212711;* e *cquest@tm.net.my*) to manage the park visits, trips and accommodation ($$–$$$). For overnight visits (the only way to see the egg-laying spectacle), there are simple but clean rooms with bathrooms in several wooden chalets spread across the island. Expect sudden power cuts as electricity is provided by a generator. The rest of your time can be spent swimming in the crystal clear waters.

Pulau Lankayan The 80-minute speedboat trip out to Lankayan, through Sandakan Bay and into the Sulu Sea, is thrilling. Boats will not go if the weather is too bad. The 14 dive sites offer an ocean cocktail of reef, wreck and macro-pelagic diving. With increased protection (relying on observation by Malaysian and Filipino fishing vessels), large marine life to the surrounding reefs is said to be making a comeback – leopard sharks, marbled stingray, mimic octopus and giant grouper. 'Jawfish Lair' is home to yellow camouflaged jawfish. 'Lankayan Wreck' – a fish-poaching vessel put out of business – lies very close to shore. The visibility here was poor when I dived, but I still saw stingrays, painted frogfish, harlequin ghost pipefish and schools of parrotfish.

Where to stay and eat It's another one-island, one-resort set-up, operated by **Pulau Sipadan Resorts & Tours** (\ *089 230782;* e *psrt@po.jaring.my; www.lankayan-island.com; $$$–$$$$*). There are 16 chalets, prettily nestled at the water's edge or near the trees, and the food served up in the main lodge is simple but fresh. Take any extras you may require as there are no shops. You don't have to be a diver to stay here; the seclusion and simple wooden chalet are heavenly.

SEPILOK AND LABUK BAY Sandakan would surely receive only a fraction of the visitors it does if it wasn't for Sepilok's famous orang-utan sanctuary to the west. Further along Labuk Bay is a proboscis monkey sanctuary, hedged in by plantations.

Getting there and away
By car Sepilok is 22km west of Sandakan, 11km from the airport, along Jalan Lintas Labuk. Labuk Bay is a further 25km in this direction. There are signs for both.

By bus Minibuses for both destinations depart from near the Central Market, Jalan Pryer.

🏠 Where to stay

🏠 **Sepilok Forest Edge Resort** (16 rooms) Jln Rambutan (off Jln Sepilok, Mile 14); \ 089 533190; e sepilok@sepilokforestedge.com; www.sepilokforestedge.com. 9 new standard & luxury chalets, plus 7-room backpacker longhouse. 'In farm environment' on edge of jungle, 10min walk from Sepilok. $–$$$$
🏠 **Sepilok Nature Resort** (17 twin rooms) \ 089 673999; e sepilok@po.jaring.my; www.sepilok.com.

A 10min walk from the orang-utan sanctuary. Twin-bed chalets by a lake, in rainforest surrounds. AC, bathrooms, hot water. Recommended. $$
🏠 **Sepilok Jungle Resort** (57 rooms) Km22 Jln Labuk; \ 089 533031; e info@sepilokjungleresort.com; www.sepilokjungleresort.com. Reported as friendly, with beautiful gardens & good food. $

What to see and do
Sepilok Orang-utan Rehabilitation Centre (*Jln Labuk, Sepilok;* \ *089 531180;* e *soutan@po.jaring.my; www.sabah.gov.my/jhl;* ⊕ *08.30–17.00 daily; adult 10MYR, 18 & under 5MYR; video/photo fees extra*) One of Borneo's orang-utan-viewing hotspots. 'SOURC' was set up in 1964 to rehabilitate orphaned orang-utans who had lost their parents and their habitat through logging. The apes were brought here to be taught the necessary survival skills before returning to the wild. Operated by Sabah's Wildlife Department, it has now branched out into tourism and education, as well as conservation of other species. A boardwalk leads to the feeding platform, perched up in the trees about 25m from the viewing area. The number of orang-

utans to be viewed depends on luck – and whether orang-utan females' favourite 'Mr B' is there. Once the huge apes are full of bananas and vitamin shakes, they set off to have a swing and a play. Macaques and gibbons also come for a bite to eat. This is a great way to get a fairly close-up view of the 'Man of the Jungle' and his primate cohorts. Feeding times are at 10.00 and 15.00 – the latter is generally quieter. The centre also has a Sumatran rhinoceros enclosure (*admission 1–2MYR*).

Kabili-Sepilok Forest Reserve Sabah's number-one tourist attraction – Sepilok's orang-utans – actually lies within an often overlooked rainforest reserve. Most visitors watch the feasting frenzy and leave but there is plenty to see in the reserve too. The 43km² of lowland rainforest contains 350 different tree species and almost 40% of the known Dipterocarpaceae flora in Sabah. There is also a 5km trekking trail through mangrove forest – for which you need to get a Sabah Parks permit.

Labuk Bay Proboscis Monkey Sanctuary (*Mile 8, Bandar Sibuga Jaya, off Jln Lintas Labuk;* ✆ *089 672133;* e *labukbay@proboscis.cc; www.proboscis.cc*) The sanctuary is billed as a chance for proboscis monkey sighting and birdwatching for those who don't have time to travel up the Kinabatangan River for an overnight stay. Located in mangrove forest along the coast near Kampung Samawang, Labuk Bay, it's about an hour's drive from Sandakan (48km) – the last 15km is along a gravel road through the centre of oil palm plantations. The best viewing times are said to be 10.30 and 16.30.

Deathly Trek While some might find this too upsetting, TYK Adventure Tours (✆ *088 720826;* e *www.sandakantrek.com*) trace the steps of the chilling Sandakan–Ranau death march of World War II POWs, on a five–seven-day trek. The trip is usually organised from Kota Kinabalu, and involves a flight to Sandakan and transfer to Tolupid (about three hours away) to begin the walk there, in order to avoid palm oil plantations. You could join the group in Sandakan rather than Kota Kinabalu if you preferred.

SUKAU A small settlement on the banks of the lower Kinabatangan River, Sukau is the jungle hub for those who want to dwell within the wildlife habitat of the Sungai Kinabatangan conservation area. Be prepared to go back to basics.

Getting there and away
By car Sukau is 80km from Sandakan and around 120km from Lahad Datu. The last 42km of road from Sukau Junction is really rough, though the road is due to be sealed by 2009 – perhaps with money from the oil palm plantations which dominate 90% of the scenery along this road.

By bus From Sandakan market to Sukau.

By boat Local tour operators and river lodges use speedboats for transfers from Sandakan's jetty and the Sepilok area to the lower Kinabatangan. A few of these operators also run lodges, but will provide transport to a different lodge. **Seagull Sea Transport** (✆ *089 215841*) in Sandakan is another port of call for independent travel transfers to Sukau and Abi.

Where to stay and eat If you are staying in a lodge, and don't have your own transport, it may be best to take a package which includes transfers as well as accommodation, meals and excursions. The area is run on generator electricity, and whilst it can be enriching to 'go back to nature' there is some room for improvement in accommodation and food. Lodges vary from being little more than a jungle camp to large bungalow-style wood-panelled rooms with modern bathrooms and power plugs. There are no luxury lodges at present, though some are being upgraded. Food can be very ordinary so take some snacks and drinks and any special dietary foods you may require.

Mid-range

🏠 **Abai Jungle Lodge & Restaurant** (20 twin rooms) ☎ 089 213502; e info@sitoursborneo.com; www.sitoursborneo.com. Set in mangroves with a 300m boardwalk through the forest, the lodge is run by S.I. Tours as a rustic ecotourism experience with biodegradable products & minimal electricity. New sister to established Kinabatangan Riverside Lodge (below) and higher in standards. Twin rooms are spacious, with powerful fans, modern bathrooms & furnishings. Food is served from a simple but dedicated restaurant, with locally sourced produce. The river-facing lodge is eco-rustic & beautiful rather than eco-chic, & you can get your hands dirty with tree planting & other local development activities. $$$

🏠 **Sukau Rainforest Lodge** (20 rooms) ☎ 088 438300; e info@borneoecotours.com; www.sukau.com/public/default.asp. Run by Borneo Eco Tours, this part solar-powered lodge has won various international prizes for its eco-approach & has been a pioneer in ecotourism. It is an intimate stay

alongside nature, with 4 bird- & wildlife-viewing decks & a 450m-long 'hornbill boardwalk' complete with 2 'elephant passes' to accommodate the huge animals' regular migration through the lodge. The restaurant-cum-jetty is complete with fishing & sunset decks. Uses electric boats for the river cruises to minimise wildlife disturbance. $$$

🏠 **Kinabatangan Riverside Lodge** (20 twin rooms) ☎ 089 213502; e info@sitoursborneo.com; www.sitoursborneo.com. On the banks of the Kinabatangan in a lush setting, also run by SI Tours. Accommodation was due for a makeover by the end of 2008, which should see the cramped rooms become more like those of newer Abai Lodge (above). Hopefully the food will also improve. B/fast consists of baked beans & egg. Little fresh fruit/veg available. However, staff are lovely & atmosphere around the main lodge is fun. River excursions are a highlight, with knowledgeable SI Tour guides. FB approx 500MYR for 2 days/1 night/pp, inc transfers, meals, accommodation & excursions. $$

Budget

🏠 **Abi Village Homestays** (approx 30 houses) Tour operators can arrange for you to stay in the Abi village in people's homes, instead of a lodge. $$–$$$

🏠 **Uncle Tan Wildlife Adventures** Mile 16, Jln Gum Gum, Sepilok; ☎ 089 531639; e eugene@uncletan.com; www.uncletan.com. If you don't mind sleeping with several people (& perhaps a monkey or 2!), this operation is basic but with its heart in the right nature-loving place. On the edge of an oxbow lake of the lower Kinabatangan, the

quasi-bush camp is remote & offers greater chances of seeing wildlife in the 'back garden' than many other river lodges. The founder, 'Uncle Tan', has passed away but his family still run the business & the guides are passionate about their work. Lodgings are open-fronted with just a mosquito net for protection. All-inclusive packages of 3 days/2 nights with transfers, 6 river & jungle excursions, start at around 350MYR pp. Bring wellies, raincoat & torch. Pick-up & transfers start from Uncle Tan's shoestring B&B on Jln Gum Gum. $$

WHAT TO SEE AND DO

River excursions All of the lodges and tour operators sail out on the Kinabatangan and its tributaries to see the wildlife from fibreglass boats. The Menanggol, a 26km offshoot heading towards the Gomantong Caves, is considered one of the best wildlife-spotting areas, taking in fig, orchid and rattan-entwined riverine environments and freshwater swamp forest. Boats leave most lodges at around 16.30 each day, for 90-minute proboscis monkey-spotting river trips. Other common sightings are pit vipers, macaques and gibbons. Orang-utans are less common here, more likely to be seen on the way up the Kinabatangan to and from Sandakan. SI Tours offer a 'Kinabatangan River Safari' from Sandakan as a day trip, setting out to Sukau by road, and then taking the boat out at dusk.

For quieter early-morning trips, try bird- and wildlife-watching on the **Oxbow lakes**. These disconnected river bends are teeming with bird life and wonderfully afloat with water hyacinths.

Firefly spotting At night, float out on a boat for some tranquil firefly spotting. The 'bioluminescence' of the fireflies is produced to attract a mate, created in their abdomens by chemical reactions that emit light. The riverbanks are lit up like Christmas trees strung with garlands of fireflies, a beautiful sight to behold.

Local kampung On a u-turn bend in the Kinabatangan River, **Abi village** lies on the other side of the water from the Abai lodge. It's about equidistant between Sukau and Sandkan, and can only be reached by a one-hour boat journey from either direction. On a visit here you might see the 60 village children studying in their longhouse school, or time your visit with the local Hari Guru festivity – a day of paying tribute to the teachers of the village. To celebrate, a day of fun, sport and music is held – one of the events is a banana-eating competition, *makan pisang* – skin and all!

Tree planting Roll up your sleeves and get involved in local tree planting, with initiatives such as Bandok Abai Jungle Tree Planting Kinabatangan Project, a joint project between WWF, a local NGO and Sabah Tourism. I planted a mango tree, and will go back to check on it in a year's time (they take around eight years to fully grow).

Gomantong Caves The Gomantong Caves are the largest limestone outcrop in Sabah. Within limestone forest in the lower Kinabatangan, the cave is home to some two million bats and two million swiftlets which produce edible mossy nests from their saliva. Locals collect the nests which hang from the cave roofs, on rattan and bamboo ladders. The dusk performance is a delight for bird enthusiasts, as bat hawks and peregrine falcons pursue the bats. Some 27 species of bat roost here, mostly wrinkled-lipped bats. The nests sell for about 2,000MYR per kilogram, though a top grade white nest can fetch more than six times that – as much as US$4,000 per kilogram in Hong Kong.

Getting there and away The caves are 95km from Sandakan along the sealed Sandakan–Sukau road, and 26km from Sukau. By boat you can visit from Sandakan or Sukau and the Kinabatangan area. Coming from the south, the caves are about a two-hour drive from Lahad Datu.

8

Southeast Sabah

Between the islands, lagoons and straits off the coast of southeast Sabah lurks a treasure chest of marine biodiversity. On its drier parts, hilly hinterlands are interspersed with some of Borneo's biggest tracts of enduring rainforest. Cocoa, rubber and coconut crops thrive in the fertile volcanic soils – though the landscape is now increasingly dominated by large palm oil plantations. The coast is inhabited by the Bajau Laut – maritime nomads whose ancestors set out from the Filipino island of Mindanao over 1,000 years ago. Many have now settled in stilt villages along the shores of the mainland as well as offshore islands and reefs. Others are still closely connected to the sea, living closer to the shores and making a living from fishing and seaweed cultivation. Local and international initiatives are under way to save the eco-region of the Sulu-Sulawesi seas. *National Geographic* magazine named it as one of the most diverse marine communities on earth – with nine times as many stony corals as the Caribbean Sea, and more than twice the number found in the Indian Ocean. Six of the world's seven species of sea turtles can be found here, along with huge whale sharks, massive manta rays, and an incredible abundance of fish species. Bordered by three densely inhabited nations, it is also a region of socio-political volatility, where ocean piracy and territorial tugs of war persist, and the population is forecast to double within three decades.

TAWAU

Spread around Sebuku Bay, the commercial port of Tawau claims a strategic sea and land location on the southeast frontier of Sabah, edging out towards Indonesia whose border towns can be seen some 30km across the bay. Since the 1990s, the population of Sabah's third-largest town has doubled to about 250,000 due to the influx of illegal immigrants from the Philippines and Indonesia. With the fastest rate of development in the state, the hilly region is upheld by the government as an agricultural beacon, being Malaysia's leader in cocoa production and research and development, as well as a centre for palm oil plantations. The port still does a lively trade in timber, the significant logging imports from poorer Kalimantan into Malaysia, and the manner in which that logging is carried out raises big questions.

A small coastal fishing village in the 19th century under the Sultan of Sulu, Tawau was ceded to the British North Borneo Company in 1878, which set up a rudimentary local government. In the 1890s its population of 200 was made up largely of immigrants from Balungan and Tawi-Tawi, who had fled Dutch rule in Kalimantan. By the end of the 1930s some 60 timber shop-houses, mostly Chinese-owned, lined the main street of Tawau. During Japanese occupation in World War II, many locals were killed. British military administration continued until July 1946, when North Borneo became a Crown Colony and civil government was resumed. The noticeable religious diversity is an indication of

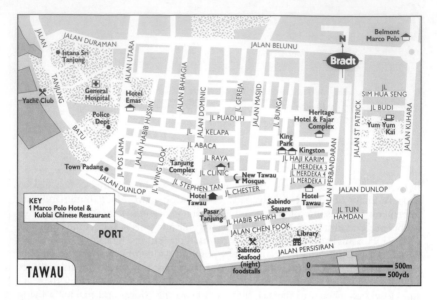

Map labels:
JALAN DURAMAN · JALAN BELUNU · Belmont Marco Polo · Istana Sri Tanjung · JALAN UTARA · Bradt · JALAN TANJUNG · General Hospital · Hotel Emas · JALAN BAHAGIA · JALAN DOMINIC · JL GEREJA · JALAN MASJID · JL BUNGA · Heritage Hotel & Fajar Complex · JL SIM HUA SENG · Yacht Club · Police Dept · JL PUADUH · JALAN ST PATRICK · JL BUDI · Yum Yum Kai · JALAN KUHARA · BATU · JL KELAPA · King Park · Kingston · JL POS LAMA · JALAN HABIB HUSSIN · JL ABACA · JL HAJI KARIM · JALAN PERBANDARAN · JL WING LOOK · JL RAYA · JL MERDEKA 1 · Town Padang · Tanjung Complex · JL CLINIC · JL MERDEKA 4 · JL MERDEKA 3 · JALAN DUNLOP · JL STEPHEN TAN · New Tawau Mosque · JL CHESTER · JALAN DUNLOP · Hotel Tawau · Sabindo Square · Hotel Tawau · JL TUN HAMDAN · KEY 1 Marco Polo Hotel & Kublai Chinese Restaurant · Pasar Tanjung · JL HABIB SHEIKH · JALAN CHEN FOOK · Library · PORT · Sabindo Seafood (night) foodstalls · JALAN PERSISIRAN · TAWAU · 0 — 500m · 0 — 500yds

mixed roots and colourful history: there is a rather gaudy green-roofed, salmon-sided Buddhist lodge, a new mosque, the Basel Christian church and Anglican church. Chinese make up about 15% of the population; Bajau and Malay peoples around the same; Indonesians comprise nearly a quarter; and there are minorities of Kadazan, Dusun and Murut. One Malay minority are the Bugis, an exuberant seafaring people who have been migrating to Sabah for centuries, from Sulawesi Island in Indonesia. As the main entry point for Indonesian traders and migrant workers, there is a thriving barter-trade economy with products from across the border. Overlooking an immense stretch of sea, the Tawau tip alone has 82km of coastline, 210 islands and 186 lagoons.

GETTING THERE AND AWAY

By air The new Tawau International Airport is located at Apas Balung, about 35km from town and 70km from Semporna. As it's the transport hub for the southeast, anyone travelling to the nearby islands or Danum Valley area will probably pass through, though there are plans for an airport in Semporna for island traffic. Daily flights link Tawau with Kota Kinabalu (Kota Kinabalu), Sandakan, Lahad Datu and Tarakan in Kalimantan. Malaysia Airlines have five flights every day to Tawau from Kota Kinabalu, a 45-minute flight. AirAsia have two direct daily flights daily from Kuala Lumpur to Tawau – a three-hour trip. MASWings operate a Fokker 50 flight from Sandakan to Tawau.

There are some buses from the airport to Tawau, operated by Kasah Transport. Some hotels operate shuttle services from the airport, charging around 18MYR for a return journey. A taxi will cost between 40 and 60MYR. If you are visiting the areas for diving, organise transfers with the dive package.

By car From Kota Kinabalu, take the east–west highway to Sandakan, then the east coast highway to Semporna and Tawau. Tawau is also connected by major roads like the Tawau–Lahad Datu Highway and the Tawau–Kunak Highway.

By bus From Kota Kinabalu and Sandakan, express buses take eight hours and cost about 60MYR. From Lahad Datu the trip is two and a half hours. The long-distance bus station in Tawau is around Sabindo Square on the waterfront, between Jalan Dunlop and Jalan Chen Fook, adjacent to the mosque. From Tawau to Kota Kinabalu, buses leave every evening at 19.45.

By ferry If you are travelling to or from East Kalimantan, there are a few daily ferry services between Tawau and Nunukan (one hour) and between Tawau and Tarakan, a three-hour journey. For travels to Indonesia you must obtain a visa beforehand, as none are issued at the border.

GETTING AROUND Due to the spread-out nature of Tawau, the best way to see its coast and hills is by car. The minibus station for local (and airport) buses is near the mosque. Taxis are easier and cost 6–10MYR for most inner-town trips.

The main town centre and wharf lies between Jalan Dunlop, Jalan Chen Fook, Jalan Stephens Tan and Jalan Chester. Kompleks Fajar commercial centre is the hub of many hotels, supermarkets, banks, ATMs and food outlets, near to the waterfront area around the Sabindo Complex.

WHERE TO STAY

🏠 **Belmont Marco Polo Hotel** (150 rooms) 3 Jln Clinic; 📞 089 777988; e bmph@tm.net.my; www.sabahhotels.net. Large, centrally located red-roofed pagoda-style. Carpets are a bit tired, but this is still considered the top hotel in town. B/fast inc in Executive Floor & suites or buffet b/fast 13MYR. Book through website. $$$–$$$$

🏠 **Heritage Hotel** (88 rooms) 210–213 Jln Bunga, Fajar Kompleks; 📞 089 766222; e info@heritagehotel.com.my; www.heritagehotel.com.my. Inside the peak shopping & commercial centre. A soberly stylish hotel with warm décor, deluxe & superior rooms & suites, Wi-Fi, sat TV, kettle. Often good promotional rates online. $$–$$$

🏠 **Hotel Emas** (126 rooms) 2103 Jln Utara (North Rd); 📞 089 762000; e emas@teckguan.com. A 3-star business hotel about 0.5km from town centre, owned by a cocoa company. Room for improvement in service but deluxe rooms are good value with modern bathrooms, tea/coffee making, AC, TV & b/fast. Premier Floor sgle/twin with b/fast still border on budget rates. Shuttle-bus service to airport 15MYR one-way/18MYR round trip. $$–$$$

🏠 **Hotel Soon Yee** (16 rooms) 1362 Jln Stephens Tan; 📞 089 772447. Heralded as friendly. Sub-shoestring. $

🏠 **Hotel Tawau** (21 rooms) 72–73 Jln Chester; 📞 089 771100; e tawauhtl@tm.net.my. Reports of the rooms being 'spartan but spacious'. Sat TV, AC, phones, bathrooms, centrally located. $

Newly opened and untried are the following three places:

🏠 **King Park Hotel** (103 rooms) 30 Jln Haji Karim; 📞 089 766699; e kingpark@streamyx.com. Health centre, shuttle service. $$–$$$

🏠 **Kuahara Court Apartment Suite** 4550, Mile 1, Jln Kuahara, Block C, Ground Floor; 📞 089 768778. About 1.3 km from town, next to huge new Eastern Plaza shopping centre. The condominium development also has deluxe rooms & 2–3-bedroom units. Available for day & monthly leases in a complex with a pool, poolside café & catering. $–$$

🏠 **Kingston Hotel** Lot 6–15, Ground Floor, Jln Haji Karim - In the Fajar commercial centre 📞 089 702288; book via www.etawau.com. $$

Out of town

🏠 **Roach Reefs Resort** (11 chalets) 📞 089 779332; e info@roachreefsresort.com; www.roachreefsresort.com. Who would want to go to a manmade tropical reef when Sipadan & other natural island paradises are just nearby? This very upmarket Japanese-owned product says you can have both private resort & Sipadan. Packages from Tawau inc transfers, reef chalet accommodation, food & PADI diving activities starting from 1,200MYR. A 25min speedboat journey from Tawau, 50 mins from Sipadan. $$$$–$$$$$

🏠 **Balung River Eco Resort** Mile 33, Apas Balung; 📞 089 761339; e seavent@po.jaring.my. In the Tawau Hills Park (55km from Tawau) on a mixed agricultural plantation. Standard rooms & 3–4-bedroom 'eco-chalets' built with river stones & local timber. Surrounded by fruit trees, rainforest & rivers where you can fish your own dinner. Restaurant, & karaoke lounge. $$–$$$

✖ WHERE TO EAT

Street food and markets Many people claim the best seafood in Malaysia is found in Tawau, and it's from here that Kota Kinabalu gets much of its fresh catch. You can sample this from small open-fronted *kedai kopi*, in under-cover markets and open-air food stalls all over town. The nightly food park **Sabindo Seafood** (*opposite the Sabindo Shopping Complex, Jln Chen Fook*) is a large open-air set-up with many food stalls, tables and chairs. At **Kam Ling Seafood**, a good dinner for two will cost under 50MYR. The larger **Good View Seafood** gets mixed reports. The whole area bustles with people from 18.00 to 23.00. There is also a seaside strip of evening food stalls selling fast Malay, Indian and Indonesian food – barbecued skewers and satays, *murtabak* and *nasi ayam*, *roti cani* – some serve *sulawesi soto makassar*, a Bugis buffalo soup dish.

Sabindo has plenty of casual eateries by day. Food courts are located in marketplaces and shopping centres, from the **Pasar Tanjung** central market to the Malay-oriented **Parkwell Food Centre** in the Parkwell supermarket (⊕ *06.00–18.00*).

Coffee shops and restaurants The **Kompleks Fajar** has cheap eateries but also some air-conditioned restaurants, including **Maxim's Seafood Restoran** (*Jln Baru, Block 30 Fajar Complex;* ✆ *089 771800*). Locals refer to the area of Jalan Budi (east of the Fajar centre) as 'Yum Cha Kai' – Yum Cha Street. All the coffee shops here serve good food and drink, try: **Kedai Kopi Kim Kim**, **Mui Lok**, and **Sin Hing**.

Nearby is a great place for vegetarian, rice and noodle dishes and soups: **Kedai Kopi Bunga** (*TB1722 Hotel Kuhara, Jln Kuahara*). Some hotel restaurants are good, with the added bonus of being off-street and air conditioned: **Kublai Chinese Restaurant** (*3 Jln Klinik;* ⊕ *11.30–14.00 & 18.00–22.00 Mon–Sat, 07.00–14.00 & 18.00–22.00 Sun & public holidays*) in the Marco Polo Hotel has a buffet lunch on weekdays for 12.99MYR, and Cantonese cuisine and dim sum in a mandarin court, and it **Venice Coffee House** (⊕ *06.00–13.00 Sun–Fri, 06.00–14.00 Sat & public holidays*) serves international and Asian dishes and is a good place for breakfast. **Cacao Palace Restaurant & Bar** in Hotel Emas goes a bit overboard on chocolate (including fish, soup and more!), but there is a good nightly steamboat buffet as well as à la carte. **Cowie Bay Restaurant** (*Rich Park, port area*) also gets good reports.

Cake shops Tawau makes excellent *kedai kek*. For all sweet and savoury bakes and cakes, head to the area around the Fajar complex; the **Southern Cake Shop** is on Jalan Merdeka next door to the more average chain **Multi Bake**, and just opposite is a coffee shop-style branch of the **Sugar Bun** (*2 Jln Merdeka*) fast-food chain.

WHAT TO SEE AND DO

Mosques *Al-Kauthar,* or New Tawau Mosque (*Jln Stephens Tan*) is the biggest mosque in Sabah. Completed in 2004, it cost 31 million MYR to build, can hold 17,000 people and has a library, seminar hall and offices.

Markets Tawau's markets are marvellous. The pastel pink-winged **pasar Tanjung** – the new central market – on Jalan Dunlop is said to be largest in Borneo, with 6,000 stalls selling fresh food and fish, salted dried fish (*ikan masin*), clothes, baskets and much more. The old market is known as the **pasar Gantung** or 'hanging market', because all the items for sale (from clothing, handicrafts and handbags to house decorations) are suspended from the stalls. Most of the produce is Indonesian. A *tamu* market is held every Sunday morning on the corner of Jalan Apas and Jalan Kuhara, with over 200 stalls starting at 06.00 and running until around midday.

Cocoa tours Tawau is trying to get people to taste its wares with its slogan of 'Asia Cocoa City'. The **Teck Guan Cocoa Village** (*Quoin Hill;* ✆ *089 772277 ext 2254 to organise tours*) dubs itself 'Cocoa Kingdom' – a cocoa plantation up in the hills near Tawau. During a two-hour tour, cocoa breakfasts and lunches can be enjoyed – with cocoa flavoured noodles, porridge, prawn and banana rolls and fresh cocoa juice on the menu. A few minutes' drive away is a hiking trail which leads to a 9m-high waterfall, the **Culture Spring**. The same factory has a museum just out of Tawau **Teck Guan Cocoa Museum** (*Mile 2, Tanjung Batu Laut;* ✆ *089 775566 ext 2601;* ⊕ *08.00–11.30 & 13.30–16.30 Mon–Fri; reservations necessary for guided visits*). Inside the Majulah Cocoa Factory, the one-hour visit is guided by factory staff and includes a quality multi-media presentation of the history of cocoa, topped off by tastings of cocoa drinks and sweets. It's a very personable, small-scale affair.

Festivals With about a fifth of Tawau's population Chinese, February's **Chinese New Year** Festival is said to paint the town red with fireworks, festivities and fun. A **Cocoa Festival** is also held, featuring colourful cocoa-inspired cultural dances.

EXCURSIONS FROM TAWAU

TAWAU HILLS PARK (Taman Bukit Tawau) (*50km from Tawau; adult 10MYR/under 18 6MYR*) This is a rainforest and lower montane park of about 28,000ha, gazetted in 1979 to preserve the Sungai Merotai, Ulung Sungai Tawau and Sungai Balung – three rivers which flow through the area – and their unique ecosystems. Over 150 flowering plants have been recorded in the park, a small island of biodiversity within a region of limestone outcrops, rich alluvial volcanic soils, cocoa and oil palm crops. The reserve is managed by Sabah Parks and boasts waterfalls (including the 30m-high Banjir Kilat) and hot springs. It also contains mountain-bike trails and jungle treks to the tops of Gunung Magdalena and Gunung Maria, on which you can encounter monkeys, hornbills and orchids. The park rangers are very helpful. The nearest lodgings are on the adjacent **Balung Plantation**, also intersected by the Sungai Balung river; a nice place for swimming, trekking, birdwatching and mountain biking.

ASIA COCOA CITY TOUR (✆ *019 8830173; adult 550MYR, child 450MYR*) Ivy Yap, local livewire and special project manager at Teck Guan Cocoa company, organises four-day/three-night packages, taking in Tawau, the Balung Eco Resort, trekking, snorkelling and Semporna's Singamata Water Chalet.

LIVE ABOARD CELEBES EXPLORER (✆ *088 223918;* e *jworld@po.jaring.my; www.borneo.org*) This Tawau-based luxury live-aboard diving company offers packages from Kota Kinabalu or Semporna. The custom-built vessel has eight en-suite air-conditioned cabins fitted out with five-star hotel equipment, a sundeck and salon. UK specialist tour group Dive Worldwide (e *sales@diveworldwide.com; www.diveworldwide.com/holiday/celebes_explorer_liveaboard.html*) offer three-, seven- and ten-day packages

MALIAU BASIN CONSERVATION AREA A 'protected forest reserve' once open to logging, Sabah's so-called 'Lost World' lies in south-central Sabah, about 40km north of the Indonesian border – an enclosed 390km² basin up to 25km across. The area is drained by tributaries of the Maliau River, one of which forms a stunning series of waterfalls, the seven-tiered **Maliau Falls**. It is a remarkable block of tropical forest – virtually the entire catchment of the Maliau River – almost encircled by a dramatic escarpment rising over 1,600m in height, insurmountable from most directions. The area was originally set aside by the Sabah Foundation and then formally upgraded to a Class 1 Reserve.

The basin has 12 different forest types, mostly Agathis tree-dominated lower montane, dry heath forest and lowland and hill dipterocarp forest. It is a faunal haven with over 1,800 species of plants and lots of wildlife including barking deer, banteng, sun bears, proboscis monkeys, clouded leopards, pythons and many species of birds including the rare Bulwer's pheasant, crimson-headed partridge and peregrine falcon. Only a couple of operators are allowed to visit this area – it is under tight wraps, and is very expensive – about 4,000–6,000MYR for five days and four nights excluding airfares, less with a bigger group. It's a tough trip – camping in tents, with lots of leeches around (including tiger leeches) and 06.00 starts. With long walking days in humid conditions, participants must be physically fit, and mentally prepared. There are about 12 licensed tour operators, both local and international, who can visit the area. **Borneo Nature Tours** (*Block 3, Ground Floor. MDLD 3285 Fajar Centre (edge of town near airport);* ☏ *089 880207; www.borneonaturetours.com*) is one. Maliau treks start with pick-up at Tawau Airport, followed by a five-hour drive in a 4x4 to the Maliau Basin Security Gate 180km away. The trip can also be done from Keningau on the west coast, with a six-hour drive in.

Those wanting to visit Maliau Basin independently must get permits and written permission from the Conservation and Environmental Management Division of

THE MALIAU EXPERIENCE

Sir Peter Crane

A few days in the Maliau Basin provides a truly authentic tropical rainforest experience. All year round, day or night, the temperature rarely deviates more than a few degrees from its average of about 30°C. The humidity is always high, so dripping with sweat becomes a way of life. Torrential downpours are a regular occurrence – the region receives more than three metres of rainfall annually, which is about a metre more than the English Lake District receives in a typical year. Clothes and camera gear – and anything else – never dry out, and even the shortest journey involves slithering up or down precipitous slopes that always seem to end in sandstone cliffs or white water torrents. The ubiquitous leeches take every opportunity to gorge themselves on any passing mammal; leech socks are a must.

The exuberance and sheer diversity of plant and animal life in Maliau more than compensate for the challenging conditions. In the valleys, immense dipterocarp trees dominate small patches of lowland rainforest containing incredible plants – such as the legendary rafflesia with its enormous, malodorous flowers, and giant strangling figs. This is also the habitat of the greatly prized ironwood – one of the most dense and resistant of all tropical hardwoods.

Sir Peter Crane is a former Director of the Royal Botanic Gardens, Kew, England. He has been at the University of Chicago since 2006, and is a frequent visitor to Borneo's forests

the Sabah Foundation (*Yayasan Sabah*) (*12th Floor, Menara Tun Mustapha Tower, Kota Kinabalu;* \ *088 326300;* e *mbca_kk@icsb-sabah.com.my*) or the Maliau Basin Conservation Area Tawau office (\ *089 759214;* e *maliau@icsb-sabah.com.my*).

The new Maliau Basin Studies Centre (MBSC) (\ *087 745100/101/103*) has a hostel, camping ground, exhibition hall, mini theatre, conference room and library.

IMBAK CANYON Just north of the Maliau Basin, this 300km^2 valley has only recently been set aside as a conservation area and looks set to become another magnet for rugged treks. It's a sweeping area of one of the largest contiguous lowland dipterocarp forests left in Sabah, enclosed by high sandstone ridges and canyon waterfalls. A vital link in the biodiversity corridor linking Maliau Basin to the Danum Valley further east, it is also an important area for research and a botanical gene bank for forest rehabilitation projects. Conditions of visiting are the same as for Maliau Basin.

SEMPORNA

Semporna means 'perfect' in Bajau language. At the end of the Semporna Peninsula, its feet bathing in the waters of the Celebes Sea, Semporna is a watery world: the bay is a whirr of engines, masts and boats of all forms. Bajau Laut, the indigenous population of the Bajau sea, live along the coast in houses perched on stilts over shallow reefs. The high rate of conversion to Islam among the Bajau people explains the large proportion of Muslims here – 90% of the 100,000 strong population in the Semporna area. Stone Age tools found in the hills above Semporna show the area was a prehistoric pottery hub.

GETTING THERE AND AWAY
By car Semporna is a 90-minute drive from Tawau town, and an hour from Tawau Airport.

By taxi A taxi ride from Tawau will cost 100MYR.

By bus Express buses from Kota Kinabalu leave daily at 07.30 and 19.30. It's a seven- or eight-hour trip and costs about 60MYR with a meal included. Minibuses between Tawau and Semporna take two hours.

WHERE TO STAY
Seafest Hotel (63 rooms) Jln Kastam; \ 089 78 2333; e info@seafesthotel.com; www.seafesthotel.com. Efficient, calm location a few blocks from town centre. Standard/deluxe rooms & suites, majority overlooking the all-surrounding water. Health centre at extra charge; kettle, AC, ceiling fan, & buffet b/fast inc – though very ordinary. 3-star excellence; by far the best hotel in town comfort wise; also lovely location at end of pier. $$–$$$
Sipadan Inn (32 rooms) Block D, Lot 19–24; \ 089 782766; e booking@sipdadan-inn.com; www.sipadan-inn.com. New hotel, looks like it lives up to its slogan ('luxury budget accommodation') in many respects; modern rooms of rich furnishings, all with AC, sat TV & free internet, & extra spacious superior rooms & ocean suites. Boutique-style at very budget prices. $–$$

Dragon Inn Floating Hotel (65 rooms) 1 Jln Custom; \ 089 781088; e info@ dragoninnfloating.com.my; www.dragoninnfloating.com.my. Ineffective AC due to natural ventilation between wooden floorboards & lack of shutters, but beautiful water-ambience & rustic charm. Family rooms and suites. $–$$
City Inn (24 rooms) Lot 2, Block K, Bangunan Hing Loong; \ 089 784733; e info@cityinn-semporna.com; www.cityinn-semporna.com. Big warmth on shoestring budget, cosy, clean & ethnic décor in common areas, sgl/dbl/family (5-bed) rooms, all with AC & showers, daily room cleaning & complimentary bottled mineral drinking water; some with sat TV. Negotiates budget weekly or monthly rates. $

8

Semporna is the springboard to Sabah's famous dive islands: Pulau Sipadan, Mabul, Kapalai and Mataking. In all, there are about 20 main dive sites: over half around Sipadan, and half a dozen around Mabul. All the resorts offer beginners and advanced diving opportunities around Sipadan, Mabul and Kapalai.

SIPADAN One hour by speedboat from Semporna, Pulau Sipadan looks like little more than a cluster of trees from above the water's surface. Formed by living corals growing on top of an extinct volcanic cone, it took thousands of years to develop and drops off 600m to the ocean floor. 'Sipadan's oceanic location keeps visibility at 30m or more, and marine life has thrived thanks to limits on the number of divers,' says dive journalist William Moss. 'Barracuda Point' is so called due to the incredible vortices of thousands of chevron barracuda which swirl through it. Close encounters with turtles and sharks (grey reef sharks, leopard sharks, scalloped hammerheads...) are common here and at the 'Pinnacle'. The drop-off is popular for shore and night diving. A Sabah Parks permit for Sipadan is 40MYR per day.

For environmental and security reasons, there are no longer resorts on Sipadan. Dive operators visit there from the mainland and the other three islands, with enforced limits of 120 people per day. Since the kidnapping of divers on Sipadan in 2000, and with 'continuing threats', the British Foreign & Commonwealth Office (www.fco.gov.uk) and the Australian Department of Foreign Affairs (www.smartraveller.gov.au) have issued warnings against travelling to these islands (see *Diving in Borneo* box in *Chapter 2*, page 39). The islands and surrounding waters are under constant military surveillance and there is a continuous military presence.

MABUL AND KAPALAI Sitting on the edge of the continental shelf, 45 minutes from Semporna, these islands have very different ecosystems, and visibility can be low – as little as 10m – because of the sandy bottoms, especially at Kapalai. However, their reefs 'host a dazzling array of odd and photogenic creatures including frogfish and leaf fish, ghost pipefish, anemone and cleaner shrimps, lionfish, octopi, venomous catfish, elusive mandarin fish, and a rainbow of nudi-branches,' says William Moss. Mabul is a beach-fringed atoll, part of a 200ha reef, and is popular for muck-diving. Kapalai sits further out to sea on the same reef, separated by a sand bar – the 'Jetty' dive has five wrecks, while the sloping 15m reefs of Kapalai are a highly photogenic place to dive.

🏠 **Scuba Junkie Backpackers** Block B Lot 36 (nr the waterfront, next door to the Scuba Junkie Dive Shop & Restaurant); e info@scuba-junkie.com; www.scuba-junkie.com. Dorm (30MYR) & standard (80MYR) rooms, 100MYR for en suite. 50% discount for their dive clients. Very professional young & dynamic operation with good website, max 12 people on the dives. $

✕ **WHERE TO EAT** Anjung Lepa (*Seafest Hotel, Jln Kastarn;* ✆ *6089 7823333*) is a small sea hut with plastic chairs, adjacent to the Seafest Hotel and hanging over the water. It does charcoal-grilled fish (*ikan panggang*), prawns and octopus by weight (2–4MYR per 100g, minimum 300g) as well as grilled satay. All food is cooked outdoors, and served with rice and fresh melon juices – no alcohol is served. The hotel also has an indoor venue, the **Lepa Café**, serving buffet lunches. Western and Eastern food, and lots of seafood, are on the lunch and dinner menu. There are food stalls day and night about town, near the market and in the area along Jalan Kastarn. **Pearl City Restaurant** (*1 Jln Custom;* ✆ *089 781 099*) is a floating restaurant, and part of the Dragon Inn stilted complex. Choose fish fresh from tank, though some is over-priced. **Seafest Café** is on Jalan Kastarn, near Seafest Inn.

MATAKING Mataking is a 40-minute boat ride from Semporna, for macro and pelagic diving with 100m reef drop-off on eastern shore.

RESORTS AND OPERATORS Most resorts offer two- four- or six-night packages, including boat transfers from Tawau Airport to Mabul, three meals a day, accommodation, three boat dives a day, and most dive gear.

Mabul
🏠 **Sipadan Water Village** (45 rooms) & **Mabul Water Bungalows** (14 units) (Explore Asia Tours) ✎ 088 230006; e mabul@po.jaring.my; www.sipadan-mabul.com.my. Both resorts are on Mabul. The water village (www.sipadanwatervillage.com) – known among divers as SMART – is very established. The water bungalows (www.mabulwaterbungalows.com) are more recent, and floating. Both are expensive (1,236–1,413MYR/night for non-divers, add about 530MYR for divers). Very upmarket with plush chalet, 5-star hotel services & dining. Prices more than halve with a 4-night diving or non-diving package. PADI dive centre. $$$$$

🏠 **Mabul Dive Resort** (Borneo Divers) ✎ 088 222226; www.borneodivers.info. Pretty wooden chalets with many simple comforts & ethnic furnishings, AC & bathrooms, in tropical gardens with pool. Good buffet meals & very friendly, helpful staff. PADI dive centre. Promotional deals & good negotiating skills can result in 2-night packages of around 1,000MYR pp, at least 100MYR less for a non-diver. $$$–$$$$

🏠 **Scuba Junkie** Block B Lot 36, Semporna; e info@scuba-junkie.com; www.scuba-junkie.com. Can arrange longhouse stays on Mabul Island for 50MYR pp inc meals. Free transfers if you are diving with them, otherwise there is a small fee. $

🏠 **Uncle Chang's Sipadan Mabul Dive Lodge** (Borneo Jungle River Island Tours) ✎ 089 781002; e info@sipadanbackpackers.com or mabulbackpackerslodge@yahoo.com; www.sipadanbackpackers. A new backpackers' option on Mabul. 50MYR/night including meals. $

Kapalai
🏠 **Pulau Sipadan Resort & Tours** ✎ 089 765200; e kapalai@tm.net.my; www.sipadan-resort.com. The only resort on Kapalai – water village resort above the water, linked by elevated paths; you can dive straight from the resort into the reefs. Very exposed in windy weather. $$$$–$$$$$

Mataking
🏠 **Reef Dive Resort** ✎ 089 770022; e sales@mataking.com; www.mataking.com. Luxury diving beach & spa resort, rising honeymoon destination. $$$$–$$$$$

WHAT TO SEE AND DO Semporna is small, and easily navigated on foot. In a matter of minutes you can journey from the pier to the bus station, markets, banks and hotels.

Semporna Ocean Tourism Centre (*1 Jln Custom;* ✎ *089 781077*) Locally called 'the floating' this is a source of local tourist information. It is built in Bajau water-village style on the pier, with a few bungalows, a hotel (the Dragon Inn), restaurant, bar and souvenir shops, all connected by duckboards.

Pasar Ikan The Fish Market is held in the beige pyramid-shaped structure right on the waterfront.

Semporna Islands The largest in view is **Pulau Bum Bum** (pronounced 'Bom Bom'), and is bigger than Singapore – 1,000 families cultivate seaweed here. Speedboats (20MYR) leave from the pier near the Seafest Hotel.

Bukit Tengkorak Archaeological Site Museum (*Kampung Tampi Tampi, 5km from Semporna;* ℡ *088 253199;* ⏲ *09.00–17.00 daily*) The Department of Natural Heritage at Sabah Museum and university researchers found of thousands of pottery residues here, with some specimens dating as far back as 8,000BC. This suggests the area was one of the largest Neolithic craft centres in southeast Asia and a major stop-off point on early Pacific trade routes.

Culture and festivities The *lepa*, a traditional wooden sailing boat with intricately carved embellishments, is an integral part of the life of the Bajau Laut people. Usually made of hardwoods, the *lepa* are decorated with a flotilla of red and yellow frilly sails (*sambulayang*) and small triangular flags (*tapis-tapis*). **The Regatta Lepa** is held in April with other traditional watersports including a rowing competition (*Lumba dayung*), in which rivals tug at the ropes of other boats, and races in small dugout boats (*kelleh-kelleh*). Traditional dances including the *daling daling* – an upbeat courting dance whose name comes from the English word 'darling' – accompany the festivities.

Diving The major 'dive islands' and their resorts are run by one operator or another (see box on page 39). Some people stay in Semporna and go diving from there by day, finding it cheaper and/or more interesting. If you have arrived without a pre-booked package and want to go diving, beware of dodgy operations – there are at least a couple in town. Check blogs and reviews on other major dive sites (such as *www.scubatravel.co.uk* and *www.scubadiving-malaysia.com*) – this is also an excellent way of getting feedback about different dive resorts and accommodation. Day diving is possible to many places such as Tampi Tampi, a dive resort ten minutes along the coast from Semporna. I have heard people ask how they get to the dozens of other small Semporna islands to dive. One answer is to not go for a prescribed dive operator–island resort package; then you are free to cherry-pick, and some more budget oriented Semporna-based operators visit such islands for day diving. Reputable operators for day dives include **Scuba Junkie** (*Block B, Lot 36 Semporna seafront;* ℡ *089 785372/019 584657;* e *info@scuba-junkie.com; www.scuba-junkie.com; 250MYR 1-day PADI Discover Scuba, 750MYR 3-day Open Water, 700MYR 3-day Advanced Open Water*) who also organise outings to some 25 islands in the area. They are a young, business-driven operation, and take groups of 12 as a maximum. **North Borneo Dive and Sea Sports** (*Semporna Ocean Tourism Centre, Dragon Inn, Jln Kastam;* ℡ *089 942788/769950;* e *borneo_tours@hotmail.com*) also arrange diving in the area.

LAHAD DATU

Lahad Datu in Bajau language means 'a place of royals' – bestowed on the town by noble-blooded Bajau peoples who migrated from the Sulu Islands in the late 19th century. It faces the Sulawesi Sea and sits within a large inlet, Darvel Bay. Palms and casuarinas line 'The Corso' which runs along the waterfront to the rather grubby old town centre. Here the streets are packed with street vendors, small shops, department stores, Islamic restaurants and food stalls. By evening, the large fish market can be a bit overbearing on the senses. The population of Bajau, Sulu islanders, illegal Filipino immigrants and minorities of 'river people' – *orang sungai sagama,* who live near the Sagama River – form an intriguing cultural pool. Lahad Datu is trying to clean up its 'cowboy' image, a campaign driven by the local mayor. Results of the sprucing-up effort can already be seen around the 'new town', an area with many new hotels and shopping centres earmarked. On the edge of town is a large immigrant *kampung* of 4,000, Filipino and Indonesian migrants: the people motoring the palm oil and construction industries with cheap labour.

GETTING THERE AND AWAY

By air MASWings fly to Lahad Datu direct from Kota Kinabalu and from Miri via Kota Kinabalu.

By bus With all the cheap flight options it's best to avoid the lengthy bus journey from Kota Kinabalu to Lahad Datu. Between Sandakan and Lahad Datu, Syarikat Chin buses (\ *019 883 4962*) leave from Sandakan open air bus terminal at Batu (2.5km from town) around 07.30 – the 179km journey takes four hours. Sida Bus Express (\ *019 8737808*) run the same trip at 07.15. Pay for tickets on board for first-in-first-served seating. There is a single daily return from Lahad Datu to Sandakan departing at 12.30.

By van/4x4 taxi Vans and 4x4 taxis run trips between Lahad Datu and Sandakan bus terminals, early morning (about 07.00), leaving only when they are full – with about six passengers. If not, they may postpone the trip till the next day! 20–25MYR per person. Regular services also go between Lahad Datu and Semporna.

WHERE TO STAY At the time of writing there was talk of a new five-star hotel ready for opening by 2009, as well as a couple of other mid- to upper-range hotels, filling a much-needed gap in the market.

Asia Hotel (60 rooms) 639 Jln Teratai; \ 009 881 771; e reservations@asiahotel.com.my; www.asiahotel.com.my. Renovated 10 storey 1960s building saw this 3-star hotel with a competitive edge, offering lots of facilities for price. AC, free Wi-Fi, sat TV, tea/coffee-making facilities, private safe. Rooms quaint but light, bright & good furnishings. $$–$$$

Executive Hotel (50 rooms) Jln Teratai; \ 089 881333; e tehotel@tm.net.my. In the heart of the 'new town' commercial area, a family-run hotel with a Chinese flavour & predominantly business clientele. Avoid the cell-like standard rooms & opt for a deluxe – very comfortable & light with modern bathrooms, TV, AC, phone & kettle. No safes or fridges. Interesting but not pretty views over town & South China Sea. As part of the mini boom in Lahad Datu, the hotel foresees an important renovation, which will see it build upwards & have up to 200 rooms by 2012. $$–$$$

Grace Hotel (58 rooms) Levels 4/5, Centre Point, Jln Kastam Lama; \ 089 881000; e grh@tm.net.my or grchotel@streamyx.com. 2-star, salmon pink building block, comfortable rooms, restaurant & business centre, suites with b/fast in budget bracket $$–$$$

There are three shoestring hotels where you should be able to count on a clean room, air conditioning and bathrooms for under 100MYR for a double:

Mido Hotel (61 rooms) Jln Teratai; \ 089 881800. Restaurant, slightly more expensive than the Jagokota and Perdana.

Hotel Jagokota (55 rooms) Jln Kampung Panji; \ 089 882000
Perdana Hotel (23 rooms) Block 31 Jln Seroja; \ 089 881400

WHERE TO EAT Lahad Datu's new split personality brings both new- and old-town eating. In the old town, a *pasar malam* is held along a paved strip in the middle of Jalan Mawar (directly opposite Emporium Ramai Ramai) – smoking, steamy stalls, of skewers and satays, whole grilled fish (*ikan panggang*), chicken wings, roasted meats and sweets, among some tables and chairs. The other side of the street is full of late-night clothes shops and Restoran Islam. There are also some stalls on Jalan Kastam Lama. In the 'new town', the pedestrian-only street of Jalan Panji leading up to the waterfront 'Corso' has food stalls day and night, as well as coffee shops and restaurants. At **Sakura Seafood Restaurant**, a dozen seafood varieties of fish, shellfish, crab and prawns can be bought and cooked per 100g, (2–8MYR). There are also many Chinese dishes: noodles, dumplings and roasted duck, all priced about 4MYR. **Choi Kee** has good noodles, clay-pot dishes, roasted pork and duck; **Ah Seng** offers chicken rice; and opposite the Kedai Kopi, **San Hoi Pow** serves homemade noodles. For vegetarian food, try **Kedai Kopi Jeet Lee** (*Block 48, Lorong 1, off Jln Teratai opposite the Executive Hotel*). The Executive Hotel's **Spring Palace Chinese Restaurant** is frequented by many local Chinese people for its Cantonese and Szechuan cuisines and dim sum. There is a more international menu of snacks and dinners in the **Plantation Coffee House**. In the Kompleks Fajar, on the edge of town near the airport, the **Unicorn Vegetarian Restaurant** (*Jln Segama*), has a Chinese buffet and menu. Also here are two Malay-Chinese eateries **Restaurant Dovist** (*Lot 73, Fajar Centre*), and **Restoran Serai Wangi** (its name comes from the Citronella plant).

WHAT TO SEE AND DO Most people come to Lahad Datu to go diving, or to visit the Danum Valley and surrounding region's natural attractions. Although the town may appear grotty in places, there is a certain charm about it. There is a Sunday market in the centre of town. A curiosity is **Kampung Cocos**, a village about 8km from town populated by a community of Cocoas islanders – Orang Cocos – originally from the Keeling Islands in Australia, they came in the 1950s to work on the coconut plantations.

SHOPPING The Sunday *tamu*, **Emporium Ramai Ramai** (*Jln Bunga Raya; ⟩ 089 880151*), is a large bustling supermarket along the main street near the fish market. It has a mix of Chinese and Asian produce, health and beauty products, as well as quite a good range of international brands of biscuits, confectionery, jams and alcohol. It is part of the multi-level **Wisma Ramai Ramai** shopping centre. The 128 million MYR Dravel Bay Plaza, to be completed by 2010, will be the district's biggest shopping mall. As part of the overall Dravel Bay commercial centre development, it will include hundreds of retail shop-lots, a supermarket, food court, house wares, IT, fashion stores and cafés, and close to 700 parking bays.

OTHER PRACTICALITIES
Intra Travel Service (⟩ *089 274988;* e *enquiry@intra-travel.com.my; www.intra-travel.com.my*) offers budget to mid-range tours in the region, including Tabin.

Health and emergency An excellent pharmacy is the well-stocked **Guardian Chemist** (*Hotel Mido, Ground Floor, Jln Teratai;* ⟩ *089 880137*), which has many international brands (UK, US and Australian).

Miscellaneous A good air-freight and transport company with a Lahad Datu office is Kangaroo Worldwide Express (*Block A, Lot A4, Jln Kastam Lama;* e *www.kangaroo.com.my*).

EXCURSIONS FROM LAHAD DATU

DANUM VALLEY It is a bitter irony that one of the greatest 'protected areas' of Sabah, the Danum Valley Conservation Area (DVCA), exists alongside some of the most severe over-logging. The 438km² reserve is promoted as 'the largest remaining area of undisturbed virgin lowland rainforest in Malaysia', which has been set aside for research and education. However, as you drive into the 'untouched' area you will undoubtedly come across well-laden log trucks on the road, which can be upsetting. As Sabah Tourism declare candidly 'a vast timber concession area borders all around Danum Valley'. The road into the reserve passes through logged and regenerating forest areas – the DVCA is touched on every side by 3–100km of commercial forest, and beyond are oil palm plantations. Guides here express their heartbreak at what is happening, and what has already happened. Together with the Maliau Basin, Danum Valley is part of the huge 10,000km^2 timber concession of Yayasan Sabah (the Sabah Foundation). Since the 1980s, it has been a Class 1 Protected Forest Reserve and part of the foundation's long-term Forest Management Plan, to remain un-logged for the purpose of wildlife conservation, education and research.

Getting there and away
By car It's about 85km from Lahad Datu, a two-hour journey first along the Lahad–Tawau road, then (two-thirds of the journey) on unsealed forestry roads.

Where to stay

Borneo Rainforest Lodge (24 chalets) www.borneorainforestlodge.com. A temple of nature, simple but beautifully built eco-cabins elevated through the forest, with a daily symphony of birds. Fan-cooled, bathrooms & forest balconies. Restaurant, good buffet food, lovely main lodge. Also a tent camp for 2–6 people. High prices of their 2–3 night packages are prohibitive for many & heavily penalise singles. Run by Borneo Nature Tours (details in Maliau Basin Conservation Area, page 216) $$$–$$$$

Danum Valley Field Centre (DVFC) Block 3, Fajar Centre, Jln Segama, Lahad Datu; ☎ 089 881688/880441. Mostly for official researchers, but overseas students & scientists can visit with written approval from centre. 'Keen naturalists' can apply for a stay with written approval from the Danum Valley Management Committee (see www.ysnet.org for more info) VIP rooms, resthouse rooms, male & female hostels & camp-site.

What to see and do Lying on the upper reaches of the Sungai Segama (Sabah's second-longest river) and its tributaries, the area is one of undulating lowland tropical rainforest – hilly but not mountainous. Gunung Danum forms its apex at 1,090m. The 438km^2 conservation area is home to 120 mammal species including the rarest – Sumatran rhino, pygmy elephant, sun bear, clouded leopard and banteng (wild cattle), ten of eastern Sabah's primates and over 340 recorded species of bird. There are amphibians and reptiles galore too, from the rare Wallace's flying frog and Bornean horned frog to turtles, geckos, pythons, vipers, cobras and coral snakes. Activities include guided jungle treks, night wildlife excursions, canopy walks, birdwatching and guided visits to the Danum Valley Field Centre.

Trekking There are many marked trails in the Danum Valley including self-guided trails, but most longer (especially overnight) treks require a guide. One such trek is to the highest mountain in the DVCA – Gunung Danum, at 1,090m. Starting from the Danum Valley Field Centre (see below), four hours into this trek (thus a possible return day trek) are the Sungai Purut river's seven-tiered waterfalls.

Danum Valley Field Centre The DVFC paints itself as 'probably the leading rainforest research centre in the Old World tropics'. Scientists come from all over the world to conduct research here – including work on the impacts of logging. All visitors must get a **permit** from the Sabah Foundation sales office in Lahad Datu (*Block 3, MDLD 3286, Ground Floor, Fajar Centre, Lahad Datu*), unless you are on an arranged tour in which case that is likely to be taken care of. Self-drivers must get a vehicle pass from the office. Viewing-spot highlights include a suspension bridge over the Sungai Segama river and 40m-high canopy observation platform.

TABIN WILDLIFE RESERVE The reserve lies on the Dent Peninsula, northeast of Lahad Datu, wedged between the lower reaches of the Segama River and the Silabukan Forest Reserve. The endangered trio – Asian elephant, Sumatran rhinoceros and clouded leopard – make another one of their rare appearances in this 122,539ha reserve of primarily logged lowland rainforest reserve, which has been put aside to protect 75 mammals including orang-utan, proboscis monkeys and three wild cats, 220 birds and 45 reptiles. Contact the Wildlife Department Office in Lahad Datu (✆ *089 884416*) to check the current situation with permits.

Getting there and away
By car It's 50km on a sealed road at first but then a very bumpy gravel road from Lahad Datu town.

By bus A daily bus from Lahad Datu (destination Tomanggong) passes the entry to Tabin, a one-hour trip.

⌂ Where to stay and eat
⌂ **Tabin Wildlife Reserve** (26 rooms) ✆ 088 267266: e enquiry@tabinwildlife.com.my; www.tabinwildlife.com.my. River & hill lodges with AC & private balconies, linked by board walks to the Sunbird Café & other facilities, plus 'eco-tented platforms' with common showers, toilets, mosquito netting & mattresses. The **Sunbird Cafe** (🕑 07.00–19.00) is a timber restaurant open on the forest, with Western & local food. Packages usually include transfers, meals, lodgings. $$–$$$$

What to see and do Selected from the exploited areas of the Silabukan Forest Reserve, and protected as a Wildlife Reserve, a core of old-growth rainforest remains in Tabin though most of it is disturbed – selectively logged and surrounded by oil palm plantations. There is also a wetland area to the northeast side, around the Segama River. Neighbouring Kulamba Wildlife Reserve, an area of 20,682ha on the east coast, is quite a different ecosystem of freshwater swamp forest, mangrove and beach vegetation. Access to it is by boat and there are no visitor facilities here at all. The chances of seeing wildlife such as rhinos and elephants in Tabin Wildlife Reserve may be just as good as in the Danum Valley – with an estimated 300 elephants, 100 banteng and 20 rhino. These animals are attracted to Tabin's mud volcanos – mounds of mud and clay – for their salt fix, and there is an observation tower above one of the muddy mounds about 700m from the chalet. Tabin is a special place for birdwatching – with eight species of hornbills, hawk-eagles and pink-necked green pigeons, attracted by the abundance of fruit trees. The giant flying squirrel glides around at night – up to 70m between trees. Some animals are more likely to look for you – leeches are particularly abundant in the wet season.

Part Four

SARAWAK

9

Kuching

The magic of Kuching, like much of Sarawak, emanates from the water that runs through it – the glorious, 120km Sungai Sarawak divides it in two. Across the water, the chants of Muslim prayer from the *kampung Melayu* (Malay villages) meet with the hustle and bustle of the old Chinese trading bazaar of the south. Under the weight of soaring urbanisation, the river has been battling pollution, mostly from untreated sewage and accumulating rubbish. Things are improving however, and Kuching has been awarded a gold star from the World Health Organisation for its efforts to become cleaner and greener. It's actually a very liveable city, rich in urban parks, and surrounded by nature reserves and wetlands.

The name 'Kuching' is said to derive from the Malay word for cat, *kucing*. One version of history says it came from the abundance of *mata kucing* ('cat's eyes') – a lychee like fruit – growing on the riverbanks of the Sungai Sarawak. Though flagrantly promoted as 'Cat City' with cat statues and museums, others say the city was baptised by early Indian and Chinese traders as *Cochin* – 'port' in Indo-Malay. A backdrop to the city skyline is provided by the Gunung Santubong. The limestone massif of the indigo mountain rises up on the shores of the South China Sea 32km away.

Partly saved from World War II bombing, many early buildings were destroyed in fires and uprisings in the 19th century, and later by developers' bulldozers. With a generous sprinkling of colonial buildings and century-old Chinese remnants, Kuching serves up an evocative brew of the past with its watery character and multi-racial tones. The odd neo-classical building and Corinthian columns add a weird and wonderful touch to the potpourri of Chinese shop-houses, mosques and Buddhist temples. Curiously, the city has two mayors – one on either side of the river. The Majilis Bandaraya Kuching Selatan (Kuching South City Council) administers on the south side and the Dewan Bandaraya Kuching Utara (Kuching North City Hall) on the northern banks. Between the vibrant city centre, old villages and modern structures of its suburbs, the 580,000 residents represent a quarter of Sarawak's population.

HISTORY

Kuching's foundations were set in silt and on stilts, like so many of Borneo's river cities today. Before James Brooke sailed up the Sungai Sarawak in *The Royalist* (see *History*, page 4) in 1839, inklings of a water village (*kampung ayer*) existed in the same area as modern Kuching, with some 600 houses built from *Nipah* palm thatch on the banks of the river. Kuching was the epicentre of control for the century of white rule in Sarawak – a period once described as an era of 'benign despots'. After Brooke had been bestowed the title of Governor and Rajah of Sarawak in 1841, roots of a colonial settlement were embedded and the town grew up on the southern banks of the river. In 1868, Brooke's nephew Charles took the helm. More an administrator than an adventurer, under his rule a government was established and Kuching's streetscape took form with forts, courthouses and museums springing up. From 1917, the third White Rajah, James's grandson Charles Vyner Brooke, expanded infrastructure and development. In 1941 he steered Sarawak towards democracy, ceding state legislative and budget issues to the Sarawak General Council. However, the empowerment of the Council, comprised of native Chiefs and Chinese and Malay representatives, was to be short-lived. The democracy gains were crushed within a few months with the onset of World War II and Japanese invasion, during which Charles Vyner Brooke took refuge in Australia.

GETTING THERE AND AWAY

BY AIR

Kuching International Airport Modernised and attractive, Kuching airport is 11km from Bandaraya Kuching (Kuching City). There is a Sarawak Tourism Board information counter at the airport (⊕ *09.00–18.00 daily, closed 13.00–14.00*). A taxi to the city costs approximately 18MYR – buy a coupon at the taxi counter inside. The Sarawak Transport Company bus No 12A leaves every 45–50 minutes.

International flights Some five airlines link Kuching with international cities including Kuala Lumpur (a flight of two and a half hours), Brunei Darussalam (one hour) and Singapore (one hour and 15 minutes). Malaysia Airlines and AirAsia both operate many daily flights between Kuching and Kuala Lumpur. MAS and Silk Air fly to Singapore. MAS has twice-weekly direct flights between both Perth and Sydney and Kuching. Royal Brunei Airlines operate flights between Bandar Seri Begawan in Brunei and Kuching. A good website for seeing all ticketing and price options is www.farecompare.com.

Domestic flights Within Sarawak, MAS and AirAsia fly to Miri (one hour flight), Sibu (40 minutes) and Bintulu (30 minutes). AirAsia fly direct between Kuching and Kota Kinabalu in Sabah (one hour and 20 minutes) as well as to Sibu, Bintulu and Miri.

Rural air services (RAS) From Kuching via Miri, MASWings (*www.maswings. com.my*) operate flights to rural airstrips including Ba'Kelalan and Bario (Kelabit Highlands), Lawas, Limbang, Marudi, Mulu, Mukah, Long Akah and Long Lelang. Helicopter services are possible to other towns and more inaccessible areas in the Sarawak interior.

Airlines

✈ **MAS** Lot 215, KCLD Block 47, Jln Song Thian Cheok; ☏ 082 246622. Located in the KCLD commercial centre.

✈ **AirAsia** No 291, Sub Lot 4, Ground Floor, Wisma Ho Ho Lim (shopping centre), Jalan Abell; ☏ 082 251491

✈ **Sarawak Convention Bureau** Lot 31, Jln Masjid; ☏ 082 242516; e info@sarawakcb.com; www.sarawakcb.com

BY CAR

The smooth-sailing Pan-Borneo Highway connects Sarawak with Brunei and Sabah. It is 842km from Kuching to Miri in the north, via Sibu (462km) and Bintulu (644km). The road system within the state is being upgraded constantly as traffic volume increases. There are excellent English-language interactive digital road maps for Kuching, Sibu, Miri, Mukah and Bintulu at http://sidra.sarawaknet.gov.my with free login.

BY BUS

Biramas Bus Express (℡ 082 610111; e bus@biramas.com; www.biramas.com. Kuching booking office on Jln Khoo Hun Yeang, nr Electra House; ℡ 082 429418) This links Kuching with Sibu, Sarikei, Miri and Bintulu, as well as Bandar Seri Begawan in Brunei and Pontianak in Indonesia. Timetables and fares can be found on the website. Child fares are mostly 40–50% cheaper, except for international trips.

Borneo Highway Express (℡ 082 453190; www.vftransportation.com.my/schedule.html) Tickets for services run by the Vital Focus Transportation (VFT) company can be purchased at **Borneo Interland Travel** (1st Floor, 63 Jln Bazaar; ℡ 082 413595; www.bitravel.com.my).

PB Coaches Another long-distance bus company, part of VFT with business-class seats available. The company has offices all over Sarawak – the Kuching sales counter is inconveniently located at 3.5 Mile, Jalan Kuching-Serian. Buses leave from the long-distance bus station.

PB Express Also part of VFT, this company has a ticket counter at the Sanjana car-park complex in Jalan Masjid, downtown Kuching (℡ 082 244349). Note some buses north to Sibu, Bintulu and Miri involve a change of bus in Sarikei so make sure you are booked direct, if that is what you want. The long-distances bus hub, 'Regional Express Bus Terminal', sometimes referred to as '3rd Mile Bus Terminal' is 5km from the city on Jalan Penrissen.

BY BOAT A company called **Express Bahagia** ('express boat services') (℡ 082 410076) connects Kuching with other coastal cities and towns: Kuching-Sibu departs daily at 08.30. The five-hour journey costs 40MYR (45MYR first class) and stops at Sarikei and Tanjung Manis. Tickets are sold at the wharf in Pending. A taxi fare to the jetty is approximately 10MYR. From Sibu boats to Kuching leave daily at 11.30, stopping at Sarikei and Tanjung Manis. Tickets are sold at the passenger terminal at Sibu's Express Wharf (℡ 084 319228; 40MYR/45MYR first class).

GETTING AROUND

ON FOOT The city centre and waterfront areas are quite compact and easy enough to walk around. You will need to rely on other transport beyond that.

BY BOAT The traditional-roofed wooden boats, *tambang* (the local version of a *sampan*), are used for Kuching river crossings around the clock. A vital means of public transport around the waterfront area, they charge 30sen per person one-way, increasing to 1MYR after 22.00. The journey takes less than five minutes. You can also charter one from any of the small jetties where they pull in, for about 30MYR an hour. Ask them to take you anywhere you like, and to use either the motor or just to gently row the boat along the Sungai Sarawak.

BY BUS Buses are the main form of public transport in and around Kuching and offer plenty of character for money, as well as reasonable efficiency and safety. Nevertheless there is room for improvement, especially as city transport congestion worsens. This improvement is expected in the coming years with the formation of Kuching City Bus Services Sdn Bhd (KCBS), a possible new affiliation between the various Kuching-based public bus companies. For now though, there is no single bus terminal, which can make travelling by bus difficult. There is, however, plenty of choice. A kind of bus-hub area lies at the western end of the waterfront near the open-air market and Electra House, between Jalan Gambier and Jalan Mosque. Several bus companies operate in this area, each with their own station, serving distinct areas and marked with a bus symbol on the *Kuching Tourist Map* which is available from most hotels and the tourism office in Kuching. You must have the correct fare on you as drivers generally do not give change. For trips within the city, fares rarely exceed 2MYR.

Sarawak Transport Company (*Jln Leboh Jawa*) STC serve Kuching and southwest Sarawak. Bus No 3A goes to the long-distance bus terminal.

Chin Lian Long (*Jln Gambier*) The company operate services to the city and suburbs with major bus stops on Jalan Gambier, as well as Jalan Masjid and outside the post office. Bus No 1 goes to the express boat jetty in Pending (see above).

Petra Jaya Transport Buses go to Bako, Damai and Santubong. The yellow buses with black-and-red stripes depart from bus stop No 1, on Jalan Leboh Jawa near Electra House.

Matang Transport Company (*Jln Masjid*) These buses go to Matang and Kubah.

BY BIKE There are some good mountain-bike trails close to Kuching, but the city itself does not lend itself to cycling. Bike rental can be arranged through many hostels and a couple of bike shops.

BY TAXI Taxi drivers in Kuching, like much of Sarawak, do not use the meters their taxis are installed with, so before you get into a cab, it is best to negotiate and agree on a price.

TOURIST INFORMATION

Kuching Visitors' Information Centre Sarawak Tourism Complex, Old Court Hse, Jln Tun Abang Haji Openg; 082 410944; e vic-kuching@ sarawaktourism.com; 08.00–18.00 Mon-Fri, 09.00–15.00 Sat/Sun & public holidays. The best port of call for maps, hotel rates & bus routes.
The National Parks & Wildlife Office Sarawak Tourism Complex as above; 082 248088; http://ebooking.com.my. The place to obtain permits & book accommodation in the Bako, Gunung Gading & Kubah national parks & the Matang Wildlife Centre. Online booking service for parks state-wide available on the website. Park entry/conservation

fees vary from park to park but mostly 10MYR adult/5MYR children.
Sarawak Tourist Association (STA) Main Bazaar, Kuching waterfront near the Square Tower; 082 240620. Another very helpful outlet for recommending & organising tour guides in Kuching & for general visitor information. They prefer you to book weeks ahead for this service, directly or through a tour agent, but last-minute arrangements are not out of the question.
Tourism Malaysia Kuching office, 2nd Floor Bangunan Rugayah, Jln Song Thian Cheok; 082 246575; e mtpbkch@tourism.gov.my

TOUR OPERATORS

Borneo Adventure 55 Main Bazaar Kuching; 082 245175; e info@borneoadventure.com; www.borneoadventure.com
Borneo Transverse No 15, Ground Floor, Jln Green Hill; 082 257784; m 019 8868948 24hr; e bntv@po.jaring.my; www.borneotransverse.com.my. Knowledgeable local people, friendly & professional. At more mid-range prices this is a good company to call

even at shorter notice, if you want to do a trip from Kuching – whether you just require the transport or want the transfers & company of a guide.
Borneo Exploration Tours & Travel 76 Wayang St; 082 252137; e chris@borneoexplorer.com.my; www.borneoexplorer.com.my. Recommended budget & independent travel group, can also help cut the costs incurred (eg: penalties) for travelling alone.

The 'Golden Triangle' riverfront area around Jalan Tunku Abdul Rahman (which locals shorten to TAR) is five-star Forte – prime location, and prime prices (for Sarawak, but still much cheaper than in Europe or the US). In the streets behind here, around China Town, you can get some excellent deals on mid-grade business and leisure hotels. More budget hotels and bed and breakfasts can be found further into this area. The vicinity of Jalan Ban Hock, known as 'new town', is within a 1km walk of the waterfront attractions; a neighbourly hub of eating and nightlife with Reservoir Park still on your doorstep. There is surprisingly little enforcement of non-smoking in hotels for such a (small-scale) international and American-loved city.

LUXURY

⌂ **Hilton Kuching** (315 rooms) Jln Tun Abdul Rahman; ☎ 082 248200; e kuching@hilton.com or sales_kuching@hilton.com; www1.hilton.com. Overlooking the river in Golden Triangle area (ask for river-view room); spacious rooms & suites inc. non/s floors; pool with faux waterfall setting; fitness & business centres, several top-notch eateries & entertainment outlets. Most consistent high service & glowing reports of all the luxury hotels. Mid-range prices possible on dbl rooms with internet specials & hotel promotions. Also very good deals for Executive Floor with b/fast, Wi-Fi & access to executive lounge (US$120 dbl). $$$–$$$$$

⌂ **Merdeka Palace Hotel & Suites** (213 rooms) Jln Tun Abang Haji Openg; ☎ 082 258000; e info@merdekapalace.com; www.merdekapalace.com. Lots of character, though faded in places in both structure & service. Some standard rooms slightly dowdy & cramped – best to opt for a deluxe room. Good choice of apts for families & couples. Well located for museums & greenery but less so for waterfront attractions. Fitness-centre facilities are ageing a little (steam bath, sauna); Wi-Fi is chargeable. Non/s floor. $$$–$$$$$

UPMARKET

⌂ **Crowne Plaza Riverside Kuching** (241 rooms) Jln Tun Abdul Rahman; ☎ 082 247777; e cprk@po.jaring.my or reservation@cprk.com.my; www.ichotelsgroup.com. Very good reports, good value & views for money, spacious rooms, service with a smile, good restaurants, non/s floor. Rooms/facilities for disabled guests, sport & fitness facilities, Club Floor & Lounge & business centre. $$$–$$$$$

⌂ **Hotel Grand Continental** (192 rooms) Lot 42, Section 46, Jln Ban Hock; ☎ 082 230399; e kuching@ghihotels.com.my or sales_reservation@ghihotels.com.my; www.ghihotels.com.my. In new town business district. Nice rooftop swimming pool & spacious attractive rooms (inc non/s & facilities for disabled) make this very good value. Choice of going upmarket to the Executive Lounge on the 12th–14th 'Continental Comfort' floors, with complimentary daily paper & Wi-Fi. Excellent spa & gym. $$–$$$$

⌂ **Holiday Inn Kuching** (305 rooms) Jln Tun Abdul Rahman; ☎ 082 423111; e hikmy@myjaring.net; www.icihotelsgroup.com. Riverfront location, good gym, business centre & outdoor pool but many find it falls short on service, that it is in need of refurbishing & that, as with some other Borneo hotels, it is not in line with standards of its international namesake. Definitely not good value compared with other offerings. $$–$$$$

MID-RANGE

⌂ **Kingwood Inn** (90 rooms) Lot 618, Section 62, Jln Padungan (approx 3km from Kuching waterfront); ☎ 082 330888; e kingwd@tm.net.my. A spic & span 3-star hotel with standard Chinese-style furnishings, rooms & suites, business centre, outdoor swimming pool. A staple business hotel with good amenities & internet promotional rates. $$–$$$

⌂ **Telang Usan Hotel** (66 rooms) Jln Ban Hock; ☎ 082 415588; e ask@telangusan.com; www.telangusan.com. Small hotel run by Orang Ulu, simply decorated with a few ethnic artefacts in open places. Loved by its faithful for friendly management, cleanliness & unquestionably good value. It is however less highly rated by others for location (10 mins' walk from waterfront area), efficiency &

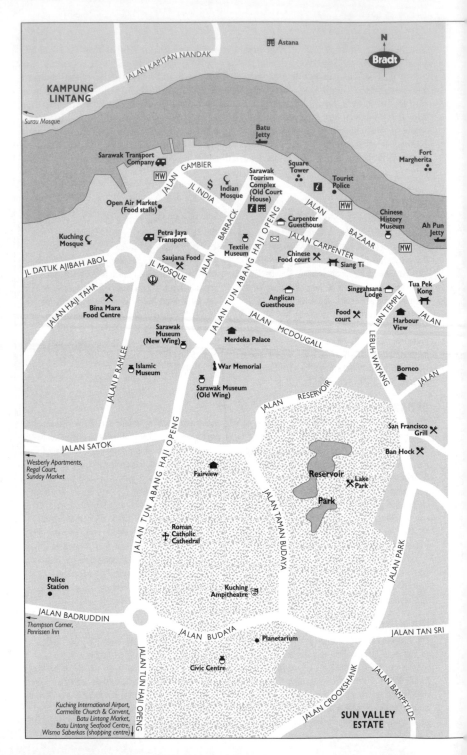

N

Bradt

KAMPUNG
LINTANG

Astana

Surau Mosque

JALAN KAPITAN NANDAK

Batu
Jetty

Fort
Margherita

Sarawak Transport
Company

GAMBIER

Square
Tower

Tourist
Police

JALAN

BAZAAR

MW

JL INDIA

Indian
Mosque

Sarawak
Tourism
Complex
(Old Court
House)

Chinese
History
Museum

Ah Pun
Jetty

Open Air Market
(Food stalls)

MW

Kuching
Mosque

Petra Jaya
Transport

BARRACK

Carpenter
Guesthouse

JALAN CARPENTER

MW

JL DATUK AJIBAH ABOL

Saujana Food

JL MOSQUE

Textile
Museum

Chinese
Food court

Siang Ti

Singgahsana
Lodge

Tua Pek
Kong

JALAN

JALAN HAJI TAHA

Bina Mara
Food Centre

JALAN

Anglican
Guesthouse

JALAN MCDOUGALL

Food
court

LBN TEMPLE

Harbour
View

Sarawak
Museum
(New Wing)

JALAN P RAMLEE

Islamic
Museum

Merdeka Palace

JALAN TUN ABANG HAJI OPENG

Borneo

LEBUH WAYANG

JALAN

War Memorial

Sarawak Museum
(Old Wing)

JALAN RESERVOIR

San Francisco
Grill

JALAN SATOK

Ban Hock

Wesberly Apartments,
Regal Court,
Sunday Market

Fairview

Reservoir

Lake
Park

JALAN TUN ABANG HAJI OPENG

Park

Roman
Catholic
Cathedral

JALAN TAMAN BUDAYA

Police
Station

Kuching
Ampitheatre

JALAN BADRUDDIN

Thompson Corner,
Penrissen Inn

JALAN BUDAYA

Planetarium

JALAN PARK

JALAN TAN SRI

Civic Centre

JALAN CROOKSHANK

JALAN BAMPFYLDE

SUN VALLEY
ESTATE

Kuching International Airport,
Carmelite Church & Convent,
Batu Lintang Market,
Batu Lintang Seafood Centre,
Wisma Saberkas (shopping centre)

JALAN TUN HAJI OPENG

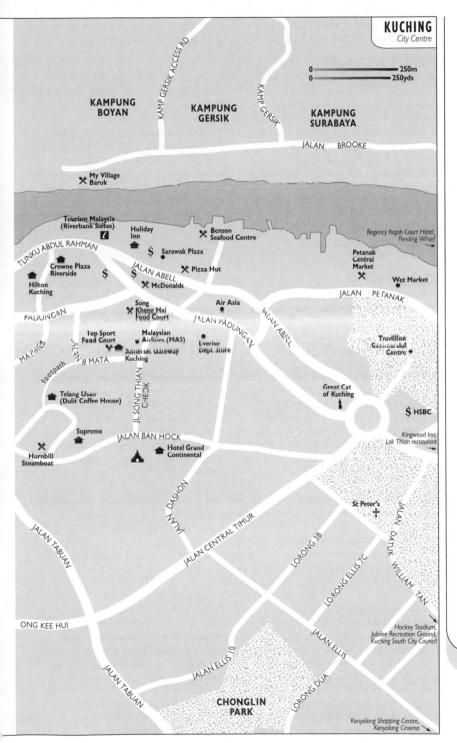

KUCHING
City Centre

0 ——————— 250m
0 ——————— 250yds

KAMPUNG BOYAN

KAMPUNG GERSIK

KAMPUNG SURABAYA

KAMP GERSIK ACCESS RD

KAMP GERSIK

JALAN BROOKE

My Village Baruk

Tourism Malaysia (Riverbank Suites)

Holiday Inn

Benson Seafood Centre

Regency Rajah Court Hotel, Pending Wharf

TUNKU ABDUL RAHMAN

Sarawak Plaza

Petanak Central Market

Crowne Plaza Riverside

JALAN ABELL

Pizza Hut

Wet Market

Hilton Kuching

McDonalds

JALAN PETANAK

PADUNGAN

Song Kheng Hai Food Court

Air Asia

MACHES

JALAN PADUNGAN

JALAN ABELL

Travillion Gateway Centre

Top Sport Food Court

Malaysian Airlines (MAS)

Somerset Gateway Kuching

Everise Dept Store

JALAN B MATA

footpath

Great Cat of Kuching

JL SONG THIAN CHECK

Telang Usan (Dulit Coffee House)

HSBC

Supreme

JALAN BAN HOCK

Kingwood Inn, Lok Thian restaurant

Hornbill Steamboat

Hotel Grand Continental

St Peter's

JALAN DASHON

JALAN CENTRAL TIMUR

LORONG 3B

JALAN DATUK WILLIAM TAN

JALAN TABUAN

LORONG ELLIS 7C

LORONG ELLIS 0

ONG KEE HUI

Hockey Stadium, Jubilee Recreation Ground, Kuching South City Council

JALAN ELLIS 0

JALAN ELLIS

JALAN TABUAN

LORONG DUA

CHONGLIN PARK

Kenyalang Shopping Centre, Kenyalang Cinema

upkeep. TV, AC, minibar in some rooms. Internet access, safe deposit box, good coffee-house food

(noodles, *laksa*), spicy Chinese, Dayak & Western cuisine between its various eateries. $$

SERVICED APARTMENTS

🏠 **Somerset Gateway** (70 apts) No 9, Jln Bukit Mata; ✆ 082 250958; e enquiry.kuching@ the-ascott.com; www.somersetgatewaykuching.com. Immaculately furnished & well located near shopping centres, airline offices & food courts. Corporate-style. Short-term & extended stays. Part of the international Ascott group, centrally located, spacious 1/2/3-bedroom apts with kitchens, rooftop swimming pool, gym, residents' lounge, meeting & business rooms, 24hr reception & security, babysitting service. $$$–$$$$

🏠 **Harbour View Hotel** (245 rooms) Lorong Temple; ✆ 082 274666; e sales@harbourview.com.my; www.harbourview.com.my. 3-star Chinese-run hotel

very popular with Malay people. Soft business feel, relaxed atmosphere & central location (opposite the Tua Pek Kong Temple), free Wi-Fi & b/fast inc with all rooms. $$, $$$$ (suites)

🏠 **Wesberly Apartments** (5 apts) Lot 2812, Block 195, Jln Rubber (West); ✆ 082 246197; f 082 243521; e enquiries@wesberly.com.my; www.wesberly.com.my. Big, bright & light 2–3-bedroom apts. In the vicinity of the Sunday Market, north of the city centre, modern-Asian furnished 110m² apts with botanically inspired names, above an art gallery (The Galleria) & next door to Wisma Sandhu shopping centre. Well equipped throughout, washing machines & parking lots. (300–400MYR per day) $$$

BUDGET There are many budget to mid-range hotels in the 'new town' area between Jalan Padungan, Jalan Tabuan and Jalan Ban Hock. Some are cell-like with no windows. Better ones have air conditioning, phone, satellite television, fridge and bathrooms. Upgrade by moving away from the waterfront.

🏠 **Borneo Hotel** (65 rooms) 30 Jln Tabuan; ✆ 082 244122. Budget-priced rooms & suites, no-frills facilities. AC, phone, sat TV, fridge & bathrooms. $$

🏠 **Rajah Court Hotel** (98 rooms) Lot 6115 Section 64 KTLD Jln Tun Razak, Pending; ✆ 082 484799; e rajcourt@tm.net.my. Located 6km out of town, 8km from airport. Suitable if you want to be near Pending wharf & industrial area. Standard & deluxe rooms plus serviced apts & a penthouse, swimming pool, & Jolly Bachelor bar/lounge. $$

🏠 **Regal Court** (42 rooms) Jln Tun Ahmad Zaidi Adruce; ✆ 082 412211; e regal_c@tm.net.my; www.borneohotels.net. Near Jln Satok & the Sunday Market, about 1.5km from the waterfront. A sweet place which sees itself as boutique; quite charmingly furnished for the price with business centre, standard to deluxe rooms & sauna. $$

🏠 **Supreme Hotel** (74 rooms) Jln Ban Hock; ✆ 082 255155. AC, phone, sat TV, fridge & bathrooms. $$

SHOESTRING Hostels and guesthouses are your best bet if you want to be among fellow travellers or want cheap family rooms. If not then some of the small, mostly Chinese, hotels can offer better value, with air-conditioned rooms and attached bathroom, television and phone.

Several hotels and inns in the area of Jalan Green Hill, Jalan Padungan and Jalan Nanas near the Sunday Market will provide you with a fan-cooled room, for between 40 and 100MYR for a family room.

🏠 **Anglican Guest House** Jln Tun Haji Openg; ✆ 082 414027. Adjoined to St Thomas Cathedral in the old town. Some residents from budget travellers to overseas researchers swear by it, others swear at it. From all reports it is not a shade of what it used to be (a more gracious guesthouse for visiting priests), having fallen into a bit of neglect. A bargain nevertheless with old charm, green surrounds & warm greeting. No AC. Fan-cooled rooms & apts with private bathroom & salons. $

🏠 **Berambih Lodge** 104 Ewe Hai/Carpenter St; ✆ 082 238589; e info@berambih.com; www.berambih.com. In old town hub, a Dayak longhouse-style hostel, beyond basic but clean, where rates include AC. Dorm/dbl/twin/family rooms with b/fast, bedlinen, coffee/tea/drinking water, Wi-Fi & individual lockers. $

🏠 **Carpenter Guesthouse** (9 rooms) 94 Ewe Hai/Carpenter St; ✆ 082 256729; e enquiry@carpenterguesthouse.com;

www.carpenterguesthouse.com. Small & sweet, clean & friendly, non/s, lounge/TV room, internet (4MYR/hr); b/fast, linen, water, coffee, tea inc; 24hr key card access, AC dorms/twin, family rooms. ⑤

🏠 **Fairview Guesthouse** 6 Jln Taman Budaya; ☎ 082 240017 e thefairview@gmail.com; www.thefairview.com.my. Family-run guesthouse in a leafy tropical garden setting, near Sarawak Museum & Reservoir Park, with possibility of longer stays & choice of dorm, dbl rooms & a 3-bed master suite good for families (100MYR with AC, dressing room & bathroom). Shared kitchen, lounge & computers. Personally organised itinerary of tours in region. ⑤

🏠 **Penrissen Inn** (42 rooms) Lot 382–386, Lorong 6, Section 10, KTLD, Jln Nanas; ☎ 082 238400. ⑤

🏠 **Singgahsana Lodge** Jln Temple 1; ☎ 082 429 277; f 082 429 267; e info@singgahsana.com; www.singgahsana.com. An ethnic-hip budget boutique somewhere between backpacker & guesthouse, in city centre with low-lit dorms & sgl/twin/dbl rooms decked out in tribal prints. The lodge oozes the friendliness & local knowledge of its team of youthful staff & owners. Access cards, AC, bedlinen (for dorms too, but not towels), continental b/fast inc, non/s premises. Recommended. ⑤

✗ WHERE TO EAT AND DRINK

FOOD COURTS AND STREET FOOD These are some of the best places for on-the-go eating – easy on the pocket, but with high-quality food and a bustling atmosphere. The indoor food courts are good if you want air conditioning. If the place serves predominantly Malay food, it will be halal. **Top Spot Food Court** (*6th Floor Taman Kerata, Jln Bukit Mata Kuching;* ☉ *17.00–22.00 daily*), is one of the best places in Kuching for cheap, quality seafood and is found on the top of a multi-level car park. The 36 food stalls here offer a bevy of grilled fish, satays, chilli crab, clay-pot dishes, oyster omelette and curries. **Song Kheng Hai Food Court** (*off Jln Padungan near cat statue*) has noodle-heavy good-food stalls operating day and night. Further east along the river on Jalan Petanak (continue on from Sarawak Plaza), there is a lively food centre in the **Petanak Central Market**. In the old town centre the daytime **Chinese Food Centre** (*opposite San Ti temple on Leboh Ewe Hai*) has several stalls with fish balls, fish soups and noodles. **Medan Pelita Food Court** (*corner of Wayang and Temple sts;* ☉ *11.00–17.00*) is a centrally located air-conditioned set-up. Near the mosque, *gerai makan* serve Malay, Chinese and seafood dishes, both day and night. The **Saujana Food Centre** (*5th Floor, Sajuana Car Park Complex, Jln Masjid*) has stalls serving mostly Malay curry and rice dishes. **Benteng Satok** (*Jln Satok, left-hand side heading out of town;* ☉ *18.00–24.00*) has many Malay food stalls along the roadside. **Thompson Corner** (*corner of Jln Nanas and Jln Palm*) is loved by locals for its stalls of clay-pot noodle (*mee*) dishes and *mee sua*.

FAST FOOD This can be found everywhere, but for sushi, burgers or KFC on the run, several fast-food chains are found at the **H20 Food Court** (*Jln Tun Abdul Rahman;* ☉ *10.00–21.30*) basement level of Sarawak Plaza shopping centre.

COFFEE SHOPS AND RESTAURANTS For cheap breakfasts or lunches, head to traditional coffee shops.

General

✗ **Min Joo** Corner of Bishopsgate and Ewe Hai/Carpenter St. They still make their own noodles here. Very popular at breakfast – you may struggle to get through the door! $–$$

✗ **Ming Heng Café** 6 Ewe Hai. Serves *laksa, kolo mee*, other noodle dishes & satay. Count on paying 4–10MYR for a Sarawak *laksa* – more according to the serving size & the size of the prawns. $–$$

✗ **Chong Choon** Jln Abell. An old-style b/fast institution where people read newspapers whilst eating bowls of steaming *kolo mee* & *laksa*. $–$$

✗ **Choon Hui** Jln Ban Hock, nr the Hindu temple. A b/fast hit for its *laksa* & *kolo* mee in unadorned surrounds. $–$$

✗ **Ting Noodle House** 117B, Lot 132, Jln Ban Hock. More a lunchtime noodle joint with a menu of dumplings & many rice & noodle dishes inc tangy Taiwanese beef noodles. $–$$

✗ **Toh Yuen** Jln Tun Abdul Rahman; ☎ 082 248200. In the Hilton Hotel. Sophisticated (& relatively pricey), with Chinese food & atmosphere. The dim sum luncheon buffet is highly recommended; the menu is a mix of Cantonese & Szechuan.

✗ **Café Harapan** Lorong Temple. The coffee shop at the Harbour View Hotel, is down to earth in décor but with good noodle dishes.

✗ **Orchid Garden Coffee House** Jln Tun Abdul Rahman; ☎ 082 423111. At the Holiday Inn hotel. Has a b/fast buffet sometimes with Sarawak *laksa*, & open 24hrs at w/ends, while its restaurant, **Meisan**, is another popular higher-end hotel Chinese eatery with (halal) Szechuan cuisine.

✗ **Dulit Coffee House** Telang Usan Hotel, Jln Ban Hock, ☎ 082 415588; ⏰ 06.30–23.00. Some say the Sarawak *laksa* here is the most consistent in quality & suitable for Western palates. There are other local & international dishes on the menu. The

hotel's **Golden Phoenix Restaurant** specialises in Szechuan food.

✗ **Hong Kong Noodle Restaurant**. Wisma Saberkas shopping centre, Jln Tun Abang Haji Openg (3km out of town). Chinese locals & Westerners 'in the know' flock here for a cheap, quality lunch. Sweet barbecued *char siew* is their speciality.

✗ **Lok Thian** 1st Floor Bangunan Bee San, Jln Padungan; ☎ 082 331310 (3km east out of town). A more urban Chinese cuisine & atmosphere, though not expensive. The same building houses the **Bangkok Thai Restaurant** & **Ten-Inchi**, an excellent Japanese restaurant.

✗ **Hornbill Corner** 85 Jln Ban Hock; ☎ 082 252670; ⏰ 17.00–12.30. Perhaps the best downtown steamboat restaurant for all-you-can-eat buffet value.

✗ **Coca Restaurant** Jln Tun Abdul Rahman (in the Crowne Plaza Riverside); ☎ 082 232133; ⏰ lunch 11.30–14.00, dinner 18.30–22.30. A good Thai steamboat on the 3rd floor.

Vegetarian While many of the above are vegetarian-friendly, the following are particularly good for vegetarian food. There are also daytime vegetarian food stalls in Jalan Green Hill, off Jalan Padungan.

✗ **Life Café** 108 Ewe Hai St; ☎ 082 411754; ⏰ 11.00–22.00 Mon–Sat. This paper-lantern-lit café serves many dedicated vegetarian dishes among its simple but spicy Szechuan fare, clay-pot dishes, spicy noodles, pork/vegetarian dumplings. Dozens of different speciality coffees & teas are served

charmingly – the teas with traditional tea service – & there are iced & fruit teas such as mango, lychee & passion fruit in tumbler glasses. $–$$

✗ **China Street Vegetarian** Leboh China, off Jln Bazaar; ⏰ 07.30-14.30. Café/restaurant serving vegetarian snacks & meals. $–$$

Malay The best Malay food is in the several *kampung* on the northern side of the river just near Fort Margherita – reached by a two-minute *tambang* ride from Ah Pun jetty to Encik Oman jetty. With bamboo ceilings, *nibong* (spiky palm) pillars and rattan blinds, the traditional Bidayuh atmosphere at **D'Baruk** (*Kampung Boyan;* ☎ *082 375470;* ⏰ *17.00–01.00*) goes beyond the décor. The Malay-Bidayuh menu has many noodle dishes, rice and soup. They don't serve alcohol.

Kampung Boyan is the first of four Malay villages along the riverbank, and there are several eating choices here at night including a few simple food kitchens and tables. These places are on temporary licences under a government programme to promote jobs for the *Melayu* (Malay) locals. Clean and simple, and you couldn't ask for a better dining location for such cheap food. Opposite, there are a few more established Malay *kedai* with under-cover areas. Given that all of these restaurants are strictly halal, this is not the place for partygoers or beer drinkers, but more for those who want to feel the romance of water-crossings and views in an inky black setting at night. Have an aperitif first before heading here.

About a kilometre from the waterfront, in the vicinity of the Sunday Market, cheap southern Indian food is served beautifully on a banana-leaf 'plate' at **Indian LL Banana Leaf** (*7G, Lorong Rubber 1, Jln Rubber;* ☎ *082 239404;* ⏰ *7.30–21.00*) with its very basic décor, indoor and outdoor tables. It's also good for takeaways and is vegetarian-friendly. The area around Jalan Rubber is Indian stamping ground – try the **Curry House** (*Lot 409, Section 10, Lorong 3A, Jln Rubber*) and the **Azreen Cafe** (*351 Lorong 12, off Jln Rubber*).

Seafood

✖ **See Good** Off Jln Ban Hock; ☎ 082 251397. Extensive & interesting menu & wine list, reasonably priced, sharp-flavoured food. Fans say it is worth every 'sen'. **$$$–$$$$**

✖ **Benson Seafood Centre** Jln Abell; ☎ 082 255262; ⏰ 18.00–22.00. On the eastern side of the riverfront, past the major hotel strip. Highly recommended. Very popular so best to book, especially on w/ends. **$$–$$$**

✖ **Rock Road Seafood** 2nd Mile, Jln Rock; ☎ 082 241575. A bit further along from Batu Lintang Seafood Centre (below). You can select your catch here – fish or crustaceans – from tanks. **$$–$$$**

✖ **Batu Lintang Seafood Centre** Off Jl Batu Lintang (3km out of town along Jln Tun Abang Haji Openg & into Jln Rock). Excellent cheap outdoor seafood, the *kedai* & stalls are open evenings only. **$–$$**

International and fusion

✖ **Magenta Restaurant** 32, Lot 141, Jln Nanas; ☎ 082 237878; ⏰ 18.00–23.00 (last orders) Tue–Sun. Antique Malay home just out of town, the restaurant oozes cool Zen fusion in décor & food, but does a better job at the former with its mix of contemporary art, artefacts & mood lighting. Good for those wanting a funky mix of traditional & modern. On the menu are duck, crème brûlée, mussels & pastas. **$$$$**

✖ **Khatulistiwa Restaurant** Jln Tunku Abdul Rahman. Perched over the river, this 24hr restaurant has a certain people-watching attraction to it. The architecture is traditional Bidayuh *baruk* warrior

style with a *belian* (ironwood) roof. The Bidayuh name means Equator. The food is a mix of Malay & Western. **$$$**

✖ **Beccari's Ristorante** Merdeka Palace Hotel, Jln Tun Abang Hj; ☎ 082 258000; ⏰ 12.00–23.00. Good Italian trattoria atmosphere, dark & woody, with lots of choices, inc wood-fired pizza **$$$**

✖ **Waterfront Café** The Hilton's turn on a coffee house is a good lunch place with daily themed buffets & both Western & local food, lots of fresh salads, good breads. Loved for its family-friendly all-day Sunday buffet & high teas during the week. **$$$**

A good steak Being vegetarian I can only point you in the direction of the recommended **San Francisco Grill** in Jalan Ban Hock and, more upmarket, **The Steakhouse** in the Hilton Hotel (⏰ *dinner only*). **The Victoria Arms** (**$$$–$$$$**) in the Merdeka Palace Hotel has lots of meat and other pub grub.

Cafés and cakes

✖ **Caffe Cino** Hilton Hotel. ⏰ late. The best Western breads (sourdoughs, baguettes, wholemeal) in Kuching. **$$$**

✖ **Seattle Coffee Co** Merdeka Palace Hotel, Jln Tun Abang Haji Openg; ⏰ 12.00–23.00. It's a rather chill-box (excessive AC) environment, but spic & span, & offers a late-night coffee kick. **$$–$$$**

✖ **Bing! Coffee Company** 84 Jln Padungan. ⏰ late. The only café in town which serves seriously European coffee & Illy is the bean. Young, laptop-loving crowd. Wi-Fi.

✖ **Black Bean Coffee & Tea Company** 87 Ewe Hai St; ☎ 082 420290. ⏰ Daytime only. An exquisite little

boutique coffee roaster, ancient-Chinese infused with wooden pigeon holes. Inside this shoebox of a shop, you can sample or purchase freshly roasted pure Borneo coffee (Sarawak Liberica, Ararbica & Robusta) & teas including Chinese Green & Taiwan Oolong, among the vintage & contemporary accessories. The minimalist environment has just 1 table & a bow-sized counter.

✖ **Coffee Bean & Tea Leaf** Sarawak Plaza street level, Jln Tun Abdul Rahman. ⏰ late. Only beans are sold here, not ground coffee. More than half of all the packets on display were out of date when I visited.

ENTERTAINMENT AND NIGHTLIFE

Kuching is not exactly a pulse-point of nightlife, but there is a burgeoning scene of late-night café-bars and clubbing between the waterfront hotel strip along Jalan

Tunku Abdul Rahman and around Jalan Padungan and Jalan Bukit Mata. Increasing urbanity seems to be accompanied by a decline of the once-prevalent karaoke culture and a greater crossover between day/night venues. The following pointers are from Gustino Basuan, at the Sarawak Tourism Board. 'A new place for clubbing and drinks is the **Travilion Mall** which consists of several bars and lounges, still considered a new place of entertainment in Kuching. Another evening hotspot is around Padungan Road – **Ipanema**, **SoHo** and **Grappa** (see below) are places to unwind and have a few drinks. They are Kuching's most fashionable entertainment outlets, playing dance-oriented music and catering to a slightly younger, mixed crowd. Other than bars, a number of cafés and restaurants transformed from old shop-house buildings are also becoming a place to hang out for nightlife. With its classy décor, **Bing! Coffee**, also on Padungan Road, is one of them. Most places like this offer free Wi-Fi – people use their laptops whilst enjoying their drinks. **Bar Zing** (*Travilion Mall, Jln Petanak*) is very popular with the younger crowd seeking urban cool; Western-style, reasonable drink prices; and pop, house and lounge music. **Ipanema** (*Jln Padungan*) is a new wine bar for style-setters, which also serves Mediterranean food à la carte. **SoHo** (*64 Jln Padungan*) has a very à la mode pub atmosphere, with Latin and jazz music, à la carte menu in the restaurant area and snacks in the bar. **Grappa** (*Jln Padungan*) plays house, R&B and '80s music and hosts a very young crowd.

Some hotel lounge-bars for more soothing cocktails and jazz or light live entertainment include **Senso** at the Kuching Hilton, an ambient-lit lounge-bar with resident band and good cocktail list. The **Victoria Arms** at Merdeka Palace is more the boisterous pub, with imported beers and live bands (⊕ *22.00 onwards Mon–Sat*) and ladies-only sessions on Fridays (⊕ *19.00–21.00*). The **YN Cellar**, also at the Merdeka, is a bit of an old boys' establishment, with a long wine list, but you must like cigar smoke. **The Club** (⊕ *17.00–01.00*) lounge-bar at the Crowne Plaza Riverside is a quieter corner for drinks, and it also has a poolside terrace bar.

FESTIVALS

GAWAI DAYAK This important Iban festival venerates rice, and is held every June at the end of harvest and has developed into a state-wide celebration among the Dayak community with many dance and cultural performances.

THE INTER-CULTURAL MOON CAKE FESTIVAL (30 Sep–6 Oct) This is more of a friendship festival between the Malay and Chinese cultures of Kuching.

GERAI RAMADAN If you are in Kuching during mid-September–October don't miss the atmosphere at one of the Ramadan bazaars such as Gerai Ramadan, held for the breaking of the month-long dawn-to-dusk fast. Around 400 stalls are held around the city serving curries, barbecued meats and satays. The most easily accessible bazaar unfurls on Jalan Satok, with another across the river in Jalan Semarak, Petra Jaya. Stalls are open 13.00–19.00.

SHOPPING

MARKETS *Pasar Satok*, the Sunday Market (which strangely enough starts on Saturday) is held along Jalan Santok, north of the city centre (*stalls* ⊕ *13.00–01.00/2.00 Sat, 06.00–12.00 Sun*). Take bus No 4a/4b from outside the post office, catch a taxi, or walk – it takes around 20 minutes. Some 1,500 traders gather here to sell food and fruit, Dayak handicrafts, forest produce such as wild honey, clothing, pets and plants. Saturday evening is a good time to go if you want to eat, otherwise Sunday morning to see it in its full daylight activity. Be on the alert for pickpockets.

HANDICRAFTS Among the copious souvenirs and carbon-copy handicrafts found along Jalan Bazaar, there are some nice and inexpensive basketry, carved objects and textiles, as well as more expensive, but authentic, *objets d'art*. The area is a treasure chest to be explored, with hidden gems to be discovered upstairs and in back rooms. Some places cater more to collectors and foreign dealers, pushing prices higher, though not necessarily out of reach. **Nelsons Gallery** (*84 Jln Bazaar*) is a floor-to-ceiling clutter of charm – tribal art, antiques, jewellery – run by members of a prominent family of Kuching art dealers, as is **Art of Dayaks** (*68 Jln Bazaar*). As well as handicraft demonstrations, the **Sarawak Handicraft Centre & Craft Council** (*Court House Complex;* ✆ *082 425652; www.sarawakhandicraft.com;* ⊕ *08.30–12.30 & 14.00–17.00 Mon-Fri, 08.30–12.00 w/ends & public holidays*) offers a 'mini-bazaar' of Sarawak handicrafts, with different ethnic groups represented each month, and a resource centre with library and handicraft videos. More handicrafts and textiles are on sale at the **Sarakraf Pavilion** (*78 Jln Tabuan, nr Reservoir Park;* ⊕ *09.00–17.00 daily*); as well as crafts for sale there are demonstrations, and workshops in handicraft and dance. **Perbadanan Kemajuan Kraftangan Malaysia** (*Lot 3057 Blok 18, Daerah Salak, Jln Stadium, Petra Jaya;* ✆ *082 444205*) sells indigenous crafts gathered and commissioned at the source.

BOOKS A good range of English-language books and maps are sold at **Bell Books** (*Sarawak Plaza*).

GENERAL Of the many shopping centres, **Riverside shopping centre** has a department store but also lots of electronic stores etc, plus a supermarket. **Sarawak Plaza** also has a supermarket at basement level.

OTHER PRACTICALITIES

BANKS AND MONEY CHANGERS Banks are generally open 09.30–15.00 Monday–Friday. Money changers are open much longer, including weekends.

$ **Bank Bumiputra-Commerce & Standard Chartered Banks** are located inside the Wisma Bukit Mata shopping centre on Jln Tun Abdul Rahman.
$ **HSBC Bank** Jln Padungan
$ **Majid & Sons** 45 Jln India; ⊕ 09.00–19.30 Mon–Sat, 09.00–15.00 Sun. Reputable money changers.

$ **Everrise Money Changer** Everrise department store, Jln Padungan; 10.00–21.00 Mon–Fri, 10.00–18.00 Sat/Sun.
$ **Mohamad Yahia & Sons** Lower Ground Floor, Sarawak Plaza; ⊕ 10.00–21.00, closed Fri afternoons. Reputable money changers.

COMMUNICATIONS AND MEDIA
✉ **Post office** Jalan Tunku Haji Openg; ⊕ 08.00–18.00 Mon–Sat, 10.00–13.00 Sun

Internet There are many cyber cafés in Kuching, charging about 3–4MYR, decreasing in price by the hour. Some offer free coffee and tea.

🄴 **Cyber City** Opposite Hilton, Taman Sri Sarawak; ⊕ 09.00–23.00 daily. 4MYR per hr for 1st hr, 3MYR thereafter, with free tea & coffee; also printing & scanning.

🄴 **Deli Café** Jln Bazaar. Wi-Fi.
🄴 **Lunch & Such** Jln Bazaar. Wi-Fi.

Tourist press The annual publication *Kuching Guide* is very handy and the attractive quarterly *Kuching Talk* has nice cultural background and human interest stories.

HEALTH AND EMERGENCY

Central Police Station Opposite Padang Merdeka (sports field); ☏ 082 241222; emergency calls 999.

Tourist Police Unit Kuching waterfront; ☏ 082 250522; ◷ 08.00–12.00 daily
Fire ☏ 994

Hospitals

✚ **Sarawak General Hospital** Jln Ong Kee Hui, about 2.5km from city centre; ☏ 082 276666. Public Accident & Emergency dept. Foreign visitors charged 50MYR for consultation, payable by cash or credit card.
✚ **Timberland Medical Centre** Jln Rock; ☏ 082 234466. Private hospital with 24hr emergency facilities.

✚ **Normah Medical Specialist Centre** Jln Tun Abdul Rahman, Petra Jaya; ☏ 082 440055; e inquiry@normah.com; www.normah.com.my. Private hospital in northern Kuching.

Doctors

✚ **The Clinic** Jln Bazaar, opposite Chinese History Museum. Highly reputable & purportedly very experienced in dealing with tourists' complaints.

Pharmacies

✚ **Apex Pharmacy** 1st Floor, Sarawak Plaza; ◷ 10.00–21.00 daily

✚ **UMH Pharmacy** Jln Song Thian Cheok (opposite Malaysia Airlines office); ◷ 09.00–18.00 Mon–Sat. Helpful staff.

MISCELLANEOUS

Sarawak State Library ☏ 082 442000; ◷ 14.00–21.00 Mon, 10.00–21.00 Tue–Sat. Petra Jaya bus No 6.

Spotfree Dry Cleaning 105 Jalan Padungan

WHAT TO SEE AND DO

While the greater city spreads out over 50km², the centre accounts for less than 4% of that (2km²). Being compact, it is easily seen on foot. Kuching feels like a very safe city but there are warnings about pickpockets on the waterfront and in the market area. There is a police booth along here in case of any problems.

KUCHING CENTRAL

The Waterfront Life ebbs and flows along the banks of the Sungai Sarawak. On one side there are the old Chinese coffee shops, with antique stores in the old town along **Jalan Bazaar** ('Main Bazaar' in English, and the oldest street in Kuching). On the other riverbank is the stroller's esplanade, known as The Waterfront. Official lines say it grew from the pyres of a drab warehouse area in the early 1990s under a programme of 'urban renewal'; critics say some old gems were cleared in the process. From the marketplaces in the west on Jalan Gambier through to the '**Golden Triangle**' on Jalan Tunku Abdul Rahman, the riverside esplanade is one of the most atmospheric places to stroll, as dozens of *tambang* slip into the night shadows of the 200m-wide river.

Little India Here, in the pedestrianised area around Jalan India (adjacent to the Open Air Market) and along Jalan Gambier, you can buy spices and textiles while absorbing the atmosphere; ideal for people-watching. Nearby is the 1850s **Masjid India**, the city's oldest Indian mosque.

China Town Some places here have historic monumental walls, others have giant modern cat statues. The monument of *Kitty Kitschery*, the **Great Cat of Kuching**, sits at the end of the street that forms the heart of China Town, *Jalan Padungan*. Most of the buildings here date to the rule of the Third Rajah, Charles Vyner Brooke, around 1910–30; a few even date back to the 1850s. Running parallel to the riverbank it's a hub of hip in the evenings, and a good street for eating.

Malay kampungs Crossing the river to these four villages (*kampungs*) is like a trip out of the city, without actually leaving. Reached from Batu jetty or Ah Pun jetty, land at Encik Omar jetty in Kampung Boyan.

Petra Jaya This northern side of the river is developing into a visionary hub of high tech and glistening new government buildings, state libraries and sports centres.

LANDMARKS

Mosques At the western end of the waterfront, **Kuching Mosque** (*Masjid*) sits like a piece of perfect Arabia on the Kuching skyline; its golden domes and minarets, and milky walled, aqua-pillared façade are most impressive when viewed from the river. The sound of evening prayer flowing from it through the marketplace and over the river adds to the spiritual high of Kuching's watery sunsets. From 1968 it was the state mosque, until a new mega-mosque with an Italian marble interior was built in Petra Jaya on the northern bank of the river.

The lime green façade announcing the Masjid Bandar Kuching – the **Indian Mosque** – looks like just another shop-house in the rather baubled Jalan Gambier – deceptive first impressions, as it is actually the oldest mosque in the whole of Sarawak. Built in 1837 by Indian Muslims who had migrated from southern India, for a long time it was called *Masjid India*. The original *nipah* palm roofs were gradually replaced by *belian* (ironwood), the floors were cemented and the mosque engulfed by new buildings so that you have to pass through a small laneway, Lorong Sempit, to reach the entrance. The sound of a *bedok* (drum) rings out at prayer times and hundreds of faithful descend upon the mosque. Tired travellers are welcome, in keeping with the mosque's tradition.

Temples At the other end of the Main Bazaar and the spiritual spectrum, the gaudy dragon-embossed pastiche of the **Tua Pek Kong Temple** (*corner of Jln Temple and Jln Padungan*) is, at heart, the city's oldest Chinese temple, dating back to 1843 but with several renovated layers, including the multi-coloured wooden and carved stone façade. The Sarawak Cultural Heritage Ordinance which protects it came too late for some other buildings. Many locals believe this temple protected the town from Japanese bombing and saved the whole row of old buildings along Jalan Bazaar from obliteration. The intersection of Jalan Bazaar and Jalan Tabuan opposite the temple has thus been christened 'Corner of Good Hope'. Among the shop-houses of Ewe Hai, the small **San Ti Temple** fades into the shadow of the city's most famous Chinese worship house, yet is a picturesque mesh of mythical figurines, ruby-coloured lanterns and baubles. It also dates back to the 1860s and is the soul place of the Teochew Chinese population. As such it is frequently the nerve centre of celebrations and street festivals.

Colonial relics Among the older buildings in the city – all along Main Bazaar – are the English-castle-like **Square Tower** which was built in 1879 as the town's jail, a

1912 **Chinese Chamber of Commerce** (now the **Chinese History Museum**) and the colonial **Court House Complex** – a stunning mix of building styles, New Orleans pavilions, white colonnades and *belian* roof tiles, it was built as the seat of Sarawak's government in 1871 and continued that way for just over a century. The colonial Baroque **Clock Tower** was added in 1883, and a 6m-high granite obelisk – the **Charles Brooke Memorial** – erected in front of the courthouse in 1924. The four decorative bronze plaques on the memorial signify the Malay, Iban, Chinese and European cultures of Sarawak. Since 2003 the restored building has housed the Sarawak Tourism Complex, Visitor Information Centre and National Park administration.

Two eminent buildings protrude from the dense slopes of greenery on the northern banks of the river. The **Astana** (a slight variation on *istana*, or palace, in Malay), was built in 1870 by Charles Brooke as a bridal gift to his wife Ranee Margaret. It was the seat of power for the White Rajahs and is now the official residence of the Governor of Sarawak and not open for visiting. The symmetrical cream-coloured citadel, **Fort Margherita,** was built in 1879 to ward off pirates. Now on state-owned grounds of the police barracks, it houses the **Police Museum,** although this is frequently closed. Check with the Visitors' Centre before venturing that way, or just enjoy the view from the water. At the time of writing Fort Margherita was completely closed due to a neighbouring construction on the riverbanks. The rather stunning spherical structure being built will be the new home of the state legislature, due for completion in 2008.

VIEWPOINTS The best 360° bird's-eye view of the whole of Kuching and outlying areas is from the lookout tower on top of the Civic Centre. From its rooftop you can see Mount Serapi and Mount Santubong, and on a clear day even the peaks rising up on the Kalimantan border.

SPORTS AND GREEN SPACES The green lung of Kuching is **Reservoir Park**, good for jogging. The **Botanical Gardens** are in the grounds of the Sarawak Museum. With national parks on its back doorstep you can go hiking for a morning or afternoon (see *Chapter 10, Southern Sarawak,* for more on surrounding national parks). Most four/five-star hotels have gyms and tennis courts. Crowne Plaza Riverside has a squash court. The public swimming pool and another recreational ground is off Jalan Padungan by the Kuching South City Council.

MUSEUMS AND GALLERIES Most Sarawak museums have free admission though some have a small camera (photo and video) fee. Most that 'open daily' are closed on the first day of major festivals and public holidays. The first five museums here come under the umbrella of the State Museums (❧ *082 244232; www.museum.sarawak.gov.my;* ⊕ *09.00–17.30 daily; free*).

Sarawak Museum (*Old Building, Jln Tun Abang Haji Openg*) Built in the style of a Normandy townhouse, the museum was opened by Charles Brooke in 1891 and is the most interesting for its ethnographic collections, artefacts and historical documents and displays of indigenous arts and crafts. The foundations of the collection were put in place by Tom Harrisson, its curator from 1947 up until Sarawak's independence in 1963. Harrisson, distinguished naturalist, archaeologist and anthropologist, is also credited with 'discovering' the 39,000-year-old skull in the Niah caves. On the other side of the overpass along the same avenue is the new wing of the museum in a former state parliament building, named after the second prime minister of Malaysia, *Dewan Tun Abdul Razak.* This houses special exhibitions and has a museum shop on the ground floor.

Natural History Museum and Sarawak Arts Museum (*opposite Sarawak Museum*) These are two recent additions. The first has vast collections of flora and fauna (some gathered by Alfred Russel Wallace in the 19th century), mounted specimens of Sarawak reptiles, birds and mammals including the near-extinct *banteng (Bos javanicus)*, or Asian wild cattle. The second houses historical paintings and photographs.

Sarawak Islamic Museum (*Jln P Ramlee*) Housed in the restored 1930s building *Maderasah Melayu* – Malay Islamic School – the Islamic Museum has seven galleries depicting the history and culture of Malay people in Sarawak and the entire Malay-Indonesia Archipelago, from weaponry and religion to literature, architecture and education.

Textile Museum (*Jln Tun Abang Haji Openg;* ✆ *082 246194*) This offers a fascinating look into the textile history of indigenous Borneans from bark cloth to Iban *pua kumbu* weaving, raw materials, textile motifs and accessories.

Pua Kumbu Museum (*4th Floor, Tun Jugah Tower;* ✆ *082 239672;* ⊕ *09.00–16.30 Mon–Fri, closed Sat, Sun and public holidays, free*) Another must for textile buffs, this museum goes a few steps further in the hands-on experience of Iban *pua kumbu* textiles – you can watch the weavers in action and take lessons, plus see antique and modern *pua kumbu*, Iban silverware and jewellery.

Cat Museum (*Lobby Floor, Kuching North City Hall;* ✆ *082 446688; www.dbku.gov.my/catmuseum;* ⊕ *09.00–17.00 daily*) Cat kitsch or kitty consecration, depending on your taste. The dedicated museum of meows plays up on the rumour that Kuching's name comes from the Chinese word for cat. It houses 2,000 cat-fetish exhibits including a mummified cat said to have been discovered in Egypt sometime between 3000BC and 3500BC. The museum is on the hilltop Bukit Siol, a 15MYR taxi ride from the city centre, or take Petra Jaya bus No 2C and walk 15 minutes up the hill to the museum from the bus stop.

Chinese History Museum (*Kuching Waterfront, nr Tua Pek Kong Temple;* ✆ *082 244232; www.museum.sarawak.gov.my;* ⊕ *09.00–17.30 daily; free*) In the old Chinese courthouse building, it shows the historical power of the Chinese as a trading people, from early trade routes and migration to modern times.

Timber Museum (*Wisma Sumber Alam, Petra Jaya;* ⊕ *08.00–13.00/14.00–17.00 Mon–Thu, 08.00–11.40/14.00–17.00 Fri; free*) A forest resources and timber industry showcase.

Timber Product and Bamboo Museum (✆ *082 368575; www.sarawakforestry.com;* ⊕ *on request 09.00–16.30 Mon–Fri; free*) Another forestry promotional point, displaying some 82 species of wood found in Sarawak and a collection of bamboo products. It's located in the Sama Jaya Nature Reserve in Stutong, 15 minutes from the city, along with the **Forest Biology Museum**.

Society Atelier Sarawak (✆ *082 243222*) Promotes arts and crafts and art happenings, and has its own gallery, Atelier Gallery.

Artrageously Ramsay Ong (*www.artrageouslyasia.com*) Art gallery open for public viewing.

The Galleria (*Wesberly Hse*) Another gallery open for public viewing.

EXCURSIONS FROM KUCHING

Easy day or half-day trips include Santubong Peninsula, the Sarawak Cultural Village and Damai Beach; Bako, Kubah and Gunung Gading National Parks; and Semenggoh Wildlife Centre. All are detailed in the following chapter, *Southern Sarawak*.

10

Southern Sarawak

From the Santubong Peninsula and Damai beach area on Kuching's doorstep, to the Borneo Highlands in the hinterland, and west towards Tanjung (Cape) Datu where Sarawak meets Indonesian territory, a lot of southern Sarawak is part of the huge Kuching Division. The district is one of 11 in Sarawak and encompasses six national parks. Stretching along the Indonesian border to the east, the Samarahan Division gives way to Sri Aman, and some of the deepest, most moving river journeys into Iban territory.

NORTH OF KUCHING

Heading north to the Semanjung Santubong (Santubong Peninsula), over the wide Sungai Santubong river, **Gunung Santubong** (810m) rises up through a swirl of clouds in the background. The peninsula is rimmed by beaches and bays: the resort area is **Pantai Damai** (Damai Beach) around which the majority of the peninsula's lodgings are located. As a popular beach getaway for Kuchingites it is still very *damai* – 'peaceful' – and one of Sarawak's special places. The big tourist beacon to the area is the Sarawak Cultural Village, but the jungle-thick landscape is a place to spend some time hiking, visiting the Malay fishing villages and nearby wetlands and mangrove environments. Some love it so much they do it in reverse – base themselves here and visit Kuching for the day.

GETTING THERE AND AWAY
By car The village of Kampong Santubong is 32km north of Kuching; Pantai Damai (Damai Beach) is slightly further at 35km. The roads are quite bumpy over the mangroves.

By taxi A one-way fare from Kuching will cost around 35MYR, from the airport 50MYR.

By bus Take Petra Jaya Transport bus No 2D to Kampung Buntal, the first fishing village on the eastern side of the peninsula where there are beaches and seafood restaurants. The bus departs from Jalan Khoo Hun Yeang, not far from the Open Air Market, every hour between 07.00 and 18.00, returning every hour from 08.00 to 18.00. A Kuching–Damai shuttle-bus service operates from outside the Holiday Inn and Crown Plaza in Kuching, with stops at the Damai Beach Holiday Inn Resort and Sarawak Cultural Village (SCV). The journey takes an hour to an hour and a half, and a one-way fare is 10MYR (for adults) or 5MYR (for children under 12). The first bus from Kuching is 07.30, the last bus back from Damai 21.00.

WHERE TO STAY There has been a shake-up in the established luxury lodgings in Damai. Damai Puri Resort morphed from a Holiday Inn in late 2007,

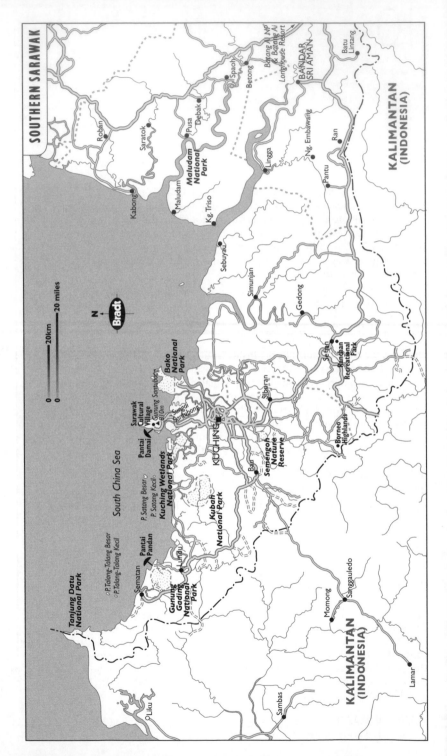

SOUTHERN SARAWAK

South China Sea

KALIMANTAN
(INDONESIA)

Tanjung Datu
National Park

P. Talang-Talang Besar
P. Talang-Talang Kecil

Sematan
Lundu
Gunung Gading
National Park

Pantai
Pandan

P. Satang Besar
P. Satang Kecil
Kuching Wetlands
National Park

Pantai
Damai

Sarawak
Cultural
Village

Gunung Santubong
810m

Sungai
Santubong

Bako National Park

Kubah
National Park

Bau

KUCHING

Siniawan

Semengoh
Nature
Reserve

Borneo
Highlands

Kabong

Maludam

Maludam National
Park

Kg. Triso

Sebuyau

Simunjan

Gedong

Roban

Saratok

Pusa
Debak

Spaoh
Betong

Lingga

Ng. Embawang

Pantu

Ran

Serian
Bandhan
Recreational
Park

Batang Ai NP
& Batang Ai
Longhouse Resort

BANDAR
SRI AMAN

Batu
Lintang

KALIMANTAN
(INDONESIA)

O Liku

Sambas

Momong

Sanggauledo

Lamar

N

Bradt

0   20km
0   20 miles

while another leading hotel is rumoured to be set to be taken over by Marriott.

⌂ **Damai Beach Resort** (224 rooms) Teluk Bandung Santubong; ☏ 082 846999; e general@ damaibeachresort.com; www.damaibeachresort.com. In a leafy beach location, this old-timer got an upmarket lift recently, with a new spa & 5-star wing of secluded hilltop rooms & suites, built in longhouse, Malay & 'Baruk' roundhouse style, private pool, water views & jacuzzi. Spacious standard rooms, good dining & entertainment — cocktail bars, pubs & cafés. **Treez Café** has good Malaysian cuisine, mid-range prices, though many find the service is slow & not 4–5 star. $$$–$$$$$

⌂ **Damai Puri Resort & Spa** (formerly Damai Lagoon Resort) (200 rooms) Teluk Penyuk; ☏ 082 846900; e info@damaipuriresort.com; www.damaipuriresort.com. With the most luxurious & beautifully located luxury lodgings on the peninsula, the resort lies on a cape with its own secluded beach on the bay of Teluk Penyuk. A US$10 million facelift in 2007 revamped all rooms & suites, added a spa village, speciality tea house & club floor. Tennis courts, fitness centre, jungle & mountain trekking, Bako Park excursions. Good eating options (Malaysian & international), all rooms have AC, sat TV, kettle, safe, hairdryer, minibar. $$$–$$$$$

⌂ **Santubong Kuching Resort** (378 rooms) Jln Pantai Damai; ☏ 082 846888; e skresort@ po.jaring.my. The biggest hotel, with big banquet & conference facilities & the Damai Golf Course on its back doorstep. Well removed from the main road, café & restaurant, good-value rooms & suites & 2-bedroom chalets all with sat TV, minibar, baths & showers. 4-star. $$–$$$

⌂ **Nanga Damai** (6 rooms) Jln Sultan Tengah; ☏ 019 8871017; e polseb@pc.jaring.my or nangadamai@hotmail.com; www.nangadamai.com. Billed as a 'luxury homestay'. Relaxed, eco-design environment in private rainforest. Wooden doors open onto a large deck. 4 dbl AC rooms on upper floors have phone, TV & jungle views. 2 cottage suites with small kitchen & forest-edge veranda. B/fast is rye bread & fresh-brewed coffee. Minimum 2 nights' stay for B&B. The owner (a lawyer & yoga teacher) considers the place unsuitable for children due to poolside sculptures; best for peace-loving singles & couples. Polycarp, a Sino-Iban, is an expert 'freelance trekker' if you are ready for an off-track jungle adventure on Mt Santubong. $$

⌂ **Permai Rainforest Resort** (formerly Camp Permai) (39 cabins plus a longhouse) ☏ 082 846487; e rosorvo@permairainforest.com, www.permairainforest.com. Back to jungle with creature comforts. 2-person, AC 'Tree Houses' are at canopy level, not in the trees themselves. B/fast inc. Also 6–10 sleeping cabins with fans & mosquito nets & a 6-bed longhouse for a family/group. In the rainforest with a jungle pool, Wi-Fi, Rainforest Café & outdoor sports, from rock climbing to trekking, organised from its Outdoor Activity Centre. Does large school & team-building groups so if tree-house calm is important, ensure you are not going to be there in the peak 'camp' periods. $–$$

⌂ **Sarawak Cultural Village** ☏ 082 846411; e info@scv.com.my. Longhouse rooms with threadbare facilities — choose from Iban, Bidayuh, Orang Ulu or Melanau style. $$

✗ **WHERE TO EAT** There are many small seafood and other restaurants on the peninsula, along the main road and in the villages. In Kampung Buntal (you will need to take a car or taxi from hotels) there are at least half a dozen inexpensive restaurants including **Lim Hock Ann** and **Teo Seafood**, all under 40MYR per person for a good feed. Many people point towards the **Palm Garden Seafood Restaurant** (*Jln Kampung Santubong*). Personally, I found the big metal structure lacking charm, and there was a strong smell of diesel; the food was average. In Kampung Santubong, **Dayang Seafood** is recommended. **Green Paradise Café** on the Jalan Santubong–Kuching road at the entrance to the Santubong mountain trek has simple but healthy rice and noodle dishes. At the Sarawak Cultural Village, the **Budaya Sarawak Restaurant** (*☏ 082 846411*) has a buffet lunch and menu, including ethnic specialities such as *manok pansoh* (chicken cooked in bamboo and served in banana stem). **Damai Lookout Point Seafood** restaurant has a good selection of dishes.

WHAT TO SEE AND DO

Trekking Gunung Santubong (Mount Santubong) is not a national park or reserve (though this may be in the pipeline), but its dense, lush beauty should not be underestimated. A mountain guide is not necessary, but can be arranged through hotel recreation desks. The trail head is on the main Kuching–Santubong Road. The **Red Trail** to the summit is about a five-hour return trip. The **Blue Trail** is an easy 2km trek around the foothills of the mountain. On any of the walks caution should be taken: there are spiders, scorpions and snakes.

Birdwatching Buntal is an important wintering ground for migratory birds. Birdlife International has registered the whole area between Teluk Buntal and Teluk Bako bays as an 'Important Bird Area'. Between October and March many migratory birds can be sighted in the estuary of the Buntal River including terns, egrets, sandpipers and godwits, as well as the resident white-bellied sea eagles and collared kingfishers. Pacific reef egrets frequently stop over on the rocky outcrop of Pulau Tokong Ara in Santubong Bay.

Kuching Wetlands National Park Damai is a good springboard for visiting the mangroves around the marine estuaries and tidal creeks which criss-cross between the Sungai Salak and Sungai Sibu rivers. Estuarine crocodiles, Irrawaddy dolphins (see box below), kingfishers, storks, silver leaf monkeys, proboscis monkeys, macaques and fireflies are some of the creatures to be sighted. Designated a 'wetlands of international importance' in 2002, the giant stretch of mangrove forest is a shadow of its former self, having been whittled down from 17,000ha to just 6,600ha through deforestation. The wetlands are 15km from Kuching and 5km from Damai Beach. Several tour operators offer coastal and river cruises; most boat trips start from either Damai Beach or the boat club in Kampung Santubong. 'Santubong Wildlife Cruises' operated by **CPH Travel** (⟍ *082 243708;* e *cphtrvl@streamyx.com; www.cphtravel.com.my*) leave from the Santubong jetty every day at around 16.00 and return at around 19.30. Transfers from Kuching can be included in a tour.

Sarawak Cultural Village (*Kampung Budaya Sarawak, Pantai Damai;* ⟍ *082 8464111;* e *info@scv.com.my; www.scv.com.my;* ⊕ *09.00–16.45 daily; dance performances 11.30 & 16.00; adult 60MYR, children 30MYR, under 6 free*) The area's most popular tourist attraction allows a look into Sarawak's rich ethno-cultural history as well as being submerged in Santubong's impressive scenery. As you wander from the recreated Melanau tall-house to the Chinese pagoda and Orang Ulu longhouse, greater vitality is lent to the museum through its setting: nestled among trees, and between lakes reflecting the summit of Mount Santubong. The depth and breadth

---

IRRAWADDY DOLPHINS

These shy cetaceans live in the coastal, brackish and fresh waters of the tropical and subtropical Indo-Pacific region. Their bulging forehead and snubbed beak give them a distinctive, friendly look, and they have been known for their friendliness towards people, helping Burmese fishermen by herding fish towards their boats. The fishermen tap their oars against the boat to attract the dolphins and share their catch with them. Not all Irrawaddy–fisherman relations are so good though – by-catch by fisheries is a major threat to the species, along with habitat degradation. With an estimated population of just 100 individuals they are critically endangered. The best time to see them in the Kuching Wetlands is from April to October, though their timid nature means they are not easily spotted, even by the guides.

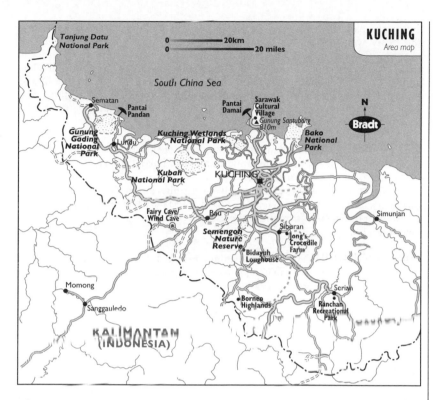

of the experience is even greater than the hyperbole surrounding it might suggest. As a living showcase of Sarawak's ethnicities, the traditional dwellings are decorated with artefacts but there are also real people from those tribes doing craftwork, cooking or chatting with visitors. The dance show is really well done – Bidayuh, Malay, Orang Ulu, Iban and Chinese dances performed by the SCV staff. There is a very down-to-earth feel about this cultural extravaganza, yet it is impeccably presented. The SCV is also home to the **Rainforest Musical Festival** (*www.rainforestmusic-borneo.com*), held every July.

Sports and leisure The Damai **Golf** Course (*Jln Santabong;* \ *082 846088*) has a Mountain Nine below the foothills of Mount Santubong. The Damai Lagoon Resort and Holiday Inn Resort offer a range of **watersports** – snorkelling, sailing, windsurfing, canoeing – and the Permai Rainforest Resort rents **sea kayaks**. **Mountain bikes** can be hired to do a whirl of the 3.5km Damai Cross Country Track.

BAKO NATIONAL PARK

The oldest national park in Sarawak and second oldest in Malaysia, Taman Bako was established in 1957 and covers 27km² at the end of the Muara Tebas Peninsula – Santubong's neighbour. Bako has a spellbinding quality, perhaps due to its astounding diversity of landscapes. From Tanjung (Cape) Rhu to Tanjung Po, and all the beaches and bays in between, it sweeps through mangrove, heath, peat swamp and mixed dipterocarp forest, grasslands, sandstone cliffs and sea-eroded coastal formations. With a population of some

10

280 in the park, the chances of seeing proboscis monkeys as you wander along the many well-marked trails are high, particularly early in the morning or towards dusk. Big-headed, bristlysnouted pigs often wander right in front of the park HQ, scavenging for scrap food or wallowing in mangrove mud. The animals to be on alert for are the macaque monkeys who are very audacious and known to raid many an unlocked room, as well as the canteen and dustbins, and even confront guests for food they might be carrying. 'Compulsive thieves' is how they are not-so-fondly described!

GETTING THERE AND AWAY Kampung Bako, the propeller-point for the boat trip to the park, is 37km north east of Kuching along Jalan Bako. Petra Jaya Transport bus No 6 runs there every hour from 07.00 to 17.00. From the jetty you must charter a motorboat to take you to the park HQ. Organise this at the booth inside the boatmen's canteen. A one-way fare is roughly 50MYR which can be shared by up to five people. The boat trip out of the estuary of the Sungai Bako into the bay is half of the fun.

OTHER PRACTICALITIES Park accommodation is extremely basic, consisting of two- and three-bedroom chalets with a fan and attached or shared bathrooms; four-bedroom hostels; and a camping ground. Cooking facilities amount to barbecue pits. There is a canteen at park HQ. The park registration desk and the Kampung Bako boat-ticketing counter are open daily (⊕ 08.00–16.15) including public holidays. A conservation fee must be paid (*adult 10MYR, children & students with international/ Malaysian student card 5MYR*). The information centre in the park shows films and slide shows on Bako's wildlife and has information on all the trails, and flora and fauna. The boatmen's canteen at Kampung Bako has cheap meals, snacks and refreshments. Bring all other necessary food and other items with you if you plan to stay.

WHAT TO SEE AND DO

Wildlife Bako is often tipped as the best park in Sarawak for wildlife experiences. Apart from the monkeys, there are otters, crabs, frogs and lots of lizards and snakes – lime green whip snakes, green spotted paradise snakes, and the only dangerous snake in Borneo, the triangular-headed pit viper. The wildlife experience starts right among the mangroves of Telok Assam, park HQ area, where many of the 150 listed birds can be sighted.

Treks Bako boasts one of the best networks of trails – 16 well-marked trails from hour-long forest strolls (1.6km return) to full-day treks (21km return). Pick up a map and flora-and-fauna guide at HQ, where you must also register for longer walks. You may find one or more of the trails closed for maintenance. It's amazing how many kinds of vegetation you will pass in an hour as you climb up a couple of cliffs, and circumnavigate the inland of a bay – Bako has 25 distinct kinds of plant life and seven ecosystems. The two supposed best trails for seeing the proboscis monkey – **Telok Delima** and **Telok Paku** – are both about 2km return from Telok Assam (park HQ), and sightings are also frequent in the mangroves around park HQ itself. Pitcher plants are found along the red-arrowed **Lintang Loop trail** (10.8km return).

Beach, bay and boat Telok Pandan Kecil, reached via the 2.5km yellow-arrowed trail, is one of the nicest beaches, nestled within a secluded bay and rocky headland. If you want to cut the journey down, or want to visit bays and coves further afield, you can charter a boat at park HQ and organise a pick-up time with a boatman for a return journey. On the way you will get to see the casuarina-topped limestone and sandstone cliffs and some of the coast's fascinating eroded rock features like the Sea Stack.

West of Kuching there are three national parks: Kubah on its doorstep; further out, Gunung Gading; and out on the end of the peninsula, Tanjung Datu. As many in the Sarawak tourism industry declare quite openly, the coasts – and beaches – along this stretch are not on the same level, in beauty or infrastructure, as those of Santubong and Bako. Others love its relaxed, undeveloped nature. The main road passes some sleepy coastal and inland towns from Lundu to Sematan. Accommodation is threadbare, and that which does exist is mostly geared to the low end of the domestic market. On weekends it will be hard to avoid the karaoke and coastal exodus from Kuching; on weekdays you might get more of a chance to discover a relaxed beach atmosphere on the flat 'Gold Coast-like' beaches of Pantai Pandan and Patai Siar. The main attraction to the Lundu area – unless you are really into silkworms – might be an outdoor escape or rafflesia flower pursuit close to Kuching, in the form of Gunung Gading National Park.

GETTING THERE AND AWAY

By car The road heads west of Kuching to Lundu and Sematan, 100km from Kuching.

By bus Matang Transport buses go to Kubah Park from outside the Saujana car park in Kuching. STC buses go to Lundu four times daily from the long distance bus terminal. From Lundu there is a connecting bus to Gunung Gading National Park or a taxi for under 10MYR. There are onward buses to Sematan from Lundu.

By boat There is no road access to Tanjung Datu area. First, you must reach the village of Telok Melano by boat from Sematan; then, access to the park HQ is either by a 15-minute boat ride from Telok Melano, or a two-and-a-half-hour walk along the Telok Melano–Telok Upas trail.

WHERE TO STAY AND EAT Aside from national park accommodation, choices in this area are sparse and the 'resorts' rather downmarket and overpriced for the services they offer.

National park accommodation
Kubah Park HQ This has five bungalows which sleep six, a ten-bed resthouse and a 12-bed hostel, all with air conditioning, television, hot water, a veranda, full kitchen facilities and barbecue area. The nearby **Matang Wildlife Centre** has more basic chalets and a hostel 'Longhouse'. $

Gunung Gading National Park The infrastructure is not in the same league – there are campsites, three-bedroom chalets, and hostel accommodation but neither a canteen nor cooking facilities – so stock up on ready-to-eat provisions, or come and go from Lundu 2km away. $

Tanjung Datu This has no accommodation in the park, but there is a community homestay in the fishing village of Teluk Melano. Call or visit the park office in Kuching for details.

Other accommodation
⌂ **Union Yes Retreat & Training Centre** Siar Beach (15min drive from Lundu); ☎ 082 453027; e headoffice@sbeu.org. Seaside retreat in a beach- garden setting, hostel, deluxe rooms & penthouse family suites with AC, fridge & bathrooms, pool & BBQ. **Café Rafflesia** serves local & Western food.

Attracts events such as weddings & conferences – can be overrun with 200 people with karaoke fever. $$–$$$

⌂ **Ocean Resort** 176 Siar Beach, Jln Pandan (10min drive from Lundu); ✆ 082 452245. 2-room AC chalets with basic self-catering facilities. $$

⌂ **Sematan Palm Beach Resort** No 12 Sematan Bazaar; ✆ 082 712388; www.sematanresort.com. Resort being revamped, chalets with AC, TV & en-suite bathroom. Individual & family rates inc b/fast & dinner. Bikes, beach (often jellyfish) & possibly loud music in public places. $$

WHAT TO SEE AND DO
Kubah National Park Some 22km from Kuching, parts of the massive sandstone ridge in this park can be seen from Kuching – the 911m peak of Gunung Serapi stands out. Predominantly mixed dipterocarp, the limestone ridges of the Serapi range, rising between 150m and 450m are punctuated by limestone-gouged waterfalls, and over 100 different palm species. The park's six marked trails range from the 255m 'Palmetum' to a 5km summit trail. The 1,429m 'Belian' trail takes in lots of Bornean ironwoods and many fruit trees. The 3,830m 'Rayu' trail passes by several *bintangor* trees, which for nearly two decades have been tapped for their sap as a hopeful cure for AIDS (the chemical costatolide is extracted from the substance). The **Matang Wildlife Centre** is adjacent to the park; orphaned orang-utans are prepped up here before graduating to Semenggoh's more open jungle.

Lundu An hour's drive from Kuching, Lundu is a small, scenic, sleepy town with a thriving *ikan pusu* (anchovy) industry. Just a couple of rows of shop-houses, and a local market, it's spread out over the riverbank in the shadow of Gunung Gading Mountain and close to the beaches of Patai Siah and Patai Pandan.

Gunung Gading National Park Another home to the rafflesia. Every park has its own signature rafflesia species; Gunung Gading hosts *Rafflesia tuanmudae*. There is a plank walk leading to a common blooming ground of the rafflesia (guiding fees 20MYR per hour per group with ranger). For rafflesia-blooming checks, ring the national parks office in Kuching (✆ 082 248088) or park HQ (✆ 082 735714). There are three trails in the park – from a two-hour trip to the six- to eight-hour return 'Gunung Gading' summit walk.

Sematan Half an hour from Lundu on the South China Sea, Sematan is a hobby barramundi fishing area – the fish were introduced by the Agriculture Department. It also has a **Silk Farm** (✆ 082 320130; www.sematansilk.com; 5MYR) where you can purchase silk quilts. In the 14km² **Tanjung Datu National Park** on the Datu Peninsula, Sarawak meets Indonesia, land meets sea and rainforest meets coral reef – and turtle conservation territory. Lack of regular viable transport makes independent travel here difficult – the boats from Sematan to Telok Melano cater to local communities and are unscheduled, but that could be an adventure in itself. Tour operators in Kuching organise transport and guided tours to the park. The area is totally off bounds during the October–February monsoon. Extreme mountain biker Hans Rey says the Sematan area is a **mountain-bike** paradise with 'an estimated 60–80km of all types of trails, with covered single-tracks, waterfalls, desert-heat, killer climbs and screaming downhills'. For tours contact **Outdoor Trek** (✆ 082 363344; e best@bikcloud.com; www.bikcloud.com).

SOUTH OF KUCHING
From the small market town of Serikin to the village of Anah Rais, the foothills of the Borneo Highlands area on the Indonesian border are Bidayuh homeland –

fleeing the coast for the hinterland earned these timid people the name of the 'land Dayaks'. Here they built their longhouses and *baruk* warrior houses from bamboo. The border is punctuated by a series of peaks rippled between 400–1,400m perfect for an off-the-beaten-track adventure. Sarawak's answer to the wildlife sanctuary of Sabah is in the neighbourhood, as are some lively Chinese market towns, caves and kayaking.

GETTING THERE AND AWAY

By car Take the Kuching–Serian road south from Kuching; for Bau (60km) veer right into Jalan Batu Kitang, for the Highlands, Jalan Penrissen.

By bus STC buses travel to Semenggoh and STC and Bau Transport company buses go to Bau.

WHERE TO STAY AND EAT

Borneo Highlands Resort (62 rooms) ✆ 088 578980; www.borneohighlands.com. A highland haven of ecotourism, organic agriculture, horticulture, rainforest – & golf. Jungle spa, 18-hole golf course, rooms, suites & several secluded chalets, ethnically refined decor. The Annah Rais Café serves organic, vegetarian, local & international food. The Hornbill's Nest is a lounge-cum-toa parlour with highland organics. Requires a 4x4 to reach it – the resort does this for 40MYR return. Good 'Jungle Spa' & other packages available online at www.sarawakresorts.com. $$$–$$$$

Annah Rais Longhouses 71 Kampung Annah Rais, Jln Padawan (60km from Kuching); ✆ 082 457941; www.longhouseadventure.com. In a traditional Bidayuh longhouse village, longhouse rooms, jungle treks, waterfalls & traditional food. 2-night packages inc transfers, accommodation, meals & activities from 368MYR adult/198MYR child. Take any additional requirements – no major shops close by. Full itinerary on website. $

WHAT TO SEE AND DO

Semenggoh Wildlife Rehabilitation Centre (*20km from Kuching;* ✆ *082 618423;* ⏱ *08.00–12.30/14.00 16.00; adult 3MYR/child 1.50MYR*) Sarawak's first forest reserve – established in 1920 and converted into a rehab centre for orang-utans, honey bears and hornbills in 1975. Now 'semi-wild' orang-utan inhabit it, having graduated from Matang Wildlife Centre. Visit during feeding times (half an hour at 08.30 and 15.00) – mornings are better as the apes roam free all day until the afternoon feed and it is not uncommon to run into some on the reserve's pathways. It is a 1km-long walk from the entrance to the feeding area. The wildlife sanctuary is part of the **Semenggoh Nature Reserve** which has an arboretum, and botanical research centre with fernariums, ethnobotanic gardens and other gardens. Visits must be booked in advance.

Bidayuh Longhouses Tour operators visit longhouses as a day trip but you can also visit several independently, including those in Kampung Annah Rais: at Kampung Benuk (*off Jln Penrissen, 50km from Kuching*) there are about 80 families in a longhouse; Kampung Pelaman Dunuk is 62km from Kuching. Admission with or without a guide is 5MYR. If you are visiting in June, the Bidayuh villages celebrate the rice festival **Gawai Padi** (*Gawai Sawa'a* in Bidayuh dialect) in their own special way, with lots of shamanistic rituals, priestesses, trance dancers and music. Contact Mr Diweng Bakir (✆ *019 8565498;* e *diweng_bakir@yahoo.com*), director of a local indigenous NGO.

Borneo highlands trekking From Annah Rais, there is a three-hour trek into the Kalimantan border region, where a large community of some 200 Bidayuh families live traditionally in four longhouses, strung each side of a suspension bridge. Two-to three-day trekking excursions taking in Gunung Penrissen (1,329m), surrounding landscapes, longhouses and villages along small trails give views over Kalimantan, Kuching and the South China Sea.

Bau The Bau region bears scars from 19th-century mining – both on the land and in the memories of the people. Antimony was discovered here in the 1820s, and the area later became a hotspot of rebellion against oppressive Brunei rulers, who forced the Bidayuh to work in the mines for a pittance and sold the women and children as slaves. Local Malays and natives rebelled in 1836, proclaiming Sarawak's independence. The rebellion dragged on with James Brooke apparently playing the role of peacemaker when he arrived on the scene in 1839. In subsequent decades the gold rush began and migrants, mostly Hakka people, came from China and Dutch Kalimantan. In 1857 there was another uprising, this time by Chinese miners against Brooke – in a massacre that is not often talked about. Up to 2,000 Chinese men, women and children were killed by the rajah's forces, smothered in caves they had taken shelter in while their mining settlement was set alight. On the way to Bau is the small market town of **Siniawan**. Composed of 1920s double-storey wooden shop-houses, Siniawan was once the rebels' headquarters. Strong on local history is Borneo Adventure Tours guide Philip Yong (❧ *082 245175;* e *info@borneoadventure.com*), also director of the Sarawak Tourist Association and son of the late Sarawak minister Stephen Yong. The opencast mine in Bau has created a small blue lake, **Tasik Biru**.

Caves and kayaking With lots of caves, rivers and limestone ridge features, the highlands area is popular for outdoor activity. The **Wind Cave** reserve towards the border is a nice picnic spot; **Fairy Cave** – which has some Chinese shrines at the entrance and interior – is also an **abseiling** destination. There are buses from Bau through to here.

Serikin At the left of the fork in the road towards the border, is another (modern) Bidayuh town – there are no longhouses here. You can buy Indonesian crafts – bags, baskets, and *kasah* floormats at the *gerai* stalls.

SOUTHEAST OF KUCHING

East of Kuching, the sinewy Sri Aman Division skirts the Indonesian border. Over 90% of the population are Iban, and their rice paddy, rubber and pepper cash crops engrave the river-lined landscape. The longhouses which start appearing in fields after the town of Serian are a mix of traditional wooden ones with modern cement structures. Deeper inland, the rivers which run through national parks and longhouse communities can only be experienced by boat trip. Allow at least a two-night stay in this area whichever way you tackle it.

GETTING THERE AND AWAY
By car Head southeast along the Serian–Kuching road.

By bus From Kuching's long-distance bus station, Sarawak Transport Company buses go to Siburan, Serian, Bandar Sri Aman and Betong. From Serian there are buses to Ranchan Pools.

By boat Use longboats and speedboats for journeys along the rivers, and to cross the Batang Ai.

SERIAN
Where to stay and eat

⌂ **KC Inn** Jln Alamanda, Serian. Recommended if you need a room mid-journey. Very clean, spacious rooms, & hot showers. $

⌂ **Ranchan Pools Chalets** ☎ 082 876681. The district council hires out several basic chalets & a 10-bed dorm room – used mostly by holidaying Malaysians & not promoted widely in tourist circles. $

✕ **Where to eat** In the 200km between Kuching and Batang Ai, the food stops are at Serian (which has fantastic market and food-stall food), Lachau and Sri Aman. Lachau – a small car and coach rest-stop – is referred to as 'cowboy town', and there is still cross-border barter going on here with travelling traders who arrive in town from Indonesia. The Chinese coffee shops along its one street are a good place to have a drink and some noodles – **Lee Chong Café** is recommended.

WHAT TO SEE AND DO

In Serian Serian, 70km from Kuching, is a small but sparkling market town of 85,000 – nearly two-thirds of the population are Bidayuh, the rest a mix of Malay, Iban and Chinese. In the middle of the market square there is **Big Durian** – a monument to the king of local fruits. The under-cover farmers' market is a maze of culinary forms: chillis, freshly picked peanuts, snake fruit and squirming *sago* worms. There are plenty of food stalls for *pisang goreng* (fried banana) and savoury snacks here. **Taman Danu** is a recreational park which is very pretty at night with lights on the lake, a couple of restaurants and some food stalls. Near Serian is the **Ranchan Recreational Park**, a waterfall, picnic spot and pool in the rainforest. The park facilities and trails have been criticised for being run-down and seem set for an upgrade; the canteen on the other hand and the park chalets are new and in a lovely setting.

In Siburban At Siburan, 30km from Kuching, is **Jong's Crocodile Farm** and mini-zoo (*off Serian Rd;* ☎ *082 863570;* ⊕ *09.00–17.00 daily, feeding times 11.00 & 15.00; adult 8MYR, child 4MYR*).

BANDAR SRI AMAN Some 194km from Kuching, 9km from turn-off on main road, Bandar Sri Aman is on the banks of the Batang Lupar River. This is the trading hub of the district for the timber, oil palm, rubber and pepper industries, and the gateway to the **Batang Ai National Park**. The city's main claim to fame is its *benak* or 'tidal bore' which rolls in through the river mouth and fills the riverbed within minutes. The tidal bore is actually a daily occurrence but on such a small scale that it is not noticeable – however, a couple of times a year it reaches speeds of 7–18km/h and heights of up to 3m. The phenomenon was immortalised by Somerset Maugham in the short story *The Yellow Streak*; he visited and was nearly drowned in 1921 while boating on the river with his companion. Sri Aman is trying to build up

---

IBAN TALK

A few handy words to have up your sleeve for longhouse visits are:

Nama berita nuan? – How are you? (used as a general greeting instead of hello)
Berita Akumana – I am well
Nyamai – It's delicious (a good one to comment on the rice wine)
Terima kasih – Thank you (the same as in Malay)

10

its tourism attraction with a **Pesta Benak** – tidal bore festival – with lots of merriment, food and dance. People even try surfing the bores. The only historical building of note, **Fort Alice**, was built out of *belian* wood in 1864, after Rajah Charles Brooke's claimed 'defeat' of the last of the great Iban chieftains, Rentap.

Batang Ai National Park A place for wildlife research more than orang-utan spotting, the national park is accessed after three to four hours of longboat journey. The newly launched (and not trailed) **Red Ape Trail** is an arduously challenging trek. Borneo Adventure mapped it out with the local Iban communities in the Batang Ai area, and it has the endorsement of the Orang-utan Foundation. The full trek is 11 days but shorter treks can be arranged. Contact **Borneo Adventure** (*55 Main Bazaar, Kuching;* ＼ *082 245175;* e *info@borneoadventure.com; www.borneoadventure.com*).

BATANG AI The water catchment of **Batang Ai Reservoir** was formed when the valley and some 30 longhouses in it were drowned in the 1980s – a very controversial move in which hundreds of locals were relocated. The power station provides half of Sarawak's daily energy needs. The area is the starting point for excursions deep along the Sungai Batang Ai and Sungai Engkari rivers, leading to huge longhouses where Iban communities lead isolated lives somewhere between tradition and modernity.

Getting there To reach Batang Ai Reservoir is tricky but possible: take the Lubock Antu bus and alight on the main road at the junction to Lubock Antu, then catch another bus the last 40km to the hydro dam. For those continuing their journey north, you can also pick up the Sibu bus at this junction.

🏠 **Longhouse experiences** Most longhouses which accept guests are in the Skrang and Lemanak river areas near Bandar Sri Aman, and the Batang Ai River and its tributaries. Most are in remote areas only reached by longboat. The easiest option is to go on a tour, but you can arrive in Betong and line up a journey directly with local Ibans for the Batang Skrang. Try:

🏠 **Hilton Batang Ai Longhouse Resort** (100 rooms) ＼ 083 584388, or via Kuching Hilton ＼ 082 248200. A 15min boat journey from the Batang Ai dam. The only hotel in the area is this 3-star, built in longhouse style on the banks of the reservoir. Wood-panelled rooms pleasantly plain, arranged in blocks facing inward, the dining veranda faces out. AC, TV, average buffet food. Good base for excursions to longhouses, jungle treks, boating & fishing. Rooms & suites. $$–$$$

🏠 **Ulung Ai Jungle Lodge** Batang Ai; ＼ 082 245175; e info@borneoadventure.com; www.borneoadventure.com. Next to the Nanga Sumpa longhouse. Ethically run lodge by Borneo Adventure; 2-night packages from 1,200MYR – less expensive are 2-night trips to a Lemanak longhouse.

🏠 **Nanga Ukum Longhouse** www.borneoecotours.com. Borneo Eco Tours do a luxury safari to this longhouse, 3 days/2 nights from Kuching, stopping on the way at Semenggoh orang-utan centre and Serian town, staying at the Hilton on Batang Ai & visiting Nanga Ukum by longboat (1,200MYR).

🏠 **Nanga Sumpa Longhouse** Batang Ai. Staying among some 10 families who live in the community. 20 mins' walk from the jetty. Facilities are basic, but rooms are clean, & fresh fish & vegetables can be enjoyed with the locals. Contact the visitors' information centre in Kuching (see page 230) or one of the tour operators to organise this budget trip.

Longhouse visits Reached either by self-chartered longboat trip or on a tour, some of the upriver longhouse communities still live a relatively isolated and traditional life which is fascinating to observe. At Kampung Mengkak Longhouse (*Rumah*

Burau, Mengkak; ☎ *013 2867451*) on the Sungai Engkari, you can mingle with some of the 26 families who live in the 200m-long structure, as they sit out in the *ruai* (communal veranda), drinking *tuak* (rice wine) and making handicrafts. The locals demonstrate their blowpipe skills, perform dances and play music in traditional dress on request, but with far more personality and passion than you could ever expect in a city cultural show. The best visits can be those to just experience 'life as usual' rather than great shows. The key to making such a visit as enriching as possible is to be humble and respectful, learn a couple of Iban greetings and mingle gently with the people. Get acquainted with the chief (Tuai Rumah), and get ready to feel your face all smiled out as the whole community turns out to welcome you.

CENTRAL SARAWAK

South China Sea

Bintulu & Miri

Pelagus
Resort

Beloga

Batang Rejang

Batang Baleh

N

Bradt

0   20km
0   20 miles

Fort
Sylvia
Kapit

Sg. Mukah

Selangau
Selangau
Rest Stop
Sg. Selangau

Song

Batang Rejang

Mukah

Dalat

Sg. Kut

Igan

Batang Igan

Kanowit

Ngemah

Sg. Julah

Sg. Ngemah

Sibu

Durin

Batang Rejang

Julau

Matu

Daro

Pulau
Beruit

Binangor

Sarikei

Pakan

Sebangkol
Recreational Park

Belawai

Rajang

Tg. Manis

Jakar
Rest Stop

Selalang

Kg. Grigat

Sri Aman, Batang Ai & Kuching

258

11

Central Sarawak

Central Sarawak is intersected by the mighty Batang Rejang and its tributaries, and the journey from the South China Sea through this vast region to remote inland areas is a compelling mix of tribal traditions, coastal modernity and mountainous isolation. River transport is a necessity for getting around the area as much as it is for getting to it. Long river journeys are rewardingly different, with the complex culturescape of the Rejang. Iban and Melenau riverbank settlements are found on its lower reaches, and way upstream is the territory of nomadic Penan hunter-gatherers and other upriver people, Orang Ulu.

SIBU

As Sibu lies at the confluence of the Rejang and the Igan, 130km from the South China Sea, river geography has played a major hand in its history. As a major transport hub for the whole Rejang Basin, parts of its harbour are over 1km in width. Sarawak's affluent second-biggest city – with a population of 180,000 – was pushed to modernity by a former mayor with the help of powerful Chinese community associations. About 60% of Sibuan are Chinese, the rest Malay, Melanau, Iban and Orang Ulu. Propelled by religious persecution and poverty, the Chinese started arriving in 1901, led by Methodist missionary Reverend Wong Nai Siong who is heralded as the town's founder. He persuaded Charles Brooke to give land to the Chinese in the Lower Rejang region for farming paddy, pepper and rubber. Sibu rebounded in the post-World War II years as a centre of the timber industry, and boomed through the 1980s in timber trade, sawmilling and shipbuilding. The town's name comes from the Iban word for rambutan – *buah sibau*.

GETTING THERE AND AWAY

By air MAS have two daily flights in both directions between Sibu and Kuching and Sibu and Kuala Lumpur. AirAsia's bargain flights from Kuching to Sibu are renowned for delays. MASWings have Fokker 50 flights between Sibu, Kuching and Miri. The airport is a few kilometres from town and there is no bus service – a taxi costs 28MYR with a coupon purchased inside the airport.

Airlines
✈ **Malaysia Airlines** Jln Tuanku Osman; ✆ 084 321055. Town office.

✈ **Air Asia** Jln Tuanku Osman; ✆ 084 307808

By car Sibu is roughly midway between Kuching (462km) and Miri (380km).

By bus The long-distance bus hub, the Sibu New Bus Terminal, is on Jalan Pahlawan 3km from the city centre. Several bus companies operate from here.

Biaramas Express have daily buses to Kuching, Bintulu and Miri. **Trans Borneo Resources** (☏ *082 452271*) also go to coastal and inland towns to the north in Mukah Division including Mukah, Oya and Dalat. Bus 21 links the long-distance bus station to the city bus 'Transit Point' in about 20 minutes.

By boat Longer-distance express boats come and go from the Express Wharf for Kuching, Belaga, Dalat, Daro, Kapit, Kanowit, Sarikei and Song. Tickets are sold at the passenger terminal at the wharf. During peak holiday periods it's best to book in advance, otherwise arrive 30 minutes before departure. For up-to-date schedules, contact the Sarawak Rivers Board (☏ *084 339936*).

GETTING AROUND The city centre is small, and pleasant to walk around.

By car For car hire contact the visitors' information centre (see below). They warn of unlicenced drivers and advise tourists to contact them for the latest details of recommended car hire companies.

By taxi Taxis do not use meters; shorter trips cost between 6 and 12MYR. Taxis are easily flagged outside the big hotels, at the taxi stand opposite the Express Wharf and on Jalan Lintang – or call the station (☏ *084 320773*). Official long-distance fares (one-way) are: Mukah 200MYR; Bawang Assan longhouse settlement 50MYR; Sarikei 100MYR; Kanowit 50MYR; and Bintangor 90MYR.

By bus The city Transit Point is opposite the Express Wharf on Jalan Khoo Peng Loong, with buses bound for the town area, Sibu region and neighbouring Sarikei. The destination is generally marked on the front of the bus.

TOURIST INFORMATION

🄴 **Sibu Visitors' Information Centre** 32 Jln Tukang Besi; ☏ 084 340980; e vic-sibu@ sarawaktourism.com; ☉ 08.00–17.00 Mon–Fri, closed Sat/Sun/public holidays. Brochures, guidebooks & maps available. The helpful staff can advise on travel plans & national park accommodation bookings in the district and whole Rejang river basin area, as well as car hire.

🏠 **WHERE TO STAY** There are a handful of very good international-class hotels in Sibu, and some excellent medium-class hotels – usually lacking pools and gyms, but often with free Wi-Fi. Some three–four-star establishments offer budget, mid-range and suite-level luxury prices under one roof.

Upmarket to mid-range

🏠 **Kingwood Hotel** (168 rooms) 12 Lorong Lanang 4; ☏ 084 335888; e kingwd@po.jaring.my. The top-notch hotel in town, 10 mins' walk to Town Square; 4-star with rooftop swimming pool, fitness centre, good coffee shop & Chinese restaurant; river views from the riverside rooms. $$, suite $$$$

🏠 **Premier Hotel** (189 rooms) Sarawak House Complex, Jln Kampung Nyabor; ☏ 084 323222; e reservation@premierh.com.my; www.premierh.com.my. A business-oriented 4-star, with restaurant, music lounge, karaoke room, Wi-Fi, 24hr business centre, nr shopping malls & Cineplex. $$, suite $$$$

🏠 **RH Hotel** (formerly the Everly Hotel) (226 rooms) Jln Kampung Nyabor; ☏ 084 365888; www.rhhotels.com.my. The newest 4-star. Swimming pool, coffee shop, music lounge, fitness centre. $$, suite $$$$

🏠 **Tanahmas Hotel** (120 rooms) Lot 277, Block 5, Jln Kampung Nyabor; ☏ 084 333188; e enquiries@tanahmas.com.my; www.tanahmas.com.my. One of the best 3-stars in town, very centrally located near the market strip with swimming pool, karaoke & restaurant. $$, suite $$$$

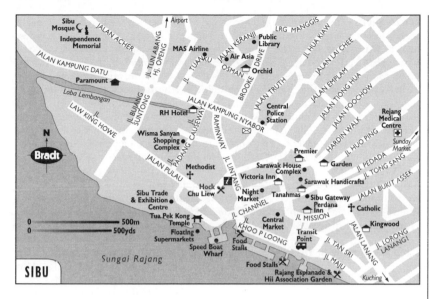

Budget to shoestring There is a big cross-over of budget/shoestring prices in Sibu. In a three-star hotel it is possible to have a large double room for 100–150MYR; this will cost around 100MYR in a two-star hotel. Meanwhile standard rooms in some of the hotels listed below cost 60–100MYR and come with bathroom, television and fan or air conditioning; some also have a fridge and kettle.

🏠 **Orchid Hotel** (48 rooms) 9 Jln Persiaran Brooke; ☎ 331999. Restaurant/lounge, conference facilities, AC, bathroom, sat TV, internet. $$

🏠 **Paramount Hotel** 3 Lorong 9A, Jln Kampung Datu (1km from town); ☎ 084 331122; e paramounthtlrdm@myjaring.net. 3-star hotel with great service & Malay courtesy, further out on town's edge in riverside area. Many Malay café & food stalls nearby. One of few hotels with non/s in lobby & some floors. Spacious comfortable rooms. Great value, b/fast inc. Only downfall is lack of sports & leisure facilities. $$

🏠 **Garden Hotel** (40 rooms) 1 Jln Huo Ping; ☎ 084 317888. From the reception you might think it's a boutique budget, but things go a bit downhill from there. Public areas & some rooms smoky & shabby. Superior rooms better. Coffee shop quite good if you order from the menu rather than b/fast buffet. $–$$

🏠 **Perdana Inn** 24 Jln Mission; ☎ 084 327007. Recommended as best 2-star, with budget prices for larger rooms. $–$$

🏠 **Victoria Inn** 80 Jln Market; ☎ 084 320099 The cleanest, good-value shoestring hotel in town, suites at budget prices. $–$$

Hostels There are a dozen very central hostels and lodging houses where you can pay under 50MYR (as low as 30MYR) for a room with fan, television and phone. Contact the tourism office for the latest recommendations on the best.

✗ **WHERE TO EAT** The food in Sibu is probably the best value in the whole of Sarawak. Food is of a high quality and most of the restaurants are as spotless as the rest of the town. Local specials include *kam pua mee* – noodles tossed in pork lard, chilli, onion and sliced pork; *mee sua* – longevity noodles in a tub of rich herbal soup with chunks of boiled chicken; *konpia* – the local 'bagel', yeast buns sandwiched together with spicy minced pork (or chicken in Muslim restaurants); and *mee udang* – river prawns with noodles in a bowl of spicy broth.

Coffee shops The streets are packed with coffee shops which serve the above specialities from early morning onwards. For *mee udang* and other local specialities, head to **Min Kong Café** (*Jln Bank;* ⊕ *lunch & evenings daily; 5–20MYR*) and **Sin Chun Hua Café** (*next to the Sibu Visitors' Information Centre*), both cheap, cheerful cafés. Moderately priced noodle dishes, steamed buns, dumplings, seafood, and barbecued pork and duck are all on the menu at **Kheng Hock Café** (*49 Jln Maju facing the Rejang Esplanade;* ⊕ *b/fast, lunch & dinner*). **Ah Hee Kopi Tiam** (⊕ *06.30–17.00*) on Leboh Market, has a very buzzy atmosphere, with a menu offering all the local dishes. Try the fresh foaming green fruit drink *sour sop*. Two cheap, good-quality Malay coffee shops are **Gaho Café** (*opposite Wisma Sanyan*) and the Chinese (halal) **Rafie Café** (*opposite the Paramount Hotel*).

Restaurants More upmarket Chinese restaurants with mostly mid-range prices are found at leading hotels: **Ming Ziang Restaurant** (✆ *084 335888*) at the Kingwood Hotel; **Golden Palace** (✆ *084 333188*) at Tanahmas Hotel and **Gold Hope Restaurant** (✆ *084 323222*) at Sarawak House near the Premier Hotel.

Seafood Esplanade Seafood (*Rejang Esplanade*), is an open-air riverfront restaurant with some Western dishes and moderate prices, open only in the evenings. **Hai Bing Seafood** (*31 Jln Maju*) offers the same, plus seafood and meat dishes, with indoor air conditioning and outdoor dining – a friendly, and recommended, place. **Sri Meranti** (*1 Jln Hardin;* ⊕ *evenings only*) is a Chinese Muslim (halal) seafood restaurant, bright and clean with air conditioned section and outdoor tables. The famous fish-head curry (*tapah*) is made from fresh river fish.

Stalls and market food The first floor of the Sibu Central Market has around 30 (mostly Chinese) stalls, offering cheap, fresh food from 06.00–1400. Some are open in the evening. There are stalls all along Jalan Market and at the *pasar malam* (**Night Market**) on Jalan Lebuh Tinggi. The **Swan Food Centre** (*Jln Temple next to Sibu Trade & Exhibition Centre;* ⊕ *morning to evening*) has mostly Chinese food stalls with lots of chicken rice and roasted pork. For food on the go, there is a food court on the first floor of Express Boat Wharf, and Malay food to go from stalls next to the wharf. **Taman Selera Harmoni** (*near the Sibu mosque*) is a vast under-roof pavilion with several Malay *restoran,* each with their own allotment of tables and chairs, and multiple television screens. A *konpia* hotspot for breakfast is **Mr & Mrs Yeo's Stall** (*Lorong Tiong Hua 26, 15 mins' walk or take a taxi*), where they serve pork buns in a pork broth with slices of stewed pork. A fantastic bakery is the **Big Thumb Cake House** (*71–73 Jln Tuanku Osman;* ✆ *084 339829*), a family business specialising in cakes, bread and Hong Kong *cha siew pau* (mini steamed bun).

ENTERTAINMENT AND NIGHTLIFE Sibu has several pubs and clubs, and even a few Iban karaoke pubs. For cocktails and sophistication, head to the international hotels – **Club Emas** for cocktails and karaoke and the **Blowpipe Lounge** (*Tanahmas Hotel, Star Cineplex 6 Jln Ramin*) for music.

SHOPPING If you are travelling by car, the **Durin Handicraft Shop** (*35km southeast from Sibu, near the Rejang's Durin ferry terminal*) has handicrafts from all over the central region. Chinese potteries are produced at several workshops near Sibu. The narrow, crowded streets of the town centre are full of clothing and high-tech stores. The 28-storey Wisma Sanyan shopping complex – the tallest building in Sarawak – is Sibu's largest retail mall. On the fourth floor is a cyber café, Forever Link.

Markets With 1,200 stalls selling everything from fish, fruits, handicrafts and live ducks, Sibu's spanking new **Central Market** is one of the biggest trading markets in Malaysia, combining the former 'wet market' and indigenous *Lembangan* market. Good, moderately priced handcrafts can be bought at the Central Market and night market stalls, often from the source. The *tamu* is also held here on Sundays. The **night bazaar** (🕙 *17.00–22.00 daily*) on Leboh Market is a colourful melange of stalls selling household goods, fashion and footwear, and a variety of foods from steamed buns to satay.

OTHER PRACTICALITIES

Health and emergency There are several downtown clinics, a public hospital out of town and two modern and central private hospitals including the **Rejang Medical Centre** (*29 Jln Pedada;* ✆ *084 330733*).

Miscellaneous The website of **Sibu Municipal Council** (*www.smc.gov.my*) is a good source of local information.

WHAT TO SEE AND DO

Around town Sibu is a compact town easily explored on foot, with taxis or buses available for out-of-town locations. Climb to the top floor of the seven-storey **Kuan Yin** ('Goddess of Mercy') **Pagoda**, which towers above the 100-year-old **Tua Pek Kong Temple** – great for seeing the day-to-day activity on the water. A huddle of colourful 'floating supermarkets', wooden boats which service Rejang longhouse communities, are anchored in port. The **Heritage Walk** links several public places and memorial gardens. One of the prettiest is the Hokkien community's **Chiang Chung Immigration Garden** on the river in front of the temple. The **Rejang Esplanade** starts from the Express Boat passenger terminal and ends near the emblematic **Swan statue**. Sibu's swans symbolise its ugly-duckling transformation, drawing on Chinese folklore about a town saved from starvation by a sago-drinking swan. The vast **Town Square** – the largest urban square in Malaysia – is the venue for the **Borneo Cultural Festival** held every July, with performances from all of Sarawak's major ethnic groups as well as some from Sabah and Kalimantan. **Bukit Aup Jubilee Park** (*TekubBus No 2/3;* 🕙 *08.00–18.00 daily; free*) is a great place for strolling, picnicking and jogging, with views from its 60m tower over the Igan River and nearby longhouses. The Iban bring offerings to the top of the hill for the benevolent spirit Naga Bari, believed to help people in need. Another workout-friendly place is the **Sungai Merah (Red River) Heritage Walk** (*Sungai Merah bus*), a landscaped river promenade area on the site of the original Chinese settlement in Sibu. True to its name, the water is rusty red in colour because of the tidal action on peat soils from upriver forests. The walk leads to the **Wong Nai Siong Memorial Garden** which is graced by a dour statue of the town's revolutionary father.

Museums and galleries

Sibu Cultural Heritage Museum (*In the Civic Centre, Jln Tun Abang Haji Openg; 2km from city, take Sungai Merah bus 1A;* 🕙 *10.30–17.30 Tue–Sun; free*) Flat yet interesting presentation of antiques, artefacts and photos on the town's history, Chinese migration and the various ethnic groups of the Rejang river basin. The Foochow presence in Sibu is elucidated at the **World Fuzou Heritage Gallery** on Jalan Salim.

EXCURSIONS FROM SIBU

LONGHOUSES Day or overnight trips to Kampung Bawang Assan, a settlement of eight Iban longhouses both modern and old (*taxi 50MYR, vans from Central Market* *every 2hrs*) are available. Andy Austin, the son of one of the longhouse chiefs, acts as a guide and can be contacted via the visitors' centre (see page 260). Frankie Ting from **Sazhong Trading & Travel Service** (*4 Jln Central;* ↘ *084 336017;* e *sazhong@tm.net.my*) does tours to nearby longhouse settlements such as Bawang Assan, upriver trips and treks (for longer trips book at least one week in advance).

SARIKEI In 1856, Sarikei town was burnt down in an uprising against the Brooke administration – waged by Iban people from the Sungai Julau river area. Situated 122km southwest of Sibu (buses leave the city station every half-hour), Sarikei is now an agro-industry hub and home of the '*ananas*' – curiously, they use the French name for pineapple. Various oranges, *pomelo* and avocado also thrive in the area's acidic soils, and Malaysia owes its ranking as the world's fifth-biggest pepper exporter to Sarikei Division, which produces more than 80% of Sarawak's crop. Tiger prawn farms and shrimp processing are being pushed with government subsidies to diversify from pepper. The town lies about 40km from the mouth of the Rejang; at the river's delta is the largest mangrove swamp in Sarawak. The coast is both a timber-processing zone and developing deep sea port.

About 15km from Sarikei, **Bintangor** is a small market town at the heart of Sarikei's fruit production renowned for its green oranges. These *agrumes* infuse the Malay dish *rojak*, a spicy salad of fruits and vegetables. Situated 25km from Sarikei, the small (13ha) **Sebangkoi Forest Park** is a good mid-journey rest spot if you are travelling along the Pan-Borneo Highway.

🏠 Where to stay and eat

🏠 **Dragon Inn** 60 Jln Masjid Lama; ↘ 084 651799. If you are travelling independently, try this plain but clean registered 2-star hotel, with a coffee shop serving noodle & rice based meals. $–$$

🏠 **The Oriental Hotel** 48 Jln Repok; ↘ 084 655559. Has a halal Chinese restaurant. $

✕ **Golden Happiness Restaurant** Jln Masjid Lama. One of the better coffee shops with Malay/Chinese basics. Seafood and venison specialities.

✕ **Hung Kiew Kee Restaurant** Jln Masjid Lama. Similar to the Golden Happiness.

✕ **KFC** Jalan Masjid Lama

✕ **Sugar Bun** Jalan Masjid Lama. Fast food.

Tours For an organised tour of Sarikei and surrounding areas, contact Ling How Kang at **Greatown Travel** (↘ *084 211243;* m *019 856 5041;* e *greatown@gmail.com*) – on regional knowledge, he is second to none. The trip focuses on Sarikei's agricultural attractions: dragon fruit and orange orchards, pineapple farms and pepper gardens, as well as visits to Kampung Rejang to see *songket* weavers, and Kampung Belawai – the heart of the smoked prawn (*sesar unjur*) processing industry. You can meet him in Sibu or in Sarikei.

MUKAH Originally from Mindano Island in the Philippines, the Melanau people have lived in Borneo since the 16th century – and Mukah is their heartland. The Melanau make a characteristically distinctive signature dish, *umai* – a spicy salad of raw shredded fish marinated with lime, ginger and chilli. Around 130,000 Melanau are spread along the coast from the Rejang Estuary to the city of Bintulu – with six distinct groups and 11 different dialects.

The Brooke dynasty rajahs and the Brunei sultans competed with each other to control the trade in *rumbia* (sago) in the late 1800s. Sago still underpins the economy and many local customs and cottage industries, but fishing and oil palm are turboing ahead. The region's façade on the South China Sea is seeing the beginnings of a riviera-effect, as the currently sparse stretch is slowly earmarked for coastal development. Many of the Melanau and Iban *kampungs* are built near rivers and above mangrove swamp around the coast.

Getting there and away

By air MASWings fly Twin Otters from Kuching to Mukah (one-hour flight), Sibu to Mukah (30 minutes) and Miri to Mukah (30 minutes).

By car It's a 159km (about two-hour) drive from Sibu, the last 40km along an unsealed and seriously pot-holed dirt road.

By bus Express buses from Sibu take about three and a half hours.

By boat The most engaging and enjoyable way to get to 'Melanau Heartland', if you have time on your hands, is by speedboat – from Sibu to Dalat, about 40km from Mukah township. Buses go onwards to Mukah from the station behind the Hiap Leong Mini Market, and there are cheap trips by van and taxi, both of which will be waiting for passengers.

Getting around The best way to see to see the coastal and inland *kampung* is by car. A mixture of boat and bus travel is possible, if you are determined to see the area, on a budget, but you must ensure that there are food options near your accommodation.

Where to stay With the advent of the new road there are sure to be more mid-range hotels.

🏠 **Kingwood Resort** (99 rooms) Lot 96, Block 17, Mukah Land District; ☏ 084 873888; e kingwoodresort_mukah@yahoo.com. Located 12km from town & facing the South China Sea, the pillared, nouveau-Chinese structure stands pretty much on its own between the oil plantations & the ocean, with totally uninterrupted 180° views to the horizon. A vigorous promoter of the culture of the area. Friendly & incredible value for money, modern, spacious, light & bright, full of high tech & leisure facilities. $$, suite $$$$
🏠 **King Ing** (19 rooms) 1–2 Jln Boyan, Mukah; ☏ 084 871400; e AcSG8@yahoo.com. Best choice

if you want to be in Mukah town itself AC, TV, bathroom, standard & superior rooms. $–$$
🏠 **Lamin Dana** (12 rooms) Kampung Tellian (4km from Mukah); ☏ 084 871543; e info@lamindana.com; www.lamindana.com. Part riverside lodge, part cultural centre, Lamin Dana is built in Melanau style at the end of a village boardwalk through mangroves. Rustically alluring, it is much like a longhouse homestay but without the crowds. Earthy décor, with beautiful crafts on display. Twin & family rooms, fans, games/computer room. Melanau meals. Mangrove tours, boat trips, bike hire. $–$$

Homestays Sarawak Tourism describe homestays in the Mukah area as 'culture-based accommodation'. The following are best arranged through Sibu Tourism (*vicsibu@sarawaktourism.com*) and fall within a budget price category.

🏠 **Oya Homestay** Kampung Senau, Oya; ☏ 084 871416; e anail@yahoo.com. Homestay programme in 10 village houses run by the Malaysian Fisheries Development Board as a rural development initiative. Locals will cook traditional Melanau food for you & perform *bermukun*, which involves playing drums, dancing & reciting poetry, & give healing Melanau massages. $$

🏠 **Dalat Homestays** In the small Melanau township of Dalat, some 20km inland from Oya, on the Batang Oya. Express boats from Sibu to Mukah arrive in Dalat. Fishing, sago gathering, taking boat trips & trekking. $$
🏠 **Pantai Harmoni Resort** Km4 Jln Mukah-Oya (4km south of Mukah on coast); ☏ 084 872566. Family-run, simple beach chalet, 2 bedrooms with dbl bed, sitting room & restaurant. $–$$

Where to eat Mukah's old town and new town districts are packed with coffee shops for cheap and charming food. A row of basic kitchens serve Chinese and

11

Malay food in a large open space. For more upmarket food (and mid-range prices) try **JS Seafood** and **River View Restaurant**, both situated near the Tua Pek Kong Temple and serving authentic Melanau food, including tasty *umai*, or **Nibong House** on Jalan Orang Kaya Setia Raja, opposite the Civic Centre. The (halal) **Palm Beach Restaurant** (⏱ *06.30–22.45 last order*) in the Kingwood Resort serves Malaysian and Melanau specialities as well as Western food. In Dalat there are several Chinese coffee shops opposite the riverfront and a Melanau restaurant, **Taku Café**, serving local specialities.

What to see and do There is a new town and an old town in Mukah – the fishing harbour is in the latter. The modern **mosque** and **civic centre** both have emblematic *terendak* (conical Melanau palm-leaf sun-hat) roofs. Melanau traditions are best seen on parade in the **Pesta Kaul**. Held at the beginning of the fishing season (usually April), to appease the spirits, a three-day taboo on leaving and entering the town precedes the festival and feasting. During the *seraheng* procession, food is carried up the Batang Mukah River by canoe – raised on bamboo poles by mask-wearing Melanau. **Fireflies** thrive in the mangroves of Mukah and one prime firefly territory is **Tanjung Pedada**, a cape in **Kampung Pedada**, just across the narrow stretch of river from Mukah town.

The award-winning **Lamin Dana Handicraft Centre** (*Kampung Tellian Tengah, 4km from Mukah town;* ✆ *084 871543*) sprung up from a Melanau performing-arts and youth development project in 1999, aimed at preserving Melanau heritage. In the first two years, 50 weavers were trained. The handicrafts are mostly woven from *sago* fronds. Each of the seven villages involved is focused on one craft industry, and receives 1,000–2,000MYR per month for their produce. The only remaining original **Melanau longhouse**, dating to 1872, is in Kampung Sok, Matu. Vans go there from Daro wharf. Arrange visits through the Mukah Resident's office (✆ *084 872596*). **Kelidieng** are ornately carved wooden burial poles made out of hollowed ironwood (*belian*) tree trunks. One of the finest is in Dalat, opposite the wharf and Chinese temple.

KAPIT AND THE UPPER REJANG The Rejang flows through administrative borders into Kapit Division, a river-ribbed area the size of Switzerland with a population density of less than three people per square kilometre. The Upper Rejang area, extending another 120km between Kapit and Belaga, is one of the last Bornean frontiers for remote, rugged adventure and deeper ethnographic encounters. Within a collection of peaks averaging 1,200m altitude are dozens of rivers – major tributaries of the Rejang flow through the region and provide the main means of transport. Thick carpets of forest are pockmarked from logging, mining and slash-and-burn agriculture – to make way for hill paddy, pepper, rubber, cocoa, fruit and vegetable crops, and increasingly for oil palm plantations. Positioning itself as a 'premier nature destination in the state', the pressure is on to sustain the natural beauty which attracts tourists.

Getting there and away
By boat Express boats run by various companies ply the Rejang daily between Kanowit, Sibu, Song and Kapit, starting as early as 05.30, through to mid-afternoon. The direct Sibu to Kapit boat takes two to three hours. The fare is 20MYR, or a first-class ticket – in a massage chair – is 25MYR. Other boats stop in Kanowit (40-minute trip, 6MYR), Song (2½ hours, 17/22MYR first class). One boat a day goes from Sibu to Belaga at 06.15 (leaving Kapit at 09.30). The journey takes eight hours and costs 35–40MYR.

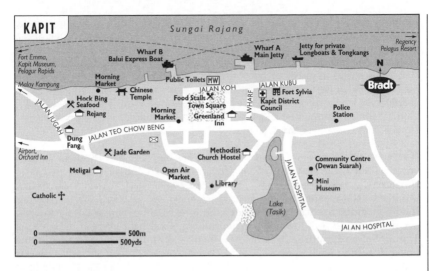

Other practicalities Foreign visitors require a permit to travel beyond Kapit to Belaga or up the Baleh River, so an overnight stay in Kapit town is mandatory except for stays at the Regency Pelagus Resort. One- and two-week permits are issued at the **Kapit Resident's Office** (*9th Floor, New State Office Complex, Beletch Commercial Centre;* ⏰ *08.00–13.00 & 14.00–17.00 Mon–Thu, 08.00–11.45 & 14.15–17.00 Fri, closed Sat/Sun & public holidays*). Take a van from Jalan Airport to reach the office. View and request information via their website (*www.kapitro.sarawak.gov.my*). Belaga is not accessible by boat when water levels are low so services may not operate during the dry season from July to September. Air conditioning in the boats (as on many forms of Malaysian transport) can be icy-cold, so bring a long-sleeved top.

Where to stay There is nothing flashy in Kapit, but there are several clean hotels with air conditioning and hot water showers and a couple with upgraded suite rooms. There is one out-of-town resort, the Regency Pelagus.

Regency Pelagus Resort (40 rooms) ✆ 084 799050/1; e pelagus@tm.net.my or rihresv@tm.net.my; www.theregencyhotel.com.my/ pelagus/. Perched over the river not far from the Pelagus rapids, Pelagus is a wooden longhouse-style resort on the hillside. Wood-panelled rooms, light & fresh furnishings. Speedboat transfers from Kapit organised on reservation. Good base for jungle treks & day tours to nearby longhouses. 6 jungle trails of varying difficulty & a guided night trek. Refreshingly local in style & names. Coffee house Bungai Nuing overlooks the jungle. The Kayan manager takes guests to see people weaving baskets & mending fishing nets. $$, FB $$$$

Greenland Inn (19 rooms) Lot 463–464, Jln Teo Chow Beng; ✆ 084 796388. Rooms & more spacious 'suites' but a bit down the scale. $–$$

Meligai Hotel (46 rooms) Lot 334, Jln Lapangan Terbang (Airport Rd); ✆ 084 796611. 2-star, AC, cable TV, bathroom. For a better room, pay for a suite. Restaurant & music lounge. $–$$

Dung Fang Hotel Lot 510 Jln Temenggong Jugah; ✆ 084 797799. $

Rejang Hotel (18 beds) 28 Jln Temenggong Jugah; ✆ 084 796709. Considered the 'backpackers' of Kapit; rooms have fans. $

Longhouse stays The Kapit Resident's office can give you an up-to-date list of longhouses accepting visitors for day/overnight visits (it often changes). An overnight stay including longboat trip will cost around 320MYR per person, with a minimum of 30MYR extra for meals. Those further upstream from Kapit on the Sungai Tisa, Sungai Kain and Sungai Mujong require overnight stays. One of the guides, Joshua Muda Guna (✆ *019 4676004;* e *joshuamuda@hotmail.com*) is a very switched-on, capable and adventurous guide. As well as standard longhouse stays, he organises trips to places such as Long Singut, a remote Kenyah longhouse on the Sungai Baleh (seven-day/six-night packages for 1,600MYR) and more arduous jungle treks and expeditions to the remote peak of Batu Tiban (12–14 days; physical fitness required), evoked in Redmond O'Hanlon's classic book *Into the Heart of Borneo* (see *Appendix 2*, page 293).

✗ **Where to eat** River prawns and fish dishes are big in Kapit. Try them at mid-priced **Hock Bing Seafood** (*off Jln Temenggong Jugah*) and air-conditioned **Jade Garden** (*Jln Lapangan Terbang, opposite the Meligai Hotel;* ⊕ *lunch & dinner*). **Orchard Restaurant** (*64 Jln Tlong Ung Hong;* ⊕ *09.00–23.00*), is also air conditioned, and has many pork dishes. Cheap coffee shops with good noodles and rice dishes are all over town. There are outdoor food stalls every evening in the **Taman Selera Empurau**, near the Eon Bank, and by day on the first floor of the **Pasar Teresang** town market – a good place to buy fresh food and fruits, sweets and cakes (*kuih*). It is possible to try the Iban cooking style *pansuh* at some local restaurants, though it's best to request ahead: chicken and fish are cooked in bamboo stems over an open fire.

What to see and do

Kapit Kapit is a lively trading centre and transport hub for the upper river regions. Express boats, longboats and steamboats converge on the wharf. Kapit was settled by Charles Brooke as a garrison town in the 1880s, using **Fort Sylvia** (⊕ *10.00–12.00 & 14.00–17.00 Tue–Sun*) to crack down on Iban warriors who were moving upriver to fight other tribes. A peacekeeping ceremony between the Iban and Orang Ulu was held at the fort in 1924. It was originally called Kapit Fort, but Brooke changed the name to honour his wife Ranee Sylvia. Once a district office and courthouse, the fort is now a small museum. More encompassing is the **Kapit Museum** (*Kapit Civic Centre;* ⊕ *09.00–13.00 & 14.00–16.15 Mon–Thu, closes 11.45 Fri*).

Belaga Beyond Kapit and up to Belaga, boat travels on the Rejang and Baleh rivers are the most unique thing to experience – with the greatest chance of traditional Kayan and Kenyah longhouse stays along the riverbanks. It's mandatory to do such trips with a licensed nature guide. Contact the Kapit Resident's office for details. Belaga is the last trading post on the Rejang – it sprang up in the early 1900s when some Chinese traders set up shop to supply goods such as kerosene, salt and cooking utensils to the Orang Ulu people upriver.

Warning There have been reports of alcoholism being rife among Belaga guides; do not use guides unless the operator can promise they will be sober. Women are advised not to travel alone.

Kanowit About 50km southeast of Sibu, Kanowit is the furthest point along the river accessible by road. A small riverside town of 1930s Chinese shop-houses, the main landmark is **Fort Emma**, a 19th-century Brooke-era wooden stockade. The area has one of the greatest concentrations of Iban longhouses in Sarawak, particularly along the Sungai Julau and the Sungai Katibas near Song.

12

Northern Sarawak

The coastline stretching north from Bintulu to Miri is not known for its stunning beaches, but it does have some beautiful coastal geology and vegetation. As oil, petroleum and gas hubs, interest in Bintulu and Miri has traditionally been mostly from business travellers, foreign investors and workers. As such, Sarawak Tourism paints Bintulu as a 'transit point' for the Niah Caves and Miri as a 'gateway' to Gunung Mulu National Park. Sometimes disproportional interest is pinned on these two must-sees to the exclusion of nearly all else. But the often overlooked coastal strip of northern Sarawak has other, quite lovely, national parks. Deep inland towards the Indonesian border, the temperate Kelabit Highlands are a haven for independent trekkers – subsisting on Bario rice and vegetables and living in basic accommodation.

BINTULU

'Boom-town Bintulu' got a real economic boost from the large natural gas and oil deposits found near its shores in the 1970s. Today, the city is a monument to the power of Petronas, the Malaysian government's oil corporation, whose subsidiary – the Malaysia Liquefied Natural Gas Corporation – owns Bintulu's natural gas processing plant, the largest in the world. Annexed as part of Sarawak by James Brooke in 1861, the town of Bintulu grew up along the banks of the Sungai Kemena river, which flows into the South China Sea. Until oil was discovered in the region, Bintulu's port was primarily a centre of the fishing and timber trades, with export wood sent downstream from the forests. Said be the most wonderfully planned city in Sarawak, the city continues to prosper and grow in an independent fashion.

GETTING THERE AND AWAY
By car Bintulu is about 644km north of Kuching, 192km north of Sibu, 214km south of Miri and 124km south of Niah National Park.

By air AirAsia/MAS flights connect Bintulu to Kuching and Kuala Lumpur. The airport is about 20km from town.

By bus There are express buses to Sibu, Miri and Kuching.

GETTING AROUND Local buses leave from the town bus station near the markets off Main Bazaar. Long-distance buses depart from the express bus terminal on Jalan Tun Hussein Onn, 3km north of the civic centre, near Medan Jaya shopping centre. The Express Wharf is off Jalan Masjid.

TOURIST INFORMATION
i Bintulu Information Centre Jln Keppel

WHERE TO STAY The downtown area – along Jalan Keppel and Jalan Abang Galau – runs parallel to the riverbank for over 0.5km where most budget hotels are found. A couple of three-stars are located a few hundred metres out of the CBD (Central Business District) toward the river's entrance and the landscaped area of Bintulu Park City. Contact Sarawak Tourism for help with arranging hotels.

Park City Everly (228 rooms) Lot 3062, Jln Tun Razak; ☎ 086 318888; e reservation.pehb@vhmis.com; www.vhhotels.com. Top business hotel in town, AC, sat TV, deluxe rooms & suites, swimming pool & gym, coffee shop, restaurant & pub. $$$, suite $$$$

Regency Plaza Hotel (161 rooms) 116 Taman Sri Dagang, Jln Abang Galau; ☎ 086 335111; e hotel@plazabintulu.com.my; www.theregency.com.my/plazabintulu. 3-star, sat TV, AC, bath & fridge, swimming pool, sauna & coffee house. $$, suite $$$$

Li Hua 36 Berjaya Commercial Centre, Jln Sultan Iskandar (1km north of town, near civic centre & temple); ☎ 086 335000; e lihuab@po.jaring.my; www.ihuahotelbtu.com. Good value – standard but solid. AC, friendly 1-star with family rooms & suites, coffee house & restaurant, buffet meals 10–15MYR. $$

🏠 **Hoover Hotel** (40 rooms) 92 Jln Keppel; ☎ 086 337166. Standard rooms for low-price bracket, AC, sat TV, fridge, Wi-Fi, coffee house. $

🏠 **Regent Hotel** (45 rooms) Kemena Commercial Centre (4km north); ☎ 086 335511. Edge of town budget hotel recommended in tourism circles, in green surrounds of Tanjung Batu. Coffee house. $
▲ There is also a **campsite** at Tanjung Batu.

✗ WHERE TO EAT

Restaurants/Coffee shops More chic and air-conditioned places with mid-range prices are found in the top hotels (see above for contact details). **M&D's Restaurant** (⊕ *06.00–24.00 daily*) at the Park City Everly has an open kitchen and international food while there are lighter snacks and drinks at its **Luconia Bay Coffee Terrace** (⊕ *10.00–01.00*). The **Kemena Coffee House** (in the Regency Plaza) has good local as well as Western dishes.

Food to go Pantai Ria Food Centre (*2km from city, by the sea;* ⊕ *evenings only*) has stalls. A ten-minute walk from most hotels is the night market *medan pasar malam*. There are many food stalls in the vicinity of the markets and Express Wharf on Main Bazaar.

SHOPPING City Point shopping mall on Jalan Keppel is the most central. The *pasar utama*, central market and *pasar tamu* handicrafts market are held by the riverside under a *terendak* (conical hat)-shaped roof.

OTHER PRACTICALITIES
Banks
$ **Standard Chartered Bank** Jln Keppel
$ **Utama Bank** Nr the jetty area off Jln Masjid

Health and emergency
Police station Jalan Queen, off Jln Keppel

✚ **Bintulu New Hospital** is on Jln Nyabau north of town.

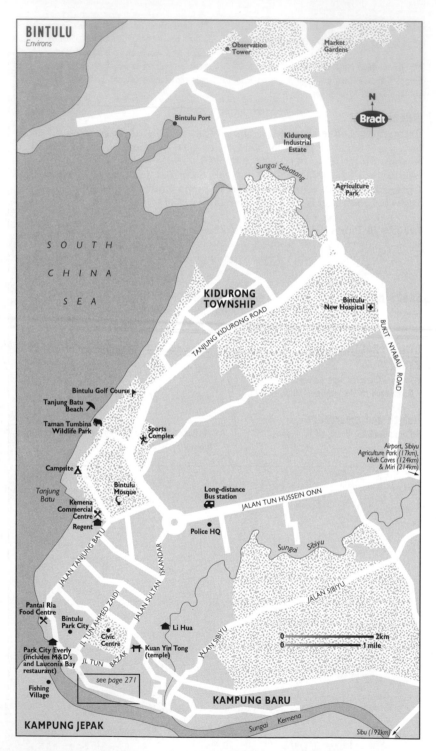

BINTULU
Environs

Observation Tower

Market Gardens

Bradt

Bintulu Port

Kidurong Industrial Estate

Sungai Sebatang

Agriculture Park

S O U T H

C H I N A

S E A

KIDURONG TOWNSHIP

Bintulu New Hospital

TANJUNG KIDURONG ROAD

BUKIT NYABAU ROAD

Bintulu Golf Course

Tanjung Batu Beach

Taman Tumbina Wildlife Park

Sports Complex

*Airport, Sibiyu
Agriculture Park (17km),
Niah Caves (124km)
& Miri (214km)*

Campsite

Tanjung Batu

Kemena Commercial Centre

Bintulu Mosque

Long-distance Bus station

JALAN TUN HUSSEIN ONN

Regent

Police HQ

Sungai Sibiyu

JALAN TANJUNG BATU

JALAN SIBIYU

Pantai Ria Food Centre

Bintulu Park City

JL TUN AHMED ZAIDI

JALAN SULTAN ISKANDAR

Civic Centre

Li Hua

JALAN SIBIYU

Park City Everly
(includes M&D's
and Lauconia Bay
restaurant)

Kuan Yin Tong
(temple)

JL TUN BAZAK

0   2km
0   1 mile

see page 271

Fishing Village

KAMPUNG BARU

KAMPUNG JEPAK

Sungai Kemena

Sibu (192km)

Miscellaneous

Public library Jalan Queen, off Jln Keppel

WHAT TO SEE AND DO Spiritual landmarks include the modern **Bintulu Mosque** *Masjid Assyakirin,* meaning 'gratefulness to God', set in landscaped surrounds on Tanjung Batu headland, and the **Kuan Yin Tong Temple** on Jalan Sultan Iskandar, 2km north of the CBD. **Kampung Jepak**, a traditional Melanau fishing village, is on the other side of Sungai Kemena near the river mouth – take a short ride over on a *bot tambang* riverboat to see fish-drying and sago-processing activities. The **Council Negeri** (State Council) **Monument** in the **Civic Centre** commemorates Sarawak's 1867 convened legislative assembly, and the oldest parliament in Malaysia, composed of five British officers and 18 Malay and Melanau chiefs. The best view is from the **Observation Tower** in Tanjung Kidurong, where you can gaze up the coast along the Bintulu Port area. Two connecting coastal parks, **Taman Tumbina** and **Taman Kidurong** start about 3km north of the town centre from the small headland of Tanjung Batu where there is a beach. Taman Tumbina has a wildlife park with a small zoo, botanical garden and butterfly world. The second-biggest port in Malaysia and an industrial port for agro-food, petrochemical and timber industries, the **Bintulu deep sea port** and container terminal covers an area of 320 acres with a total quay length of nearly 0.5km.

Sports The sports complex in Taman Tumbina parklands has a swimming pool and tennis courts and the **Bintulu Golf Course** is located on the headland of Tanjung Kidurong.

EXCURSION FROM BINTULU

SIMILAJAU NATIONAL PARK Some 30km north of Bintulu on an unsealed road, with no regular bus service, this park lives largely in the shadow of the Niah Caves, but is really a great nature getaway with lovely brackish water beaches, skirted in *kerangas* and rainforest. Stretching 32km up the coast in a 1.5km-wide strip, the park covers an area of over 9,000ha. There is just one main trail with a few possible deviations along the coast to various beaches – where turtles come ashore to lay eggs. You could easily spend a day here. The park is home to saltwater crocodiles and though there have been no attacks reported, it is advisable to be alert and avoid swimming.

Where to stay Park accommodation is disappointing – the chalets (which sleep four) have electricity and running water but not much more. There is also a campsite and barbecue pits. That doesn't necessarily mean seclusion however, and holiday periods can be particularly busy. Accommodation can be booked at the park HQ Registration and Information Desk (there is also a canteen here) (✆ *086 391 284; www.forestry.sarawak.gov.my/forweb/homepage/contact.htm;* ⊕ *08.00–12.30 & 13.30–17.15 daily*), through the Miri office, online, or by calling the park direct.

NIAH NATIONAL PARK

Rising up dramatically behind the small township of Batu Niah, the 388m limestone massif of Gunung Subis dominates the Niah National Park, and hosts the famous archaeological site of the Niah Caves among its huge outcrops. First gazetted as a National Historic Monument in 1958 after the find of a 44,000-year-old skull at the entrance to the caves, 3,100ha of surrounding rainforest and limestone hills were swept into the park's realm when it was created in 1974. Most people visit for the day from either Miri or Bintulu, though the visitors' accommodation facilities are among the better maintained of Sarawak's parks. The discovery of coffins, urns, pottery, paintings, textiles, tools and ornaments in Niah show consistent habitation over thousands of years – the area within and around the caves is full of archaeological, cultural and natural history.

GETTING THERE AND AWAY

By car The Niah National Park HQ are located at Pengkalan Batu, 109km south of Miri and 131km north of Bintulu. The closest town to HQ is Batu Niah, which is also the public transport hub for the caves.

By bus Syarikat Bas Suria has regular bus services from Miri's express bus terminal and from Bintulu to Batu Niah. From there the park office is 3km away. You can

THE GREAT CAVE OF NIAH – A BRIEF HISTORY

Dr Huw Barton

The Great Cave of Niah is enormous by any measure. The floor area of the cave has been calculated at almost 10ha, and in places the majestic cave roof rises 75m above the rubble-strewn floor. As well as being home to multitudes of bats, darting swiftlets (their nests are the famous ingredient of Chinese bird's nest soup) and the occasional snake, it is also the site of human occupation dating back at least 46,000 years. The richness of the deposits at Niah, and the great span of time they encompass, marks the site as one of the most important archaeological sites in southeast Asia.

The site was first excavated by the brilliant but cantankerous Tom Harrisson, a self-trained archaeologist, curator and ethnologist of the Sarawak Museum, who realised the enormous potential of the site and began excavation in 1954. In 1958 came the discovery of a 44,000-year-old human skull at the front of the West Mouth (an area affectionately referred to as 'Hell' – due to the working conditions in the heat of the day!) The skull has since been determined to belong to a 15–17 year old, probably female. Flaked stone and other evidence of human activity were found as well.

Food remains recovered more recently show people had a fairly broad diet, using a wide range of plant and animal foods from the forest and nearby freshwater streams. Recent analysis of bone fragments shows evidence that people were hunting arboreal primates, butchering them on-site, and manufacturing bone tools. A favoured food appears to have been the bearded pig, *Sus barbatus* – still a popular food today. Fabulous preservation of plant remains at Niah has shed new light on ancient diet and foraging knowledge. Charred remains of edible but toxic tubers and nuts have been recovered, indicating a degree of sophistication in food processing not previously believed to occur this early. We have also found evidence that these early foragers knew how to make complex multi-component tools: some of these tools included jagged stingray spines and bone splinters finely worked to make spears or arrows.

Use of the cave changed over time. At one time used occasionally by roaming foragers, it later became a major repository of the dead around 4,000 years ago. At this time, there is evidence for the use of pottery as funerary gifts and burial jars, with later evidence of imported metals, ceramics and glass. Remarkably, even textiles were recovered from some graves. Some of the recovered material is on display at the site museum at Niah Cave, and also in the Sarawak Museum in Kuching.

reach it either by foot – a 45-minute plankwalk along the riverbank – by motorised longboat, or taxi. Tour buses go all the way to HQ.

OTHER PRACTICALITIES The park has a visitor centre and canteen and an extensive network of plankwalks to and throughout the caves. The caves are about a 3km walk from park HQ. A torch and good walking shoes are recommended as the caves are unlit and the plankwalk can be slippery. Conservation fee is 10MYR.

WHERE TO STAY AND EAT

National Park accommodation (9 chalets) ☎ 085 737450. Basic 2-room chalets (4-beds), with attached bathroom, some with AC, plus a 'Forest Hostel' sleeping 16 in 4 rooms, & a 30-site campsite. All have 24hr electricity & piped water, but there are no cooking facilities. Common park facilities include washrooms, a canteen, an AV room & information centre. $

If you choose to stay in Batu Niah, there are some basic lodging houses and coffee shops in this one-street township.

Niah Cave Inn Lot 621, Batu Niah Bazaar; ☎ 085 737 333. TV, AC. $

WHAT TO SEE AND DO The **Great Cave** is just over 3km from HQ along a path buttressed with huge *tapang* trees, *pandanus* plants, orchids and fungi – sightings of monkeys, lizards, butterflies, hornbills and squirrels are likely. The caves' spectacular entrance (West Mouth) is over 60m high and 250m wide – inside, guano collectors gather bat excrement to sell as fertiliser. The walls of the nearby **Painted Cave** feature a set of etchings in red hematite depicting boat journeys of the dead into the afterlife. The wall paintings tie in with the discovery of a number of 'death ships' in the cave – boat-shaped coffins containing human remains and a selection of 'grave goods' considered useful in the afterlife, such as Chinese ceramics, ornaments and glass beads. The death ships date to sometime between AD1 and AD780, although local Penan folklore tells of death-ship burials as late as the 19th century. Some birdwatching enthusiasts come just to witness the sunset 'changing of the guard' which happens when up to half a million swiftlets return to their nests, and the bats swarm out to forage in the forest.

From HQ there are two other well-marked but short trails of 2–3km: the Bukit **Kasut Trail** through rainforest and *Kerangas* forest to the top of a hill; and the **Madu Trail** along the Sungai Subis river through peat and alluvial swamp forest to the base of Bukit Kasut.

MIRI

Determined to shake its reputation as an industrial oil town, Miri has become an important leisure stretch for the expat community in the region, and a weekend playground for escaping Bruneians. If you want a bit of a beach atmosphere before, in between or after backcountry trips, Miri is the best place with its big choice of classy-to-budget hotels and relaxed social buzz. Evolving from the oil slick of its past, Miri's future as a self-made resort town is positively glowing with more coastal condominiums and luxury hotels planned. Sarawak's second metropolis with a population of 300,000, Miri is still enjoying its new-found city status, proclaimed in 2005. People live, eat, work and play well here – the rich cultural infusion is largely Chinese and Iban; Malay and Orang Ulu make up the rest.

12

GETTING THERE AND AWAY

By car Miri is 215km north of Bintulu, and 30km to Kuala Belait in Brunei via the Sungai Tujuh immigration checkpoint, a journey which can take over two hours depending on the queues. Make sure you have passport and money for a visa – there are no ATMs or credit card facilities.

By air Miri's modern airport is a major midway hub in northern Borneo. MAS and AirAsia have several daily flights between Miri and Kuala Lumpur, Kuching and Kota Kinabalu. MASWings (*www.maswings.com.my*) operate rural air services on both Fokker 50s and Twin Otters from Miri to Gunung Mulu National Park, Ba'Kelalan and Bario (Kelabit Highlands), Marudi, Lawas, Limbang and Labuan, Sibu and Bintulu. Most of these 30–50-minute flights cost under 100MYR one-way.

Airlines
✈ **MAS** 1st Floor, Lot 239, Beautiful Jade Centre; ⟍ 085 417315, toll free 1 300 88 3000;

e info@maswings.com.my; www.malaysianailines.com.my

By bus Express air-conditioned buses connect Miri to Kuching, Sibu and Bintulu (Biramas, Suria Bus Express and Borneo Highway Express). They arrive at Miri's edge-of-town express bus terminal, with connecting minibuses to the city's central bus station on Jalan Padang. There are no direct buses between Miri and Brunei. From the Jalan Padang bus station, Miri-Belait bus company run several daily services to Kuala Belait, switching buses at the Sungai Tujuh border checkpoint. Between there and Brunei's capital, there are another two changes of bus – allow for the best part of a day for the whole journey.

By boat Ferries go to and from Kuala Baram, near the Brunei border.

GETTING AROUND Miri is a spread-out town and walking around can be tiring. Buses for the city area and surrounds leave from the central bus station on Jalan Padang, a couple of hundred metres from the visitors information centre on Jalan Melayu. The Taman Selera/Hawaii Beach buses Nos 11/13 go towards the marina, beach and luxury resort area.

TOURIST INFORMATION
ℹ **Visitor Information Centre** Lot 452 Jln Melayu (entry off Jln Padang); ⟍ 085 434181;

e vic-miri@sarawaktourism.com. The national park booking office is at the same office.

Tour operators
Borneo LI-SU Tours ⟍ 012 8509970; e andyson_sulang@yahoo.com.my. Andyson Sulang, ex-park ranger, leads nature conservation tours from

Miri to Niah and the Kelabit Highlands, with mountaineering & trekking, birdwatching, rock climbing, white-water rafting, fishing & diving excursions.

⌂ **WHERE TO STAY** Ever-tougher competition in resort city is pushing standards higher and higher, with prices still available across the board. A new five-star hotel (Convention Hotel) is being built in the Miri Marina Park development.

Upmarket
⌂ **Miri Marriott Resort & Spa** (220 rooms) Lot 779, Jln Temenggong Datuk Oyong Lawai, 2km from city; ⟍ 085 421121; e sales@mirimarriott.com; www.marriott.com. A liveable luxury hotel, spacious well-furnished garden & sea-facing rooms, with

balconies arranged in breezy wings, well away from lobby area. Possibly the best hotel b/fast in Borneo. Large pool, gym, spa, free parking. $$$, suite $$$$$

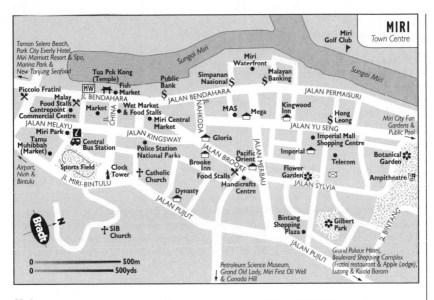

MIRI
Town Centre

Miri Golf Club

Taman Selera Beach, Park City Everly Hotel, Miri Marriott Resort & Spa, Marina Park & New Tanjung Seafood

Sungai Miri

Sungai Miri

Miri Waterfront

Tua Pck Kong (Temple)
Fish Market
Public Bank
Simpanan Nasional
Malayan Banking
JALAN PERMAISURI

Piccolo Fratini
Malay Food Stalls
Centrepoint Commercial Centre
JL BENDAHARA
MW
JALAN BENDAHARA
MAS
Mega
Kingwood Inn
Hong Leong
Miri City Fan Gardens & Public Pool

JALAN MELAYU
Miri Park
Market
Wet Market & Food Stalls
Miri Central Market
JALAN YU SENG

Tamu Muhibbah (Market)
Central Bus Station
JALAN KINGSWAY
Police Station National Parks
Gloria
Pacific Orient
Imperial Mall Shopping Centre
Imperial
Telecom
Botanical Garden

Airport, Niah & Bintulu
Sports Field
Clock Tower
Catholic Church
Brooke Inn
Food Stalls
JALAN BROOKE
JALAN MERBAU
Flower Garden
JALAN SYLVIA
Ampitheatre

JL MIRI-BINTULU
Dynasty
Handicrafts Centre

Bradt
Z
SIB Church
JALAN PUJUT

Bintang Shopping Plaza
Gilbert Park
JL BINTANG

0 — 500m
0 — 500yds

JALAN PUJUT
Petroleum Science Museum, Grand Old Lady, Miri First Oil Well & Canada Hill

Grand Palace Hotel, Boulevard Shopping Complex (Fratini restaurant & Apple Lodge), Lutong & Kuala Baram

Mid-range
The suites of the following hotels cost 500–1,000MYR; standard rooms are at budget prices and deluxe rooms at mid-range.

🏠 **Park City Everly Hotel** (168 rooms) Jln Temenggong Datuk Oyong Lawai; ☎ 085 418888; e reservation.pehm@vhmis.com. More business-oriented than the Marriott, but bright, upbeat, beachside location near Miri Marina. Well-furnished rooms with balcony & Executive Club floor. 4-star. Very affordable Malay & international food at Melinau Terrace Coffee House with in/outdoor dining & entertainment. Shuttle service to city. $$ $$$$

🏠 **Grand Palace Hotel** (125 rooms) KM2 (north of city centre) Pelita Commercial Centre, Jln Miri-Pujut; ☎ 085 428888; e gpalace@po.jaring.my. A big pink hotel in popular shopping/entertainment complex. Family-run 4-star; large rooms with elegant Chinese-style furnishings, free broadband, sat TV,

coffee house & Han Palace Cantonese restaurant, pool terrace. $$, suite $$$$

🏠 **Imperial Hotel** (96 rooms/144 apts) Jln Pos; ☎ 085 431133; e enquiries@imperialhotel.com.my; www.imperialhotel.com.my. In Imperial Mall, stylish rooms & self-catering apt suites, good online promotional rates of up to 40% off. Fitness centre, sauna & swimming pool. $$, suite $$$$

🏠 **Mega Hotel** (293 rooms) Lot 907, Jln Merbau; ☎ 085 432432; e info@megahotel.com.my; www.megahotel.com.my. Standard & deluxe rooms are budget price, large junior & executive suites mid-range. Free Wi-Fi, AC, sat TV, non/s floor, babysitting service, business centre, fitness & sauna, plus its own bakery, coffee house (⏰ 05.00–24.00) Chinese restaurant & pub. $$–$$$

Budget

🏠 **Dynasty Hotel** (130 rooms) Lot 683, Town Centre, Block 9, Jln Pujut-Lutong; ☎ 085 421111; e dyhlmyy@streamyx.com; www.dynastyhotelmiri.com. 3-star, eastern edge of town, comfortable well-equipped rooms, sat TV, AC, 2 non/s floors, coffee house & gym. $$

🏠 **Pacific Orient Hotel** (66 rooms) 49 Jln Brooke; ☎ 085 413333; e ynt@pd.jaring.my. AC, sat TV, fridge, central location, big noisy street. $–$$

Shoestring

🏠 **Gloria Hotel** (42 rooms) 27 Jln Brooke; ☎ 085 416699. AC, sat TV, fridge, bath & shower. $

🏠 **Apple Lodge** (31 rooms) Lot 343–344, Block 7, MCLD, Jln Miri Pujut; ☎ 085 419696. Orang Ulu owned. Clean; varying room standards. $

There are many Orchid-classified hotels for under 100MYR for a double (some less than 50MYR). One of the best is the Brooke Inn.

⌂ **Brooke Inn** (15 rooms) 14 Jln Brooke; ☏ 085 412881. AC, shower, clean & comfortable. Very central. $

✖ **WHERE TO EAT** There are food stalls in streets and at markets everywhere, though the waterfront's messy streets can make it less appealing. Some riverfront restaurants do not display prices, so enquire ahead of eating.

Seafood The open-air **Taman Selera** food park (*3km from city past Marina Park, Jln Temenggong Datuk; bus Taman Selera No 11;* ⊕ *about 17.00–late*) has about 12 stalls serving seafood (by weight), Chinese and Malay dishes at cheap to mid-range prices, outside and under-cover seating overlooking Brighton Beach. On the same stretch (opposite the Miri Marriott) is a cluster of seafood restaurants, with indoor/outdoor seating, where you can pick your fish from the aquarium. The last restaurant is perhaps the best, **New Tanjung Seafood** (*Jln Temenggong Datuk;* ☏ *085 433401*); look out for its big lantern with Carlsberg sign. It serves cheap to mid-range Chinese seafood, game and noodle dishes. A good seafood restaurant in the Miri waterfront vicinity in town is **Yi Hah Hai** (*Jln Bendahara*), with indoor and outdoor seating.

Chinese The **Boulevard Restaurant** (*Boulevard Commercial Centre, not city centre;* ☏ *085 436936*) serves excellent, mid-priced Chinese, favourites with locals. **Dynasty Chinese Restaurant** at the Dynasty Hotel, and the **Han Palace** in the Grand Palace Hotel are good for their air-conditioned environments, big choice and mid-range prices. The Chinese coffee shops on the street-level shop-lots of **Centrepoint commercial centre** have excellent cheap local dishes cooked on the spot – **Tian Tian Café** has lots of *laksa, mee sua, kolok mee* and other noodle dishes. **Lok Thian Restaurant** (*Jln Merbau*) is part of a chain, and makes great fresh buns.

Western and international **Piccolo Fratini** (*off Jln Kubu, heading towards Marina Park;* ☏ *085 430255*) is in a new district, opposite Centrepoint commercial centre. Mediterranean food. There is a bigger **Fratini** in the Boulevard shopping centre (⊕ *lunch & dinner*). The **Boulevard** and the **Bintang** shopping plaza are the places to head for pizza, burgers and other fast-food chains. The **Boulevard commercial centre** also has Japanese and Korean restaurants and a huge **food court** with Chinese, Malay, clay-pot dishes, Western meals, steaks and snacks. **San Francisco Coffee** (with free Wi-Fi) is in the Miri Square shopping complex, and **Coffee Bean** is in the Bintang plaza. A good chain bakery is **Hot Cross Buns** (*Jln Kubu*).

ENTERTAINMENT AND SHOPPING Miri is set out between shopping centres – the most central are the **Imperial Mall** and **Wisma Pelita**; the **Boulevard commercial centre** is to the north of town – the latter two also have nightspots, bars and lounges. There is a **Handicraft Centre** (⊕ *09.00–18.00 daily*) on Jalan Merbau.

OTHER PRACTICALITIES
Emergency
Police Central Police Station, Balai Polis Sentral, Jln Kingsway; ☏ 085 433730/085 433222

Media and communications

✉ **Post office** Corner of Jln Post & Jln Syliva, towards Miri City Fan.

WHAT TO SEE AND DO Miri is rather raffish and relaxed. A spread-out city, it stretches in a thin lip along the estuary of the Sungai Miri for over 2km. Some of the prettiest parts, such as gardens and recreational areas, lie at either end. Though it is billed as a 'resort town', the beach is out of sight from the city centre. The **Marina Park Project** (*www.mirimarina.com*) has involved re-channelling the river to create a 3km canal, along which sits a world-class marina, hotels, harbour, festival park, business and retail park, leisure strip and luxury accommodation. Typical of the new face of Miri, it's a world away from the sometimes grubby town centre. Many attractions lie just out of town. The best 360° view of Miri is from **Canada Hill**, a ridge above town where Miri's '**Grand Old Lady**' – an endearing term for Malaysia's first oil well – struck good in 1910. There's also a **Petroleum Museum** here. On the way up you will see a couple of giant sea horses – Miri's mascot.

About 3km from the city, people stop to gaze and walk around a geological marvel – a cliff face of multi-dimensions and myriad colours known rather unromantically as the **Airport Road Outcrop**, as it was exposed during the road's construction. The large **public park** is near here. Modern Miri is park upon park – underpinning Miri's vision to become a health-resort city. At the city's northern end, the **City Fan** is a 10.5ha green space with promenades, fountains, public pools, amphitheatres, Islamic and Chinese cultural gardens, botanical gardens and IT library. Even the temples are well out of town – the **Lian Hua San** (Lotus Hill) **Temple** is a strange apparition planted in the nouveau residential area of Krokop in 2000. Far more charming is the **Tua Pek Kong Temple** in the old town near the river (*Jln Bendahara*) – the central market, fish market and spice-laden Malay *tamu lama* are all in this area. Orang Ulu people bring all kinds of Bario rice, highland fruit and vegetables, wild ferns and fruit, rattan mats and baskets to the fascinating under-cover **Tamu Muhibbah** and **Tamu Khas** (*opposite the visitor information centre, Jln Padang*).

South of Miri, the **beach** area begins. Near the **Taman Selera** recreational park and children's playground is Brighton Beach. Nine kilometres further on is the **Luak Bay Esplanade** picnic spot.

Diving Miri Reef is a developing dive area – within the 150km² triangle offshore are drop-offs, reefs and shipwrecks. There is good beginner and advanced diving in the patch reefs: 7–22m depth, few currents and visibility of 10–30m. The further out you go, the better it gets. The best local operation to contact is **Tropical Dives** (*Lot 273, Ground Floor, Brighton Centre, Jln Temenggong Datuk Oyong Lawai*; ☏ *085 414300*; e *info@tropical-dives.com; www.tropical-dives.com*).

EXCURSIONS FROM MIRI

You may not even pass through Miri to visit the mountainous area of Sarawak: the Kelabit Highlands, Bario region and the Gunung Mulu National Park. It is however the region's commercial and transport nexus, and the most common departure point for locals and tourists alike heading inland.

MARUDI Marudi is the commercial centre of the Sungai Baram river district. Before there were planes to Gunung Mulu National Park and highland areas, it was a major starting point for river trips to these areas. Some people trek from Marudi to the Kelabit Highlands over four days, or do the 'old-fashioned' river trip starting from Kuala Baram (15km north of Miri) then up the Sungai Baram river

12

to Marudi, where a second boat takes you to Long Terawan. From there you have to charter a longboat to deliver you to the park. The price is restrictive for most people, but it is bound to put some wonder back into the Mulu trip. For overnight stays in Marudi, the **Mount Mulu Hotel** (60 rooms; ☏ *085 756671;* $$) is a one-star, with air conditioning and television.

The waterfalls, rainforest and low-lying peaks of the **Lambir Hill National Park** are the closest green lung to Miri, 30km south of the city along the Miri–Bintulu road. There are over a dozen trails, from 20-minute walks to the 7km Pancur Waterfall walk, and 6km Summit Trail to Bukit Lambir. The 25m **Latak Waterfalls** is a popular bathing spot, less than 200m from park HQ. There is basic park accommodation (☏ *085 491030*) here. Local buses run from the park to Batu Niah caves and Bintulu.

LOAGAN BUNUT NATIONAL PARK Some 120km southeast of Miri via Beluru, the park centres on Sarawak's largest natural lake, which sometimes dries up into an expanse of cracked mud, surrounded by mixed peat swamp forest. There are many wading birds, reptiles and small mammals here. The lake is fished by Berawan people, with whom you can charter rides on the lake and Baram River (60MYR per hour for 4 people). There's a forest hostel with seven bunk beds, small canteen, and generator electricity from 06.00–24.00. A Berawan family run the **Mutiara Hostel** (☏ *011 292164 or reserve via Miri's national park office*), with 9 twin bedrooms, simple cooking facilities, and floating grocery nearby. Buses from Miri go to Lapok Bridge, 15km before the park HQ. Head to the coffee shops to arrange a lift, or arrange with the Mutiara Hostel.

GUNUNG MULU NATIONAL PARK

Deep in the northern Sarawak interior is an isolated area of rivers and mountains, bordered on the eastern side by the Tama Abu Range – which faces Kalimantan's

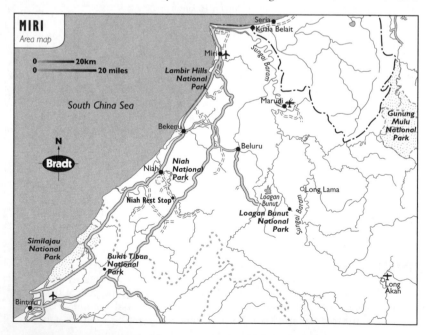

Apo Duat Range across the Indonesian–Malaysian border. The World Heritage Site of Gunung Mulu National Park is part of a corridor of lowland rainforest criss-crossed by rivers and streams and surrounded by peaks and pinnacles. The 53,000ha park is overseen by three mountains – Gunung Mulu, Gunung Api and Gunung Benarat – and contains the largest limestone cave system in the world, formed from thousands of years of erosion. Since a National Geographic expedition started in 1977, over 300km of caves have been surveyed, though it is believed that there could be at least twice as many more. Only four of the 25 caves and passages discovered are open to the public.

Within the park, there are 17 different habitat types including primary lowland rainforest, limestone forest, alluvial forest, tropical heath forest, peat swamp and riparian forest. Between altitudes of 35m and 2,375m, the park contains a staggering 3,500 plant species, 4,000 types of fungi, 80 mammals, 270 birds, 130 reptiles and amphibians, 50 fish types and 2,000 different bugs, beetles and butterflies. Like Kinabalu Park it's an entomologists dream, with hundreds of distinctive insect species including stick insects (*Phasmids*), camouflaged crawlies and butterflies (including *Trogonoptera brookiana* – Brooke's birdwing butterfly).

Indigenous people were the first naturalists of the region. Penan and Berawan people lived in the area for centuries, hunting and gathering. In the 1920s a Berawan rhino hunter, Tama Nilong, discovered the southwest ridge of Gunung Mulu and opened the way for its successful ascent. Nilong led South Pole explorer Lord Shackleton and an Oxford University expedition to the summit in 1932. The National Geographic Society subsequently lobbied for the creation of a national park there in 1976 – the 544km² area was opened to visitors in 1985. Listed as a World Heritage Site in December 2000, this is one UNESCO nature site where the negative effects are on show just as much as positive ones. Threats to the environment other than logging include pollution from locals, tourist hordes and slack tour companies.

GETTING THERE

By plane There are a couple of daily flights in both directions between Miri and Mulu, and one between Kota Kinabalu and Mulu, though none which make a comfortable day trip possible. It is best to check the latest schedules with the new carrier MASWings.

By boat It's an eight-hour river trip leaving Kampung Kuala Baram (15km north of Miri), and heading along the Baram River to Marudi, where a second boat takes you to Long Terawan. From there you have to hire a longboat to deliver you to the park.

OTHER PRACTICALITIES There is quite a lot of red tape around getting to Gunung Mulu. All visitors must be accompanied by a guide, making it mandatory to book a package through a tour operator who takes care of the three necessary **permits**: one from the national parks, another from the Resident's Office and the final one a police clearance. You can check directly with the Miri office of National Parks and Wildlife (✆ 085 436637), or on Sarawak Park's website (*www.sarawakforestry.com/htm/snp.asp*). National Park **entrance fees** are paid on arrival at the HQ (⊕ 08.00–17.00 daily). Single entry costs 10MYR, a five-entry pass 40MYR. Students, senior citizens and disabled persons get 50% off and children aged six and under go free. The park has no ATM or credit card facilities so you must carry cash. Transport within the park is by longboat, van or foot with all but the national park lodgings 3km from park HQ.

12

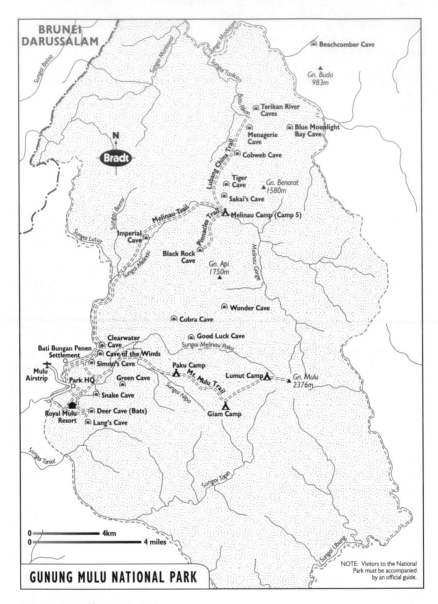

Map labels:

BRUNEI DARUSSALAM

Bradt

N

Beachcomber Cave

Gn. Buda 983m

Terikan River Caves

Menagerie Cave

Blue Moonlight Bay Cave

Cobweb Cave

Tiger Cave

Gn. Benarat 1580m

Sakai's Cave

Melinau Camp (Camp 5)

Imperial Cave

Black Rock Cave

Gn. Api 1750m

Wonder Cave

Cobra Cave

Good Luck Cave

Clearwater Cave

Bati Bungan Penen Settlement

Cave of the Winds

Simon's Cave

Paku Camp

Lumut Camp

Gn. Mulu 2376m

Mulu Airstrip

Park HQ

Green Cave

Snake Cave

Deer Cave (Bats)

Lang's Cave

Royal Mulu Resort

Giam Camp

Lubang China Trail

Melinau Trail

Pinnacles Trail

Mt. Mulu Trail

Melinau Gorge

Sungai Bunut

Sungai Lutut

Sungai Melinau

Sungai Melinau Paku

Sungai Nipa

Sungai Tapin

Sungai Ubong

Sungai Taniol

Sungai Belait

Sungai Mentawai

Sungai Tanikan

Batu Pikan

0 ____ 4km
0 ____ 4 miles

NOTE: Visitors to the National Park must be accompanied by an official guide.

GUNUNG MULU NATIONAL PARK

WHERE TO STAY AND EAT There are limited accommodation choices in the Gunung Mulu park which is good news for nature, but the options fall short on several levels. Take any extras you may require, as shopping for food or other things is very limited and there is no self-catering accommodation, so you are captive to the food on offer.

Royal Mulu Resort (188 rooms) ☏ 085 790100; e sales@royalmuluresort.com; www.royalmuluresort.com. Despite the grand name, these wood-panelled chalets are rather dated and unstylish. Average buffet & menu food, drink & food prices are relatively high as are other costs (internet etc). If you don't like the sound of karaoke in the jungle, this might not be for you. 3km (30–40min walk) to the park. Lots of activities & traditional treatments at the spa. 2-night packages inc FB. A basic café is 50m away – noodles & Western b/fasts 5–10MYR. $$$

⌂ **Asia Budget Holidays** (4 huts) www.asiabudgetholidays.com. Little huts run by budget operator, on the littered river bank opposite. The food is terrible. Price includes 3 meals with AC or fan. $

⌂ **National park accommodation** ✆ 085 433561; e enquiries@mulupark.com; www.mulupark.com. By far the best for location – at the entrance of the park. Near to walks & no need to pay extra for longboat transfers. Various longhouse & chalet rooms, dbl/sgl en-suite bathroom, AC or fans, plus a 21-bed hostel dormitory with fans & bedlinen (but not towels) & lockers for luggage. Cheap basic local & Western food at **Café Mulu**. Reservation essential. $

WHAT TO DO AND SEE It is worth taking one cave trip as well as a longer jungle trek or river safari to experience the incredibly beautiful forest world. Freedom to enjoy the park in a more independent manner is difficult due to a highly bureaucratised park service. I found that the best way to enjoy the area was to see past the caves and enjoy the rainforest which houses them, and the traditional people who have lived there.

Caves All caves are reached along solid timber-plank walks, and have eco-lit cement paths through them. The 3km duckboard walk through rainforest to reach **Deer Cave** and neighbouring **Lang's Cave** is a lovely experience in itself, passing peat swamp, alluvial flats, streams and some spectacular limestone outcrops. Two-hour return treks led by park guides leave daily at 13.45 and 14.30 from park HQ. **Clearwater Cave** and **Cave of the Winds** are reached from park HQ by longboat along the Melinau River in about 15 minutes (27MYR per person return), or along the almost 4km Moonmilk Walk which hugs the riverbanks much of the way. Park guides lead tours to the Cave of the Winds at 09.45 and 10.30 from the entrance. The most impressive for stalactites and other formations is Lang's Cave, but the most amazing overall for its size and cavernous pit is Deer Cave, *Gua Rusa*. At a staggering 2km in length it is the largest cave passage in the world. Its main chamber would have enough room for five St Paul's cathedrals!

Caving Speak with the park HQ or a tour organiser about adventure caving at Mulu. A park brochure on this subject outlines eight cave escapades from beginner to advanced level, lasting from 45 minutes to ten hours. Some popular caves have been fitted with fixed ropes on the short descents and traverses, but you are advised to bring your own equipment for anything beyond that. The **Sarawak Chamber** – on the way to Gunung Api – is compared to an aircraft hanger which would house 40 Boeing 747s. The day trip starts at 07.30, following the Summit Trail for about three hours.

Trekking There is no doubt that trekking – away from the headquarters and hotels – is the best way to feel the wonder of the park's nature and to get up close to the wildlife. There are many treks in the park, some which require a guide and some which can be done independently. Inform park officers before you do an unguided walk as they are aware of weather conditions, including dangerously high water levels. Unguided treks include the four-hour **Paku Waterfall** through rainforest to a good swimming spot and the three-hour **Long Lansat River Walk** (180MYR for the longboat return transfer, 3 people minimum). The day walk to 'Camp 1' (guided) follows part of the **Mulu Summit Trail** and concludes at one of the camps used during the 1977 Royal Geographical Society expedition. The **Summit** (guided) trek to the top of solitary-standing **Gunung Mulu** (2,376m) – Sarawak's second-highest peak – is a 24km climb, over two to three

12

nights with lodgings in forest huts with basic cooking facilities (park guide costs 1,000MYR for 1–5 people). *En route* to Gunung Api (1,750m) the **Pinnacles** is a 50m-high series of razor-shaped limestone outcrops, pointing skyward and interlinked with several caves. This tough (and guided) climb requires at least one overnight stay at Melinau Camp ('Camp 5'). Most people will stay two nights; it depends on fitness levels. The first day's trekking takes in visits to a couple of Mulu's caves. Lodgings consist of sleeping mats in five open rooms, a self-catering kitchen (cooking equipment and utensils provided) and a dining room. You have to carry all of your own food, a sleeping bag and appropriate clothing. It costs 250–800MYR, depending on numbers. Accommodation costs 22MYR per person per night; park guide 400MYR for one to five people; longboat return 370MYR for a group of one to four.

The popular tour-operated **Headhunters' Trail** combines 15km of deep jungle trekking over two days with longboat journeys and an optional longhouse stay, along a route taken by Kayan headhunting parties who paddled up the Melinau River to Melinau Gorge before launching raids against the people of the Limbang area. This trip can also be done from Limbang to Mulu Park HQ. Another option is to add a night and include the Pinnacles climb (from Camp 5) in the trip.

Longboat safaris A couple of trips visit Penan settlements along the Sungai Tutoh and Sungai Melinau rivers. These are very prescriptive though, so if you prefer to explore more independently then take your own day trip on the rivers.

KELABIT HIGHLANDS

The isolation of the Kelabit Highlands did not save it from the snowballing appropriation of Sarawak territory by Rajah Brooke, and his corps claimed it in 1911. It was, however, one of the only Bornean regions which didn't fall into Japanese hands during World War II. Allied troops led by Tom Harrisson, the future curator of the Sarawak Museum in Kuching, had bases in the area. During the Konfrontasi with Indonesian militants in the 1960s, people from settlements near the Indonesian border fled further inland and **Bario** came into existence. Geographical isolation continued to play a big hand in shaping its culture – there was very little in the way of telecommunications or reliable power sources until early 2000. There are still no paved roads. All this means a great sense of remoteness and peace for the highland trekker or visitor. The rounded, velvet upholstered peaks fall off to valleys of temperate crops – Bario rice, oranges, pineapples, highland coffee, and sugar cane – between villages and longhouse settlements of Kelabit, Kenyah, Kayan and Penan peoples. Hopefully the area will retain its secluded charm with the onset of tourism and technology.

GETTING THERE AND AWAY MASWings (*www.maswings.com.my/route.html*) have three direct flights daily each way between Miri and Bario, and one flight to Ba'kelalan; two flights either way between Marudi and Bario; one daily flight each way between Bario and Ba'kelalan; and one between Ba'kelalan and Lawas. Check full updated schedules and fares on the website.

WHERE TO STAY/EAT A good website with listings and online booking for several lodges and homestays (and guides) is www.ebario.com. All the lodgings are cheap: some offer packages of 50MYR a day for airport transfer, bed and three meals – 30–40MYR extra for a guide; others are rooms only for about 20MYR per person with lots of options for guided activities. The most recommended are **Nancy Harris Homestay** (10 rooms), **De Plateau Lodge** (8 rooms) and the very basic

Barview Lodge (1 room). **Tarawe's Lodge** (7 rooms) is right in Bario town, with satellite television, back-up solar power and electricity from 18.00 to 23.00.

OTHER PRACTICALITIES

Climate At 1,000m above sea level, average day temperatures are usually between 21 and 26°C, whereas nights can be as cool as 15°C. Walking conditions can be muddy, with many leeches, and you need good shoes and protective clothing including leech socks.

Electricity and communications The town runs on a diesel generator boosted by solar power. A UNESCO-backed engineering project has helped set up the E-Bario Telecentre – a cyber café – which is open about three days a week, with phones and internet provided via solar-powered VSAT.

Shops Bario's town centre has just a row of small bazaars, coffee shops and grocery stores. Sundries are more expensive because everything is flown in.

WHAT TO SEE AND DO

Treks and walks Most of the Bario highland treks follow the network of muddy trails and dirt roads that link the community longhouses and villages, so expect to share the trails with locals on foot and on bike, and the odd buffalo. The treks take in the Bario valley area, longhouse settlements, local markets, rice paddy, and some primary and secondary rainforest. Organised trips of four to seven days from Miri stay in longhouses and jungle camps but you can also organise your guide and accommodation independently in either Bario or Ba'kelalan.

Note that women travellers are said to be in safe hands in Bario where there is not the same problem with alcohol among guides as in Belaga region. Walks include Bario to Pa Ukat and Pa Lungan, four to five hours each way with a stay at the Pa Lungan longhouse. The hardy trek to the small settlement of Ba'Kelalan is two days – some trails go via Pa Rupai in Kalimantan.

Mountaineering The Kelabit Highlands make for some of the most challenging non-national park climbing in Borneo – the region is flanked by Sarawak's highest mountain, Gunung Murud (2,423m) – the five–six-hour trail goes from Bario through a couple of longhouse settlements. Considered more tricky is Batu Lawi (2,043m).

LIMBANG AND LAWAS

Separated by a section of Brunei, Limbang Division's two main towns are typical border-town thoroughfares – both have track records as small-scale sin-city destinations full of sleazy pubs, massage parlours and prostitution – at the centre of timber, agricultural and oil palm industries. It is rare to hear Sarawak Tourism allude to these two towns, other than as transit points. Lawas sits the prettier, bound by forest and river on one side and Brunei Bay to the northwest.

GETTING THERE

By car Lawas and Limbang are near-border checkpoints with Brunei and Lawas about 20km to the Merapok-Sindumin checkpoint into Sabah. Limbang is two hours' drive from Miri.

By air MASWings have flights from Limbang and Lawas to Kota Kinabalu and to Miri and one daily flight between the two towns.

By bus Express buses run to Brunei, Kota Kinabalu and Miri.

WHERE TO STAY If you are passing through Limbang, the most recommended lodging is the **Purnama Hotel** (*Jln Buangsiol;* \ *085 216700;* $) where a deluxe costs just 3MYR more than a standard room; in Lawas, **Mega Inn** (15 rooms; *1 Tingkat, Lot 152, Jln Muhibbah;* \ *085 283888*) has rooms with air conditioning, satellite television, fridge and bathroom.

Appendix I

LANGUAGE

A good dictionary for reference is the *Periplus Pocket Malay Dictionary* (available online from www.peripluspublishinggroup.com for about €5). Berlian are another publisher (Malaysian) of good Bahasa Melayu-Bahasa Inggeris dictionaries.

PRONUNCIATION Vowels differ from English pronunciation but words are relatively phonetic and consistent. Consonant sounds are mostly the same as English, with a couple of exceptions.

a	as in father or calm
e	there are two e sounds, a low sound like a in about (eer); and high sound like e in met, lend
i	as in fit, win
o	as in ok or note
u	as in put or could
sy	sounds like sh as in shoot (also applies to English words used widely in Malaysia, eg. 'fashion' is spelt *fesyen* to bring it in line with standard Malay pronunciation)
c	ch as in chain/cheese
sy	sh as in shut
ng	sounds like ny – banyan/oignon

BASIC GRAMMAR

- There is no verb 'to be' in Malaysian. The word saya means 'I', 'me' and 'my'.
- There is also no word for 'is' in Malay, so for example *apa nama anda* ('What is your name?') literally means 'What name you?'
- There are no gender prounouns – *dia* means both he and she …
- Bahasa Malaysia – commonly referred to as BM - is an *agglutinative* language – a word can be changed simply by adding various prefixes and suffixes to root words, both nouns and verbs. Eg: Makan is the verb to eat, and can become memakan – eating/is eating … dimakan (eaten), and the noun makanan – food.
- Plurals are formed by repetition though sometimes with slight variations: *rumah-rumah* (houses) from *rumah* (house) and *gunung-gunang* (mountains) from *gunung* (mountain)

VOCABULARY
Greetings

English	Malay	English	Malay
Hello	hello	Good evening	selamat petang
Goodbye	selamat tinggal	Welcome	selamat dating
Good morning	selamat pagi	See you again	jumpa lagi
Good afternoon	selamat tengahari	(literally 'meet again')	

Basic vocabulary

English	Malay	English	Malay
Please	*tolong*	I am from England	*saya datang dari England*
Thank you	*terima kasih*	How are you?	*apa khabar?*
You are welcome	*sama sama*	I am fine	*khabar baik terima kasih,*
yes	*ya*		or simply *baik*
no	*tidak* – also means 'not'.	Do you understand?	*faham anda?*
	Tak is an informal	I don't understand	*saya tidak faham*
	abbreviation.	Excuse me	*maafkan saya*
What is your name?	*apa nama anda*	you	*anda*
My name is	*nama saya/*	we/us/our	*kita*
(eg: Tamara)	*saya Tamara*	they/their	*mereka*
Where are you from?	*kamu datang dari mana?*	Where is the toilet?	*tandas di mana?*

Questions

English	Malay	English	Malay
How?	*bagaimana?*	Who?	*siapa?*
What?	*apa?*	How much?	*berapa?*
Where?	*di mana?*	How long?/	*berapa lama?*
What is it/this?	*apa ini?*	How long will it	
Which?	*yang mana?*	take?	*berapa lama?*
When? (also 'if')	*bila?*	How far?	*berapa jauh?*
Why?	*mengapa?* or *apa sebab?*		

Numbers

English	Malay	English	Malay
one	*satu*	11	*sebelas*
two	*dua*	12	*dua belas*
three	*tiga*	13	*tiga belas* etc
four	*empat*	20	*dua puluh*
five	*lima*	21	*dua puluh satu* etc
six	*enam*	30	*tiga puluh* etc
seven	*tujuh*	99	*sembilan puluh sembilan*
eight	*lapan*	100	*seratus*
nine	*sembilan*	1,000	*seribu*
ten	*sepuluh*		

Time

English	Malay	English	Malay
What time is it?	*pukul berapa sekarang*	tomorrow	*esok*
It is…am/pm	*Sekarang pukul… pagi/*	yesterday	*semalam* or *kelmarin*
	malam	morning	*pagi*
eg: it is 7am/7pm	*Sekarang pukul tujuh pagi/*	evening	*waktu malam/petang*
	tujuh malam	day	*hari*
today	*hari ini*	month	*bulan*
tonight	*malam ini*		

Days of the week

Monday	*Isnin*	Friday	*Jumaat*
Tuesday	*Selasa*	Saturday	*Sabtu*
Wednesday	*Rabu*	Sunday	*Ahad*
Thursday	*Khamis*		

Months

English	Malay	English	Malay
January	*Januari*	July	*Julai*
February	*Februari*	August	*Ogos*
March	*Mac*	September	*September*
April	*April*	October	*Oktober*
May	*Mei*	November	*November*
June	*Jun*	December	*Disember*

Public transport

English	Malay	English	Malay
in 30 minutes	*dalam masa 30 minit*	tour bus	*bas persiaran*
car	*kereta*	bus station	*stesen* or *perhentian bas*
taxi	*teksi*	airport	*lapangan terbang*
minibus	*bas mini*	fare	*tambang*
boat	*perahu*		

Directions

English	Malay	English	Malay
to	*ke*	to the left	*kiri*
from	*dari*	to the right	*kanan*
here	*sini*	north	*utara*
there	*sana*	south	*selatan*
Can you help me?	*bolehkah anda tolong saya?*	east	*timur*
Where is…?	*di manakah…?*	west	*barat*
Where would you like to go?	*anda hendak ke mana?*	behind	*di belakang*
I would like to go…	*saya hendak ke…*	in front of you	*di hadapan anda*
Can you give me the address of…?	*bolehkah kamu beri saya alamat untuk…?*	straight	*ke hadapan*
How far is it from here?	*berapakah jauhnya dari sini?*	near	*dekat*
		far	*jauh*

Road signs

English	Malay	English	Malay
stop	*berhenti*	exit	*keluar*
toll	*tol*	street	*jalan*
enter	*masuk*		

Other signs

English	Malay	English	Malay
open	*buka* or *terbuka*	level	*aras*
closed	*tutup*	toilets	*tandas*
floor	*tingkat*	danger	*bahaya*

Food

English	Malay	English	Malay
food	*makanan*	What would you like to drink/eat?	*anda hendak minum apa/ makan apa?*
eat	*makan*		
drink	*minum* (v), *minuman* (n)	Do you have any vegetarian dishes?	*anda ada makanan vegetarian* or *anda ada makanan sayu sayuran?*
menu	*menu*		
drinks price list	*harga minuman*		
food price list	*harga makanan*	Please can I have…?	*boleh saya …?*
I am a vegetarian	*saya vegetarian*	want	*mahu*

English	Malay	English	Malay
don't want	*tak mahu*	Please bring the bill	*tolong bawa/bawakan bil*
a lot/plenty/many	*banyak*	hot (temperature)	*panas*
a little	*sedikit*	hot (spicy)	*pedas*
more	*lebih banyak labi*	cold	*sejuk*
less	*kurang*	sweet	*manis*
without	*tanpa*	sour	*masam*

Basics

bread	*roti*	salt	*garam*
cheese	*keju*	pepper	*lada*
rice	*nasi*	sugar	*gula*
noodles	*mee*	cake	*kuih* or *kueh*
oil	*minyak*	curry	*kari*
sago	*sagu*		

Fruit

fruit	*buah*	mango	*buah mangga*
apples	*epal*	mangosteen	*buah manggis*
coconut	*kelapa*	oranges	*limau manis*
bananas	*pisang*	lime	*kapur limau nipis*
lemon	*limau* or *lemon*		

Vegetables

mixed vegetables	*sayur campur*	broccoli	*brokoli*
garlic	*bawang putih*	potato	*ubi kentang*
onion	*bawang*	yam	*ubi keladi*
carrot	*lobak merah*	eggplant	*terung*
cabbage	*kubis*		

Fish

fish	*ikan*	prawns/shrimp	*udang*

Meat

beef	*daging lembu*	pork	*daging babi*
chicken	*daging ayam*		

Condiments

chilli	*cabai*	chilli paste	*sambal*
shrimp paste	*sambal belacan*	sauce	*sos*

Drinks

water	*air*	alcohol	*minuman keras* or
fruit juice	*jus*		*alkohol*
coffee	*kopi*	wine	*wain*
tea	*teh*	rice wine	*tuak*
milk	*susu*	beer	*bir minuman*

Shopping

English	Malay	English	Malay
I'd like to buy…	*saya hendak beli…*	It's too expensive	*mahal*
How much is it?	*berapa harga ini?*	cheap	*murah*
Do you have…?	*anda ada…?*	more	*lebih lagi*
I'm just looking	*saya pandang*	less	*kurang*

Can you give it to me a bit cheaper?	*Boleh bagi saya murah sikit?*	rural market	*tamu*
		night market	*pasar malan*
Market	*pasar*		

Communications

English	Malay	English	Malay
I am looking for…	*saya ingin mencari…*	post office	*pos*
I wish to go to …	*saya ingin pergi ke …*	telephone	*telefon*
bank	*bank*	mobile phone	*hand phone* (HP)

Emergency

English	Malay	English	Malay
Help!	*tolong!*	police	*polis*
I'm lost	*saya hilang*	fire	*api*
Leave me alone	*tinggalkan saya sendirian*	ambulance	*ambulans*
		hospital	*hospital*
		doctor	*doktor*
		I am ill/in pain	*saya sakit*
		thief	*pencuri*

NB If you are trying to get rid of peddlers, it suffices to say *tak mahu*, meaning 'I don't want it'.

Health/Medical

English	Malay	English	Malay
prescription	*preskripsi*	nausea	*rasa hendak muntah* or *rasa muul*
medicine	*ubat*		
pharmacy	*farmasi*	headache	*(sakit) kepala*
painkiller	*ubat sakit*	stomach ache	*(sakit) perut*
antibiotics	*antibiotik*	fever	*demam*
antiseptic	*antiseptik*	asthma	*asma*
I am ill	*saya sakit*	epilepsy	*epilepsi*
I have…	*sakit*	diabetes	*diabetes* or *kencing manis*
diarrhoea	*cirit* or *cirit-birit*	allergic	*alergi*

Other useful words

English	Malay	English	Malay
my	*saya punya*	forest	*hutan* or *rimba*
mine	*kepunyaan saya*	beach	*pantai*
yours	*kepunyaanmu* or *kepunyaan tuan*	shop	*kedai*
		room	*bilik*
white person	*orang putih*	island	*pulau*
and/but	*dan/tetapi*		

Appendix 2

FURTHER INFORMATION
BOOKS
General history/reference
Bellwood, P *Prehistory of the Indo-Malaysian Archipelago* Academic Press, 1986. 'Landmark work in southeast Asian archeology and prehistory'. Peter Bellwood is Professor of Archaeology at the School of Archaeology and Anthropology, Australian National University.

Payne, R *The White Rajahs of Sarawak* Oxford University Press, 1960.

Runciman, S *The White Rajahs: A History of Sarawak from 1841 to 1946* Cambridge University Press, 1960.

Saunders, G E *A History of Brunei* Routledge, 2002.

Turnbull, M C *A History of Malaysia, Singapore and Brunei* Allen & Unwin, Australia, 1989. Revised sub-edition.

Wallace, A R *The Malay Archipelago: The Land of the Orang-Utan and the Bird of Paradise. A Narrative of Travel, with Studies of Man and Nature.* London, 1869. Newer editions by various publishers. The legendary Alfred Rusell Wallace's defining work from his travels around the Malay Archipelago. Stanfords Books (www.stanfords.co.uk) have recently republished this as part of their Travel Classics series.

Historic memoirs/biographies
Brooke, C *Ten Years in Sarawak* London, 1866. Available online as a Google book (*http://books.google.com/books?id=61oLAAAAIAAJ&printsec=frontcover&dq=Charles+Brooke*).

Brooke, Ranee M *My Life in Sarawak* Oxford University Press, Singapore, 1913 (reprint 1986).

Brooke, Ranee S *Sylvia of Sarawak: An Autobiography* Hutchinson, 1936, and *Queen of the Headhunters* Oxford University Press, London 1970. The two-volume autobiography of the last Ranee of Sarawak.

Eade, P *Sylvia, Queen of the Headhunters: An Outrageous Woman and Her Lost Kingdom* Weidenfeld & Nicolson, 2007. A biography of Lady Sylvia Brooke.

Keith, A N *Three Came Home* Mermaid Books, London 1955.

Keith, A N *Land Below the Wind* Michael Joseph, London 1958.

Keith, A N *White Man Returns* Mass, Little Brown and Company, Boston 1951.

Reece, R H W *The Name of Brooke: The End of White Rajah Rule in Sarawak* Oxford University Press, South East Asia, 1982.

Culture
Ave, J B and King, V T *People of the Weeping Forest: Tradition and Change in Borneo* Leiden, National Museum of Ethnology, 1986. An informative introduction to the region's contemporary cultures.

Davis, W *Nomads of the Dawn: The Penan of the Borneo Rainforest* Pomegranate, 1995. Wade Davis is an anthropologist/ethnobotanist.

Geddes, W R *Nine Dayak Nights* Oxford University Press, 1985. Anthropologist Geddes spent two years in a remote inland village of Sarawak after World War II.

Hose, C and McDougall, W *The Pagan Tribes of Borneo* 1912 (reprinted Oxford University Press, USA 1993). Charles Hose spent 24 years as a civil officer under James Brooke's rajah-ship – mostly in Baram but also in Rejang District – and McDougall was part of the Cambridge anthropological expedition, in Baram area, in 1898. The magnum opus of ethnology can be read as an e-book.

Jones, L V *The Population of Borneo: A Study of the Peoples of Sarawak, Sabah and Brunei*; Athlone Press, 1966.

King, V T *The Peoples of Borneo* Blackwell, 1993. A pace-setting anthropological history.

Lasimbang, Rita and Moo-Tan, Stella eds *An Introduction to the Traditional Costumes of Sabah* Natural History Publications in association with Department of Sabah Museum, 1997

Sather, C *The Bajau Laut: Adaptation, History and Fate in a Maritime Fishing Society of South-eastern Sabah* (South-East Asian Social Science Monographs) Oxford University Press. Interesting cultural and historic portrait of the Bajau Laut peoples.

Travel literature

Hansen, E *Stranger in the Forest: On Foot Across Borneo* 1988, reprinted in 2001 by Methuen, London/Vintage Books, USA. The best classic travel literature on Borneo – an account of Hansen's 4,000km of tripping by foot across Borneo, in the company of Penan hunter-gatherers in 1976.

Hansen, E *Orchid Fever: A Horticultural Tale of Love, Lust and Lunacy* Vintage Books, 2001. Hansen brings his wit to our fascination with orchids, with some of the action set in Borneo.

Hatt, J *The Tropical Traveller: An Essential Guide to Travel in Hot Climates* Penguin Travel Library, London, 1982. Good background on travel in sticky places.

Maugham, S *Borneo Stories* Heinemann Educational Books, Kuala Lumpur 1976. A collection of stories about expatriate Englishmen and women in exotic settings. Also included in his *Collected Short Stories*.

Munan, H *Culture Shock! A Guide to Customs and Etiquette, Borneo* Times Books International, Singapore, 1988 (revised 1992, reprinted 1996). A personal, engaging account of expat life in Borneo, social etiquette, customs and insider views on subjects as varied as 'Do You Speak Bahasa?', 'Bornean Social Circles' and 'Lo! The Cute Native'. The author was born in Switzerland, brought up in New Zealand and moved to Sarawak in 1965 where she continues to work as a journalist and cultural historian.

O'Hanlon, R *Into the Heart of Borneo* Salamander Press, Edinburgh, 1984. An account of a journey made in 1983 into the mountains of Batu Tiban on the Sarawak–West Kalimantan border, with James Fenton.

St John, S *Life in the Forests of the Far East* Elder Smith, London, 1862.

St John, S *Thirteen Years of Spencer St John's Travels in North and Western Borneo* Elder Smith, London, 1862.

Wassner, J *Espresso with the Headhunters: A Journey Through the Jungles of Borneo* Summersdale, Australia, 2001. A light but personal account of travels in Sarawak, by a Sydney advertising executive turned writer.

Natural history If your interests lie in flora and the fauna, it's worth checking the list of titles published by Sabah-based **Natural History Publications**. The **Sabah Society** (*Kota Kinabalu;* ✆ *088 250443; www.sabahsociety.com*), responsible for the establishment of the Sabah Museum and Sabah Parks, is an NGO with natural heritage at its heart, and brings together a very interesting circle of local experts – a good source of information.

ARBEC *ASEAN Review of Biodiversity and Environmental Conservation* Available online at www.arbec.com.my. Web journal published by MIMCED in conjunction with the Malaysian University of Science and Technology.

Beaman, J H, Anderson, C and Beaman, R S *The Plants of Mount Kinabalu* Natural History Publications, Borneo, 2001. Fourth volume in a series with sections on the history of plant collecting on Mount Kinabalu and a biographical sketch of two of the most important collectors, Mary Strong and Joseph Clemens. Analysis and indexes of collections, and list of plants. Information on each species on habitat, elevation range, literature and specimens upon which the study is based.

Cranbrook, Earl of (ed); *Wonders of Nature in Southeast Asia* Oxford University Press, 1997. Compilation of excerpts from famous and obscure works by the great explorers, with comments by Cranbrook.

Davidson, G *A Photographic Guide to the Birds of Borneo* New Holland, 4th edition due in 2009. Illustrated pocket field guide of 250 species found in Borneo.

Francis, Charles M *Pocket Guide to the Birds of Borneo* Sabah Society, 1984. Very popular, easy-to-use pocket guide for field reference.

Garbutt, N and Prudente, C *Wild Borneo: The Wildlife and Scenery of Sabah, Sarawak, Brunei and Kalimantan* MIT Press, Massachusetts, 2006. Illustrated book with 250 colour photographs and accompanying essays on Borneo's fauna and flora and conservation (including a chapter on the Heart of Borneo project). Published in association with WWF.

Inger, Robert F and Stuebing, Robert B *A Field Guide to the Frogs of Borneo* Natural History Publications, Malaysia, 1997.

Myers, Susan *Field Guide to the Birds of Borneo* New Holland, forthcoming.

Nais, J *Rafflesia of the World* Natural History Publications, 2001. By the assistant director of Sabah Parks. Can be ordered through Royal Botanic Gardens, Kew Books (*www.kewbooks.com*).

Payne, J and Cubitt, G; *Wild Malaysia: The Wildlife and Scenery of Peninsular Malaysia, Sarawak, and Sabah* 2nd edition, New Holland, 1999. Another coffee-table book with photographs of Malaysian wildlife and natural history.

Smythies, B E *The Birds of Borneo* 4th edition, Natural History Publications, Borneo, 2000. Essential reference on Borneo ornithology; still considered by many to be the most comprehensive guide.

Tweedie, M W F *Malayan Animal Life (and the Common Birds of the Malay Peninsula)* University of Chicago Press, 1954.

Whitehead, J *The Exploration of Mount Kina Balu, North Borneo* Graham Brash, 1993. Revised edition of the classic work published in 1893. Whitehead was the first European to reach the summit of Mount Kinabalu in 1888. The first edition included hand-coloured plates and is now rare and valuable.

Whitmore, T C *An Introduction to Tropical Rain Forests* 2nd edition, Oxford University Press, 1998. Tim Whitmore was a tropical botanist at the Geology Department of the University of Cambridge until his death in 2002. He produced several major reference works on tropical rainforests – see also *Tropical Rainforests of the Far East* Clarendon Press, 1984 and *Palms of Malaya*: *White Lotus* White Lotus Co Ltd, 2nd edition, 1998.

Conservation

Bevis, W *Borneo Log: The Struggle for Sarawak's Forests* University of Washington Press, 1995. An account of travels in Sarawak; travel narrative and environmental observation.

Harrison, B *Orang-utan* Collins,1962.

Health

Wilson-Howarth, Dr Jane, and Ellis, Dr Matthew *Your Child Abroad: A Travel Health Guide* Bradt Travel Guides, 2005

Wilson-Howarth, Dr Jane *Bugs, Bites & Bowels* Cadogan, 2006

WEBSITES

www.brunei.gov.bn Brunei government
www.gov.my Malaysian government
www.sabah.gov.my Sabah State government
www.sarawak.gov.my Sarawak State government

OTHER SOURCES OF INFORMATION

Institute of East Asian Studies (*Universiti Malaysia, Sarawak;* **e** *aroshima@ieas.unimas.my; www.ieas.unimas.my*) Publishes many books on historical and contemporary culture in Borneo, anthropology and Dayak society. Recent titles include: *Mapping the Peoples of Sarawak; The Malay Population of Sarawak; Suket: Penan Folk Stories; Changing Borders and Identities in the Kelabit Highlands;* and *Life in the Malay Kampongs of Kuching Fifty Years Ago.*

Natural History Publications (*9th Floor, Wisma Merdeka Kota Kinabalu, Sabah;* ✆ *088 233098;* **e** *chan@nhpborneo.com; www.nhpborneo.com*) A very active local publisher of nature titles by international experts in their field, headed by C L Chan. Their latest (2007) titles include books on rafflesia and rhododendrons of Sabah, the ferns of Mount Kinabalu and the *Nepenthes* (pitcher plants) of Borneo. They have also published historical documents such as *A Botanist in Borneo: Hugh Low's Sarawak Journals from 1844–46.* Some books have been published in conjunction with the Royal Botanic Gardens, Kew, England.

WWF *Terrestrial Ecoregions of the Indo-Pacific: A Conservation Assessment.* WWF report, Island Press, December 2001. WWF reports are available online at ww.panda.org. Include *Borneo's Lost World: Newly Discovered Species on Borneo 2005.*

Bradt Travel Guides

www.bradtguides.com

Africa

Africa Overland	£15.99
Algeria	£15.99
Benin	£14.99
Botswana: Okavango, Chobe, Northern Kalahari	£15.99
Burkina Faso	£14.99
Cameroon	£15.99
Cape Verde Islands	£14.99
Congo	£15.99
Eritrea	£15.99
Ethiopia	£15.99
Gambia, The	£13.99
Ghana	£15.99
Johannesburg	£6.99
Madagascar	£15.99
Malawi	£13.99
Mali	£13.95
Mauritius, Rodrigues & Réunion	£13.99
Mozambique	£13.99
Namibia	£15.99
Niger	£14.99
Nigeria	£17.99
Rwanda	£14.99
São Tomé & Principe	£14.99
Seychelles	£14.99
Sudan	£13.95
Tanzania, Northern	£13.99
Tanzania	£16.99
Uganda	£15.99
Zambia	£17.99
Zanzibar	£14.99

Britain and Europe

Albania	£15.99
Armenia, Nagorno Karabagh	£14.99
Azores	£13.99
Baltic Cities	£14.99
Belarus	£14.99
Belgrade	£6.99
Bosnia & Herzegovina	£13.99
Bratislava	£9.99
Budapest	£9.99
Bulgaria	£13.99
Cork	£6.99
Croatia	£13.99
Cyprus see North Cyprus	
Czech Republic	£13.99
Dresden	£7.99
Dubrovnik	£6.99
Estonia	£13.99
Faroe Islands	£15.99
Georgia	£14.99

Helsinki	£7.99
Hungary	£14.99
Iceland	£14.99
Kosovo	£14.99
Lapland	£13.99
Latvia	£13.99
Lille	£6.99
Lithuania	£14.99
Ljubljana	£7.99
Luxembourg	£13.99
Macedonia	£14.99
Montenegro	£14.99
North Cyprus	£12.99
Paris, Lille & Brussels	£11.95
Riga	£6.99
River Thames, In the Footsteps of the Famous	£10.95
Serbia	£14.99
Slovakia	£14.99
Slovenia	£13.99
Spitsbergen	£14.99
Switzerland: Rail, Road, Lake	£13.99
Tallinn	£6.99
Transylvania	£14.99
Ukraine	£14.99
Vilnius	£6.99
Zagreb	£6.99

Middle East, Asia and Australasia

China: Yunnan Province	£13.99
Great Wall of China	£13.99
Iran	£14.99
Iraq: Then & Now	£15.99
Israel	£15.99
Kazakhstan	£15.99
Kyrgyzstan	£15.99
Maldives	£15.99
Mongolia	£16.99
North Korea	£14.99
Oman	£13.99
Shangri-La: A Travel Guide to the Himalayan Dream	£14.99
Sri Lanka	£15.99
Syria	£14.99
Tibet	£13.99
Turkmenistan	£14.99
Yemen	£14.99

The Americas and the Caribbean

Amazon, The	£14.99
Argentina	£15.99

Bolivia	£14.99
Cayman Islands	£14.99
Chile	£16.95
Colombia	£16.99
Costa Rica	£13.99
Dominica	£14.99
Falkland Islands	£13.95
Grenada, Carriacou & Petite Martinique	£14.99
Guyana	£14.99
Panama	£13.95
Peru & Bolivia: The Bradt Trekking Guide	£12.95
St Helena	£14.99
Turks & Caicos Islands	£14.99
USA by Rail	£14.99

Wildlife

100 Animals to See Before They Die	£16.99
Antarctica: Guide to the Wildlife	£15.99
Arctic: Guide to the Wildlife	£15.99
Central & Eastern European Wildlife	£15.99
Chinese Wildlife	£16.99
East African Wildlife	£19.99
Galápagos Wildlife	£15.99
Madagascar Wildlife	£16.99
New Zealand Wildlife	£14.99
North Atlantic Wildlife	£16.99
Peruvian Wildlife	£15.99
Southern African Wildlife	£18.95
Sri Lankan Wildlife	£15.99
Wildlife and Conservation Volunteering: The Complete Guide	£13.99

Eccentric Guides

Eccentric Australia	£12.99
Eccentric Britain	£13.99
Eccentric California	£13.99
Eccentric Cambridge	£6.99
Eccentric Edinburgh	£5.95
Eccentric France	£12.95
Eccentric London	£13.99

Others

Your Child Abroad: A Travel Health Guide	£10.95
Something Different for the Weekend	£9.99

WIN £100 CASH!

READER QUESTIONNAIRE

Send in your completed questionnaire for the chance to win £100 cash in our regular draw

All respondents may order a Bradt guide at half the UK retail price – please complete the order form overleaf.

(Entries may be posted or faxed to us, or scanned and emailed.)

We are interested in getting feedback from our readers to help us plan future Bradt guides. Please answer ALL the questions below and return the form to us in order to qualify for an entry in our regular draw.

Have you used any other Bradt guides? If so, which titles? . . . .

. . . .

What other publishers' travel guides do you use regularly? . . . .

. . . .

Where did you buy this guidebook? . . . .

What was the main purpose of your trip to Borneo (or for what other reason did you read our guide)? eg: holiday/business/charity etc.. . . . .

. . . .

What other destinations would you like to see covered by a Bradt guide?

. . . .

Would you like to receive our catalogue/newsletters?

YES / NO (If yes, please complete details on reverse)

If yes – by post or email? . . . .

Age (circle relevant category) 16–25   26–45   46–60   60+

Male/Female (delete as appropriate)

Home country . . . .

Please send us any comments about our guide to Borneo or other Bradt Travel Guides. . . . .

. . . .

. . . .

. . . .

Bradt Travel Guides
23 High Street, Chalfont St Peter, Bucks SL9 9QE, UK
✆ +44 (0)1753 893444 **f** +44 (0)1753 892333
e info@bradtguides.com
www.bradtguides.com

CLAIM YOUR HALF-PRICE BRADT GUIDE!

Order Form

To order your half-price copy of a Bradt guide, and to enter our prize draw to win £100 (see overleaf), please fill in the order form below, complete the questionnaire overleaf, and send it to Bradt Travel Guides by post, fax or email.

Please send me one copy of the following guide at half the UK retail price

Title	Retail price	Half price
. . .	. . . .	. . . .

Please send the following additional guides at full UK retail price

No	Title	Retail price	Total
. . .	. . . .	. . . .	. . . .
. . .	. . . .	. . . .	. . . .
. . .	. . . .	. . . .	. . . .

Sub total . . . .
Post & packing . . . .
(£2 per book UK; £4 per book Europe; £6 per book rest of world)
Total . . . .

Name . . . .

Address. . . . .

Tel . . . .   Email . . . .

☐ I enclose a cheque for £ . . . . made payable to Bradt Travel Guides Ltd

☐ I would like to pay by credit card. Number: . . . .

Expiry date: . . . / . . .   3-digit security code (on reverse of card) . . . . .

Issue no (debit cards only) . . . . .

☐ Please add my name to your catalogue mailing list.

☐ I would be happy for you to use my name and comments in Bradt marketing material.

Send your order on this form, with the completed questionnaire, to:

Bradt Travel Guides BOR1
23 High Street, Chalfont St Peter, Bucks SL9 9QE
☎ +44 (0)1753 893444   f +44 (0)1753 892333
e info@bradtguides.com   www.bradtguides.com

NOTES

NOTES

NOTES

NOTES

NOTES

Index